STUCK RUBBER BABY

BY HOWARD CRUSE

VERTIGO

OTHER BOOKS BY HOWARD CRUSE

WENDEL

WENDEL ON THE REBOUND

DANCIN' NEKKID WITH THE ANGELS

EARLY BAREFOOTZ

STUCK RUBBER BABY

BY HOWARD CRUSE

STUCK RUBBER BABY Published by DC Comics. Cover © 2010 Howard Cruse. All rights reserved. Introduction copyright © 2010
DC Comics. All rights reserved. Original publication © 1995 Howard Cruse. Introduction © 1995 Tony Kushner.
Author photograph Copyright © 1995 Ed Sedarbaum. Vertigo, all characters, their distinctive likenesses and related elements
are trademarks of DC Comics. The stories, characters and incidents featured in this publication are entirely fictional.
DC Comics, 1700 Broadway, New York, NY 10019. A Warner Bros. Entertainment Company.
Printed in the USA.
HC ISBN: 978-1-4012-2713-5   SC ISBN: 978-1-4012-2703-6
Cover illustration by Howard Cruse.
Author photograph by Ed Sedarbaum.

SUSTAINABLE
FORESTRY
INITIATIVE

Certified Fiber Sourcing
www.sfiprogram.org
Fiber used in this product line meets the
sourcing requirements of the SFI program.
www.sfiprogram.org NFS-SPICOC-C0001801

Dedication

For Kim,

for Pam,

and

(as always)

for Eddie

INTRODUCTION

Icould go on at great length about my debt to Howard Cruse—how he inspired me as a young cartoonist and a newly out lesbian; the integral part his work played in my own political and artistic growth; how vitally important his comics have been to the LGBT movement in particular and the progressive movement in general; how personally generous and kind he has been to me over the years. But in my allotted space, I can't possibly elaborate on all these things and properly introduce his masterwork to you.

I had the honor of receiving a visit from Howard during the time he was drawing *Stuck Rubber Baby*. He and his partner Eddie were in Vermont for a little vacation, though of course it was a working vacation for Howard. He went out to the car to get some of his pages to show me.

This was over fifteen years ago, but my memory of it is very clear. As Howard came back inside with a large flat box, time seemed to slow down. I won't claim that I could see Howard's aura, or that the artwork vibrated in my hands as I examined it. But there was something numinous going on here. There was an energy emanating from these sheets of Bristol board that could not be accounted for merely by the exquisitely designed, lettered, and inked details that met my eyes.

I expect that I was experiencing a reverberation of the intense mental, emotional, and above all physical effort that Howard had invested, and would continue to invest for some time, in this drawn world. Indeed, there was something almost unbearably intimate about touching and looking at those pages, as if I were holding Howard's very self in my hands.

And if I felt like I was holding Howard as I read those freshly inked pages, I felt like Howard was holding me when I read the finished book. The formal virtuosity of *Stuck Rubber Baby*, its ambitious historic sweep, its rich characters, its unflinching look at sex, race, violence, hate, and love, make it an immersive, truly novelistic reading experience in a way that's still uncommon for graphic narrative to achieve.

I identify uncomfortably with the young Toland Polk, the archetypal nice person. A white southerner who grew up steeped in the casual as well as institutional racism of Jim Crow, he wouldn't intentionally hurt anyone—but then again, he doesn't intentionally do much of anything at all. He's drifting along, equally disengaged from himself and from the world. But inevitably, he's caught up in the forces of change sweeping past him, and as his engagement builds, so does ours.

This is not a revisionist fantasy in which the white hero flings himself wholeheartedly into the Civil Rights Movement. Toland's transformation is tentative, conflicted, alternately self-flagellating and self-serving—it's a scathingly honest portrayal.

He's surrounded by more active participants in the struggle, but they're as finely drawn as Toland is. The patient, simmering Reverend Pepper. His wife Anna Dellyne, the ex-jazz singer who now only sings hymns and freedom songs. Their gay son Les who turns from party boy to preacher's kid "at the flick of a switch." The flamboyant, wounded Sammy. And the brave but exacting Ginger Raines, the woman Toland convinces himself he's in love with. Ginger is a curious pivot for Toland, leading him toward the truth of civil rights activism, but also affording him the false front of heterosexuality.

Because what complicates and expands this story like a fifth dimension is Toland's growing acceptance of his desire for other men. I suspect this also complicated the reception of *Stuck Rubber Baby* when it was first published in 1995. The parallels Cruse establishes between racism and homophobia were perhaps just a little too ahead of their time to allow the broad mainstream embrace the book should have received.

The "fag bar," the Rhombus, is Toland's first encounter with a roomful of gay men and lesbians, but it's also the first racially integrated social space he's been in. The black drag queen Esmeraldus does Doris Day, singing "When I was just a little girl, I asked my mother, 'What will I be?'" In simple scenes like this, without ever resorting to rhetoric, Cruse deftly deconstructs race and sexuality more effectively than a shelf full of theory. In a way, *Stuck Rubber Baby* is an equal and opposite reaction to the vicious bombing at the center of its narrative. Cruse lays bare the mechanics of oppression like an explosives expert taking apart and defusing a ticking lethal device.

Clayfield is a thinly disguised version of racially riven Birmingham in the early 1960s. The pivotal episodes of violence and protest in the book are based on real events. And although the characters and story are made up, Cruse doesn't shy away from the fact that he has drawn readily on his personal experience, notably his "encounter with unintended fatherhood." This blend of documentary and fiction yields the best of both worlds—the suspense of a carefully crafted plot and the vivid immediacy of an eyewitness account.

Although the story is told by a middle-aged Toland looking back on his life, and is thus, strictly speaking, a first-person narrative, his take on the events is panoramic and omniscient. It was risky and ambitious for a white author to write about African-American characters, particularly ones at such a momentous historic juncture, but Howard nimbly clears the bar he set for himself.

The image of Anna Dellyne standing at the edge of the crowd at the jazz club, Alleysax, is one of my favorite moments in the book. She's aloof, regal, and wistful, half in the light, half in dense black shadow, a distillation of all the opposing tensions that push and pull this book along.

This brings me at last to the drawing. I know it took Howard years to draw this book, but even so, I don't see how one human being could possibly lay down this much ink in that span of time, even if they never stopped to eat or sleep. Many of the pages are so densely cross-hatched with such delicate texture that they look as if they have a nap—as if, if you ran your hand over them, you would feel velvet.

One stunning thing this technique affords is an incredibly rich palette of skin tones. White and black characters alike are shaded with loving nuance. Indeed, everything in the book is drawn with manifest love and a profound generosity. Howard recreates the visual details of life in the South during "Kennedytime" with a staggering archival fidelity. In less sensitive hands, this could be obtrusive. But the painstakingly rendered parking meters, textile patterns, vintage appliances and record sleeves are woven into a meticulous backdrop that allows us to believe in and surrender to the story completely.

I should point out that this feat was accomplished long before there was such a thing as Google Image Search. Howard gathered references not with a few mouse clicks, but by digging around in library picture files, hitting the street with a camera and sketchbook, and by engaging in god knows what other time-consuming analog practices.

It's always tempting to cheat when drawing, to gloss things over. Like a crowd scene, for example. But look at the people gathered outside the funeral at the opening of Chapter 14. The back of each infinitesimal head is never a mere oval, but always a particular person's head. Howard's benevolent Rapidograph achieves transcendence here.

Despite the sometimes microscopic level of detail, this book is always eloquently legible. Howard is so fluent with so many comics conventions that these too could threaten to intrude on the story. But his innovative page layouts and panel shapes, the bleeds and fades, the fragmented breakdown of crucial scenes—all these things combine to transmit a densely layered story with seamless coherence.

Stuck Rubber Baby is a story, but it's also a history—or perhaps more accurately a story about how history happens, one person at a time. What does it take to transcend our isolation and our particular internalized oppressions to touch—and change—the outside world? As Toland Polk begins to engage truthfully with his inner self, his outer self is able to connect with others more authentically and powerfully. Actually, it's just as accurate to put this the other way around. The two things are inextricable.

Toland lives in a place and time where not just black people but "white niggers" are routinely terrorized, and where being a "nigger-loving queer" has dire consequences. The landscape is very different half a century later. The achievements of the Civil Rights and LGBT movements appear monumental, given our African-American president and the escalating moral urgency of the battle for same-sex marriage—neither of which I had any expectation of seeing in my lifetime.

But of course, appearance isn't everything. Racism continues to fester, even though the vast majority of people in this country believe in racial equality. And although each successive generation grows more tolerant, roughly half the public still has an "unfavorable opinion" of gay men and lesbians. The civil rights of gay people remain a matter of public debate.

Howard Cruse's visceral, visual account of America's recent past contributes with grace and force to what we can only continue to hope is history's bend toward justice. And it makes just as vital a contribution to the evolving power of graphic narrative to take life—in this case the confusion and exhilaration of social upheaval—and reflect it back to us in all its glorious chaos.

Alison Bechdel
August 2009
Vermont

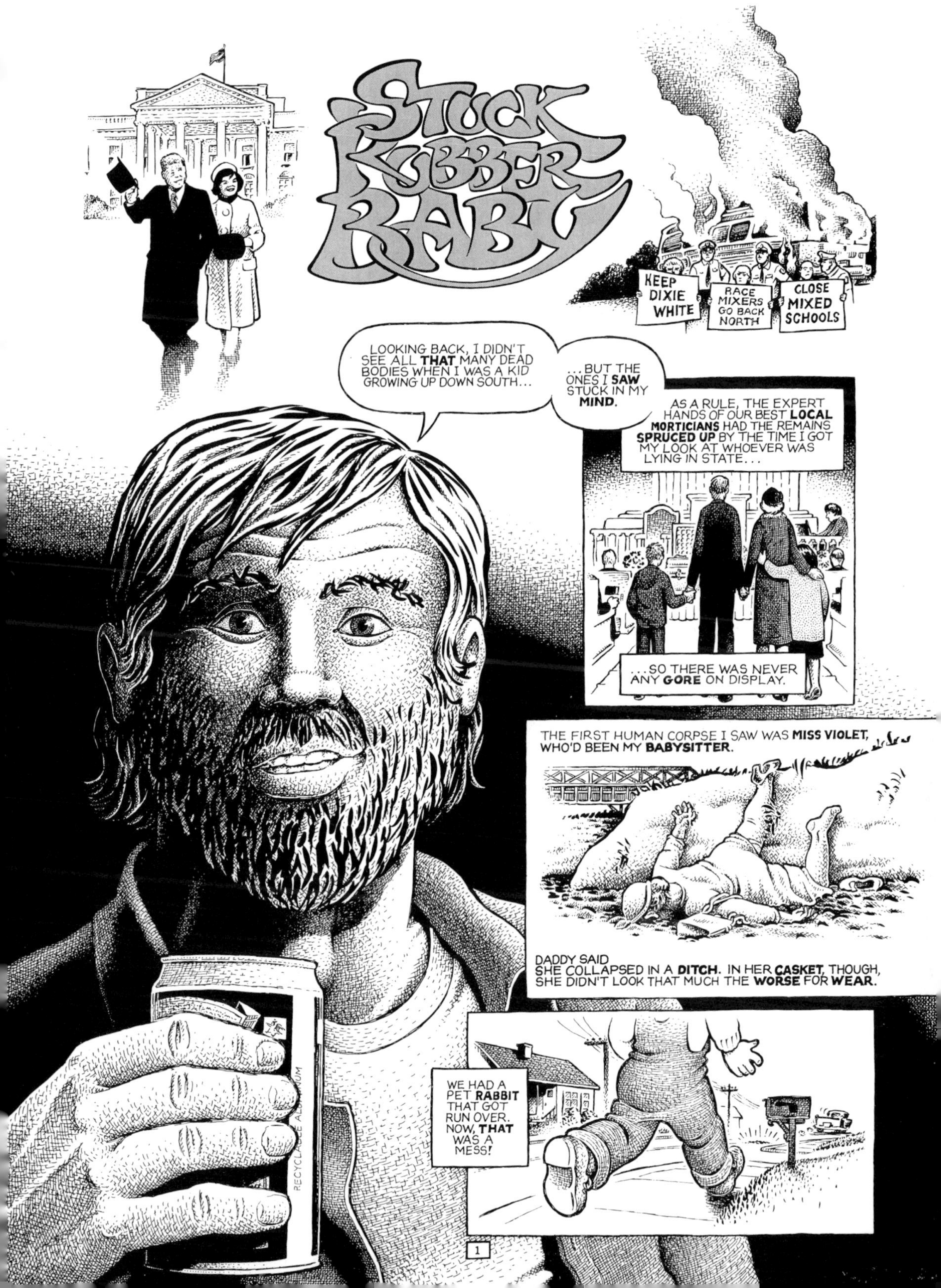
STUCK RUBBER BABY
KEEP DIXIE WHITE
RACE MIXERS GO BACK NORTH
CLOSE MIXED SCHOOLS
LOOKING BACK, I DIDN'T SEE ALL THAT MANY DEAD BODIES WHEN I WAS A KID GROWING UP DOWN SOUTH...
...BUT THE ONES I SAW STUCK IN MY MIND.
AS A RULE, THE EXPERT HANDS OF OUR BEST LOCAL MORTICIANS HAD THE REMAINS SPRUCED UP BY THE TIME I GOT MY LOOK AT WHOEVER WAS LYING IN STATE...
...SO THERE WAS NEVER ANY GORE ON DISPLAY.
THE FIRST HUMAN CORPSE I SAW WAS MISS VIOLET, WHO'D BEEN MY BABYSITTER.
DADDY SAID SHE COLLAPSED IN A DITCH. IN HER CASKET, THOUGH, SHE DIDN'T LOOK THAT MUCH THE WORSE FOR WEAR.
WE HAD A PET RABBIT THAT GOT RUN OVER. NOW, THAT WAS A MESS!

AS A DUMB **KID**, THOUGH, I CONVINCED MYSELF THAT HUMAN BEINGS WERE **DIFFERENT** FROM ANIMALS.

THE **FUNERALS** I ATTENDED LEFT ME REASSURED THAT, WHATEVER TOLL GOT TAKEN ON MY **OTHER** BODY PARTS, MY **HEAD** WOULD SURVIVE DEATH **INTACT**.

THEN MY FRIEND BO WISED ME UP.

WANNA SEE SOMETHIN' **GROSS**, TOLAND?

SURE.

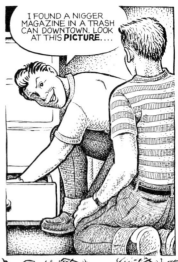

I FOUND A NIGGER MAGAZINE IN A TRASH CAN DOWNTOWN. LOOK AT THIS **PICTURE**....

IT WAS A CLOSE-UP PHOTOGRAPH OF A **DEAD BLACK PERSON** WHOSE **SKULL** WAS ALL CAVED IN.

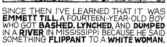

SINCE THEN I'VE LEARNED THAT IT WAS **EMMETT TILL**, A FOURTEEN-YEAR-OLD BOY WHO GOT **BASHED**, **LYNCHED**, AND **DUMPED** IN A **RIVER** IN MISSISSIPPI BECAUSE HE SAID SOMETHING **FLIPPANT** TO A **WHITE WOMAN**.

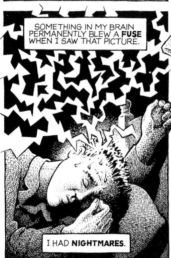

SOMETHING IN MY BRAIN PERMANENTLY BLEW A **FUSE** WHEN I SAW THAT PICTURE.

I HAD **NIGHTMARES**.

I WAS WORRIED ABOUT MY **SKULL**.

DADDY, IS THERE ANY **DIFFERENCE** BETWEEN **NEGRO SKULLS** AND **WHITE PEOPLE'S SKULLS**?

HOW D'YA **MEAN**, SON?

ARE WHITE PEOPLE'S SKULLS **HARDER** THAN NEGRO SKULLS?

OH, I **DOUBT** IT, TOLAND. I DOUBT IT **SERIOUSLY**.

IF **ANYTHING**, NEGRO BONES ARE PROBABLY **TOUGHER**, SINCE COLORED FOLKS ARE CLOSER TO THE **ANIMAL STATE** THAN WE ARE AND HAVE GOTTEN **STRONGER** FROM HAVIN' TO GET BY IN THE **WILD**.

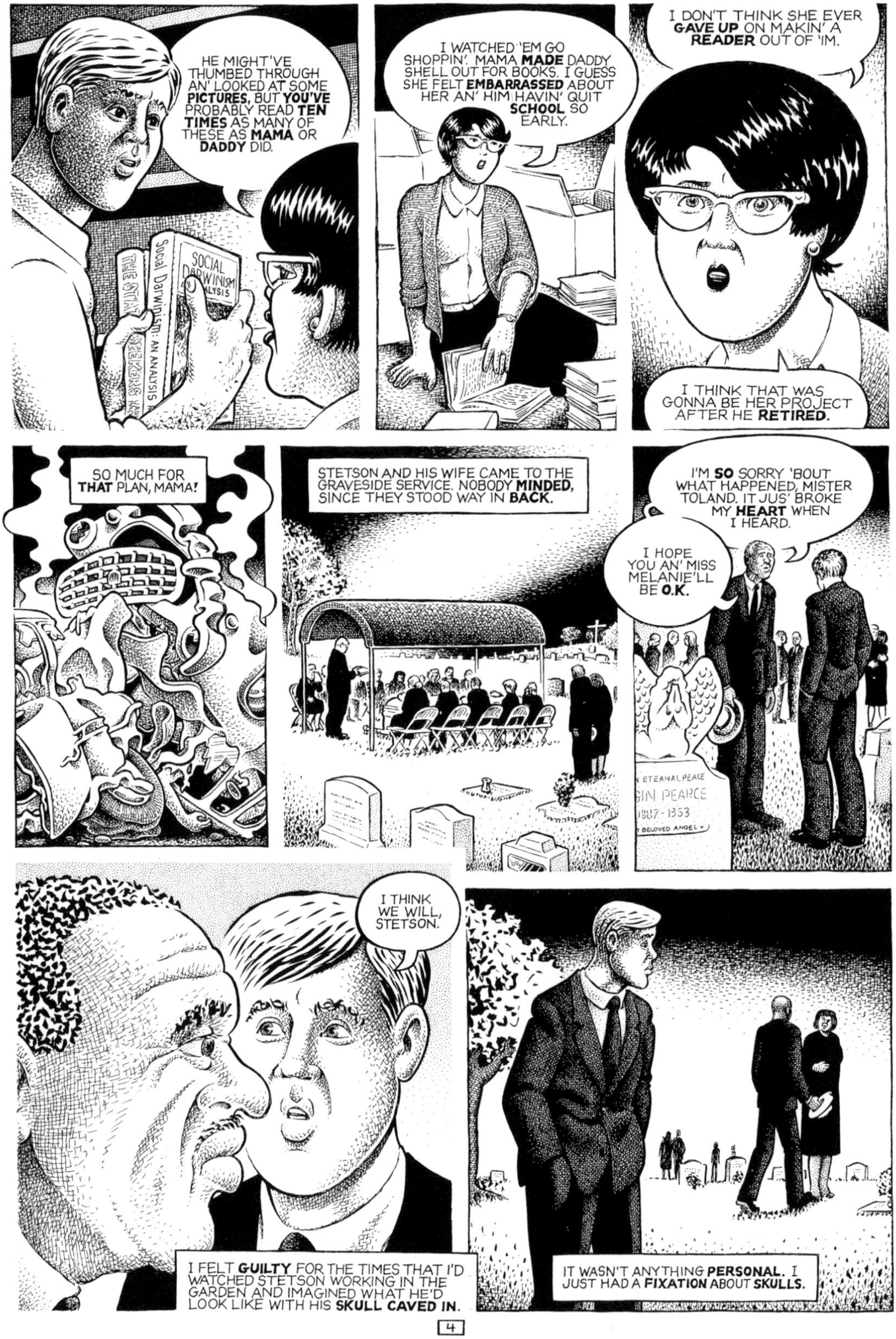
HE MIGHT'VE THUMBED THROUGH AN' LOOKED AT SOME **PICTURES**, BUT **YOU'VE** PROBABLY READ **TEN TIMES** AS MANY OF THESE AS **MAMA** OR **DADDY** DID.
SOCIAL DARWINISM AN ANALYSIS
Social Darwinism: AN ANALYSIS
I WATCHED 'EM GO SHOPPIN'. MAMA **MADE** DADDY SHELL OUT FOR BOOKS. I GUESS SHE FELT **EMBARRASSED** ABOUT HER AN' HIM HAVIN' QUIT **SCHOOL** SO EARLY.
I DON'T THINK SHE EVER **GAVE UP** ON MAKIN' A **READER** OUT OF 'IM.
I THINK THAT WAS GONNA BE HER PROJECT AFTER HE **RETIRED**.
SO MUCH FOR **THAT** PLAN, MAMA!
STETSON AND HIS WIFE CAME TO THE GRAVESIDE SERVICE. NOBODY **MINDED**, SINCE THEY STOOD WAY IN **BACK**.
I'M **SO** SORRY 'BOUT WHAT HAPPENED, MISTER TOLAND. IT JUS' BROKE MY **HEART** WHEN I HEARD.
I HOPE YOU AN' MISS MELANIE'LL BE **O.K.**
ETERNAL PEACE
GIN PEARCE
1887 - 1953
BELOVED ANGEL
I THINK WE WILL, STETSON.
I FELT **GUILTY** FOR THE TIMES THAT I'D WATCHED STETSON WORKING IN THE GARDEN AND IMAGINED WHAT HE'D LOOK LIKE WITH HIS **SKULL CAVED IN**.
IT WASN'T ANYTHING **PERSONAL**. I JUST HAD A **FIXATION** ABOUT **SKULLS**.

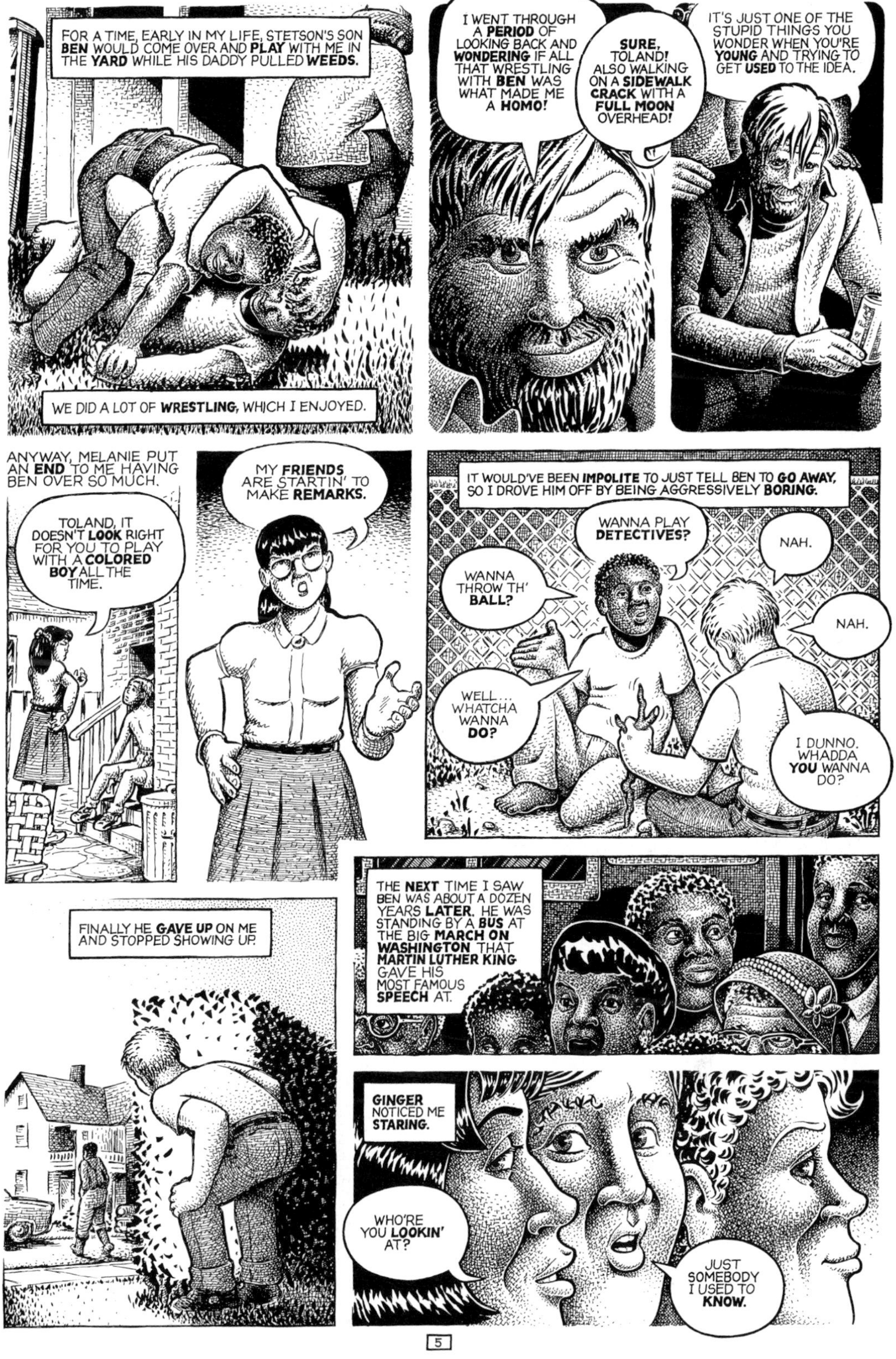
FOR A TIME, EARLY IN MY LIFE, STETSON'S SON BEN WOULD COME OVER AND PLAY WITH ME IN THE YARD WHILE HIS DADDY PULLED WEEDS.
WE DID A LOT OF WRESTLING, WHICH I ENJOYED.
I WENT THROUGH A PERIOD OF LOOKING BACK AND WONDERING IF ALL THAT WRESTLING WITH BEN WAS WHAT MADE ME A HOMO!
SURE, TOLAND! ALSO WALKING ON A SIDEWALK CRACK WITH A FULL MOON OVERHEAD!
IT'S JUST ONE OF THE STUPID THINGS YOU WONDER WHEN YOU'RE YOUNG AND TRYING TO GET USED TO THE IDEA.
ANYWAY, MELANIE PUT AN END TO ME HAVING BEN OVER SO MUCH.
TOLAND, IT DOESN'T LOOK RIGHT FOR YOU TO PLAY WITH A COLORED BOY ALL THE TIME.
MY FRIENDS ARE STARTIN' TO MAKE REMARKS.
IT WOULD'VE BEEN IMPOLITE TO JUST TELL BEN TO GO AWAY, SO I DROVE HIM OFF BY BEING AGGRESSIVELY BORING.
WANNA THROW TH' BALL?
WANNA PLAY DETECTIVES?
NAH.
NAH.
WELL... WHATCHA WANNA DO?
I DUNNO. WHADDA YOU WANNA DO?
FINALLY HE GAVE UP ON ME AND STOPPED SHOWING UP.
THE NEXT TIME I SAW BEN WAS ABOUT A DOZEN YEARS LATER. HE WAS STANDING BY A BUS AT THE BIG MARCH ON WASHINGTON THAT MARTIN LUTHER KING GAVE HIS MOST FAMOUS SPEECH AT.
GINGER NOTICED ME STARING.
WHO'RE YOU LOOKIN' AT?
JUST SOMEBODY I USED TO KNOW.

I TOLD GINGER **WHO** BEN **WAS**. **SAMMY NOONE** OVERHEARD AND SAID I SHOULD GO OVER AND GIVE THE DUDE A BIG **HELLO**.

WHO **KNOWS**? THOSE MOMENTS HE SPENT **WRITHING** WITH YOU IN THE **DUST** MAY BE AMONG BEN'S MOST **CHERISHED** MEMORIES!

NOT TOO **LIKELY**, SAMMY!

I'D FEEL MORE **PLEASED** WITH MYSELF IF I COULD CLAIM THAT IT WAS PURE **SOCIAL CONSCIENCE** THAT GOT MY ASS OUT TO THE LINCOLN MEMORIAL THAT SUMMER, OR THE **MEMORY** OF HOW I HAD FELT ABOUT **EMMETT TILL**...

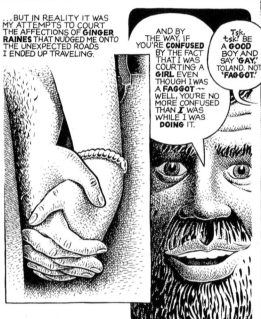

...BUT IN REALITY IT WAS MY ATTEMPTS TO COURT THE AFFECTIONS OF **GINGER RAINES** THAT NUDGED ME ONTO THE UNEXPECTED ROADS I ENDED UP TRAVELING.

AND BY THE WAY, IF YOU'RE **CONFUSED** BY THE FACT THAT I WAS COURTING A **GIRL** EVEN THOUGH I WAS A **FAGGOT**~~ WELL, YOU'RE NO MORE CONFUSED THAN **I** WAS WHILE I WAS **DOING** IT.

TSK, TSK! BE A **GOOD** BOY AND SAY 'GAY,' TOLAND. NOT '**FAGGOT**!'

I DIDN'T **FEEL** 'GAY' BACK THEN. I FELT LIKE A **FAGGOT!**

ANYWAY, MY **INTENTION** FOR QUITE SOME TIME WAS TO TURN MYSELF AROUND AND **NOT** BE GAY...

...WHICH I **KIDDED** MYSELF INTO VIEWING AS AN **OPTION.**

YOU'VE GOTTA BE AT LEAST A **LITTLE** BIT **UN-SCREWED-UP** TO BE 'GAY'!

I SUBSCRIBED TO **PLAYBOY** AND HAD AN ABSOLUTE **RULE** THAT I WOULDN'T LET MYSELF **MASTURBATE** UNLESS I WAS LOOKING AT ONE OF THE **CENTERFOLD PLAYMATES** AT THE TIME.

I HELD TO THAT RULE FOR OVER **THREE YEARS**, WITH ONLY A **COUPLE** OF LAPSES.

WET DREAMS DIDN'T **COUNT.**

UNH-H-H...

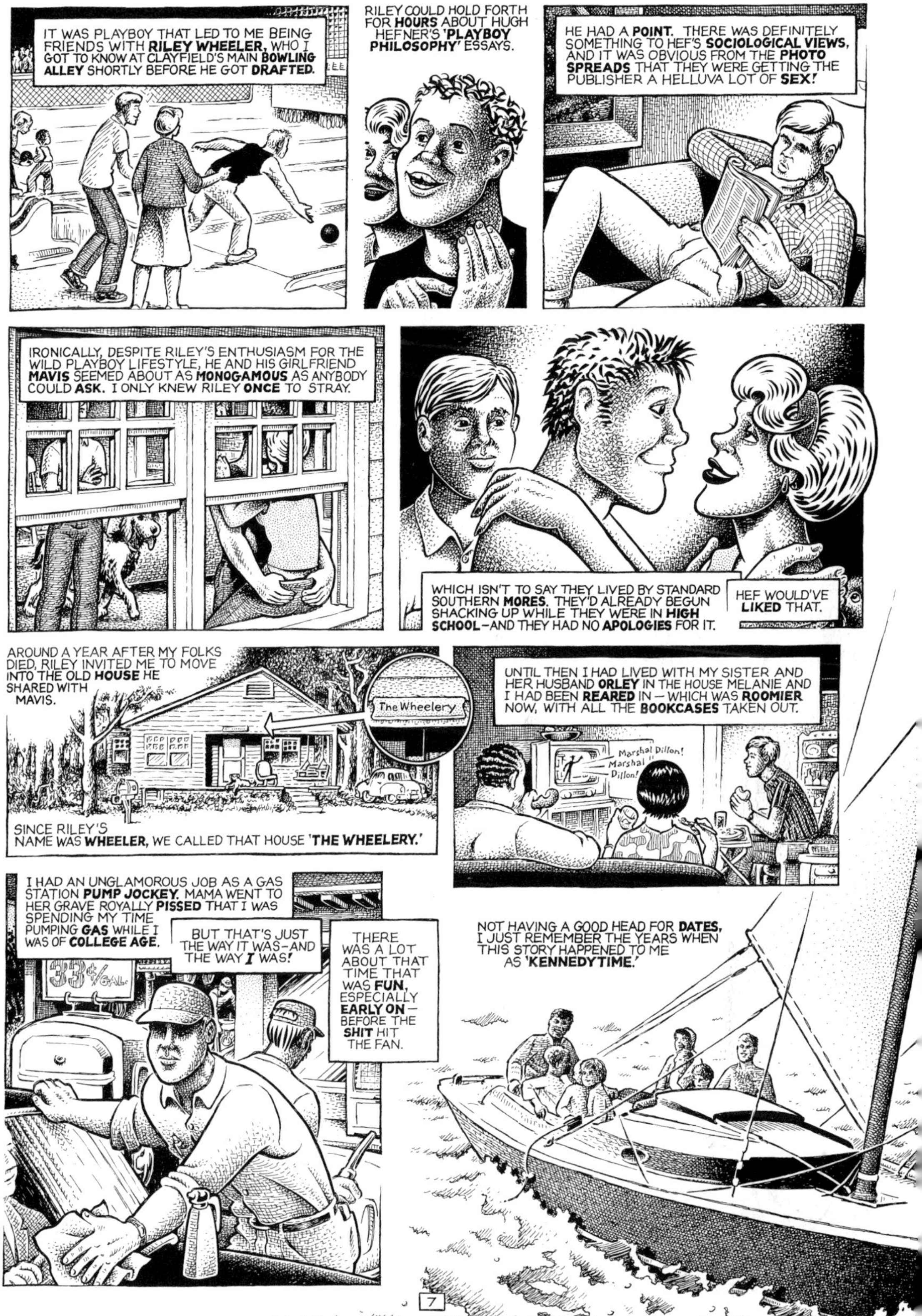
IT WAS PLAYBOY THAT LED TO ME BEING FRIENDS WITH RILEY WHEELER, WHO I GOT TO KNOW AT CLAYFIELD'S MAIN BOWLING ALLEY SHORTLY BEFORE HE GOT DRAFTED.
RILEY COULD HOLD FORTH FOR HOURS ABOUT HUGH HEFNER'S 'PLAYBOY PHILOSOPHY' ESSAYS.
HE HAD A POINT. THERE WAS DEFINITELY SOMETHING TO HEF'S SOCIOLOGICAL VIEWS, AND IT WAS OBVIOUS FROM THE PHOTO SPREADS THAT THEY WERE GETTING THE PUBLISHER A HELLUVA LOT OF SEX!
IRONICALLY, DESPITE RILEY'S ENTHUSIASM FOR THE WILD PLAYBOY LIFESTYLE, HE AND HIS GIRLFRIEND MAVIS SEEMED ABOUT AS MONOGAMOUS AS ANYBODY COULD ASK. I ONLY KNEW RILEY ONCE TO STRAY.
WHICH ISN'T TO SAY THEY LIVED BY STANDARD SOUTHERN MORES. THEY'D ALREADY BEGUN SHACKING UP WHILE THEY WERE IN HIGH SCHOOL—AND THEY HAD NO APOLOGIES FOR IT.
HEF WOULD'VE LIKED THAT.
AROUND A YEAR AFTER MY FOLKS DIED, RILEY INVITED ME TO MOVE INTO THE OLD HOUSE HE SHARED WITH MAVIS.
The Wheelery
SINCE RILEY'S NAME WAS WHEELER, WE CALLED THAT HOUSE 'THE WHEELERY.'
UNTIL THEN I HAD LIVED WITH MY SISTER AND HER HUSBAND ORLEY IN THE HOUSE MELANIE AND I HAD BEEN REARED IN—WHICH WAS ROOMIER NOW, WITH ALL THE BOOKCASES TAKEN OUT.
Marshal Dillon! Marshal Dillon!
I HAD AN UNGLAMOROUS JOB AS A GAS STATION PUMP JOCKEY. MAMA WENT TO HER GRAVE ROYALLY PISSED THAT I WAS SPENDING MY TIME PUMPING GAS WHILE I WAS OF COLLEGE AGE.
BUT THAT'S JUST THE WAY IT WAS—AND THE WAY I WAS!
THERE WAS A LOT ABOUT THAT TIME THAT WAS FUN, ESPECIALLY EARLY ON—BEFORE THE SHIT HIT THE FAN.
33¢/GAL.
NOT HAVING A GOOD HEAD FOR DATES, I JUST REMEMBER THE YEARS WHEN THIS STORY HAPPENED TO ME AS 'KENNEDYTIME.'

Chapter 2

I SHOULD MENTION HOW I GOT BROUGHT OUT OF THE **CLOSET** BY THE UNITED STATES **ARMY.**

...AND HOW YOU BROKE ALL **RECORDS** TRYING TO SCRAMBLE BACK **IN!**

THAT WAS BACK WHEN MY **FOLKS** WERE STILL **ALIVE.** I HAD RECENTLY TURNED **EIGHTEEN,** AND **UNCLE SAM** WAS KEEPING **TRACK.**

SOMETHIN' FOR YOU FROM **SELECTIVE SERVICE.**

plop!

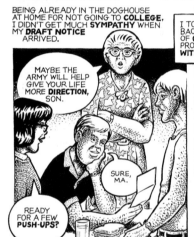

BEING ALREADY IN THE DOGHOUSE AT HOME FOR NOT GOING TO **COLLEGE,** I DIDN'T GET MUCH **SYMPATHY** WHEN MY **DRAFT NOTICE** ARRIVED.

MAYBE THE ARMY WILL HELP GIVE YOUR LIFE MORE **DIRECTION,** SON.

SURE, MA.

READY FOR A FEW **PUSH-UPS?**

I TOOK IT IN **STRIDE.** I VIEWED THE **MILITARY** BACK THEN AS A MODERATELY ANNOYING MIXTURE OF **CALISTHENICS** AND **HARASSMENT** THAT I WAS PROBABLY GONNA HAVE TO **PUT UP WITH** ONE WAY OR **ANOTHER.**

IT COULD EVEN BE **FUN,** JUDGING FROM **'SGT. BILKO'** ON **TV.**

Hide, everybody! Colonel Hall's coming!

But we can't leave Pvt. Doberman dressed up like a pineapple!

Ha ha ha heh ha ha ha h ha heh heh ha ha ha

I SHOWED UP AT THE **RECRUITMENT CENTER** AS INSTRUCTED AND GOT HAULED WITH THE OTHER DRAFTEES OFF TO THE **CENTRAL ARMORY** FOR MY **INDUCTION PHYSICAL.**

MY MOMENT OF **TRUTH** CAME WHEN A COUPLA HUNDRED OF US, STILL ALL BUT **NAKED** FROM GETTING INSPECTED FOR **LICE** AND **HEMORRHOIDS,** GOT HERDED INTO A BIG, SWEATY HALL FULL OF **SCHOOLROOM CHAIRS** AND TOLD TO FILL OUT LONG MEDICAL-HISTORY **QUESTIONNAIRES**...

...WHEREUPON, THE KID SITTING **NEXT** TO ME, FOR REASONS KNOWN ONLY TO **HIM,** GOT A **HARD-ON.**

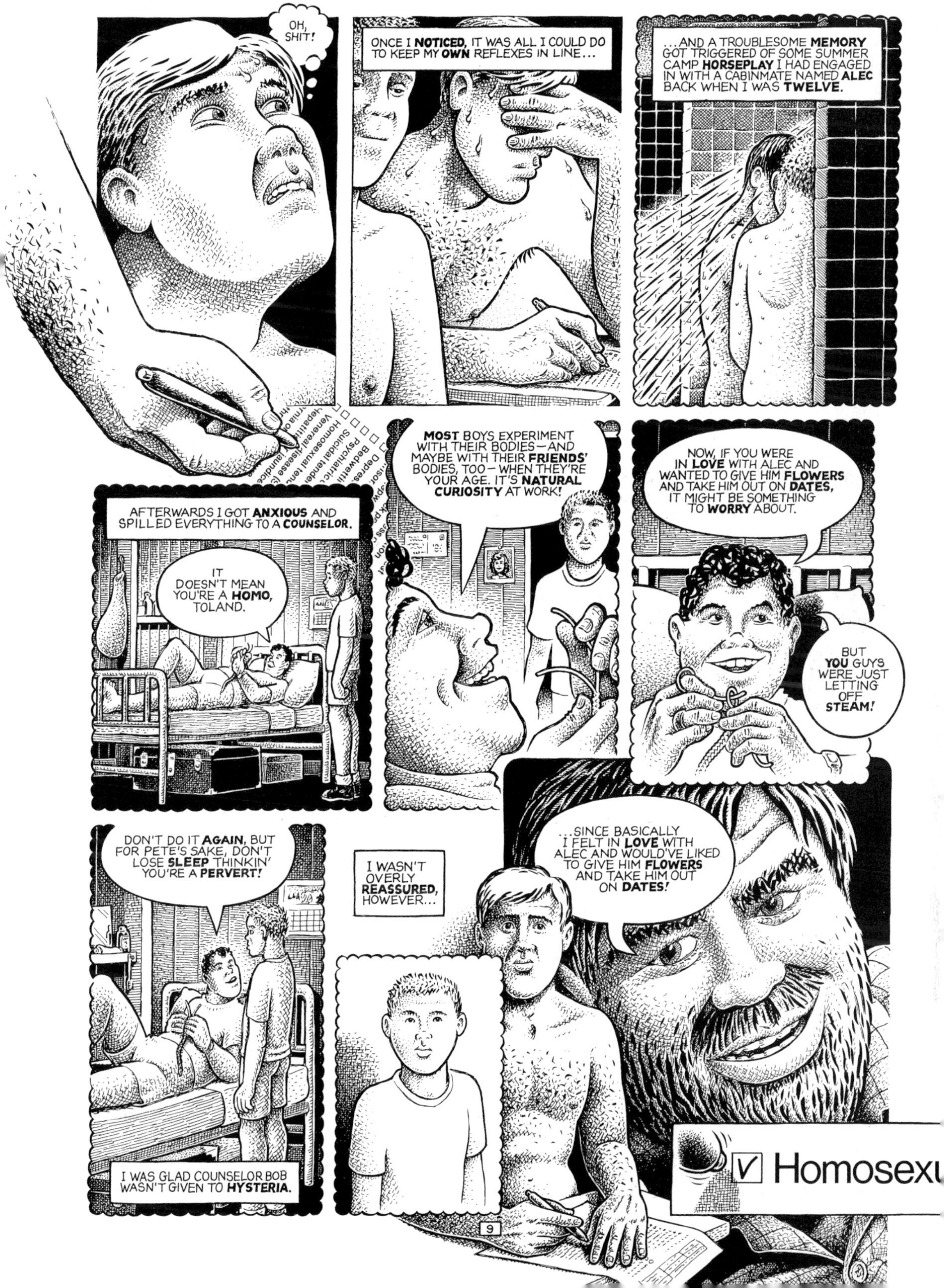
OH, SHIT!
ONCE I NOTICED, IT WAS ALL I COULD DO TO KEEP MY OWN REFLEXES IN LINE...
...AND A TROUBLESOME MEMORY GOT TRIGGERED OF SOME SUMMER CAMP HORSEPLAY I HAD ENGAGED IN WITH A CABINMATE NAMED ALEC BACK WHEN I WAS TWELVE.
AFTERWARDS I GOT ANXIOUS AND SPILLED EVERYTHING TO A COUNSELOR.
IT DOESN'T MEAN YOU'RE A HOMO, TOLAND.
MOST BOYS EXPERIMENT WITH THEIR BODIES—AND MAYBE WITH THEIR FRIENDS' BODIES, TOO—WHEN THEY'RE YOUR AGE. IT'S NATURAL CURIOSITY AT WORK!
NOW, IF YOU WERE IN LOVE WITH ALEC AND WANTED TO GIVE HIM FLOWERS AND TAKE HIM OUT ON DATES, IT MIGHT BE SOMETHING TO WORRY ABOUT.
BUT YOU GUYS WERE JUST LETTING OFF STEAM!
DON'T DO IT AGAIN, BUT FOR PETE'S SAKE, DON'T LOSE SLEEP THINKIN' YOU'RE A PERVERT!
I WAS GLAD COUNSELOR BOB WASN'T GIVEN TO HYSTERIA.
I WASN'T OVERLY REASSURED, HOWEVER...
...SINCE BASICALLY I FELT IN LOVE WITH ALEC AND WOULD'VE LIKED TO GIVE HIM FLOWERS AND TAKE HIM OUT ON DATES!

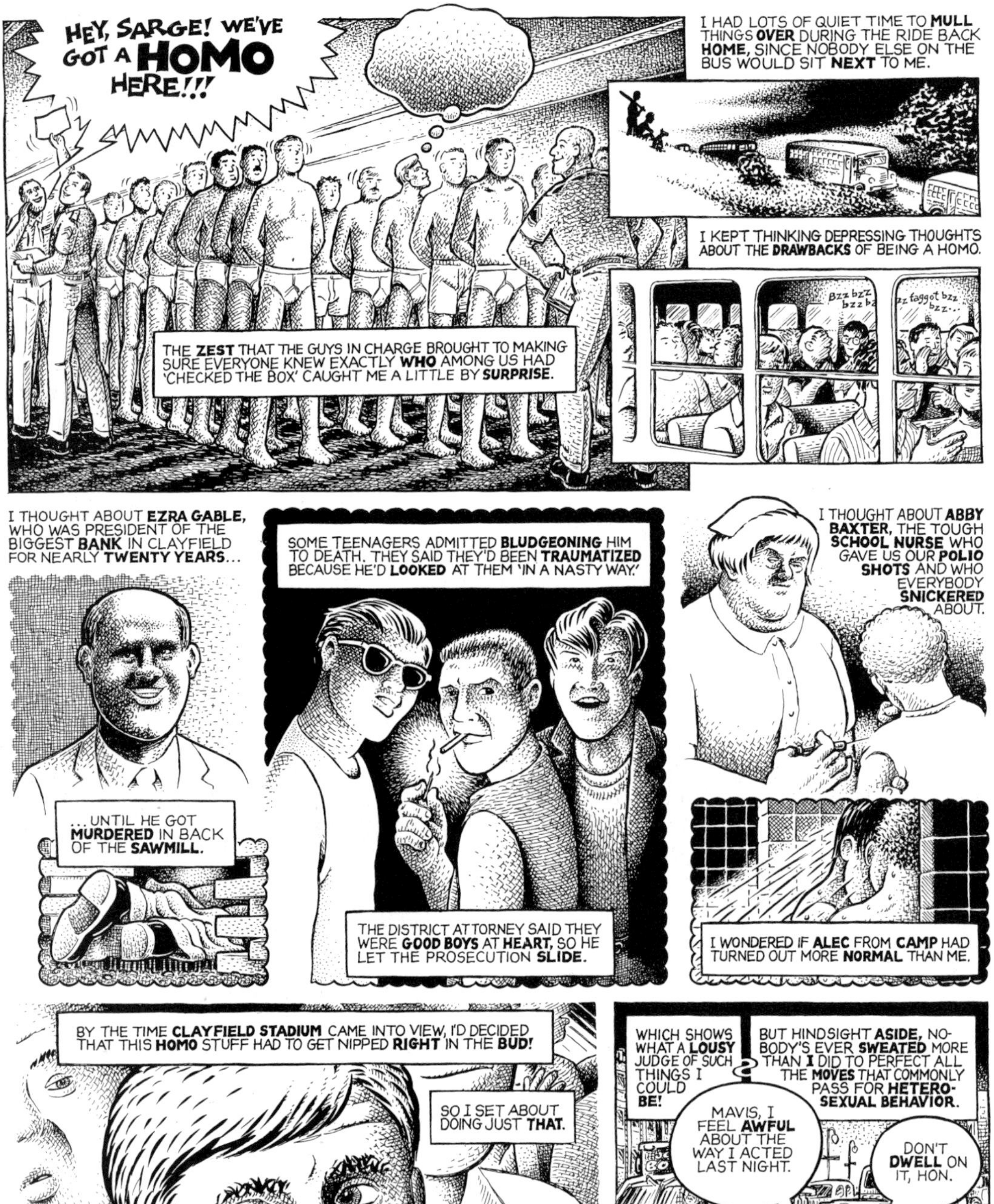

HEY, SARGE! WE'VE GOT A HOMO HERE!!!
THE ZEST THAT THE GUYS IN CHARGE BROUGHT TO MAKING SURE EVERYONE KNEW EXACTLY WHO AMONG US HAD 'CHECKED THE BOX' CAUGHT ME A LITTLE BY SURPRISE.
I HAD LOTS OF QUIET TIME TO MULL THINGS OVER DURING THE RIDE BACK HOME, SINCE NOBODY ELSE ON THE BUS WOULD SIT NEXT TO ME.
I KEPT THINKING DEPRESSING THOUGHTS ABOUT THE DRAWBACKS OF BEING A HOMO.
Bzz bzz bzz b
zz faggot bzz bzz...
I THOUGHT ABOUT EZRA GABLE, WHO WAS PRESIDENT OF THE BIGGEST BANK IN CLAYFIELD FOR NEARLY TWENTY YEARS...
...UNTIL HE GOT MURDERED IN BACK OF THE SAWMILL.
SOME TEENAGERS ADMITTED BLUDGEONING HIM TO DEATH. THEY SAID THEY'D BEEN TRAUMATIZED BECAUSE HE'D LOOKED AT THEM 'IN A NASTY WAY.'
THE DISTRICT ATTORNEY SAID THEY WERE GOOD BOYS AT HEART, SO HE LET THE PROSECUTION SLIDE.
I THOUGHT ABOUT ABBY BAXTER, THE TOUGH SCHOOL NURSE WHO GAVE US OUR POLIO SHOTS AND WHO EVERYBODY SNICKERED ABOUT.
I WONDERED IF ALEC FROM CAMP HAD TURNED OUT MORE NORMAL THAN ME.
BY THE TIME CLAYFIELD STADIUM CAME INTO VIEW, I'D DECIDED THAT THIS HOMO STUFF HAD TO GET NIPPED RIGHT IN THE BUD!
SO I SET ABOUT DOING JUST THAT.
AND PRETTY SUCCESSFULLY, TOO, AS BEST I COULD JUDGE.
WHICH SHOWS WHAT A LOUSY JUDGE OF SUCH THINGS I COULD BE!
BUT HINDSIGHT ASIDE, NOBODY'S EVER SWEATED MORE THAN I DID TO PERFECT ALL THE MOVES THAT COMMONLY PASS FOR HETEROSEXUAL BEHAVIOR.
MAVIS, I FEEL AWFUL ABOUT THE WAY I ACTED LAST NIGHT.
DON'T DWELL ON IT, HON.

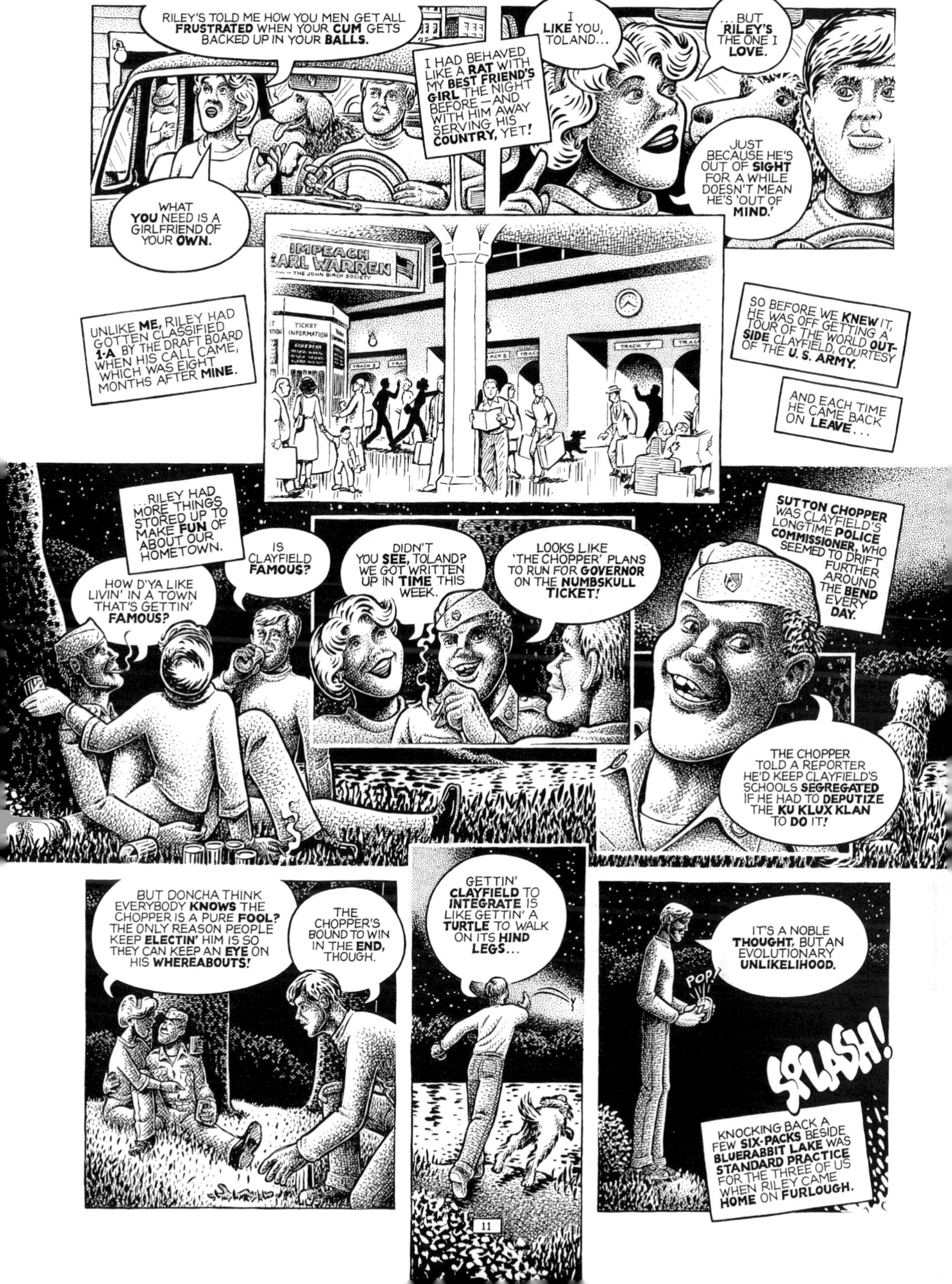

RILEY'S TOLD ME HOW YOU MEN GET ALL **FRUSTRATED** WHEN YOUR **CUM** GETS BACKED UP IN YOUR **BALLS.**
WHAT **YOU** NEED IS A GIRLFRIEND OF YOUR **OWN.**
I HAD BEHAVED LIKE A **RAT** WITH MY **BEST FRIEND'S GIRL** THE NIGHT BEFORE—AND WITH HIM AWAY SERVING HIS **COUNTRY,** YET!
I **LIKE** YOU, TOLAND...
...BUT **RILEY'S** THE ONE I **LOVE.**
JUST BECAUSE HE'S OUT OF **SIGHT** FOR A WHILE DOESN'T MEAN HE'S 'OUT OF **MIND.**'
UNLIKE **ME,** RILEY HAD GOTTEN CLASSIFIED **1-A** BY THE DRAFT BOARD WHEN HIS CALL CAME, WHICH WAS EIGHT MONTHS AFTER **MINE.**
IMPEACH EARL WARREN
THE JOHN BIRCH SOCIETY
TICKET INFORMATION
TRACK 7
SO BEFORE WE **KNEW** IT, HE WAS OFF GETTING A TOUR OF THE WORLD **OUT-SIDE** CLAYFIELD, COURTESY OF THE **U. S. ARMY.**
AND EACH TIME HE CAME BACK ON **LEAVE**...
...RILEY HAD MORE THINGS STORED UP TO MAKE **FUN** OF ABOUT OUR HOMETOWN.
HOW D'YA LIKE LIVIN' IN A TOWN THAT'S GETTIN' **FAMOUS?**
IS CLAYFIELD **FAMOUS?**
DIDN'T YOU **SEE,** TOLAND? WE GOT WRITTEN UP IN **TIME** THIS WEEK.
LOOKS LIKE 'THE CHOPPER' PLANS TO RUN FOR **GOVERNOR** ON THE **NUMBSKULL TICKET!**
SUTTON CHOPPER WAS CLAYFIELD'S LONGTIME **POLICE COMMISSIONER,** WHO SEEMED TO DRIFT FURTHER AROUND THE **BEND** EVERY **DAY.**
THE CHOPPER TOLD A REPORTER HE'D KEEP CLAYFIELD'S SCHOOLS **SEGREGATED** IF HE HAD TO **DEPUTIZE** THE **KU KLUX KLAN** TO **DO** IT!
BUT DONCHA THINK EVERYBODY **KNOWS** THE CHOPPER IS A PURE **FOOL?** THE ONLY REASON PEOPLE KEEP **ELECTIN'** HIM IS SO THEY CAN KEEP AN **EYE** ON HIS **WHEREABOUTS!**
THE CHOPPER'S BOUND TO WIN IN THE **END,** THOUGH.
GETTIN' **CLAYFIELD** TO **INTEGRATE** IS LIKE GETTIN' A **TURTLE** TO WALK ON ITS **HIND LEGS**...
IT'S A NOBLE **THOUGHT,** BUT AN EVOLUTIONARY **UNLIKELIHOOD.**
POP!
SPLASH!
KNOCKING BACK A FEW **SIX-PACKS** BESIDE **BLUERABBIT LAKE** WAS **STANDARD PRACTICE** FOR THE THREE OF US WHEN RILEY CAME **HOME** ON **FURLOUGH.**

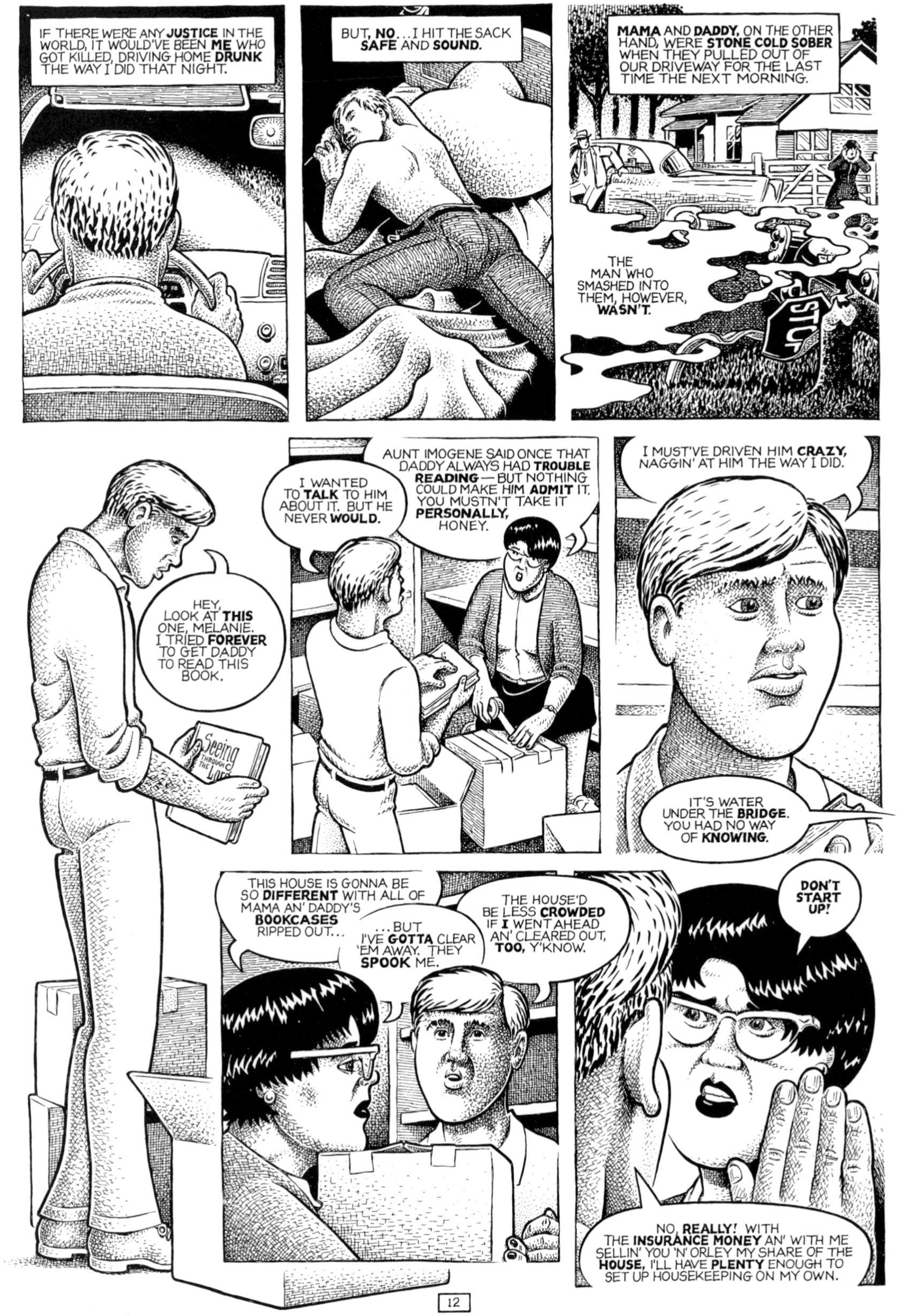

IF THERE WERE ANY **JUSTICE** IN THE WORLD, IT WOULD'VE BEEN **ME** WHO GOT KILLED, DRIVING HOME **DRUNK** THE WAY I DID THAT NIGHT.
BUT, **NO**... I HIT THE SACK **SAFE** AND **SOUND**.
MAMA AND **DADDY**, ON THE OTHER HAND, WERE **STONE COLD SOBER** WHEN THEY PULLED OUT OF OUR DRIVEWAY FOR THE LAST TIME THE NEXT MORNING.
THE MAN WHO SMASHED INTO THEM, HOWEVER, **WASN'T**.
HEY, LOOK AT **THIS** ONE, MELANIE. I TRIED **FOREVER** TO GET DADDY TO READ THIS BOOK.
I WANTED TO **TALK** TO HIM ABOUT IT. BUT HE NEVER **WOULD**.
AUNT IMOGENE SAID ONCE THAT DADDY ALWAYS HAD **TROUBLE READING** — BUT NOTHING COULD MAKE HIM **ADMIT** IT. YOU MUSTN'T TAKE IT **PERSONALLY**, HONEY.
I MUST'VE DRIVEN HIM **CRAZY**, NAGGIN' AT HIM THE WAY I DID.
IT'S WATER UNDER THE **BRIDGE**. YOU HAD NO WAY OF **KNOWING**.
THIS HOUSE IS GONNA BE SO **DIFFERENT** WITH ALL OF MAMA AN' DADDY'S **BOOKCASES** RIPPED OUT...
... BUT I'VE **GOTTA** CLEAR 'EM AWAY. THEY **SPOOK** ME.
THE HOUSE'D BE LESS **CROWDED** IF **I** WENT AHEAD AN' CLEARED OUT, **TOO**, Y'KNOW.
DON'T START UP!
NO, **REALLY!** WITH THE **INSURANCE MONEY** AN' WITH ME SELLIN' YOU 'N' ORLEY MY SHARE OF THE **HOUSE**, I'LL HAVE **PLENTY** ENOUGH TO SET UP HOUSEKEEPING ON MY OWN.

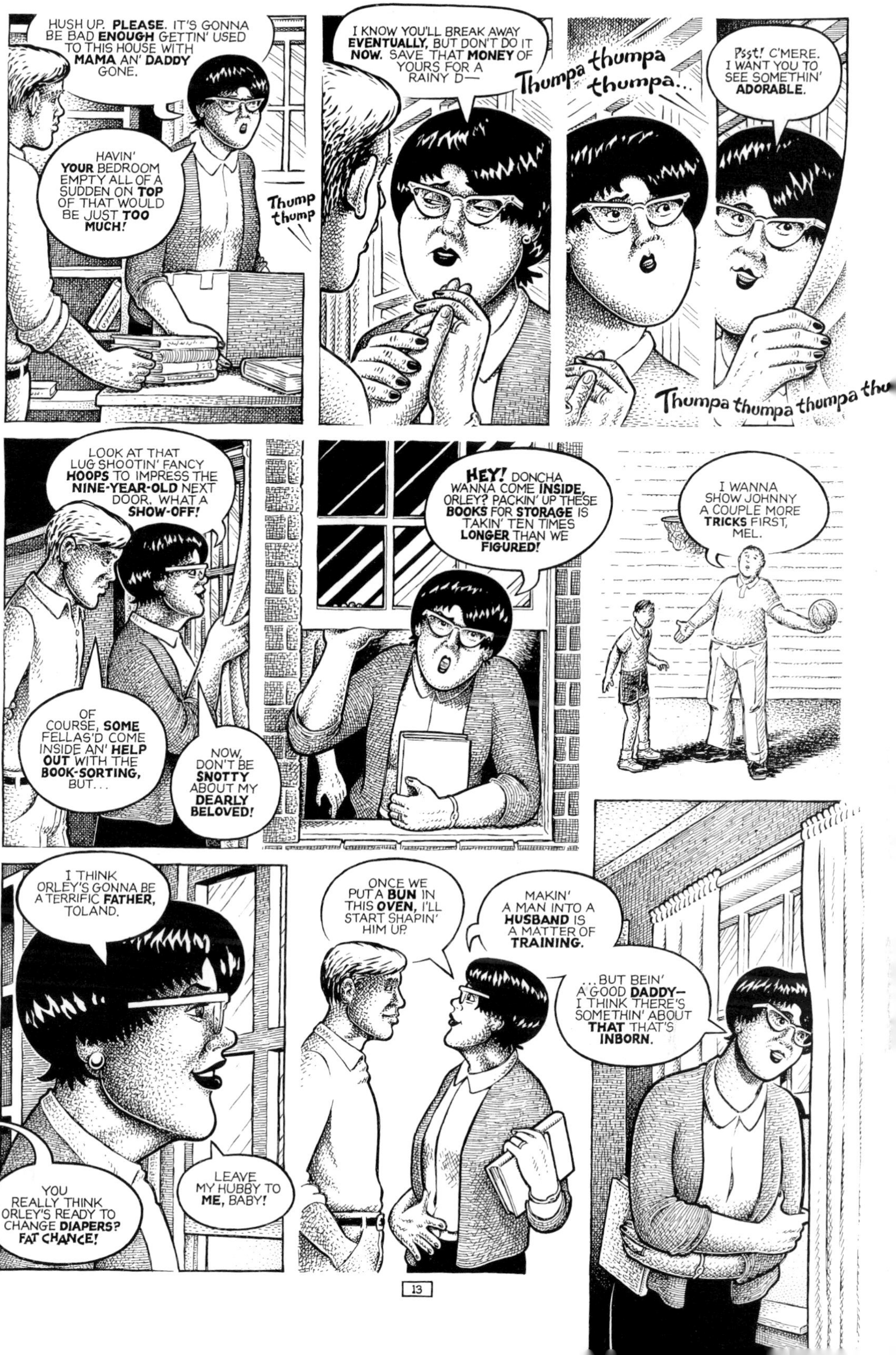
HUSH UP. **PLEASE**. IT'S GONNA BE BAD **ENOUGH** GETTIN' USED TO THIS HOUSE WITH **MAMA** AN' **DADDY** GONE.
HAVIN' **YOUR** BEDROOM EMPTY ALL OF A SUDDEN ON **TOP** OF THAT WOULD BE JUST **TOO MUCH!**
Thump thump
I KNOW YOU'LL BREAK AWAY **EVENTUALLY,** BUT DON'T DO IT **NOW.** SAVE THAT **MONEY** OF YOURS FOR A RAINY D—
Thumpa thumpa thumpa...
Psst! C'MERE. I WANT YOU TO SEE SOMETHIN' **ADORABLE.**
Thumpa thumpa thumpa thu
LOOK AT THAT LUG SHOOTIN' FANCY **HOOPS** TO IMPRESS THE **NINE-YEAR-OLD** NEXT DOOR. WHAT A **SHOW-OFF!**
OF COURSE, **SOME** FELLAS'D COME INSIDE AN' **HELP OUT** WITH THE **BOOK-SORTING,** BUT...
NOW, DON'T BE **SNOTTY** ABOUT MY **DEARLY BELOVED!**
HEY! DONCHA WANNA COME **INSIDE,** ORLEY? PACKIN' UP THESE **BOOKS** FOR **STORAGE** IS TAKIN' TEN TIMES **LONGER** THAN WE **FIGURED!**
I WANNA SHOW JOHNNY A COUPLE MORE **TRICKS** FIRST, MEL.
I THINK ORLEY'S GONNA BE A TERRIFIC **FATHER,** TOLAND.
YOU REALLY THINK ORLEY'S READY TO CHANGE **DIAPERS? FAT CHANCE!**
LEAVE MY HUBBY TO **ME,** BABY!
ONCE WE PUT A **BUN** IN THIS **OVEN,** I'LL START SHAPIN' HIM UP.
MAKIN' A MAN INTO A **HUSBAND** IS A MATTER OF **TRAINING.**
...BUT BEIN' A GOOD **DADDY**— I THINK THERE'S SOMETHIN' ABOUT **THAT** THAT'S **INBORN.**

Chapter 3

PUMPING **GAS** HAD NEVER BEEN **HIGH** ON MY LIST OF **PREFERRED OCCUPATIONS**. BUT THE **JOB MARKET** HAD BEEN **WORSE** THAN **PUNY** WHEN I FINISHED HIGH SCHOOL, THANKS TO A **BOYCOTT** BY LOCAL **BLACKS** OF ALL THE WHITE-OWNED DOWNTOWN **BUSINESSES**.

I'D LIKE TO **HELP** YOU, SON, BUT WE'RE **LETTIN' PEOPLE GO**, NOT **HIRIN'**.

ALTHOUGH CLAYFIELD'S BLACK FOLKS HAD BEEN **MAD** FOR A **LONG TIME** OVER THE WIDESPREAD **INJUSTICES** OF **RACIAL SEGREGATION**, AND ALTHOUGH VARIOUS **LEGAL CHALLENGES** WERE ALREADY IN THE **WORKS**, WHAT ACTUALLY **SPARKED** THE BOYCOTT WAS A RELATIVELY **PETTY** AGGRAVATION THAT TURNED OUT TO BE **ONE** PETTY AGGRAVATION TOO **MANY**!

HEY, DON'T GIMME **LIP**, BOY. AIN'T NO SHORTAGE OF PARKIN' FOR COLORED FOLKS OUT THERE ON THE **STREET**.

BUT I'M GON' HAVE SOME **BIG, HEAVY PACKAGES** TO BE PUTTIN' IN THE **TRUNK**....

THE **CARRYHOME DISCOUNT STORE** HAD SPENT MONTHS BALLYHOOING THE ROOMY NEW **PARKING DECK** IT WAS BUILDING FOR ITS CUSTOMERS. BUT WHEN IT OPENED, ONLY **WHITE** PEOPLE WERE ALLOWED TO **PARK** IN IT.

REVEREND HARLAND PEPPER TOLD HIS CONGREGATION AT THE **SMITH PARK BAPTIST CHURCH** HOW **FED UP** HE WAS WITH CARRYHOME. THEN HE CALLED FOR A **PROTEST RALLY**.

MISS MABEL, I WANT YOU TO GRACE THIS FLOCK WITH SOME **FERVENT MUSIC** NOW, 'CAUSE I WANT **EVERYBODY** AND HIS **COUSIN** OUT AND HOPPING AT THIS **RALLY** ON TUESDAY!

LEAVE 'EM TO **ME**, REV!

EVERYBODY THERE **KNEW** HOW MUCH MONEY GOT SPENT BY BLACKS EVERY DAY AT CARRYHOME. IT WASN'T **PEANUTS**!

AS TENSIONS ROSE, THE EVER-HELPFUL **SUTTON CHOPPER** SPOKE HIS MIND TO **REPORTERS** WHILE THE LEADERSHIP OF CLAYFIELD'S **DOWNTOWN MERCHANTS LEAGUE** NODDED ITS **APPROVAL**.

MY JOB AS **POLICE COMMISSIONER** IS TO DEFEND OUR CITY'S **FINE, TAXPAYING BUSINESSMEN** AGAINST THE IRRESPONSIBLE ACTIONS OF A BUNCH OF **UNRULY, MALODOROUS, COMMUNIST-INSPIRED NIGGER AGITATORS**!

IT WAS THE **STRAW** THAT BROKE THE **CAMEL'S BACK**.

OVERNIGHT, THE BEEF AGAINST CARRYHOME **MUSHROOMED** INTO A GENERALIZED FURY OVER **EVERYTHING** ABOUT THE WAY CLAYFIELD VIEWED ITS BLACK CITIZENS, AND THE **WHITE COMMERCIAL ESTABLISHMENT** DOWNTOWN FOUND ITSELF COLLECTIVELY TARGETED FOR AN EYE-OPENING LESSON IN **ECONOMICS**.

TIME PASSED, **HOPE** ESCALATED, **NEW ISSUES** GOT MIXED IN WITH THE **OLD** ONES—AND EVENTUALLY IT SEEMED LIKE YOU'D NEVER BE ABLE TO SET FOOT ON A **DOWNTOWN SIDEWALK** AGAIN WITHOUT HAVING SOMEBODY WITH **DARK SKIN** AND A **PICKET SIGN** SING A **FREEDOM SONG** AT YOU.

ON THE WHOLE, WHITE PEOPLE BEGAN FINDING IT TOO **STRESSFUL** TO SHOP DOWNTOWN, WHERE THEY WERE FORCED TO LOOK AT DISQUIETING SIGNS OF **SOCIAL TURMOIL**...

...SO THEY CHANGED THEIR **SHOPPING HABITS**, PREFERRING LEISURELY DRIVES TO **STRESS-FREE MALLS** IN THE **SUBURBS**...

YOO-HOO! TOLAND!

...WHICH PUT EXTRA CASH IN THE TILLS OF **SERVICE STATIONS** ALONG THE **ROUTE**, SUCH AS THE ONE THAT CHOSE TO HIRE ME.

2 MILES TO GREEN LAWN MALL

GLENN'S GULF & TUNE-UP

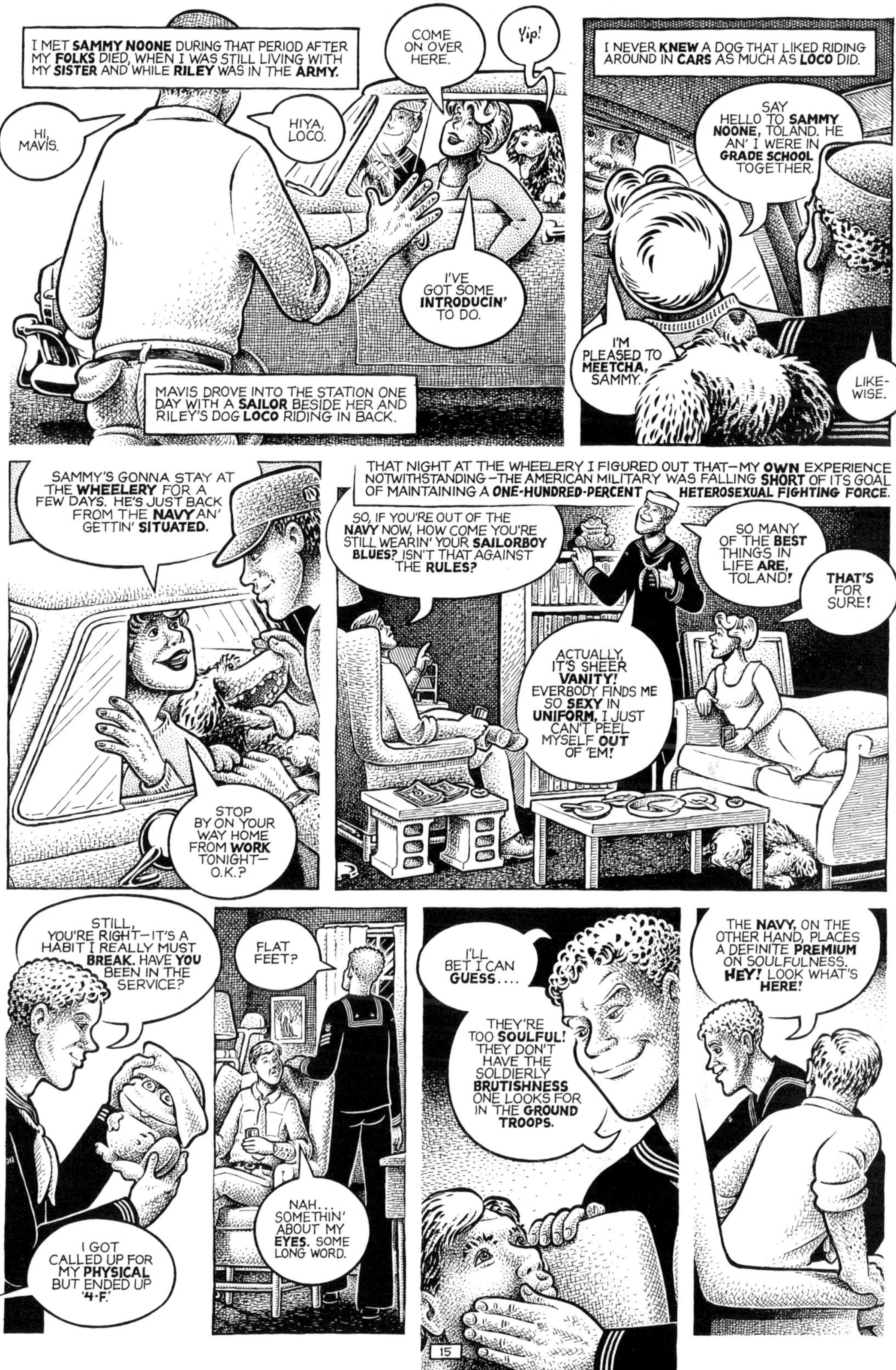
I MET **SAMMY NOONE** DURING THAT PERIOD AFTER MY **FOLKS** DIED, WHEN I WAS STILL LIVING WITH MY **SISTER** AND WHILE **RILEY** WAS IN THE **ARMY.**
COME ON OVER HERE.
Yip!
HI, MAVIS.
HIYA, LOCO.
I'VE GOT SOME **INTRODUCIN'** TO DO.
MAVIS DROVE INTO THE STATION ONE DAY WITH A **SAILOR** BESIDE HER AND RILEY'S DOG **LOCO** RIDING IN BACK.
I NEVER **KNEW** A DOG THAT LIKED RIDING AROUND IN **CARS** AS MUCH AS **LOCO** DID.
SAY HELLO TO **SAMMY NOONE,** TOLAND. HE AN' I WERE IN **GRADE SCHOOL** TOGETHER.
I'M PLEASED TO **MEETCHA,** SAMMY.
LIKE-WISE.
SAMMY'S GONNA STAY AT THE **WHEELERY** FOR A FEW DAYS. HE'S JUST BACK FROM THE **NAVY** AN' GETTIN' **SITUATED.**
STOP BY ON YOUR WAY HOME FROM **WORK** TONIGHT— O.K.?
THAT NIGHT AT THE WHEELERY I FIGURED OUT THAT—MY **OWN** EXPERIENCE NOTWITHSTANDING—THE AMERICAN MILITARY WAS FALLING **SHORT** OF ITS GOAL OF MAINTAINING A **ONE-HUNDRED-PERCENT HETEROSEXUAL FIGHTING FORCE.**
SO, IF YOU'RE OUT OF THE **NAVY** NOW, HOW COME YOU'RE STILL WEARIN' YOUR **SAILORBOY BLUES?** ISN'T THAT AGAINST THE **RULES?**
ACTUALLY, IT'S SHEER **VANITY!** EVERBODY FINDS ME SO **SEXY** IN **UNIFORM,** I JUST CAN'T PEEL MYSELF **OUT** OF 'EM!
SO MANY OF THE **BEST** THINGS IN LIFE **ARE,** TOLAND!
THAT'S FOR SURE!
STILL, YOU'RE RIGHT—IT'S A HABIT I REALLY MUST **BREAK.** HAVE **YOU** BEEN IN THE SERVICE?
I GOT CALLED UP FOR MY **PHYSICAL** BUT ENDED UP **'4-F.'**
FLAT FEET?
NAH... SOMETHIN' ABOUT MY **EYES.** SOME LONG WORD.
I'LL BET I CAN **GUESS....**
THEY'RE TOO **SOULFUL!** THEY DON'T HAVE THE SOLDIERLY **BRUTISHNESS** ONE LOOKS FOR IN THE **GROUND TROOPS.**
THE **NAVY,** ON THE OTHER HAND, PLACES A DEFINITE **PREMIUM** ON SOULFULNESS. **HEY!** LOOK WHAT'S **HERE!**

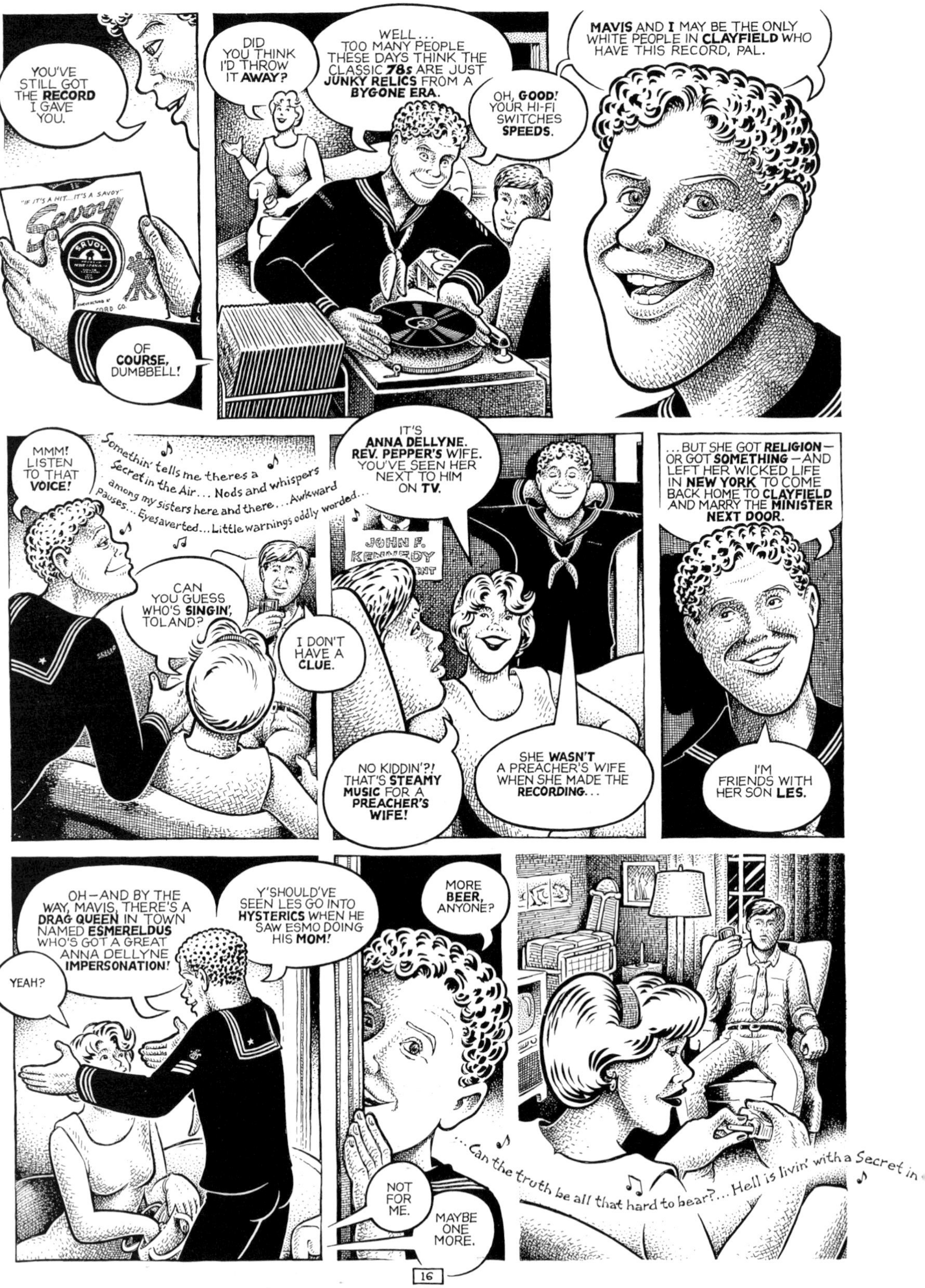
YOU'VE STILL GOT THE RECORD I GAVE YOU.
"IF IT'S A HIT... IT'S A SAVOY"
Savoy
OF COURSE, DUMBBELL!
DID YOU THINK I'D THROW IT AWAY?
WELL... TOO MANY PEOPLE THESE DAYS THINK THE CLASSIC 78s ARE JUST JUNKY RELICS FROM A BYGONE ERA.
OH, GOOD! YOUR HI-FI SWITCHES SPEEDS.
MAVIS AND I MAY BE THE ONLY WHITE PEOPLE IN CLAYFIELD WHO HAVE THIS RECORD, PAL.
MMM! LISTEN TO THAT VOICE!
Somethin' tells me theres a Secret in the Air... Nods and whispers among my sisters here and there... Awkward pauses... Eyes averted... Little warnings oddly worded...
CAN YOU GUESS WHO'S SINGIN', TOLAND?
I DON'T HAVE A CLUE.
IT'S ANNA DELLYNE. REV. PEPPER'S WIFE. YOU'VE SEEN HER NEXT TO HIM ON TV.
JOHN F. KENNEDY
NO KIDDIN'?! THAT'S STEAMY MUSIC FOR A PREACHER'S WIFE!
SHE WASN'T A PREACHER'S WIFE WHEN SHE MADE THE RECORDING...
...BUT SHE GOT RELIGION— OR GOT SOMETHING —AND LEFT HER WICKED LIFE IN NEW YORK TO COME BACK HOME TO CLAYFIELD AND MARRY THE MINISTER NEXT DOOR.
I'M FRIENDS WITH HER SON LES.
OH—AND BY THE WAY, MAVIS, THERE'S A DRAG QUEEN IN TOWN NAMED ESMERELDUS WHO'S GOT A GREAT ANNA DELLYNE IMPERSONATION!
YEAH?
Y'SHOULD'VE SEEN LES GO INTO HYSTERICS WHEN HE SAW ESMO DOING HIS MOM!
MORE BEER, ANYONE?
NOT FOR ME.
MAYBE ONE MORE.
...Can the truth be all that hard to bear?... Hell is livin' with a Secret in

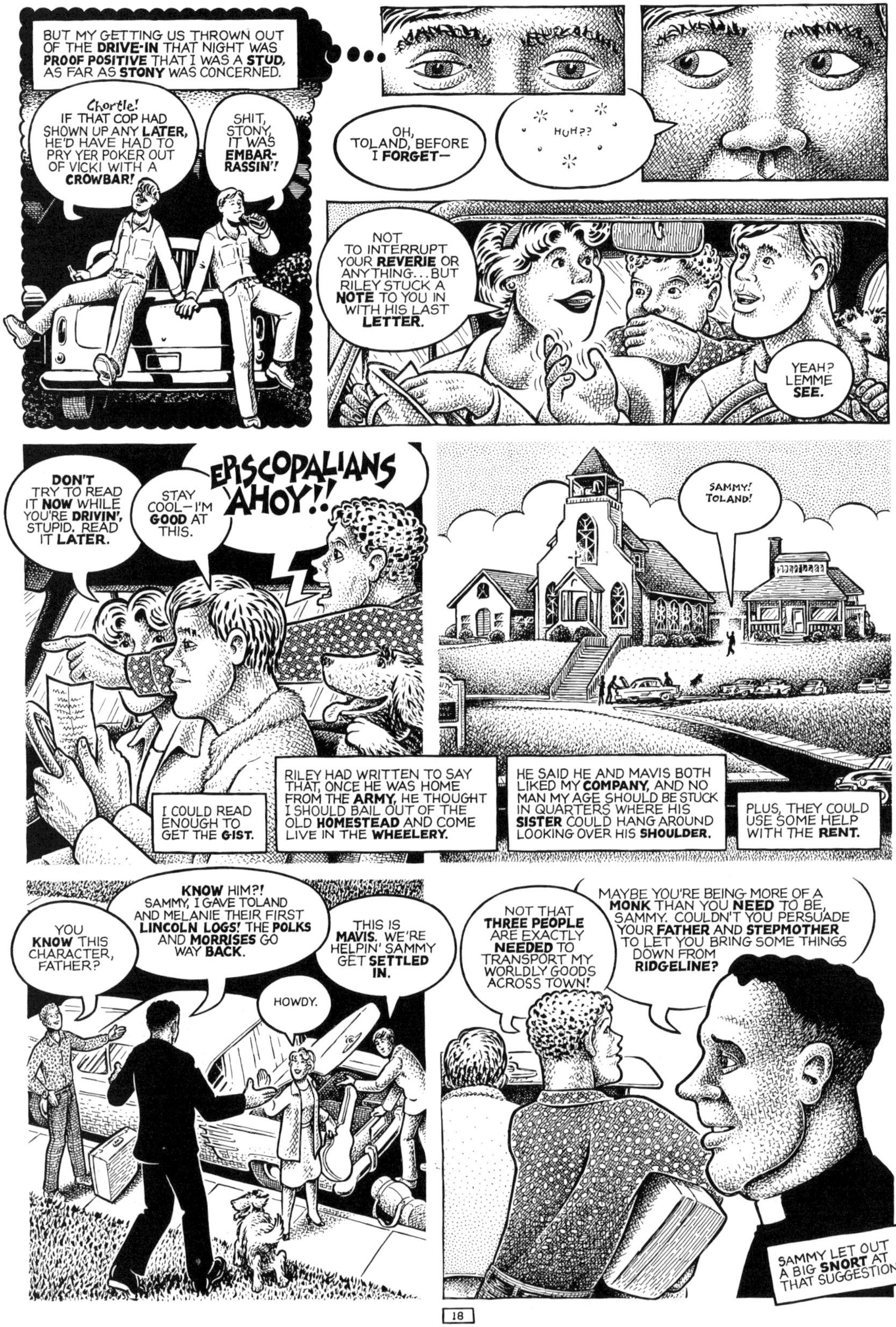
BUT MY GETTING US THROWN OUT OF THE **DRIVE-IN** THAT NIGHT WAS **PROOF POSITIVE** THAT I WAS A **STUD**, AS FAR AS **STONY** WAS CONCERNED.
Chortle! IF THAT COP HAD SHOWN UP ANY **LATER**, HE'D HAVE HAD TO PRY YER POKER OUT OF VICKI WITH A **CROWBAR**!
SHIT, STONY, IT WAS **EMBAR-RASSIN'**!
OH, TOLAND, BEFORE I **FORGET**—
HUH??
NOT TO INTERRUPT YOUR **REVERIE** OR ANYTHING... BUT RILEY STUCK A **NOTE** TO YOU IN WITH HIS LAST **LETTER**.
YEAH? LEMME **SEE**.
DON'T TRY TO READ IT **NOW** WHILE YOU'RE **DRIVIN'**, STUPID. READ IT **LATER**.
STAY COOL—I'M **GOOD** AT THIS.
EPISCOPALIANS AHOY!!
I COULD READ ENOUGH TO GET THE **GIST**.
RILEY HAD WRITTEN TO SAY THAT, ONCE HE WAS HOME FROM THE **ARMY**, HE THOUGHT I SHOULD BAIL OUT OF THE OLD **HOMESTEAD** AND COME LIVE IN THE **WHEELERY**.
SAMMY! TOLAND!
HE SAID HE AND MAVIS BOTH LIKED MY **COMPANY**, AND NO MAN MY AGE SHOULD BE STUCK IN QUARTERS WHERE HIS **SISTER** COULD HANG AROUND LOOKING OVER HIS **SHOULDER**.
PLUS, THEY COULD USE SOME HELP WITH THE **RENT**.
YOU **KNOW** THIS CHARACTER, FATHER?
KNOW HIM?! SAMMY, I GAVE TOLAND AND MELANIE THEIR FIRST **LINCOLN LOGS**! THE **POLKS** AND **MORRISES** GO WAY **BACK**.
THIS IS **MAVIS**. WE'RE HELPIN' SAMMY GET **SETTLED IN**.
HOWDY.
NOT THAT **THREE PEOPLE** ARE EXACTLY **NEEDED** TO TRANSPORT MY WORLDLY GOODS ACROSS TOWN!
MAYBE YOU'RE BEING MORE OF A **MONK** THAN YOU **NEED** TO BE, SAMMY. COULDN'T YOU PERSUADE YOUR **FATHER** AND **STEPMOTHER** TO LET YOU BRING SOME THINGS DOWN FROM **RIDGELINE**?
SAMMY LET OUT A BIG **SNORT** AT THAT SUGGESTION.

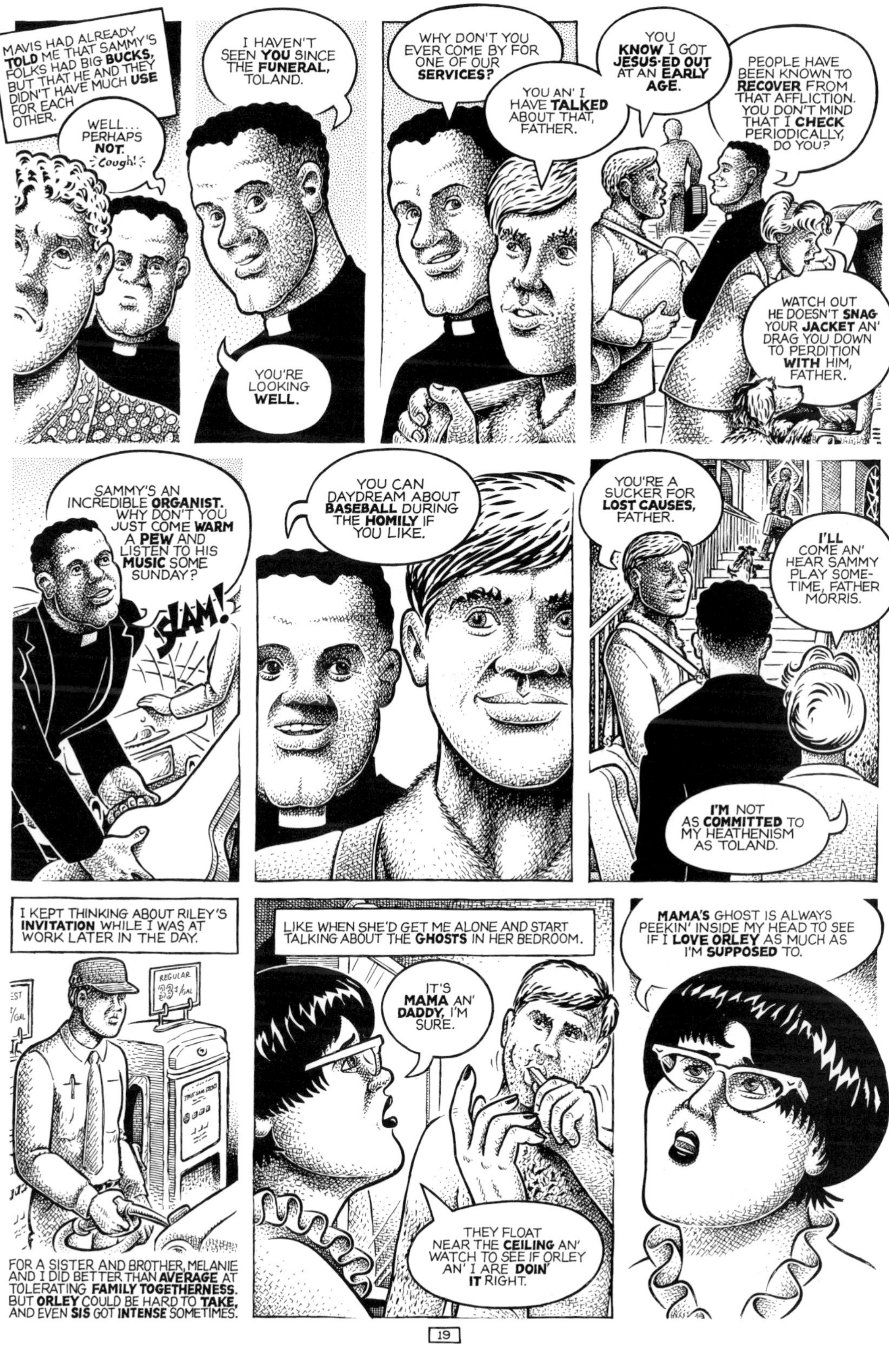
MAVIS HAD ALREADY TOLD ME THAT SAMMY'S FOLKS HAD BIG BUCKS, BUT THAT HE AND THEY DIDN'T HAVE MUCH USE FOR EACH OTHER.
WELL... PERHAPS NOT. Cough!
I HAVEN'T SEEN YOU SINCE THE FUNERAL, TOLAND.
YOU'RE LOOKING WELL.
WHY DON'T YOU EVER COME BY FOR ONE OF OUR SERVICES?
YOU AN' I HAVE TALKED ABOUT THAT, FATHER.
YOU KNOW I GOT JESUS-ED OUT AT AN EARLY AGE.
PEOPLE HAVE BEEN KNOWN TO RECOVER FROM THAT AFFLICTION. YOU DON'T MIND THAT I CHECK PERIODICALLY, DO YOU?
WATCH OUT HE DOESN'T SNAG YOUR JACKET AN' DRAG YOU DOWN TO PERDITION WITH HIM, FATHER.
SAMMY'S AN INCREDIBLE ORGANIST. WHY DON'T YOU JUST COME WARM A PEW AND LISTEN TO HIS MUSIC SOME SUNDAY?
SLAM!
YOU CAN DAYDREAM ABOUT BASEBALL DURING THE HOMILY IF YOU LIKE.
YOU'RE A SUCKER FOR LOST CAUSES, FATHER.
I'LL COME AN' HEAR SAMMY PLAY SOME-TIME, FATHER MORRIS.
I'M NOT AS COMMITTED TO MY HEATHENISM AS TOLAND.
I KEPT THINKING ABOUT RILEY'S INVITATION WHILE I WAS AT WORK LATER IN THE DAY.
REGULAR 33¢/GAL
FOR A SISTER AND BROTHER, MELANIE AND I DID BETTER THAN AVERAGE AT TOLERATING FAMILY TOGETHERNESS. BUT ORLEY COULD BE HARD TO TAKE, AND EVEN SIS GOT INTENSE SOMETIMES.
LIKE WHEN SHE'D GET ME ALONE AND START TALKING ABOUT THE GHOSTS IN HER BEDROOM.
IT'S MAMA AN' DADDY, I'M SURE.
THEY FLOAT NEAR THE CEILING AN' WATCH TO SEE IF ORLEY AN' I ARE DOIN' IT RIGHT.
MAMA'S GHOST IS ALWAYS PEEKIN' INSIDE MY HEAD TO SEE IF I LOVE ORLEY AS MUCH AS I'M SUPPOSED TO.

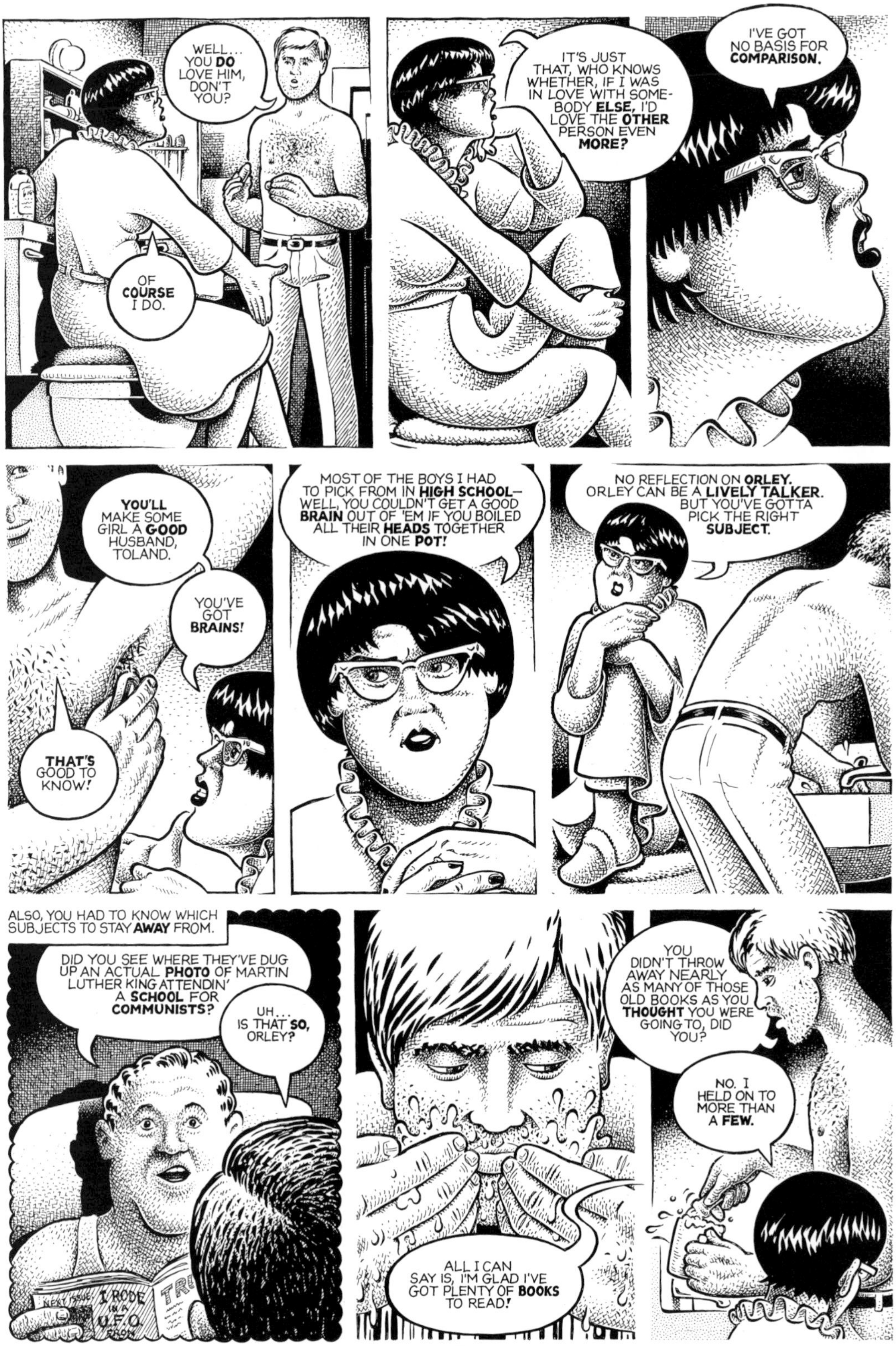
WELL... YOU DO LOVE HIM, DON'T YOU?
OF COURSE I DO.
IT'S JUST THAT, WHO KNOWS WHETHER, IF I WAS IN LOVE WITH SOMEBODY ELSE, I'D LOVE THE OTHER PERSON EVEN MORE?
I'VE GOT NO BASIS FOR COMPARISON.
YOU'LL MAKE SOME GIRL A GOOD HUSBAND, TOLAND.
YOU'VE GOT BRAINS!
THAT'S GOOD TO KNOW!
MOST OF THE BOYS I HAD TO PICK FROM IN HIGH SCHOOL— WELL, YOU COULDN'T GET A GOOD BRAIN OUT OF 'EM IF YOU BOILED ALL THEIR HEADS TOGETHER IN ONE POT!
NO REFLECTION ON ORLEY. ORLEY CAN BE A LIVELY TALKER. BUT YOU'VE GOTTA PICK THE RIGHT SUBJECT.
ALSO, YOU HAD TO KNOW WHICH SUBJECTS TO STAY AWAY FROM.
DID YOU SEE WHERE THEY'VE DUG UP AN ACTUAL PHOTO OF MARTIN LUTHER KING ATTENDIN' A SCHOOL FOR COMMUNISTS?
UH... IS THAT SO, ORLEY?
NEXT ISSUE I RODE IN A U.F.O.
ALL I CAN SAY IS, I'M GLAD I'VE GOT PLENTY OF BOOKS TO READ!
YOU DIDN'T THROW AWAY NEARLY AS MANY OF THOSE OLD BOOKS AS YOU THOUGHT YOU WERE GOING TO, DID YOU?
NO. I HELD ON TO MORE THAN A FEW.

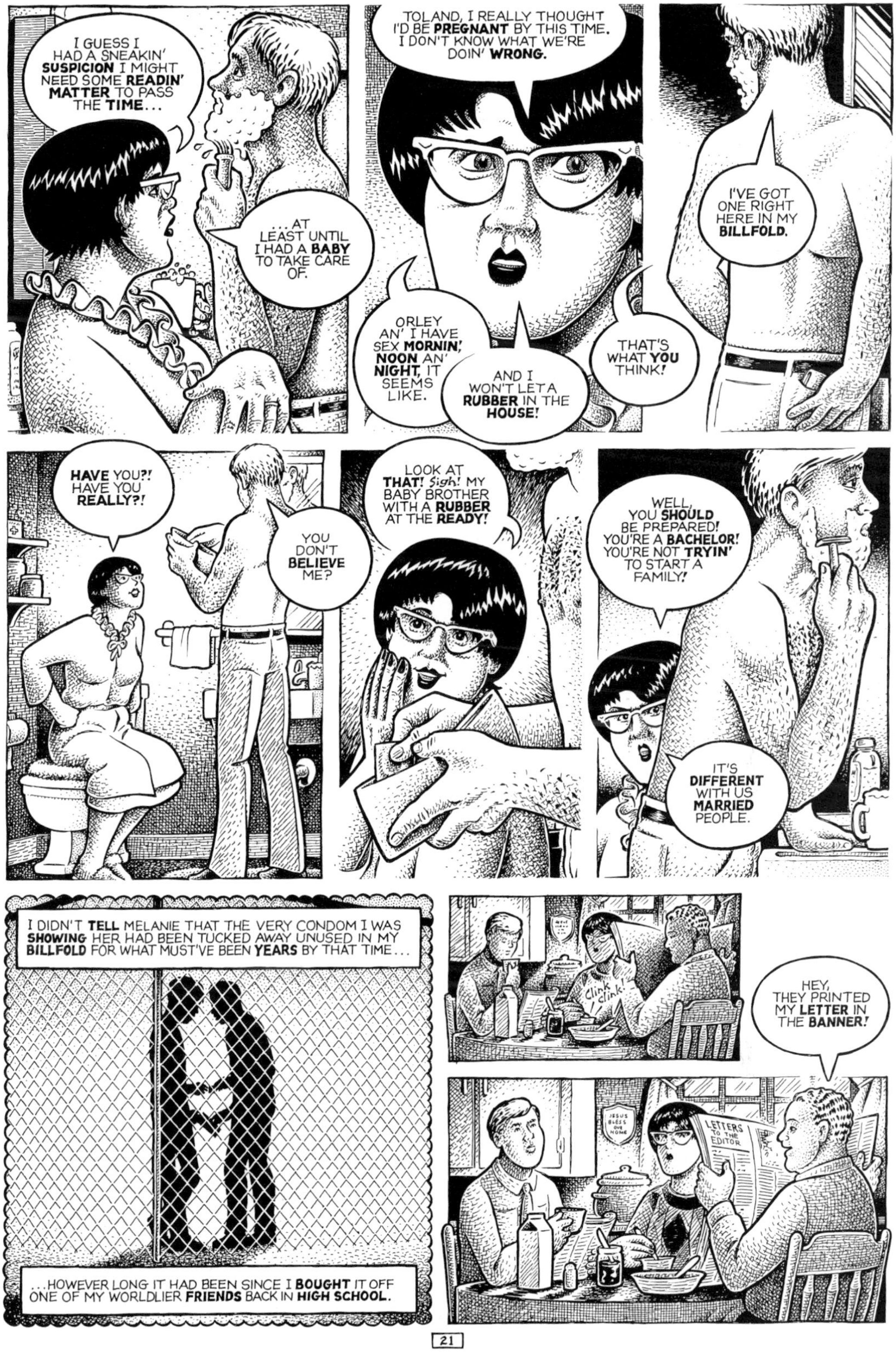
I GUESS I HAD A SNEAKIN' **SUSPICION** I MIGHT NEED SOME **READIN' MATTER** TO PASS THE **TIME**...
...AT LEAST UNTIL I HAD A **BABY** TO TAKE CARE OF.
TOLAND, I REALLY THOUGHT I'D BE **PREGNANT** BY THIS TIME. I DON'T KNOW WHAT WE'RE DOIN' **WRONG**.
ORLEY AN' I HAVE SEX **MORNIN', NOON** AN' **NIGHT**, IT SEEMS LIKE.
AND I WON'T LET A **RUBBER** IN THE **HOUSE**!
THAT'S WHAT **YOU** THINK!
I'VE GOT ONE RIGHT HERE IN MY **BILLFOLD**.
HAVE YOU?! HAVE YOU **REALLY**?!
YOU DON'T **BELIEVE** ME?
LOOK AT **THAT!** *Sigh!* MY BABY BROTHER WITH A **RUBBER** AT THE **READY**!
WELL, YOU **SHOULD** BE PREPARED! YOU'RE A **BACHELOR**! YOU'RE NOT **TRYIN'** TO START A FAMILY!
IT'S **DIFFERENT** WITH US **MARRIED** PEOPLE.
I DIDN'T **TELL** MELANIE THAT THE VERY CONDOM I WAS **SHOWING** HER HAD BEEN TUCKED AWAY UNUSED IN MY **BILLFOLD** FOR WHAT MUST'VE BEEN **YEARS** BY THAT TIME...
...HOWEVER LONG IT HAD BEEN SINCE I **BOUGHT** IT OFF ONE OF MY WORLDLIER **FRIENDS** BACK IN **HIGH SCHOOL**.
Clink clink!
LETTERS TO THE EDITOR
HEY, THEY PRINTED MY **LETTER** IN THE **BANNER**!

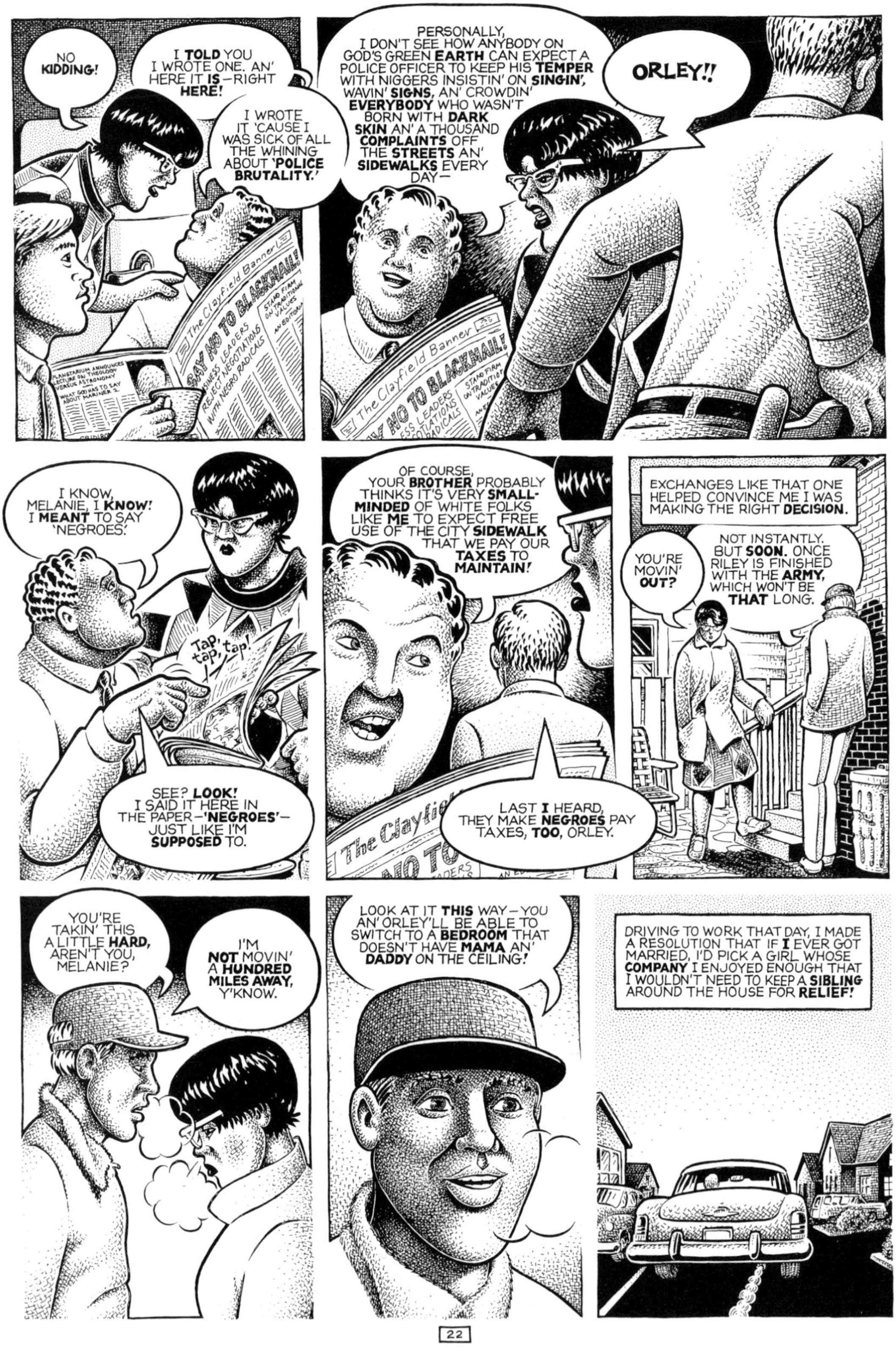

NO KIDDING!
I TOLD YOU I WROTE ONE. AN' HERE IT IS—RIGHT HERE!
I WROTE IT 'CAUSE I WAS SICK OF ALL THE WHINING ABOUT 'POLICE BRUTALITY.'
The Clayfield Banner
SAY NO TO BLACKMAIL!
BUSINESS LEADERS REJECT NEGOTIATIONS WITH NEGRO RADICALS
STAND FIRM ON TRADITIONAL VALUES
AN EDITORIAL
PLANETARIUM ANNOUNCES LECTURE ON THEOLOGY VERSUS ASTRONOMY
WHAT GOD HAS TO SAY ABOUT MARINER 2
PERSONALLY, I DON'T SEE HOW ANYBODY ON GOD'S GREEN EARTH CAN EXPECT A POLICE OFFICER TO KEEP HIS TEMPER WITH NIGGERS INSISTIN' ON SINGIN', WAVIN' SIGNS, AN' CROWDIN' EVERYBODY WHO WASN'T BORN WITH DARK SKIN AN' A THOUSAND COMPLAINTS OFF THE STREETS AN' SIDEWALKS EVERY DAY—
ORLEY!!
I KNOW, MELANIE, I KNOW! I MEANT TO SAY 'NEGROES.'
Tap, tap, tap!
SEE? LOOK! I SAID IT HERE IN THE PAPER—'NEGROES'—JUST LIKE I'M SUPPOSED TO.
OF COURSE, YOUR BROTHER PROBABLY THINKS IT'S VERY SMALL-MINDED OF WHITE FOLKS LIKE ME TO EXPECT FREE USE OF THE CITY SIDEWALK THAT WE PAY OUR TAXES TO MAINTAIN!
LAST I HEARD, THEY MAKE NEGROES PAY TAXES, TOO, ORLEY.
EXCHANGES LIKE THAT ONE HELPED CONVINCE ME I WAS MAKING THE RIGHT DECISION.
YOU'RE MOVIN' OUT?
NOT INSTANTLY. BUT SOON. ONCE RILEY IS FINISHED WITH THE ARMY, WHICH WON'T BE THAT LONG.
YOU'RE TAKIN' THIS A LITTLE HARD, AREN'T YOU, MELANIE?
I'M NOT MOVIN' A HUNDRED MILES AWAY, Y'KNOW.
LOOK AT IT THIS WAY—YOU AN' ORLEY'LL BE ABLE TO SWITCH TO A BEDROOM THAT DOESN'T HAVE MAMA AN' DADDY ON THE CEILING!
DRIVING TO WORK THAT DAY, I MADE A RESOLUTION THAT IF I EVER GOT MARRIED, I'D PICK A GIRL WHOSE COMPANY I ENJOYED ENOUGH THAT I WOULDN'T NEED TO KEEP A SIBLING AROUND THE HOUSE FOR RELIEF!

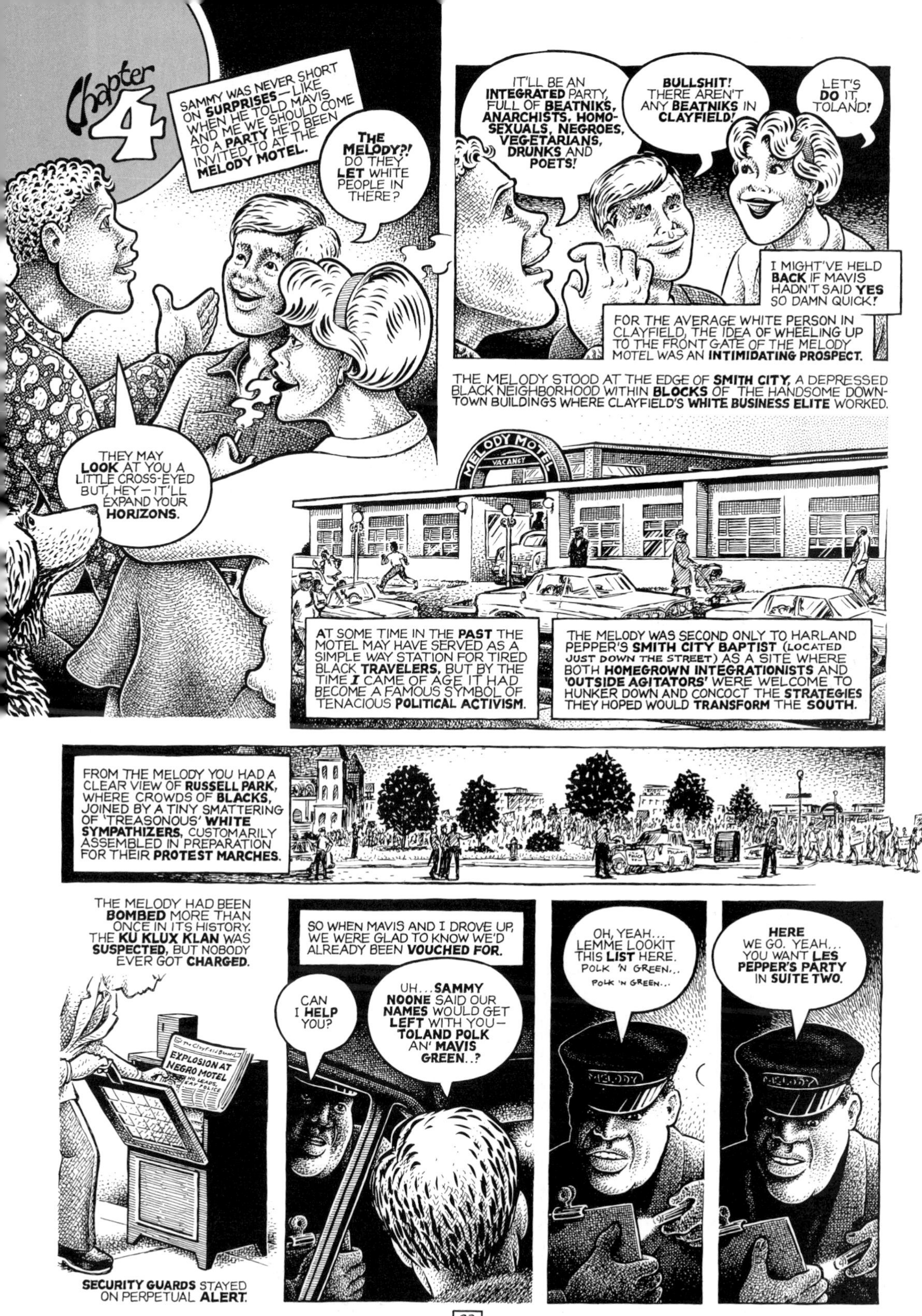
Chapter 4
SAMMY WAS NEVER SHORT ON SURPRISES—LIKE WHEN HE TOLD MAVIS AND ME WE SHOULD COME TO A PARTY HE'D BEEN INVITED TO AT THE MELODY MOTEL.
THE MELODY?! DO THEY LET WHITE PEOPLE IN THERE?
THEY MAY LOOK AT YOU A LITTLE CROSS-EYED BUT, HEY—IT'LL EXPAND YOUR HORIZONS.
IT'LL BE AN INTEGRATED PARTY, FULL OF BEATNIKS, ANARCHISTS, HOMO-SEXUALS, NEGROES, VEGETARIANS, DRUNKS AND POETS!
BULLSHIT! THERE AREN'T ANY BEATNIKS IN CLAYFIELD!
LET'S DO IT, TOLAND!
I MIGHT'VE HELD BACK IF MAVIS HADN'T SAID YES SO DAMN QUICK!
FOR THE AVERAGE WHITE PERSON IN CLAYFIELD, THE IDEA OF WHEELING UP TO THE FRONT GATE OF THE MELODY MOTEL WAS AN INTIMIDATING PROSPECT.
THE MELODY STOOD AT THE EDGE OF SMITH CITY, A DEPRESSED BLACK NEIGHBORHOOD WITHIN BLOCKS OF THE HANDSOME DOWN-TOWN BUILDINGS WHERE CLAYFIELD'S WHITE BUSINESS ELITE WORKED.
MELODY MOTEL
VACANCY
AT SOME TIME IN THE PAST THE MOTEL MAY HAVE SERVED AS A SIMPLE WAY STATION FOR TIRED BLACK TRAVELERS, BUT BY THE TIME I CAME OF AGE IT HAD BECOME A FAMOUS SYMBOL OF TENACIOUS POLITICAL ACTIVISM.
THE MELODY WAS SECOND ONLY TO HARLAND PEPPER'S SMITH CITY BAPTIST (LOCATED JUST DOWN THE STREET) AS A SITE WHERE BOTH HOMEGROWN INTEGRATIONISTS AND 'OUTSIDE AGITATORS' WERE WELCOME TO HUNKER DOWN AND CONCOCT THE STRATEGIES THEY HOPED WOULD TRANSFORM THE SOUTH.
FROM THE MELODY YOU HAD A CLEAR VIEW OF RUSSELL PARK, WHERE CROWDS OF BLACKS, JOINED BY A TINY SMATTERING OF 'TREASONOUS' WHITE SYMPATHIZERS, CUSTOMARILY ASSEMBLED IN PREPARATION FOR THEIR PROTEST MARCHES.
THE MELODY HAD BEEN BOMBED MORE THAN ONCE IN ITS HISTORY. THE KU KLUX KLAN WAS SUSPECTED, BUT NOBODY EVER GOT CHARGED.
EXPLOSION AT NEGRO MOTEL
SECURITY GUARDS STAYED ON PERPETUAL ALERT.
SO WHEN MAVIS AND I DROVE UP, WE WERE GLAD TO KNOW WE'D ALREADY BEEN VOUCHED FOR.
CAN I HELP YOU?
UH... SAMMY NOONE SAID OUR NAMES WOULD GET LEFT WITH YOU—TOLAND POLK AN' MAVIS GREEN..?
OH, YEAH... LEMME LOOKIT THIS LIST HERE. POLK 'N GREEN... POLK 'N GREEN...
MELODY
HERE WE GO. YEAH... YOU WANT LES PEPPER'S PARTY IN SUITE TWO.

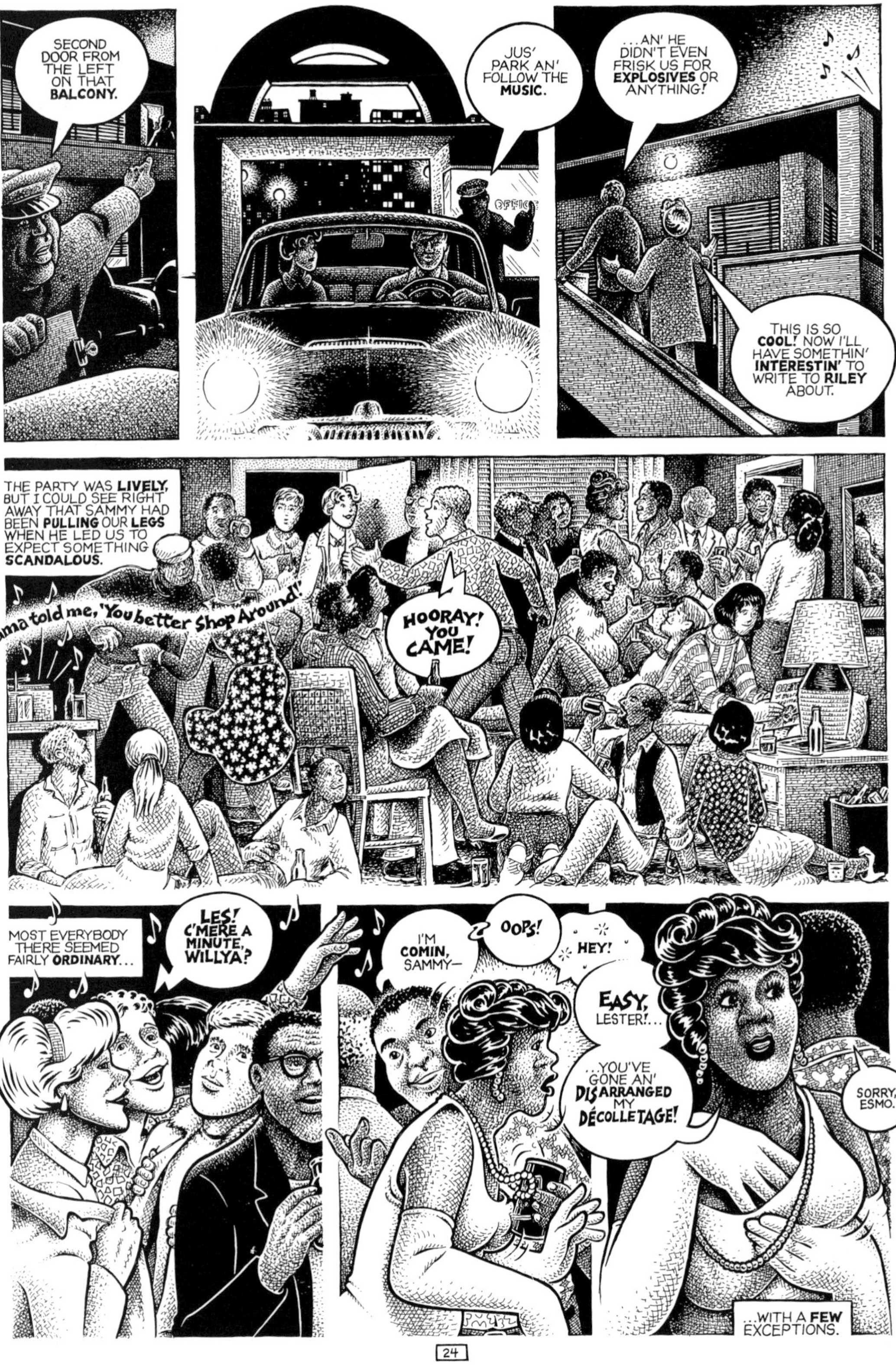

SECOND DOOR FROM THE LEFT ON THAT BALCONY.
JUS' PARK AN' FOLLOW THE MUSIC.
...AN' HE DIDN'T EVEN FRISK US FOR EXPLOSIVES OR ANYTHING!
THIS IS SO COOL! NOW I'LL HAVE SOMETHIN' INTERESTIN' TO WRITE TO RILEY ABOUT.
THE PARTY WAS LIVELY, BUT I COULD SEE RIGHT AWAY THAT SAMMY HAD BEEN PULLING OUR LEGS WHEN HE LED US TO EXPECT SOMETHING SCANDALOUS.
My mama told me, 'You better Shop Around!'
HOORAY! YOU CAME!
MOST EVERYBODY THERE SEEMED FAIRLY ORDINARY...
LES! C'MERE A MINUTE, WILLYA?
I'M COMIN, SAMMY—
OOPS!
HEY!
EASY, LESTER!...
...YOU'VE GONE AN' DISARRANGED MY DÉCOLLETAGE!
SORRY, ESMO.
...WITH A FEW EXCEPTIONS.

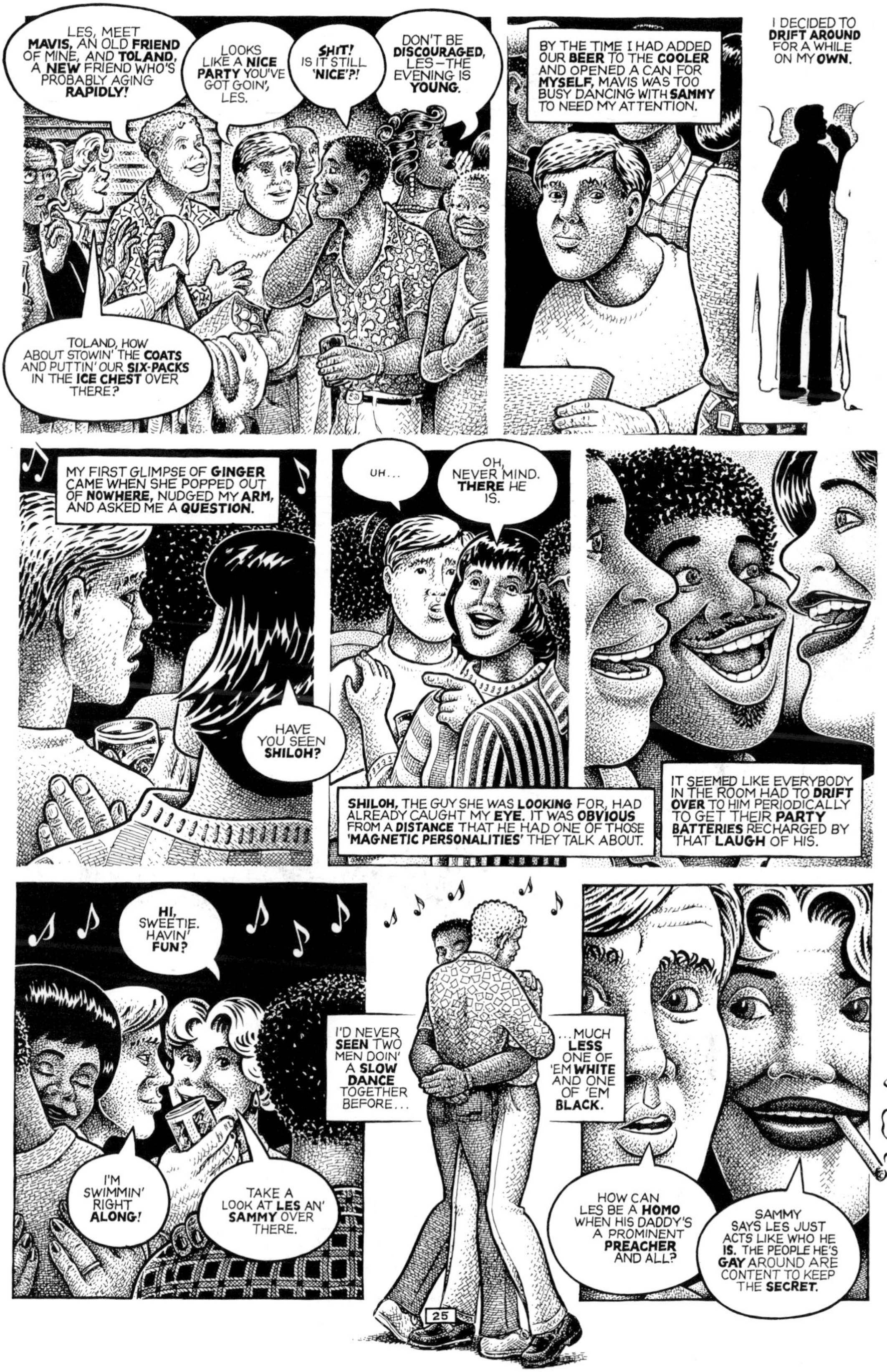
LES, MEET MAVIS, AN OLD FRIEND OF MINE, AND TOLAND, A NEW FRIEND WHO'S PROBABLY AGING RAPIDLY!
LOOKS LIKE A NICE PARTY YOU'VE GOT GOIN', LES.
SHIT! IS IT STILL 'NICE'?!
DON'T BE DISCOURAGED, LES—THE EVENING IS YOUNG.
TOLAND, HOW ABOUT STOWIN' THE COATS AND PUTTIN' OUR SIX-PACKS IN THE ICE CHEST OVER THERE?
BY THE TIME I HAD ADDED OUR BEER TO THE COOLER AND OPENED A CAN FOR MYSELF, MAVIS WAS TOO BUSY DANCING WITH SAMMY TO NEED MY ATTENTION.
I DECIDED TO DRIFT AROUND FOR A WHILE ON MY OWN.
MY FIRST GLIMPSE OF GINGER CAME WHEN SHE POPPED OUT OF NOWHERE, NUDGED MY ARM, AND ASKED ME A QUESTION.
HAVE YOU SEEN SHILOH?
UH...
OH, NEVER MIND. THERE HE IS.
SHILOH, THE GUY SHE WAS LOOKING FOR, HAD ALREADY CAUGHT MY EYE. IT WAS OBVIOUS FROM A DISTANCE THAT HE HAD ONE OF THOSE 'MAGNETIC PERSONALITIES' THEY TALK ABOUT.
IT SEEMED LIKE EVERYBODY IN THE ROOM HAD TO DRIFT OVER TO HIM PERIODICALLY TO GET THEIR PARTY BATTERIES RECHARGED BY THAT LAUGH OF HIS.
HI, SWEETIE. HAVIN' FUN?
I'M SWIMMIN' RIGHT ALONG!
TAKE A LOOK AT LES AN' SAMMY OVER THERE.
I'D NEVER SEEN TWO MEN DOIN' A SLOW DANCE TOGETHER BEFORE...
...MUCH LESS ONE OF 'EM WHITE AND ONE OF 'EM BLACK.
HOW CAN LES BE A HOMO WHEN HIS DADDY'S A PROMINENT PREACHER AND ALL?
SAMMY SAYS LES JUST ACTS LIKE WHO HE IS. THE PEOPLE HE'S GAY AROUND ARE CONTENT TO KEEP THE SECRET.

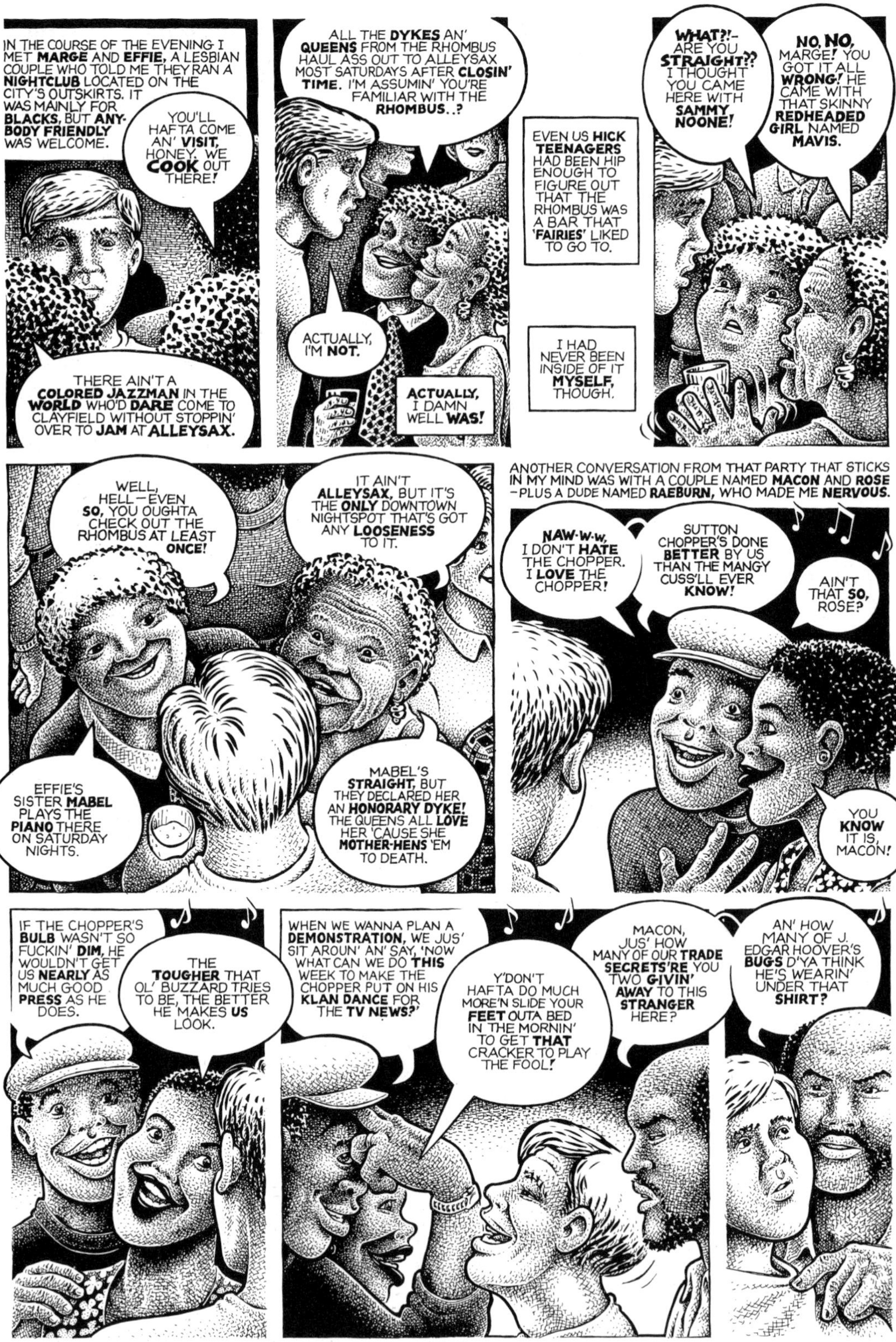

IN THE COURSE OF THE EVENING I MET MARGE AND EFFIE, A LESBIAN COUPLE WHO TOLD ME THEY RAN A NIGHTCLUB LOCATED ON THE CITY'S OUTSKIRTS. IT WAS MAINLY FOR BLACKS, BUT ANYBODY FRIENDLY WAS WELCOME.
YOU'LL HAFTA COME AN' VISIT, HONEY. WE COOK OUT THERE!
THERE AIN'T A COLORED JAZZMAN IN THE WORLD WHO'D DARE COME TO CLAYFIELD WITHOUT STOPPIN' OVER TO JAM AT ALLEYSAX.
ALL THE DYKES AN' QUEENS FROM THE RHOMBUS HAUL ASS OUT TO ALLEYSAX MOST SATURDAYS AFTER CLOSIN' TIME. I'M ASSUMIN' YOU'RE FAMILIAR WITH THE RHOMBUS..?
ACTUALLY, I'M NOT.
ACTUALLY, I DAMN WELL WAS!
EVEN US HICK TEENAGERS HAD BEEN HIP ENOUGH TO FIGURE OUT THAT THE RHOMBUS WAS A BAR THAT 'FAIRIES' LIKED TO GO TO.
I HAD NEVER BEEN INSIDE OF IT MYSELF, THOUGH.
WHAT?!– ARE YOU STRAIGHT?? I THOUGHT YOU CAME HERE WITH SAMMY NOONE!
NO, NO, MARGE! YOU GOT IT ALL WRONG! HE CAME WITH THAT SKINNY REDHEADED GIRL NAMED MAVIS.
WELL, HELL—EVEN SO, YOU OUGHTA CHECK OUT THE RHOMBUS AT LEAST ONCE!
IT AIN'T ALLEYSAX, BUT IT'S THE ONLY DOWNTOWN NIGHTSPOT THAT'S GOT ANY LOOSENESS TO IT.
EFFIE'S SISTER MABEL PLAYS THE PIANO THERE ON SATURDAY NIGHTS.
MABEL'S STRAIGHT, BUT THEY DECLARED HER AN HONORARY DYKE! THE QUEENS ALL LOVE HER 'CAUSE SHE MOTHER-HENS 'EM TO DEATH.
ANOTHER CONVERSATION FROM THAT PARTY THAT STICKS IN MY MIND WAS WITH A COUPLE NAMED MACON AND ROSE –PLUS A DUDE NAMED RAEBURN, WHO MADE ME NERVOUS.
NAW-W-W, I DON'T HATE THE CHOPPER. I LOVE THE CHOPPER!
SUTTON CHOPPER'S DONE BETTER BY US THAN THE MANGY CUSS'LL EVER KNOW!
AIN'T THAT SO, ROSE?
YOU KNOW IT IS, MACON!
IF THE CHOPPER'S BULB WASN'T SO FUCKIN' DIM, HE WOULDN'T GET US NEARLY AS MUCH GOOD PRESS AS HE DOES.
THE TOUGHER THAT OL' BUZZARD TRIES TO BE, THE BETTER HE MAKES US LOOK.
WHEN WE WANNA PLAN A DEMONSTRATION, WE JUS' SIT AROUN' AN' SAY, 'NOW WHAT CAN WE DO THIS WEEK TO MAKE THE CHOPPER PUT ON HIS KLAN DANCE FOR THE TV NEWS?'
Y'DON'T HAFTA DO MUCH MORE'N SLIDE YOUR FEET OUTA BED IN THE MORNIN' TO GET THAT CRACKER TO PLAY THE FOOL!
MACON, JUS' HOW MANY OF OUR TRADE SECRETS'RE YOU TWO GIVIN' AWAY TO THIS STRANGER HERE?
AN' HOW MANY OF J. EDGAR HOOVER'S BUGS D'YA THINK HE'S WEARIN' UNDER THAT SHIRT?

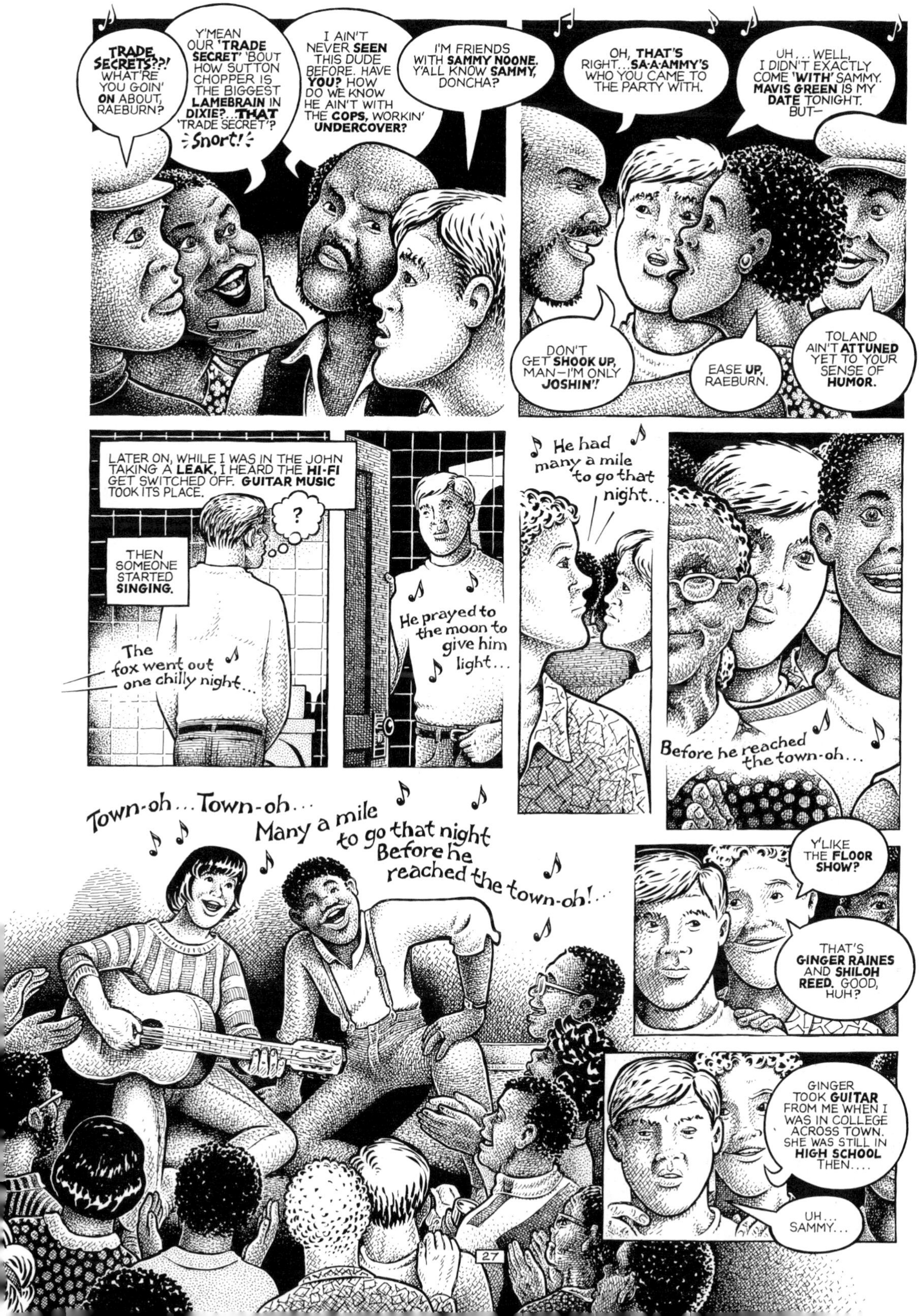
TRADE SECRETS??! WHAT'RE YOU GOIN' ON ABOUT, RAEBURN?
Y'MEAN OUR 'TRADE SECRET' 'BOUT HOW SUTTON CHOPPER IS THE BIGGEST LAMEBRAIN IN DIXIE?...THAT 'TRADE SECRET'?
Snort!
I AIN'T NEVER SEEN THIS DUDE BEFORE. HAVE YOU? HOW DO WE KNOW HE AIN'T WITH THE COPS, WORKIN' UNDERCOVER?
I'M FRIENDS WITH SAMMY NOONE. Y'ALL KNOW SAMMY, DONCHA?
OH, THAT'S RIGHT...SA-A-AMMY'S WHO YOU CAME TO THE PARTY WITH.
UH... WELL, I DIDN'T EXACTLY COME 'WITH' SAMMY. MAVIS GREEN IS MY DATE TONIGHT. BUT—
DON'T GET SHOOK UP, MAN—I'M ONLY JOSHIN'!
EASE UP, RAEBURN.
TOLAND AIN'T ATTUNED YET TO YOUR SENSE OF HUMOR.
LATER ON, WHILE I WAS IN THE JOHN TAKING A LEAK, I HEARD THE HI-FI GET SWITCHED OFF. GUITAR MUSIC TOOK ITS PLACE.
?
THEN SOMEONE STARTED SINGING.
The fox went out one chilly night...
He prayed to the moon to give him light...
He had many a mile to go that night...
Before he reached the town-oh...
Town-oh... Town-oh...
Many a mile to go that night Before he reached the town-oh!...
Y'LIKE THE FLOOR SHOW?
THAT'S GINGER RAINES AND SHILOH REED. GOOD, HUH?
GINGER TOOK GUITAR FROM ME WHEN I WAS IN COLLEGE ACROSS TOWN. SHE WAS STILL IN HIGH SCHOOL THEN....
UH... SAMMY...

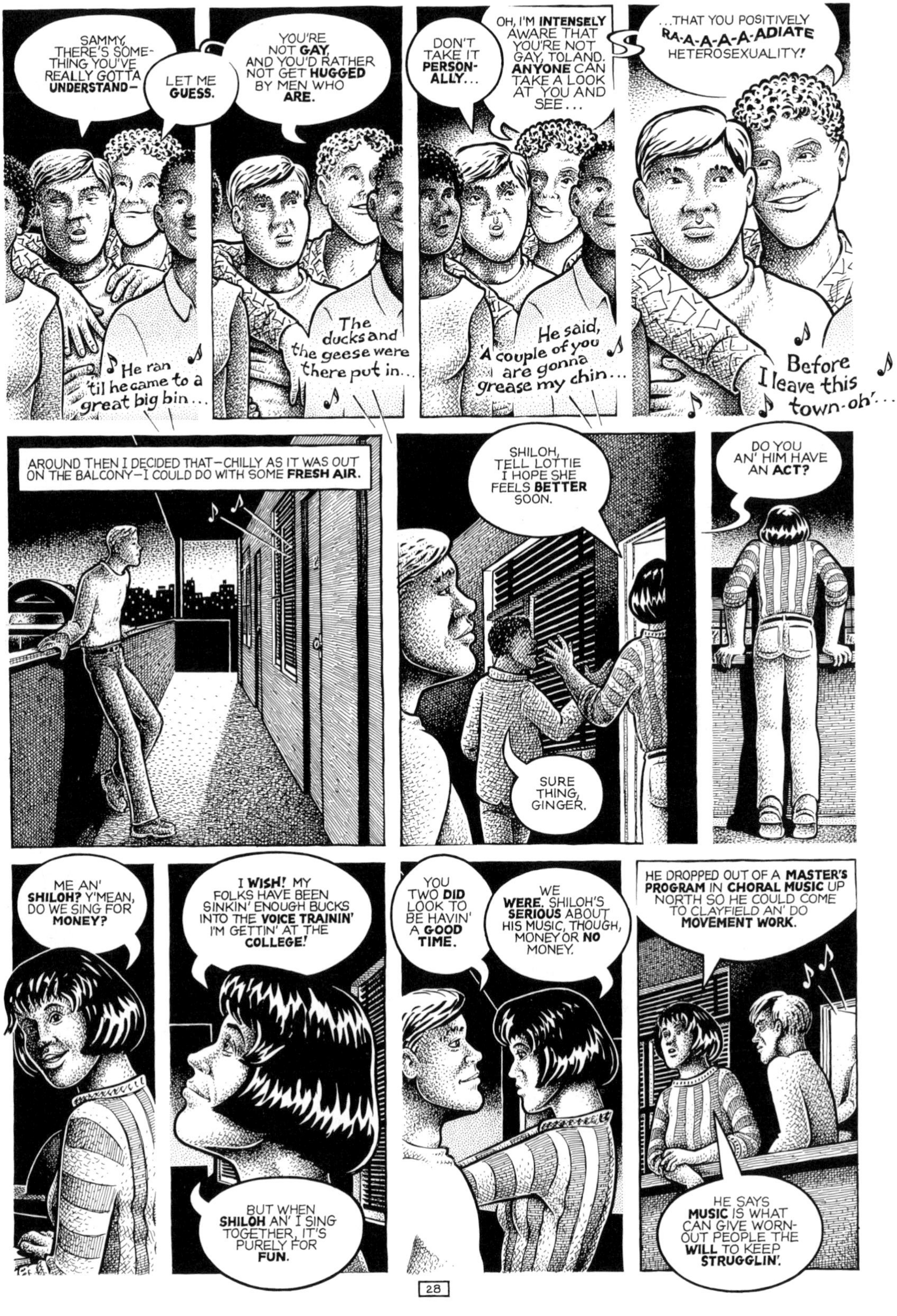
SAMMY, THERE'S SOMETHING YOU'VE REALLY GOTTA UNDERSTAND—
LET ME GUESS.
YOU'RE NOT GAY, AND YOU'D RATHER NOT GET HUGGED BY MEN WHO ARE.
He ran 'til he came to a great big bin...
The ducks and the geese were there put in...
DON'T TAKE IT PERSONALLY...
OH, I'M INTENSELY AWARE THAT YOU'RE NOT GAY, TOLAND. ANYONE CAN TAKE A LOOK AT YOU AND SEE...
He said, 'A couple of you are gonna grease my chin...
...THAT YOU POSITIVELY RA-A-A-A-A-ADIATE HETEROSEXUALITY!
Before I leave this town-oh'...
AROUND THEN I DECIDED THAT—CHILLY AS IT WAS OUT ON THE BALCONY—I COULD DO WITH SOME FRESH AIR.
SHILOH, TELL LOTTIE I HOPE SHE FEELS BETTER SOON.
SURE THING, GINGER.
DO YOU AN' HIM HAVE AN ACT?
ME AN' SHILOH? Y'MEAN, DO WE SING FOR MONEY?
I WISH! MY FOLKS HAVE BEEN SINKIN' ENOUGH BUCKS INTO THE VOICE TRAININ' I'M GETTIN' AT THE COLLEGE!
BUT WHEN SHILOH AN' I SING TOGETHER, IT'S PURELY FOR FUN.
YOU TWO DID LOOK TO BE HAVIN' A GOOD TIME.
WE WERE. SHILOH'S SERIOUS ABOUT HIS MUSIC, THOUGH, MONEY OR NO MONEY.
HE DROPPED OUT OF A MASTER'S PROGRAM IN CHORAL MUSIC UP NORTH SO HE COULD COME TO CLAYFIELD AN' DO MOVEMENT WORK.
HE SAYS MUSIC IS WHAT CAN GIVE WORN-OUT PEOPLE THE WILL TO KEEP STRUGGLIN'.

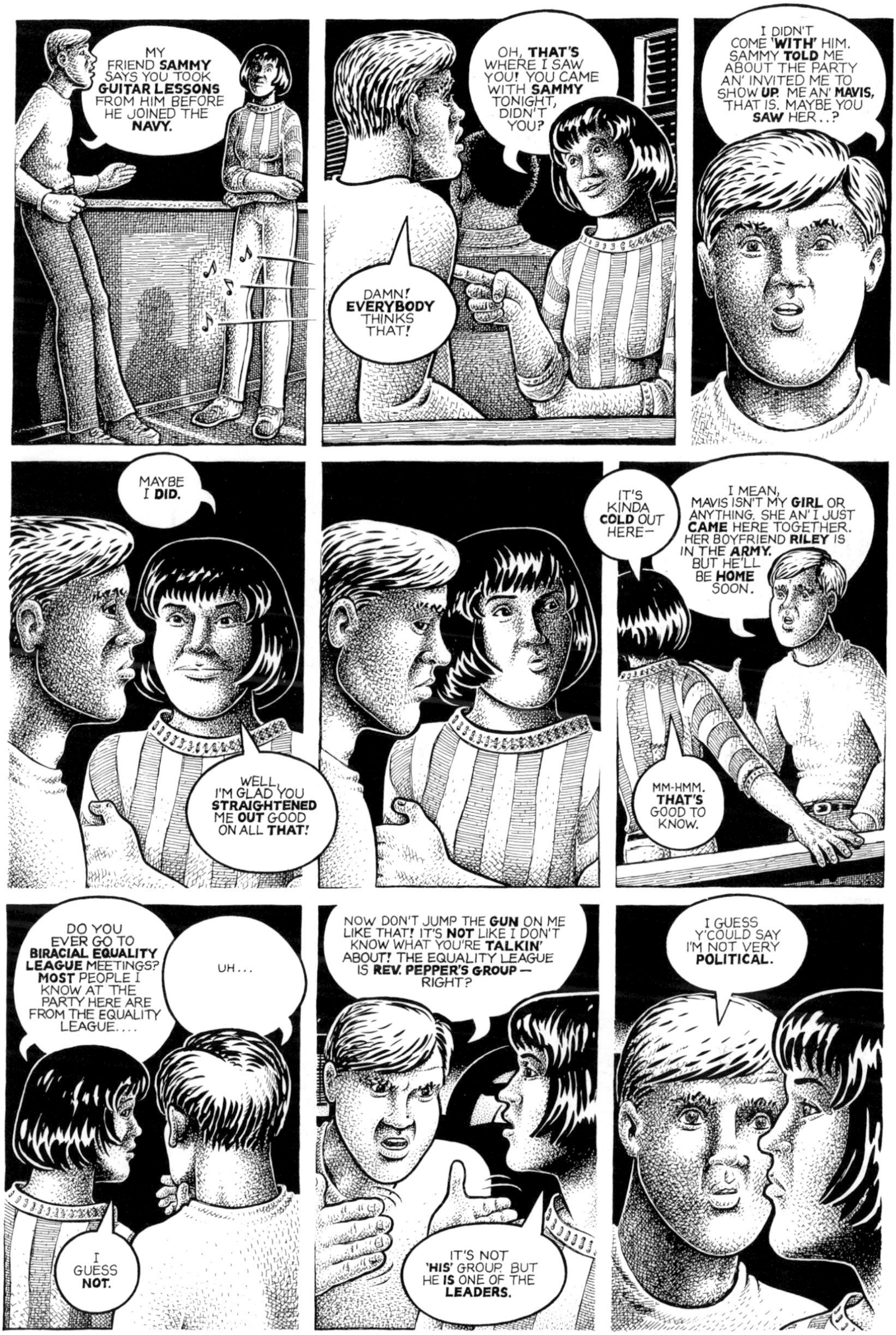
MY FRIEND SAMMY SAYS YOU TOOK GUITAR LESSONS FROM HIM BEFORE HE JOINED THE NAVY.
OH, THAT'S WHERE I SAW YOU! YOU CAME WITH SAMMY TONIGHT, DIDN'T YOU?
DAMN! EVERYBODY THINKS THAT!
I DIDN'T COME 'WITH' HIM. SAMMY TOLD ME ABOUT THE PARTY AN' INVITED ME TO SHOW UP. ME AN' MAVIS, THAT IS. MAYBE YOU SAW HER..?
MAYBE I DID.
WELL, I'M GLAD YOU STRAIGHTENED ME OUT GOOD ON ALL THAT!
IT'S KINDA COLD OUT HERE—
I MEAN, MAVIS ISN'T MY GIRL OR ANYTHING. SHE AN' I JUST CAME HERE TOGETHER. HER BOYFRIEND RILEY IS IN THE ARMY. BUT HE'LL BE HOME SOON.
MM-HMM. THAT'S GOOD TO KNOW.
DO YOU EVER GO TO BIRACIAL EQUALITY LEAGUE MEETINGS? MOST PEOPLE I KNOW AT THE PARTY HERE ARE FROM THE EQUALITY LEAGUE....
UH...
I GUESS NOT.
NOW DON'T JUMP THE GUN ON ME LIKE THAT! IT'S NOT LIKE I DON'T KNOW WHAT YOU'RE TALKIN' ABOUT! THE EQUALITY LEAGUE IS REV. PEPPER'S GROUP — RIGHT?
IT'S NOT 'HIS' GROUP, BUT HE IS ONE OF THE LEADERS.
I GUESS Y'COULD SAY I'M NOT VERY POLITICAL.

NOT TO **PUT DOWN** THE EQUALITY LEAGUE OR ANYTHING...

...BUT THESE **MARCHES** AN' **DEMONSTRATIONS** COME **ONE** ON TOP OF THE **OTHER** FOR MONTHS ON END —AND WHAT REALLY GETS **ACCOMPLISHED?**

PEOPLE ARE JUST AS **SCREWED UP** AN' **HATEFUL** TO EACH OTHER AS THEY'VE **EVER** BEEN, AS FAR AS I CAN TELL.

OH. WELL, MAYBE WE OUGHT TO STOP **DOIN'** IT, THEN.

WE CAN LEAVE THINGS THE WAY THEY **ARE** AN' PUT OUR ENERGIES INTO SOME-THIN' **USEFUL.**

I'LL BRING THAT UP AT THE NEXT **MEETING.**

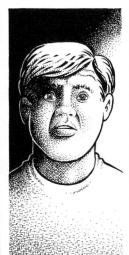

I'M **SLEEPY**, TOLAND, CAN YOU TAKE ME **HOME?**

I'LL BE READY IN JUST A **MINUTE**, MAVIS.

EXCUSE ME... I DON'T MEAN TO BE A **NUISANCE—**

—BUT IF YOU'RE NOT EVEN GONNA **ARGUE** WITH ME, WHAT'S THE POINT IN MY BOTHERIN' TO SAY SOMETHIN' **ASININE?**

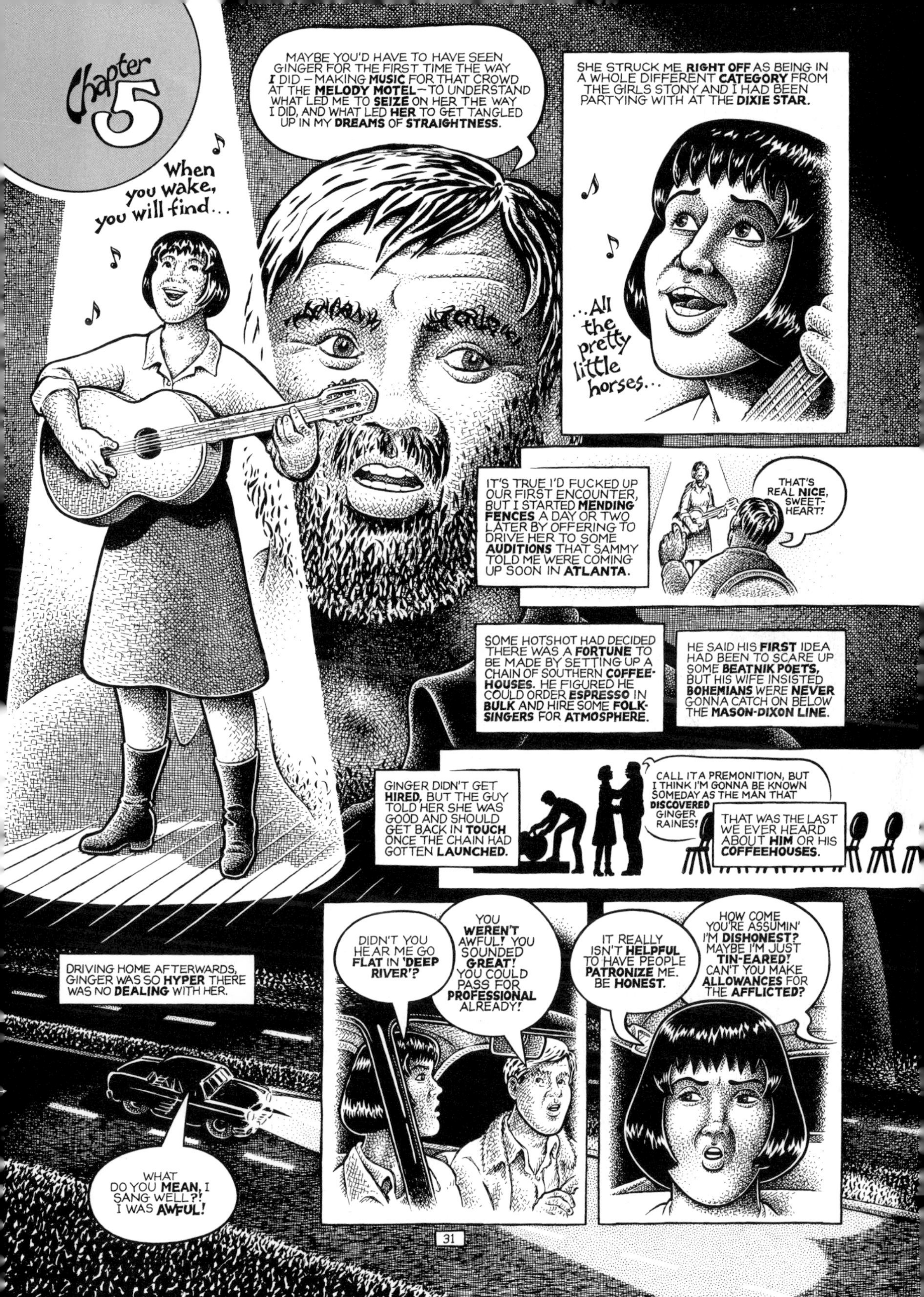
Chapter 5
MAYBE YOU'D HAVE TO HAVE SEEN GINGER FOR THE FIRST TIME THE WAY I DID — MAKING MUSIC FOR THAT CROWD AT THE MELODY MOTEL — TO UNDERSTAND WHAT LED ME TO SEIZE ON HER THE WAY I DID, AND WHAT LED HER TO GET TANGLED UP IN MY DREAMS OF STRAIGHTNESS.
SHE STRUCK ME RIGHT OFF AS BEING IN A WHOLE DIFFERENT CATEGORY FROM THE GIRLS STONY AND I HAD BEEN PARTYING WITH AT THE DIXIE STAR.
When you wake, you will find...
...All the pretty little horses...
IT'S TRUE I'D FUCKED UP OUR FIRST ENCOUNTER, BUT I STARTED MENDING FENCES A DAY OR TWO LATER BY OFFERING TO DRIVE HER TO SOME AUDITIONS THAT SAMMY TOLD ME WERE COMING UP SOON IN ATLANTA.
THAT'S REAL NICE, SWEET-HEART!
SOME HOTSHOT HAD DECIDED THERE WAS A FORTUNE TO BE MADE BY SETTING UP A CHAIN OF SOUTHERN COFFEE-HOUSES. HE FIGURED HE COULD ORDER ESPRESSO IN BULK AND HIRE SOME FOLK-SINGERS FOR ATMOSPHERE.
HE SAID HIS FIRST IDEA HAD BEEN TO SCARE UP SOME BEATNIK POETS, BUT HIS WIFE INSISTED BOHEMIANS WERE NEVER GONNA CATCH ON BELOW THE MASON-DIXON LINE.
GINGER DIDN'T GET HIRED, BUT THE GUY TOLD HER SHE WAS GOOD AND SHOULD GET BACK IN TOUCH ONCE THE CHAIN HAD GOTTEN LAUNCHED.
CALL IT A PREMONITION, BUT I THINK I'M GONNA BE KNOWN SOMEDAY AS THE MAN THAT DISCOVERED GINGER RAINES!
THAT WAS THE LAST WE EVER HEARD ABOUT HIM OR HIS COFFEEHOUSES.
DRIVING HOME AFTERWARDS, GINGER WAS SO HYPER THERE WAS NO DEALING WITH HER.
WHAT DO YOU MEAN, I SANG WELL?! I WAS AWFUL!
DIDN'T YOU HEAR ME GO FLAT IN 'DEEP RIVER'?
YOU WEREN'T AWFUL! YOU SOUNDED GREAT! YOU COULD PASS FOR PROFESSIONAL ALREADY!
IT REALLY ISN'T HELPFUL TO HAVE PEOPLE PATRONIZE ME. BE HONEST.
HOW COME YOU'RE ASSUMIN' I'M DISHONEST? MAYBE I'M JUST TIN-EARED! CAN'T YOU MAKE ALLOWANCES FOR THE AFFLICTED?

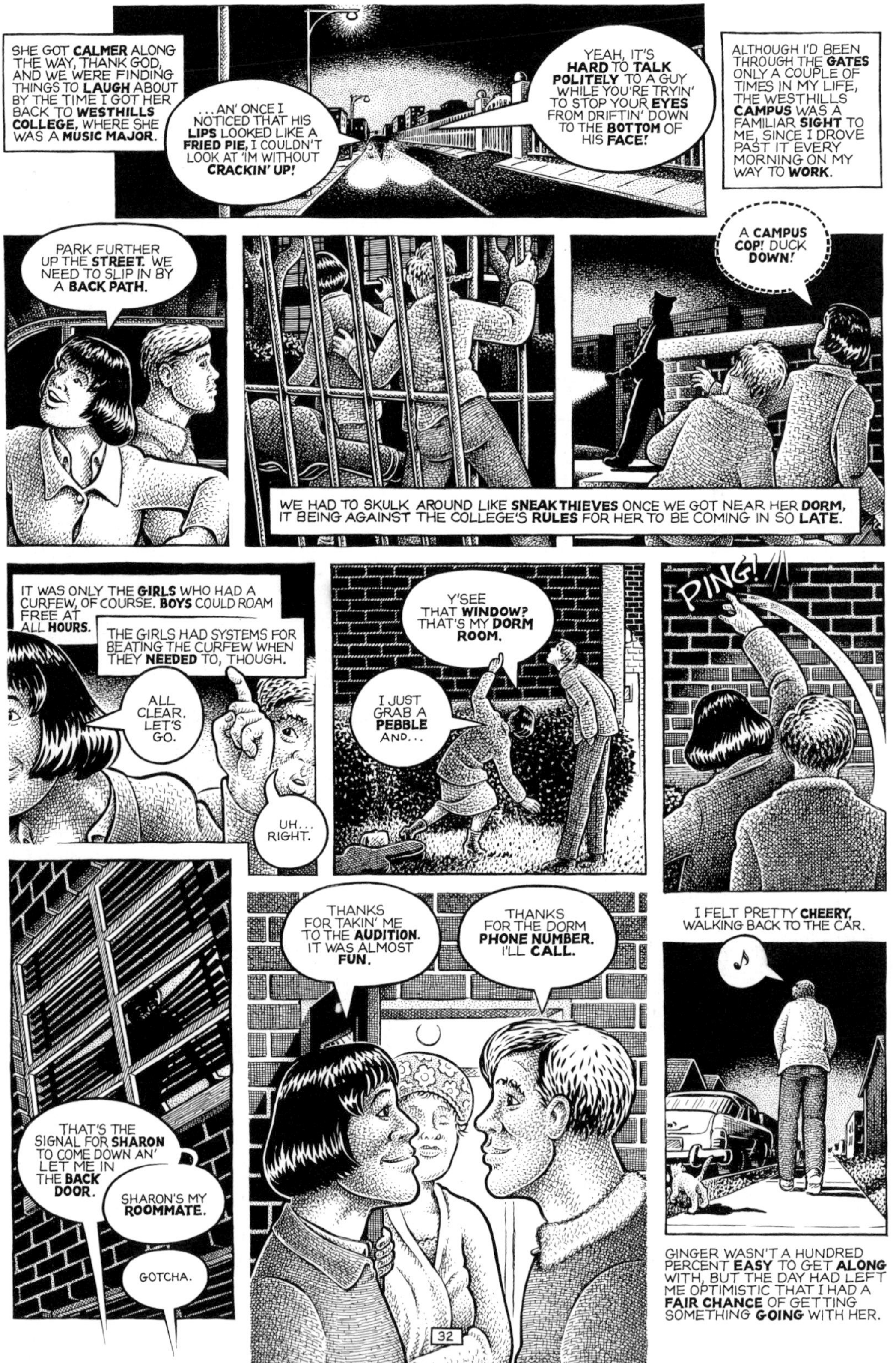

SHE GOT CALMER ALONG THE WAY, THANK GOD, AND WE WERE FINDING THINGS TO LAUGH ABOUT BY THE TIME I GOT HER BACK TO WESTHILLS COLLEGE, WHERE SHE WAS A MUSIC MAJOR.
...AN' ONCE I NOTICED THAT HIS LIPS LOOKED LIKE A FRIED PIE, I COULDN'T LOOK AT 'IM WITHOUT CRACKIN' UP!
YEAH, IT'S HARD TO TALK POLITELY TO A GUY WHILE YOU'RE TRYIN' TO STOP YOUR EYES FROM DRIFTIN' DOWN TO THE BOTTOM OF HIS FACE!
ALTHOUGH I'D BEEN THROUGH THE GATES ONLY A COUPLE OF TIMES IN MY LIFE, THE WESTHILLS CAMPUS WAS A FAMILIAR SIGHT TO ME, SINCE I DROVE PAST IT EVERY MORNING ON MY WAY TO WORK.
PARK FURTHER UP THE STREET. WE NEED TO SLIP IN BY A BACK PATH.
A CAMPUS COP! DUCK DOWN!
WE HAD TO SKULK AROUND LIKE SNEAK THIEVES ONCE WE GOT NEAR HER DORM, IT BEING AGAINST THE COLLEGE'S RULES FOR HER TO BE COMING IN SO LATE.
IT WAS ONLY THE GIRLS WHO HAD A CURFEW, OF COURSE. BOYS COULD ROAM FREE AT ALL HOURS.
THE GIRLS HAD SYSTEMS FOR BEATING THE CURFEW WHEN THEY NEEDED TO, THOUGH.
ALL CLEAR. LET'S GO.
UH... RIGHT.
Y'SEE THAT WINDOW? THAT'S MY DORM ROOM.
I JUST GRAB A PEBBLE AND...
PING! //
THAT'S THE SIGNAL FOR SHARON TO COME DOWN AN' LET ME IN THE BACK DOOR.
SHARON'S MY ROOMMATE.
GOTCHA.
THANKS FOR TAKIN' ME TO THE AUDITION. IT WAS ALMOST FUN.
THANKS FOR THE DORM PHONE NUMBER. I'LL CALL.
I FELT PRETTY CHEERY, WALKING BACK TO THE CAR.
♪
GINGER WASN'T A HUNDRED PERCENT EASY TO GET ALONG WITH, BUT THE DAY HAD LEFT ME OPTIMISTIC THAT I HAD A FAIR CHANCE OF GETTING SOMETHING GOING WITH HER.

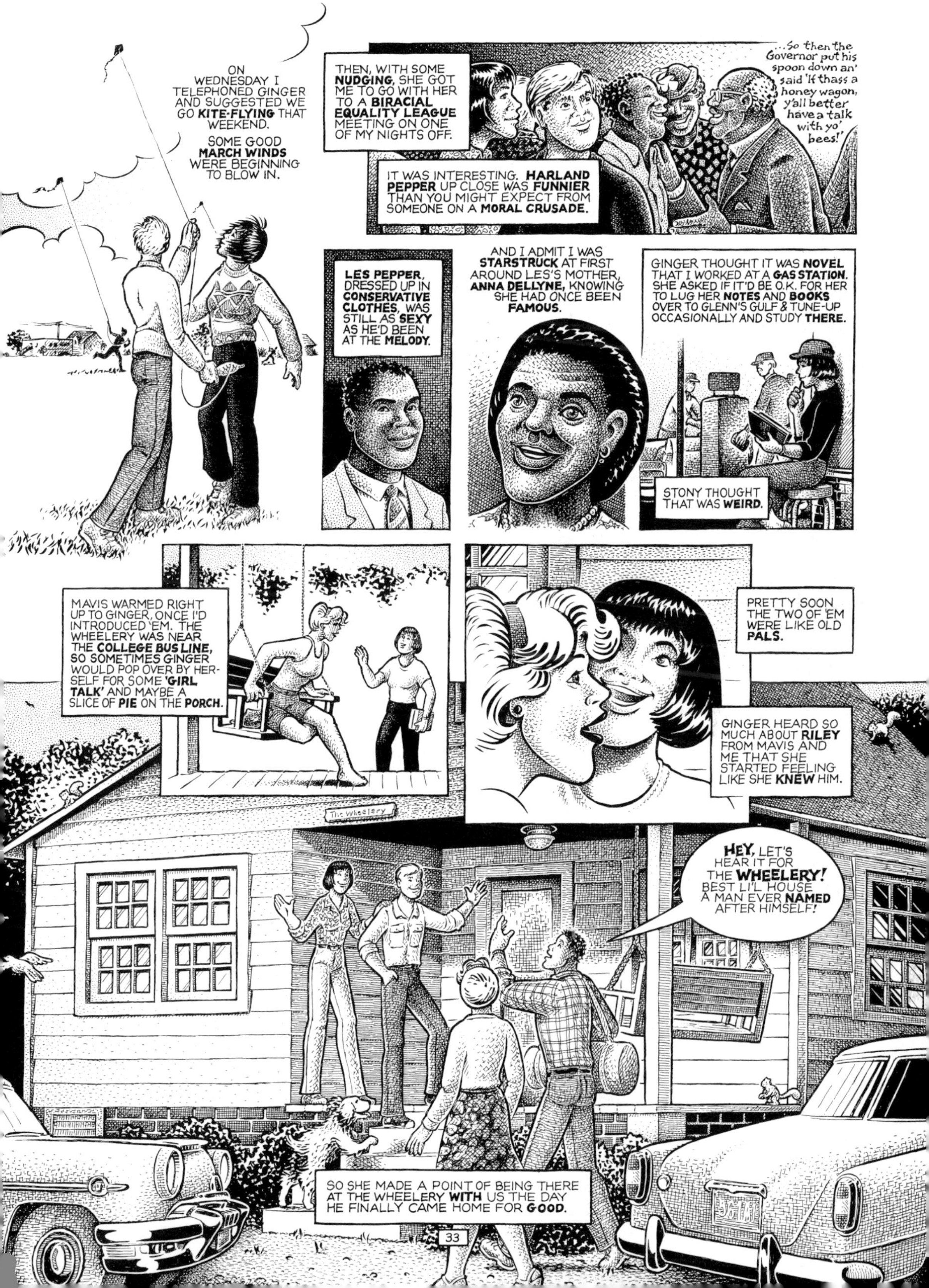

ON WEDNESDAY I TELEPHONED GINGER AND SUGGESTED WE GO KITE-FLYING THAT WEEKEND.
SOME GOOD MARCH WINDS WERE BEGINNING TO BLOW IN.
THEN, WITH SOME NUDGING, SHE GOT ME TO GO WITH HER TO A BIRACIAL EQUALITY LEAGUE MEETING ON ONE OF MY NIGHTS OFF.
...So then the Governor put his spoon down an' said 'If thass a honey wagon, y'all better have a talk with yo' bees!'
IT WAS INTERESTING. HARLAND PEPPER UP CLOSE WAS FUNNIER THAN YOU MIGHT EXPECT FROM SOMEONE ON A MORAL CRUSADE.
LES PEPPER, DRESSED UP IN CONSERVATIVE CLOTHES, WAS STILL AS SEXY AS HE'D BEEN AT THE MELODY.
AND I ADMIT I WAS STARSTRUCK AT FIRST AROUND LES'S MOTHER, ANNA DELLYNE, KNOWING SHE HAD ONCE BEEN FAMOUS.
GINGER THOUGHT IT WAS NOVEL THAT I WORKED AT A GAS STATION. SHE ASKED IF IT'D BE O.K. FOR HER TO LUG HER NOTES AND BOOKS OVER TO GLENN'S GULF & TUNE-UP OCCASIONALLY AND STUDY THERE.
STONY THOUGHT THAT WAS WEIRD.
MAVIS WARMED RIGHT UP TO GINGER, ONCE I'D INTRODUCED 'EM. THE WHEELERY WAS NEAR THE COLLEGE BUS LINE, SO SOMETIMES GINGER WOULD POP OVER BY HERSELF FOR SOME 'GIRL TALK' AND MAYBE A SLICE OF PIE ON THE PORCH.
PRETTY SOON THE TWO OF 'EM WERE LIKE OLD PALS.
GINGER HEARD SO MUCH ABOUT RILEY FROM MAVIS AND ME THAT SHE STARTED FEELING LIKE SHE KNEW HIM.
The Wheelery
HEY, LET'S HEAR IT FOR THE WHEELERY! BEST LI'L HOUSE A MAN EVER NAMED AFTER HIMSELF!
SO SHE MADE A POINT OF BEING THERE AT THE WHEELERY WITH US THE DAY HE FINALLY CAME HOME FOR GOOD.

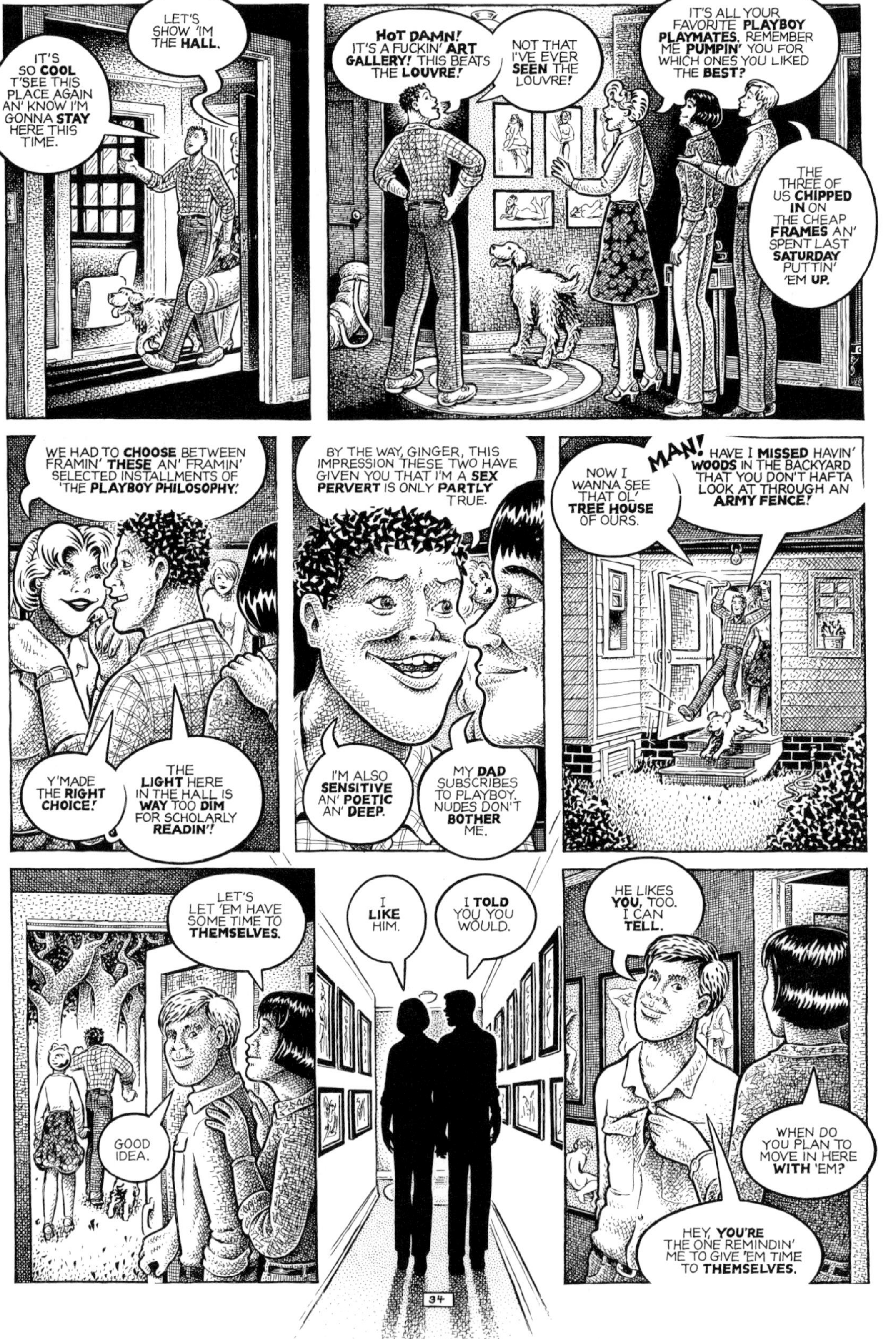
IT'S SO COOL T'SEE THIS PLACE AGAIN AN' KNOW I'M GONNA STAY HERE THIS TIME.
LET'S SHOW 'IM THE HALL.
HOT DAMN! IT'S A FUCKIN' ART GALLERY! THIS BEATS THE LOUVRE!
NOT THAT I'VE EVER SEEN THE LOUVRE!
IT'S ALL YOUR FAVORITE PLAYBOY PLAYMATES. REMEMBER ME PUMPIN' YOU FOR WHICH ONES YOU LIKED THE BEST?
THE THREE OF US CHIPPED IN ON THE CHEAP FRAMES AN' SPENT LAST SATURDAY PUTTIN' 'EM UP.
WE HAD TO CHOOSE BETWEEN FRAMIN' THESE AN' FRAMIN' SELECTED INSTALLMENTS OF 'THE PLAYBOY PHILOSOPHY.'
Y'MADE THE RIGHT CHOICE!
THE LIGHT HERE IN THE HALL IS WAY TOO DIM FOR SCHOLARLY READIN'!
BY THE WAY, GINGER, THIS IMPRESSION THESE TWO HAVE GIVEN YOU THAT I'M A SEX PERVERT IS ONLY PARTLY TRUE.
I'M ALSO SENSITIVE AN' POETIC AN' DEEP.
MY DAD SUBSCRIBES TO PLAYBOY. NUDES DON'T BOTHER ME.
NOW I WANNA SEE THAT OL' TREE HOUSE OF OURS.
MAN!
HAVE I MISSED HAVIN' WOODS IN THE BACKYARD THAT YOU DON'T HAFTA LOOK AT THROUGH AN ARMY FENCE!
LET'S LET 'EM HAVE SOME TIME TO THEMSELVES.
GOOD IDEA.
I LIKE HIM.
I TOLD YOU YOU WOULD.
HE LIKES YOU, TOO. I CAN TELL.
WHEN DO YOU PLAN TO MOVE IN HERE WITH 'EM?
HEY, YOU'RE THE ONE REMINDIN' ME TO GIVE 'EM TIME TO THEMSELVES.

SOON. I **HOPE**.

DO YOU THINK YOU'LL **ENJOY** SLEEPIN' IN A BEDROOM THAT DOESN'T COME WITH A **SISTER** AN' **BROTHER-IN-LAW** NEXT DOOR?

DEFINITELY.

I JUST NEED AN **ALL-CLEAR** FROM RILEY.

'**SPECIALLY** IF RILEY AN' MAVIS'LL LET ME INVITE A CERTAIN **FRIEND** TO SLEEP OVER....

A KISS **HERE**. AN INNUENDO **THERE**.

LOVE **BLOOMS**.

IF **INNUENDOES** COULD MAKE YOU **PREGNANT**, GINGER AND I WOULD'VE HAD A **HEFTY BROOD** BY THE TIME **SPRING** AND **RILEY** CAME BACK TO CLAYFIELD.

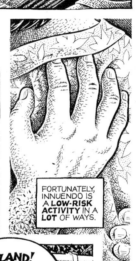

FORTUNATELY, INNUENDO IS A **LOW-RISK ACTIVITY** IN A **LOT** OF WAYS.

MY KISSES WEREN'T **INSINCERE**. BY THEN I HAD WORKED UP A BONA FIDE, AUTHENTIC **CRUSH** ON GINGER.

I TOOK ITS MEASURE EVERY MORNING AND WATERED IT LIKE A **BEGONIA**.

STILL, IN LIGHT OF THE **PERSONALITY QUIRKS** I'VE ALREADY MENTIONED...

...IT SEEMED BEST TO TAKE THINGS **SLOW** UNTIL, WELL...

TOLAND! GINGER! **COME ON OUT!** MAVIS AN' ME ARE GETTIN' A YEN FOR **BARBEQUE!**

IT'S GREAT TO **SEE** YA AGAIN, OL' BUDDY. AN' GINGER—HEY, **WELCOME** TO THE GANG!

IT'S GREAT TO SEE **YOU**, TOO, RILEY. WELCOME **HOME!**

...JUST, **UNTIL!**

SAMMY HAD NEVER **MET** RILEY BUT HE WORKED UP A **WELCOME-HOME TREAT** FOR HIM **ANYWAY**.

HE PROMISED THAT, IF WE'D JUST GO TO THE MORNING SERVICE AT TRINITY AND LISTEN TO HIM **PLAY**, WE WOULDN'T BE **SORRY**.

I **RESISTED**, BUT GINGER AND MAVIS WERE SO **TAKEN** WITH THE IDEA THAT I **GAVE IN**.

THEN— **SURPRISE!** MY **SISTER**, WHO HAD GOTTEN WIND FROM MAVIS THAT HER WAYWARD **BROTHER** HAD BEEN ROPED INTO SITTING STILL FOR A **CHURCH SERVICE**, DECIDED THAT SHE AND ORLEY SHOULD **CRASH** THE **PARTY**.

WELL, LOOK WHO'S **HERE!**

SAMMY PLAYED **BEAUTIFULLY**—EVEN MY **'TIN EARS'** COULD TELL **THAT!** MEANWHILE, HIS PRIVATE JOKE TO **US** WAS THROWING IN FRAGMENTS OF **BOB DYLAN SONGS** DURING SUCH MUSICAL INTERLUDES AS ALLOWED FOR **IMPROVISATION**.

IT WASN'T AS **WICKED** AS IT SOUNDS IN THE **TELLING**, SINCE SAMMY WAS A MASTER AT **CHURCHING UP** HIS **ARRANGEMENTS**.

IS IT MY **IMAGINATION** OR AM I HEARIN' **'DON'T THINK TWICE'**...?

AS FAR AS **MOST** OF THE WORSHIPERS WERE CONCERNED HE COULD JUST AS WELL HAVE BEEN PLAYING SOME **BACH GOLDEN OLDIE!**

ORLEY **NEVER** CAUGHT ON.

WHAT TH' DINGDONG ARE ALL YOU PEOPLE **GIGGLIN'** ABOUT?

I'LL TELL YOU **LATER**.

I GUESS YOU'D HAVE TO CLASSIFY IT ALL AS **BAD BEHAVIOR**. STILL, THE CHURCH CAME OUT **AHEAD** ON THE DEAL, SINCE I ENDED UP PUTTING MORE IN THE **COLLECTION PLATE** THAN I PROBABLY WOULD HAVE IF I HADN'T FELT **GUILTY**.

FATHER MORRIS HAD ME **PEGGED**, THOUGH: AS SOON AS HE STARTED IN WITH THE **PREACHING**, I WAS OFF IN A **DAYDREAM**.

BUT NOT ABOUT **BASEBALL**. WHAT WAS ON MY MIND WAS A **BOOK** THAT HAD NAGGED AT ME EVER SINCE I CAME ACROSS IT YEARS BEFORE IN ONE OF MY PARENTS' **BOOKCASES**.

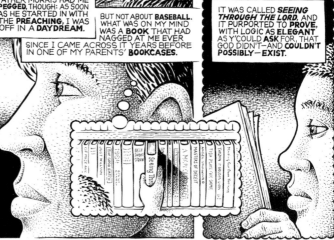

IT WAS CALLED **SEEING THROUGH THE LORD**, AND IT PURPORTED TO **PROVE**, WITH LOGIC AS **ELEGANT** AS Y'COULD **ASK** FOR, THAT GOD DIDN'T—AND **COULDN'T POSSIBLY**— EXIST.

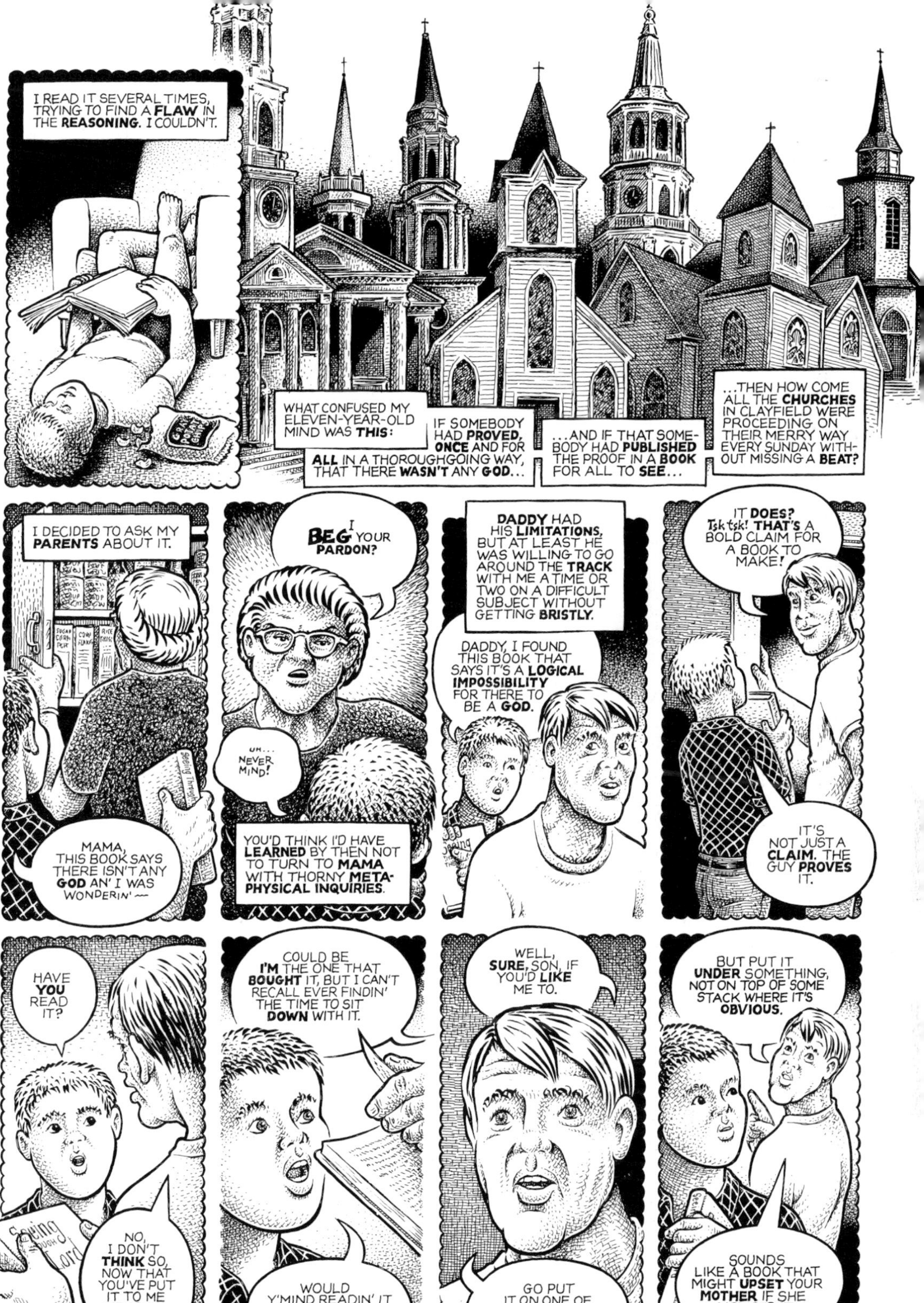

I READ IT SEVERAL TIMES, TRYING TO FIND A FLAW IN THE REASONING. I COULDN'T.
WHAT CONFUSED MY ELEVEN-YEAR-OLD MIND WAS THIS:
IF SOMEBODY HAD PROVED, ONCE AND FOR ALL IN A THOROUGHGOING WAY, THAT THERE WASN'T ANY GOD...
...AND IF THAT SOMEBODY HAD PUBLISHED THE PROOF IN A BOOK FOR ALL TO SEE...
...THEN HOW COME ALL THE CHURCHES IN CLAYFIELD WERE PROCEEDING ON THEIR MERRY WAY EVERY SUNDAY WITHOUT MISSING A BEAT?
I DECIDED TO ASK MY PARENTS ABOUT IT.
MAMA, THIS BOOK SAYS THERE ISN'T ANY GOD AN' I WAS WONDERIN'—
BEG I YOUR PARDON?
UH... NEVER MIND!
YOU'D THINK I'D HAVE LEARNED BY THEN NOT TO TURN TO MAMA WITH THORNY METAPHYSICAL INQUIRIES.
DADDY HAD HIS LIMITATIONS, BUT AT LEAST HE WAS WILLING TO GO AROUND THE TRACK WITH ME A TIME OR TWO ON A DIFFICULT SUBJECT WITHOUT GETTING BRISTLY.
DADDY, I FOUND THIS BOOK THAT SAYS IT'S A LOGICAL IMPOSSIBILITY FOR THERE TO BE A GOD.
IT DOES? Tsk tsk! THAT'S A BOLD CLAIM FOR A BOOK TO MAKE!
IT'S NOT JUST A CLAIM. THE GUY PROVES IT.
HAVE YOU READ IT?
NO, I DON'T THINK SO, NOW THAT YOU'VE PUT IT TO ME DIRECTLY.
COULD BE I'M THE ONE THAT BOUGHT IT, BUT I CAN'T RECALL EVER FINDIN' THE TIME TO SIT DOWN WITH IT.
WOULD Y'MIND READIN' IT SOON, THEN, SO WE CAN TALK ABOUT IT?
WELL, SURE, SON, IF YOU'D LIKE ME TO.
GO PUT IT ON ONE OF THOSE SHELVES BY MY BED SO I'LL REMEMBER.
BUT PUT IT UNDER SOMETHING, NOT ON TOP OF SOME STACK WHERE IT'S OBVIOUS.
SOUNDS LIKE A BOOK THAT MIGHT UPSET YOUR MOTHER IF SHE NOTICED IT.

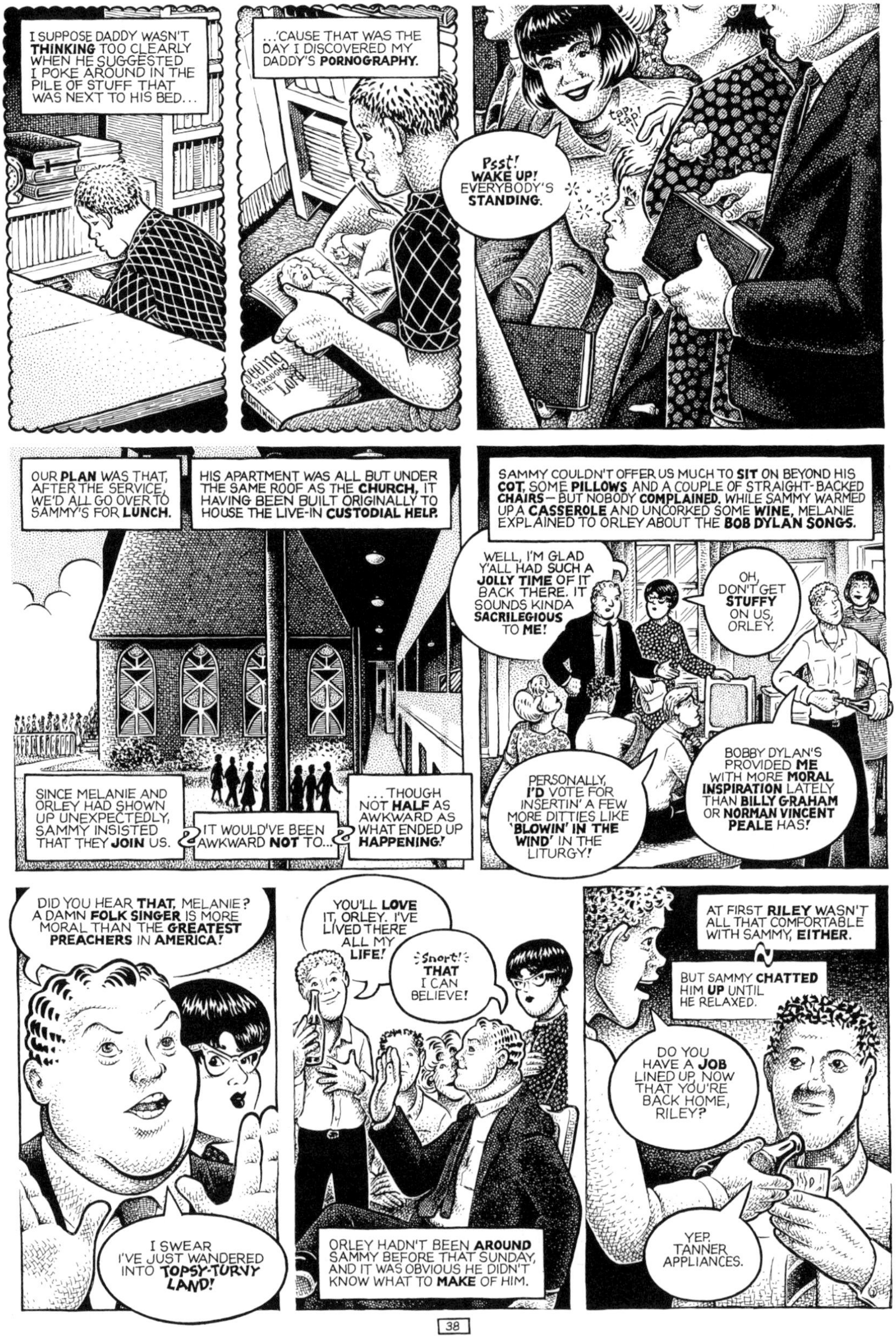

I SUPPOSE DADDY WASN'T **THINKING** TOO CLEARLY WHEN HE SUGGESTED I POKE AROUND IN THE PILE OF STUFF THAT WAS NEXT TO HIS BED...
...'CAUSE THAT WAS THE DAY I DISCOVERED MY DADDY'S **PORNOGRAPHY**.
Loving Through the Lord
tap tap!
Psst! **WAKE UP!** EVERYBODY'S **STANDING**.
OUR **PLAN** WAS THAT, AFTER THE SERVICE, WE'D ALL GO OVER TO SAMMY'S FOR **LUNCH**.
HIS APARTMENT WAS ALL BUT UNDER THE SAME ROOF AS THE **CHURCH**, IT HAVING BEEN BUILT ORIGINALLY TO HOUSE THE LIVE-IN **CUSTODIAL HELP**.
SINCE MELANIE AND ORLEY HAD SHOWN UP UNEXPECTEDLY, SAMMY INSISTED THAT THEY **JOIN** US.
IT WOULD'VE BEEN AWKWARD **NOT** TO...
...THOUGH NOT **HALF** AS AWKWARD AS WHAT ENDED UP **HAPPENING**!
SAMMY COULDN'T OFFER US MUCH TO **SIT** ON BEYOND HIS **COT**, SOME **PILLOWS** AND A COUPLE OF STRAIGHT-BACKED **CHAIRS**— BUT NOBODY **COMPLAINED**. WHILE SAMMY WARMED UP A **CASSEROLE** AND UNCORKED SOME **WINE**, MELANIE EXPLAINED TO ORLEY ABOUT THE **BOB DYLAN SONGS**.
WELL, I'M GLAD Y'ALL HAD SUCH A **JOLLY TIME** OF IT BACK THERE. IT SOUNDS KINDA **SACRILEGIOUS** TO **ME**!
OH, DON'T GET **STUFFY** ON US, ORLEY.
PERSONALLY, **I'D** VOTE FOR INSERTIN' A FEW MORE DITTIES LIKE **'BLOWIN' IN THE WIND'** IN THE LITURGY!
BOBBY DYLAN'S PROVIDED **ME** WITH MORE **MORAL INSPIRATION** LATELY THAN **BILLY GRAHAM** OR **NORMAN VINCENT PEALE** HAS!
DID YOU HEAR **THAT**, MELANIE? A DAMN **FOLK SINGER** IS MORE MORAL THAN THE **GREATEST PREACHERS** IN **AMERICA**!
I SWEAR I'VE JUST WANDERED INTO **TOPSY-TURVY LAND**!
YOU'LL **LOVE** IT, ORLEY. I'VE LIVED THERE ALL MY **LIFE**!
Snort! **THAT** I CAN BELIEVE!
ORLEY HADN'T BEEN **AROUND** SAMMY BEFORE THAT SUNDAY, AND IT WAS OBVIOUS HE DIDN'T KNOW WHAT TO **MAKE** OF HIM.
AT FIRST **RILEY** WASN'T ALL THAT COMFORTABLE WITH SAMMY, **EITHER**.
BUT SAMMY **CHATTED** HIM **UP** UNTIL HE RELAXED.
DO YOU HAVE A **JOB** LINED UP, NOW THAT YOU'RE BACK HOME, RILEY?
YEP. TANNER APPLIANCES.

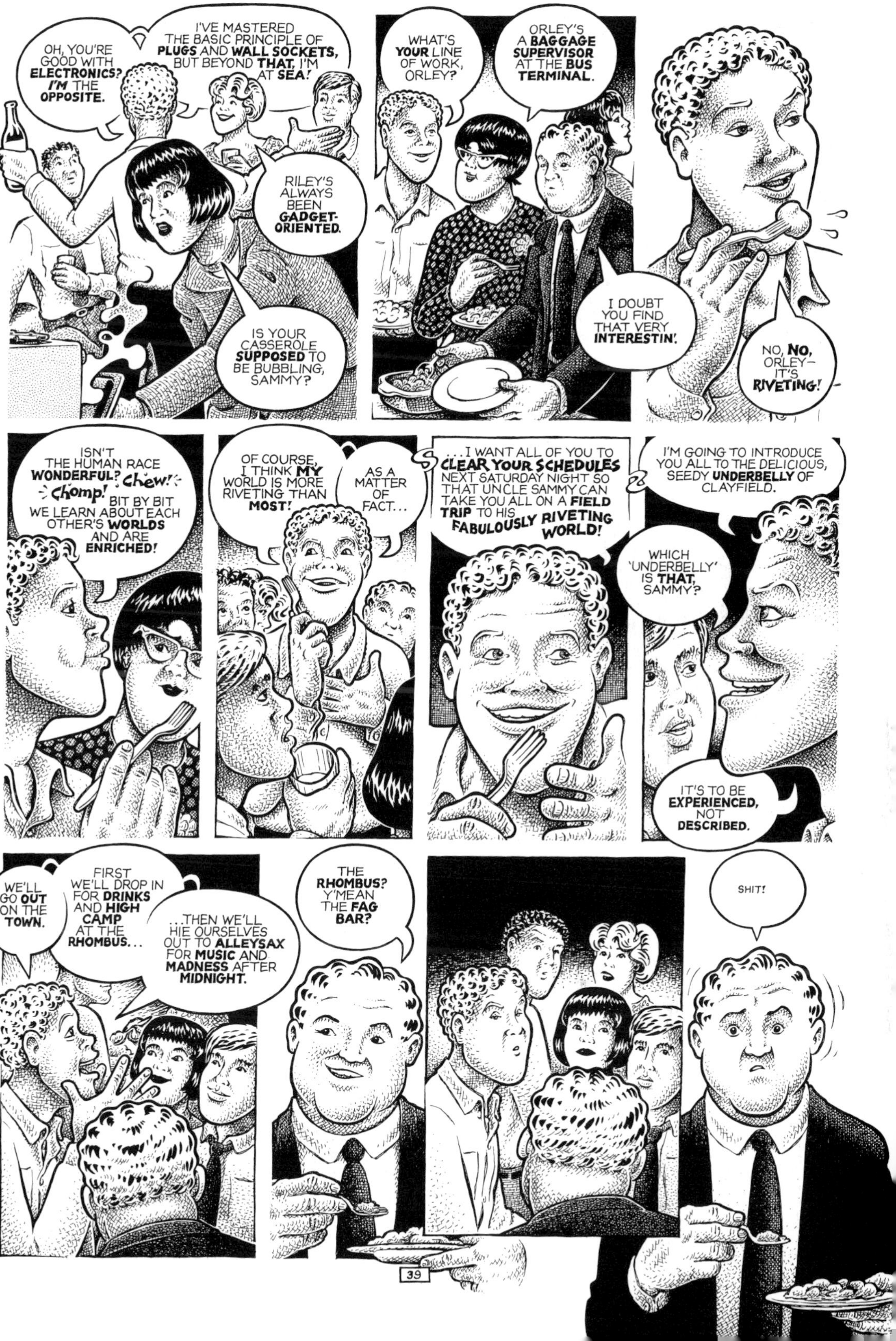
OH, YOU'RE GOOD WITH ELECTRONICS? I'M THE OPPOSITE.
I'VE MASTERED THE BASIC PRINCIPLE OF PLUGS AND WALL SOCKETS, BUT BEYOND THAT, I'M AT SEA!
RILEY'S ALWAYS BEEN GADGET-ORIENTED.
IS YOUR CASSEROLE SUPPOSED TO BE BUBBLING, SAMMY?
WHAT'S YOUR LINE OF WORK, ORLEY?
ORLEY'S A BAGGAGE SUPERVISOR AT THE BUS TERMINAL.
I DOUBT YOU FIND THAT VERY INTERESTIN'.
NO, NO, ORLEY— IT'S RIVETING!
ISN'T THE HUMAN RACE WONDERFUL? Chew! Chomp! BIT BY BIT WE LEARN ABOUT EACH OTHER'S WORLDS AND ARE ENRICHED!
OF COURSE, I THINK MY WORLD IS MORE RIVETING THAN MOST!
AS A MATTER OF FACT...
...I WANT ALL OF YOU TO CLEAR YOUR SCHEDULES NEXT SATURDAY NIGHT SO THAT UNCLE SAMMY CAN TAKE YOU ALL ON A FIELD TRIP TO HIS FABULOUSLY RIVETING WORLD!
I'M GOING TO INTRODUCE YOU ALL TO THE DELICIOUS, SEEDY UNDERBELLY OF CLAYFIELD.
WHICH 'UNDERBELLY' IS THAT, SAMMY?
IT'S TO BE EXPERIENCED, NOT DESCRIBED.
WE'LL GO OUT ON THE TOWN.
FIRST WE'LL DROP IN FOR DRINKS AND HIGH CAMP AT THE RHOMBUS...
...THEN WE'LL HIE OURSELVES OUT TO ALLEYSAX FOR MUSIC AND MADNESS AFTER MIDNIGHT.
THE RHOMBUS? Y'MEAN THE FAG BAR?
SHIT!

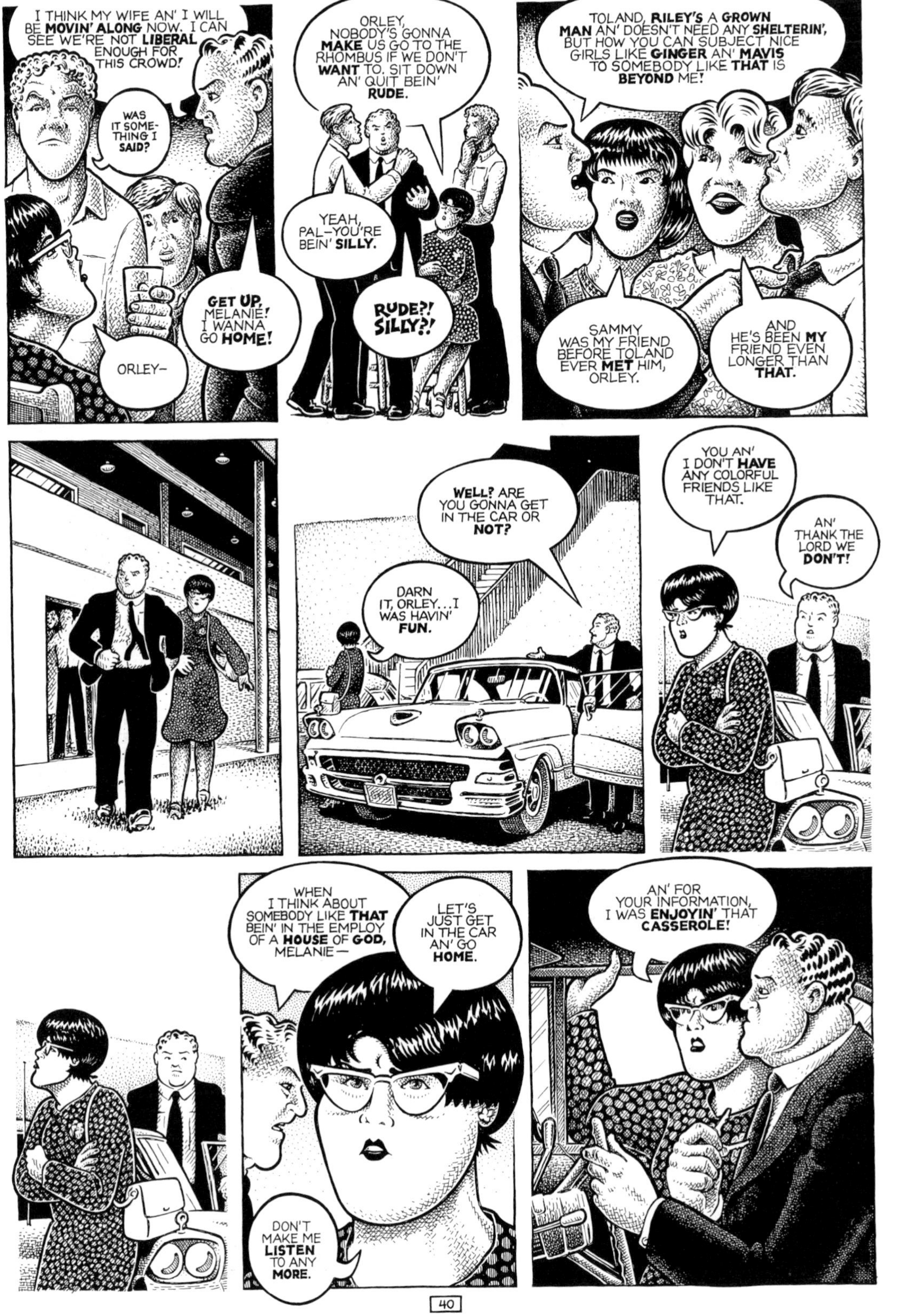
I THINK MY WIFE AN' I WILL BE MOVIN' ALONG NOW. I CAN SEE WE'RE NOT LIBERAL ENOUGH FOR THIS CROWD!
WAS IT SOMETHING I SAID?
GET UP, MELANIE! I WANNA GO HOME!
ORLEY—
ORLEY, NOBODY'S GONNA MAKE US GO TO THE RHOMBUS IF WE DON'T WANT TO. SIT DOWN AN' QUIT BEIN' RUDE.
YEAH, PAL—YOU'RE BEIN' SILLY.
RUDE?! SILLY?!
TOLAND, RILEY'S A GROWN MAN AN' DOESN'T NEED ANY SHELTERIN', BUT HOW YOU CAN SUBJECT NICE GIRLS LIKE GINGER AN' MAVIS TO SOMEBODY LIKE THAT IS BEYOND ME!
SAMMY WAS MY FRIEND BEFORE TOLAND EVER MET HIM, ORLEY.
AND HE'S BEEN MY FRIEND EVEN LONGER THAN THAT.
WELL? ARE YOU GONNA GET IN THE CAR OR NOT?
DARN IT, ORLEY... I WAS HAVIN' FUN.
YOU AN' I DON'T HAVE ANY COLORFUL FRIENDS LIKE THAT.
AN' THANK THE LORD WE DON'T!
WHEN I THINK ABOUT SOMEBODY LIKE THAT BEIN' IN THE EMPLOY OF A HOUSE OF GOD, MELANIE—
LET'S JUST GET IN THE CAR AN' GO HOME.
DON'T MAKE ME LISTEN TO ANY MORE.
AN' FOR YOUR INFORMATION, I WAS ENJOYIN' THAT CASSEROLE!

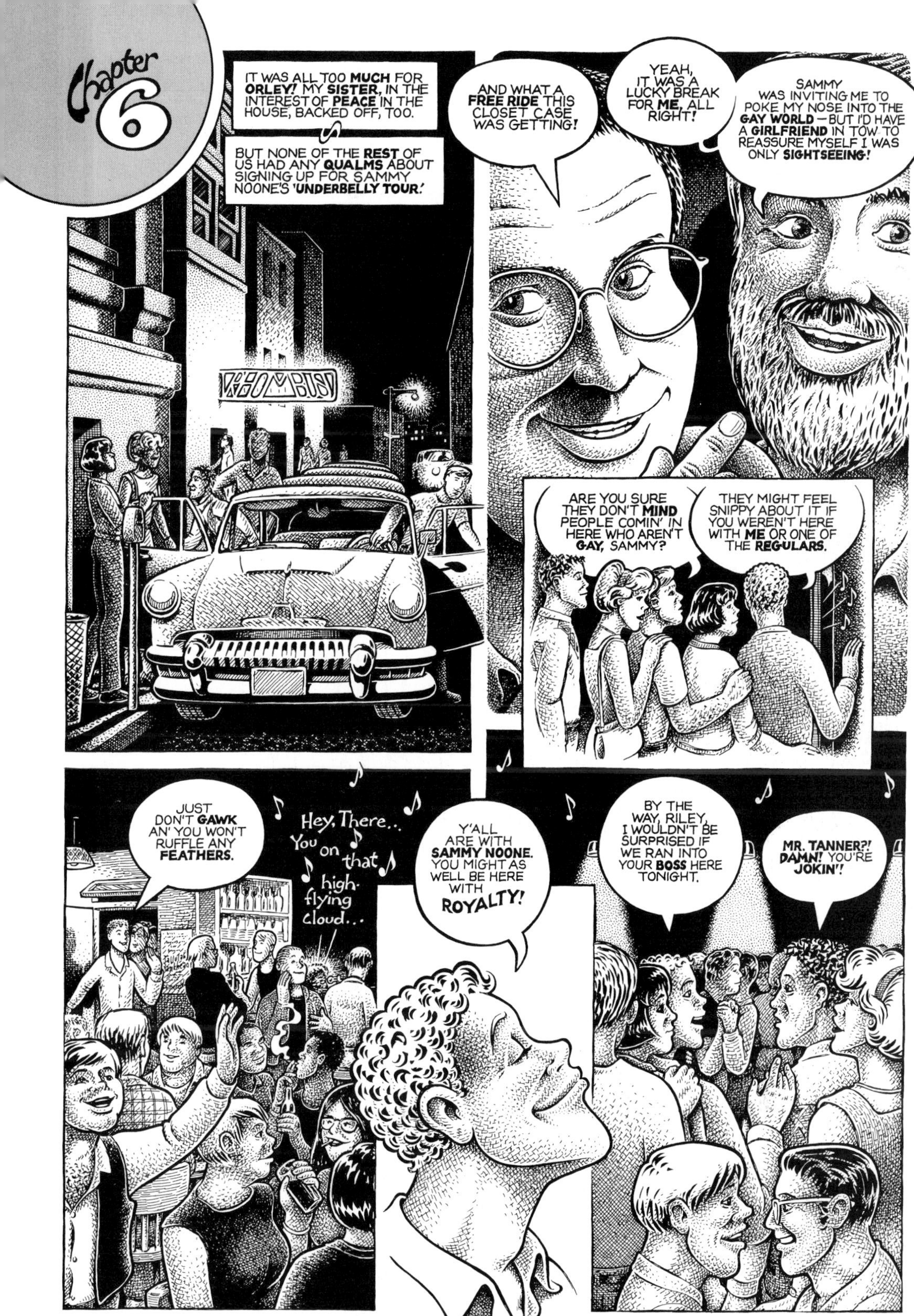
Chapter 6
IT WAS ALL TOO MUCH FOR ORLEY! MY SISTER, IN THE INTEREST OF PEACE IN THE HOUSE, BACKED OFF, TOO.
BUT NONE OF THE REST OF US HAD ANY QUALMS ABOUT SIGNING UP FOR SAMMY NOONE'S 'UNDERBELLY TOUR.'
AND WHAT A FREE RIDE THIS CLOSET CASE WAS GETTING!
YEAH, IT WAS A LUCKY BREAK FOR ME, ALL RIGHT!
SAMMY WAS INVITING ME TO POKE MY NOSE INTO THE GAY WORLD — BUT I'D HAVE A GIRLFRIEND IN TOW TO REASSURE MYSELF I WAS ONLY SIGHTSEEING!
ARE YOU SURE THEY DON'T MIND PEOPLE COMIN' IN HERE WHO AREN'T GAY, SAMMY?
THEY MIGHT FEEL SNIPPY ABOUT IT IF YOU WEREN'T HERE WITH ME OR ONE OF THE REGULARS.
JUST DON'T GAWK AN' YOU WON'T RUFFLE ANY FEATHERS.
Hey, There.. You on that high-flying cloud...
Y'ALL ARE WITH SAMMY NOONE. YOU MIGHT AS WELL BE HERE WITH ROYALTY!
BY THE WAY, RILEY, I WOULDN'T BE SURPRISED IF WE RAN INTO YOUR BOSS HERE TONIGHT.
MR. TANNER?! DAMN! YOU'RE JOKIN'!

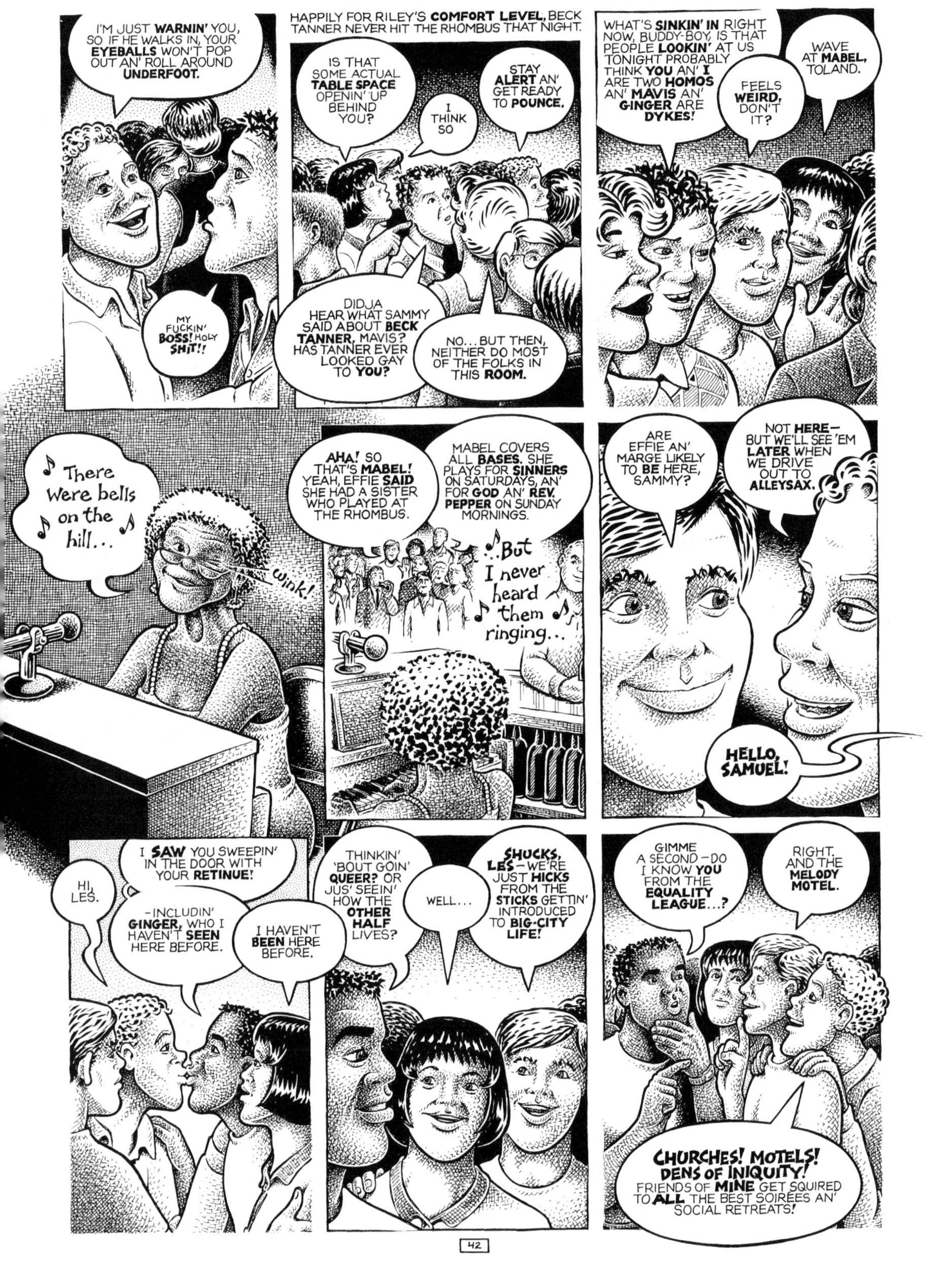
I'M JUST WARNIN' YOU, SO IF HE WALKS IN, YOUR EYEBALLS WON'T POP OUT AN' ROLL AROUND UNDERFOOT.
MY FUCKIN' BOSS! HOLY SHIT!!
HAPPILY FOR RILEY'S COMFORT LEVEL, BECK TANNER NEVER HIT THE RHOMBUS THAT NIGHT.
IS THAT SOME ACTUAL TABLE SPACE OPENIN' UP BEHIND YOU?
I THINK SO
STAY ALERT AN' GET READY TO POUNCE.
DIDJA HEAR WHAT SAMMY SAID ABOUT BECK TANNER, MAVIS? HAS TANNER EVER LOOKED GAY TO YOU?
NO... BUT THEN, NEITHER DO MOST OF THE FOLKS IN THIS ROOM.
WHAT'S SINKIN' IN RIGHT NOW, BUDDY-BOY, IS THAT PEOPLE LOOKIN' AT US TONIGHT PROBABLY THINK YOU AN' I ARE TWO HOMOS AN' MAVIS AN' GINGER ARE DYKES!
FEELS WEIRD, DON'T IT?
WAVE AT MABEL, TOLAND.
There were bells on the hill...
wink!
AHA! SO THAT'S MABEL! YEAH, EFFIE SAID SHE HAD A SISTER WHO PLAYED AT THE RHOMBUS.
MABEL COVERS ALL BASES. SHE PLAYS FOR SINNERS ON SATURDAYS, AN' FOR GOD AN' REV. PEPPER ON SUNDAY MORNINGS.
But I never heard them ringing...
ARE EFFIE AN' MARGE LIKELY TO BE HERE, SAMMY?
NOT HERE— BUT WE'LL SEE 'EM LATER WHEN WE DRIVE OUT TO ALLEYSAX.
HELLO, SAMUEL!
HI, LES.
I SAW YOU SWEEPIN' IN THE DOOR WITH YOUR RETINUE!
-INCLUDIN' GINGER, WHO I HAVEN'T SEEN HERE BEFORE.
I HAVEN'T BEEN HERE BEFORE.
THINKIN' 'BOUT GOIN' QUEER? OR JUS' SEEIN' HOW THE OTHER HALF LIVES?
WELL...
SHUCKS, LES—WE'RE JUST HICKS FROM THE STICKS GETTIN' INTRODUCED TO BIG-CITY LIFE!
GIMME A SECOND—DO I KNOW YOU FROM THE EQUALITY LEAGUE...?
RIGHT. AND THE MELODY MOTEL.
CHURCHES! MOTELS! DENS OF INIQUITY! FRIENDS OF MINE GET SQUIRED TO ALL THE BEST SOIRÉES AN' SOCIAL RETREATS!

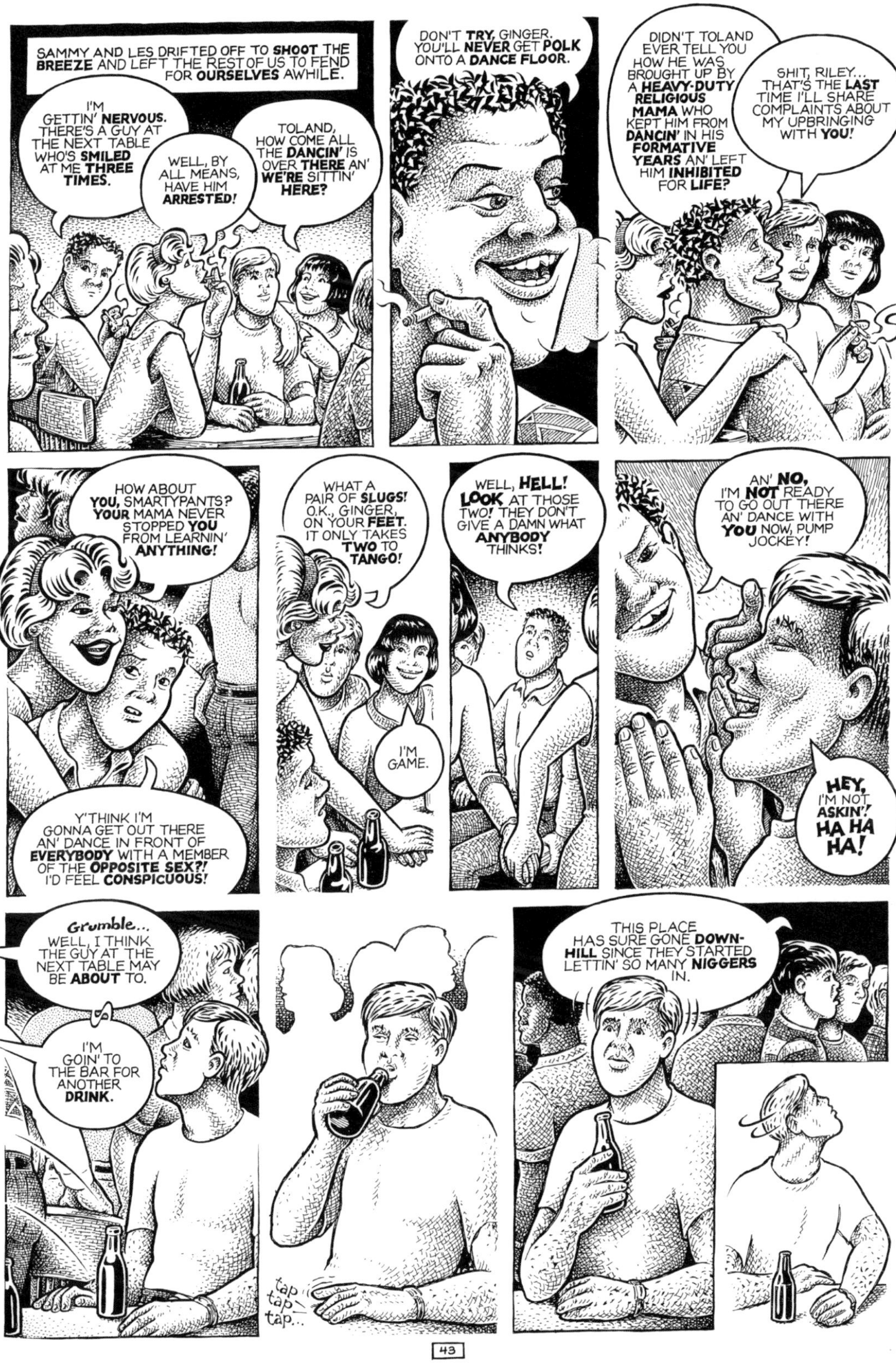
SAMMY AND LES DRIFTED OFF TO SHOOT THE BREEZE AND LEFT THE REST OF US TO FEND FOR OURSELVES AWHILE.
I'M GETTIN' NERVOUS. THERE'S A GUY AT THE NEXT TABLE WHO'S SMILED AT ME THREE TIMES.
WELL, BY ALL MEANS, HAVE HIM ARRESTED!
TOLAND, HOW COME ALL THE DANCIN' IS OVER THERE AN' WE'RE SITTIN' HERE?
DON'T TRY, GINGER. YOU'LL NEVER GET POLK ONTO A DANCE FLOOR.
DIDN'T TOLAND EVER TELL YOU HOW HE WAS BROUGHT UP BY A HEAVY-DUTY RELIGIOUS MAMA WHO KEPT HIM FROM DANCIN' IN HIS FORMATIVE YEARS AN' LEFT HIM INHIBITED FOR LIFE?
SHIT, RILEY... THAT'S THE LAST TIME I'LL SHARE COMPLAINTS ABOUT MY UPBRINGING WITH YOU!
HOW ABOUT YOU, SMARTYPANTS? YOUR MAMA NEVER STOPPED YOU FROM LEARNIN' ANYTHING!
Y'THINK I'M GONNA GET OUT THERE AN' DANCE IN FRONT OF EVERYBODY WITH A MEMBER OF THE OPPOSITE SEX?! I'D FEEL CONSPICUOUS!
WHAT A PAIR OF SLUGS! O.K., GINGER, ON YOUR FEET. IT ONLY TAKES TWO TO TANGO!
I'M GAME.
WELL, HELL! LOOK AT THOSE TWO! THEY DON'T GIVE A DAMN WHAT ANYBODY THINKS!
AN' NO, I'M NOT READY TO GO OUT THERE AN' DANCE WITH YOU NOW, PUMP JOCKEY!
HEY, I'M NOT ASKIN'! HA HA HA!
Grumble... WELL, I THINK THE GUY AT THE NEXT TABLE MAY BE ABOUT TO.
I'M GOIN' TO THE BAR FOR ANOTHER DRINK.
tap tap tap...
THIS PLACE HAS SURE GONE DOWN-HILL SINCE THEY STARTED LETTIN' SO MANY NIGGERS IN.

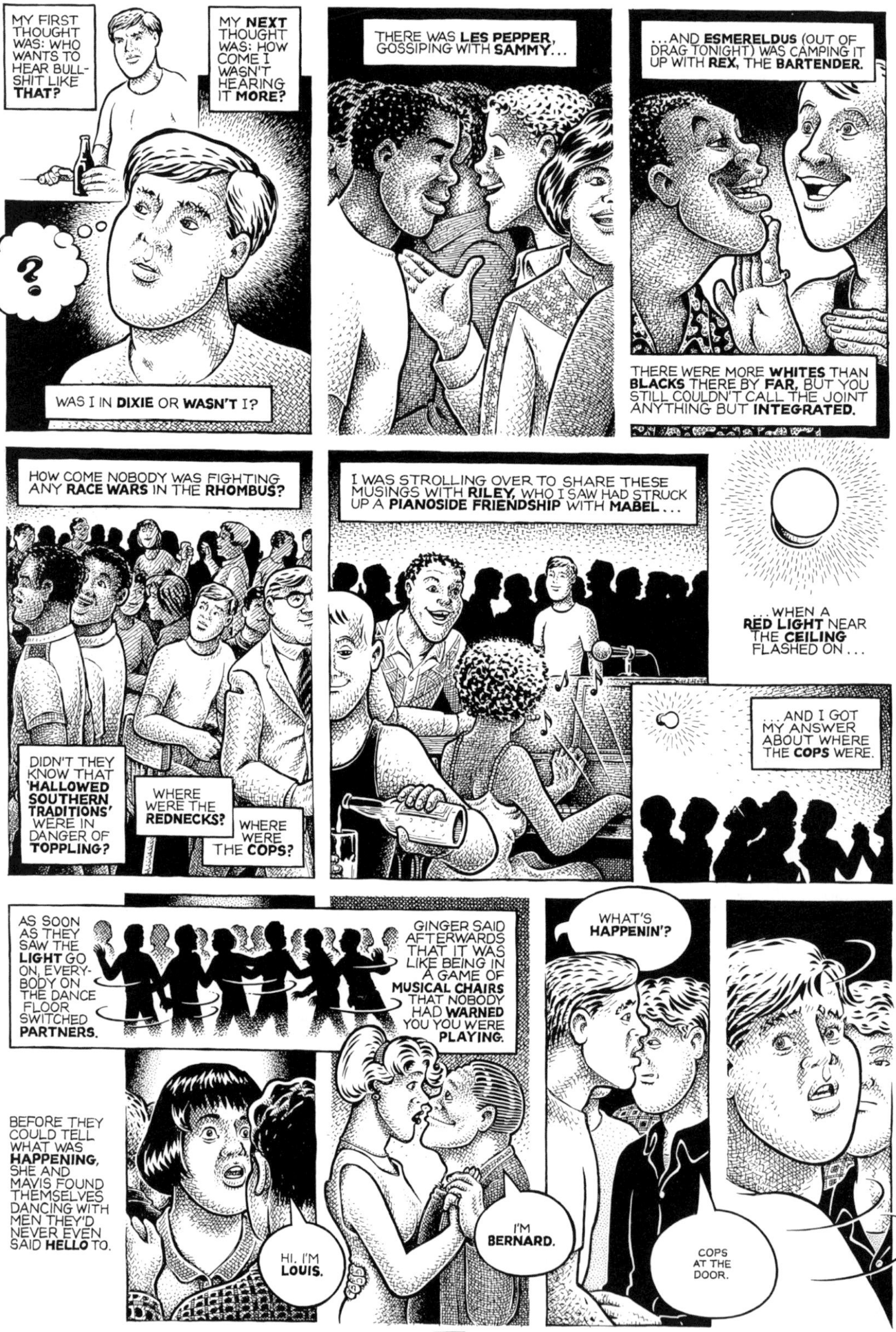

MY FIRST THOUGHT WAS: WHO WANTS TO HEAR BULL-SHIT LIKE THAT?
MY NEXT THOUGHT WAS: HOW COME I WASN'T HEARING IT MORE?
?
WAS I IN DIXIE OR WASN'T I?
THERE WAS LES PEPPER, GOSSIPING WITH SAMMY...
...AND ESMERELDUS (OUT OF DRAG TONIGHT) WAS CAMPING IT UP WITH REX, THE BARTENDER.
THERE WERE MORE WHITES THAN BLACKS THERE BY FAR, BUT YOU STILL COULDN'T CALL THE JOINT ANYTHING BUT INTEGRATED.
HOW COME NOBODY WAS FIGHTING ANY RACE WARS IN THE RHOMBUS?
DIDN'T THEY KNOW THAT 'HALLOWED SOUTHERN TRADITIONS' WERE IN DANGER OF TOPPLING?
WHERE WERE THE REDNECKS?
WHERE WERE THE COPS?
I WAS STROLLING OVER TO SHARE THESE MUSINGS WITH RILEY, WHO I SAW HAD STRUCK UP A PIANOSIDE FRIENDSHIP WITH MABEL...
...WHEN A RED LIGHT NEAR THE CEILING FLASHED ON...
...AND I GOT MY ANSWER ABOUT WHERE THE COPS WERE.
AS SOON AS THEY SAW THE LIGHT GO ON, EVERY-BODY ON THE DANCE FLOOR SWITCHED PARTNERS.
GINGER SAID AFTERWARDS THAT IT WAS LIKE BEING IN A GAME OF MUSICAL CHAIRS THAT NOBODY HAD WARNED YOU YOU WERE PLAYING.
BEFORE THEY COULD TELL WHAT WAS HAPPENING, SHE AND MAVIS FOUND THEMSELVES DANCING WITH MEN THEY'D NEVER EVEN SAID HELLO TO.
HI. I'M LOUIS.
I'M BERNARD.
WHAT'S HAPPENIN'?
COPS AT THE DOOR.

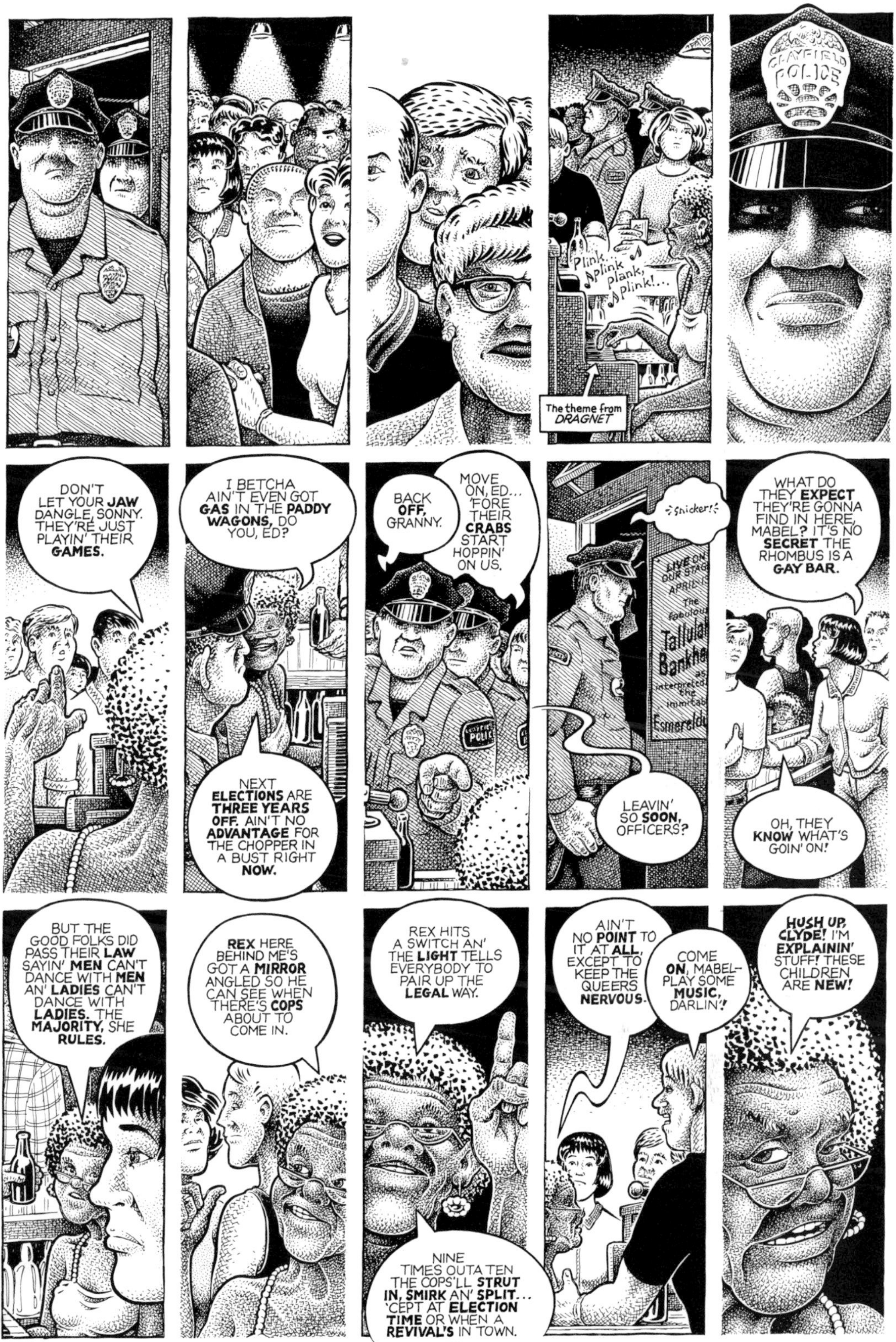

Plink.. plink plank, plink!..
The theme from DRAGNET
DON'T LET YOUR JAW DANGLE, SONNY. THEY'RE JUST PLAYIN' THEIR GAMES.
I BETCHA AIN'T EVEN GOT GAS IN THE PADDY WAGONS, DO YOU, ED?
NEXT ELECTIONS ARE THREE YEARS OFF. AIN'T NO ADVANTAGE FOR THE CHOPPER IN A BUST RIGHT NOW.
BACK OFF, GRANNY.
MOVE ON, ED... 'FORE THEIR CRABS START HOPPIN' ON US.
Snicker!
LEAVIN' SO SOON, OFFICERS?
WHAT DO THEY EXPECT THEY'RE GONNA FIND IN HERE, MABEL? IT'S NO SECRET THE RHOMBUS IS A GAY BAR.
OH, THEY KNOW WHAT'S GOIN' ON!
BUT THE GOOD FOLKS DID PASS THEIR LAW SAYIN' MEN CAN'T DANCE WITH MEN AN' LADIES CAN'T DANCE WITH LADIES. THE MAJORITY, SHE RULES.
REX HERE BEHIND ME'S GOT A MIRROR ANGLED SO HE CAN SEE WHEN THERE'S COPS ABOUT TO COME IN.
REX HITS A SWITCH AN' THE LIGHT TELLS EVERYBODY TO PAIR UP THE LEGAL WAY.
NINE TIMES OUTA TEN THE COPS'LL STRUT IN, SMIRK AN' SPLIT... 'CEPT AT ELECTION TIME OR WHEN A REVIVAL'S IN TOWN.
AIN'T NO POINT TO IT AT ALL, EXCEPT TO KEEP THE QUEERS NERVOUS.
COME ON, MABEL- PLAY SOME MUSIC, DARLIN'!
HUSH UP, CLYDE! I'M EXPLAININ' STUFF! THESE CHILDREN ARE NEW!

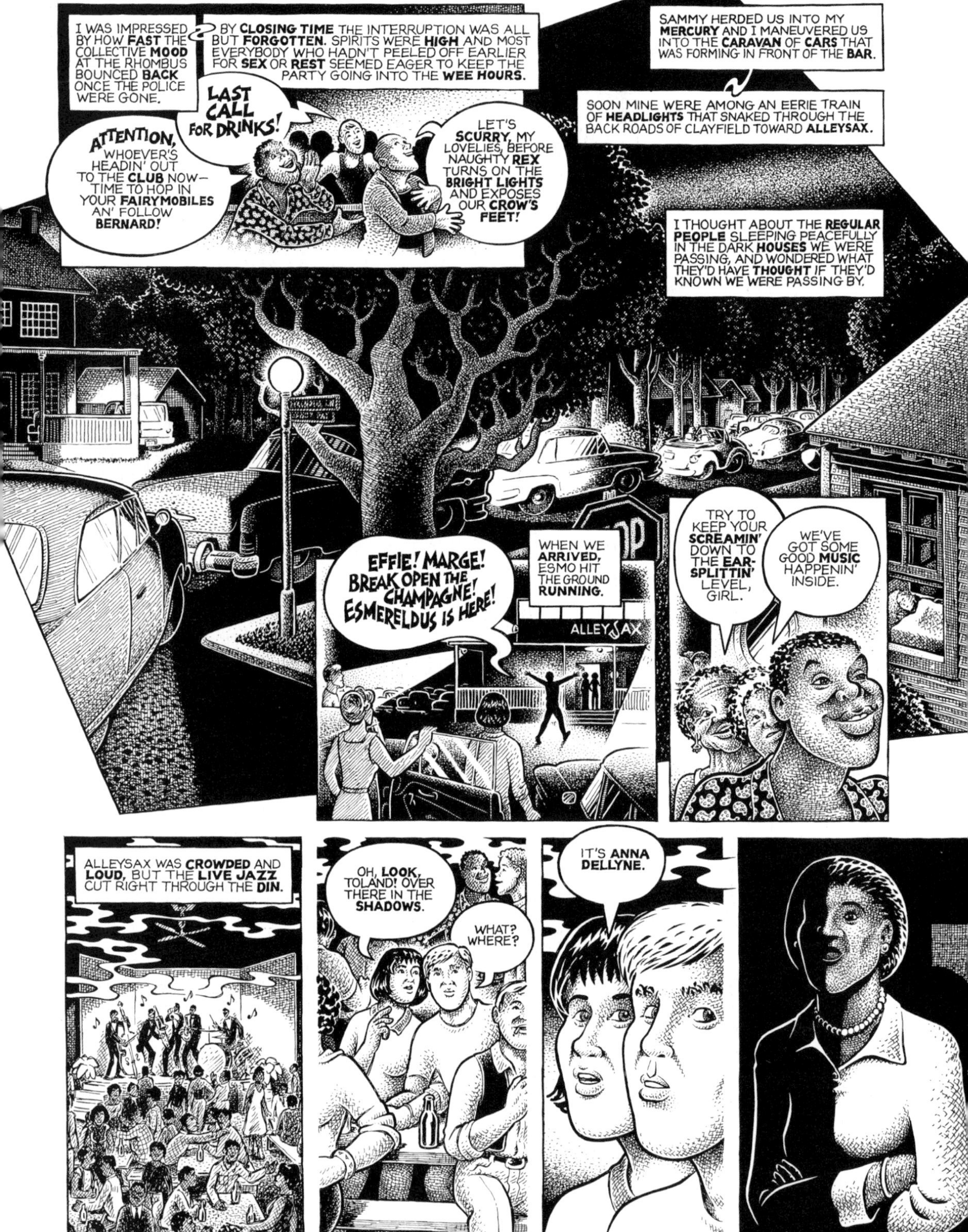
I WAS IMPRESSED BY HOW FAST THE COLLECTIVE MOOD AT THE RHOMBUS BOUNCED BACK ONCE THE POLICE WERE GONE.
BY CLOSING TIME THE INTERRUPTION WAS ALL BUT FORGOTTEN. SPIRITS WERE HIGH AND MOST EVERYBODY WHO HADN'T PEELED OFF EARLIER FOR SEX OR REST SEEMED EAGER TO KEEP THE PARTY GOING INTO THE WEE HOURS.
LAST CALL FOR DRINKS!
ATTENTION, WHOEVER'S HEADIN' OUT TO THE CLUB NOW— TIME TO HOP IN YOUR FAIRYMOBILES AN' FOLLOW BERNARD!
LET'S SCURRY, MY LOVELIES, BEFORE NAUGHTY REX TURNS ON THE BRIGHT LIGHTS AND EXPOSES OUR CROW'S FEET!
SAMMY HERDED US INTO MY MERCURY AND I MANEUVERED US INTO THE CARAVAN OF CARS THAT WAS FORMING IN FRONT OF THE BAR.
SOON MINE WERE AMONG AN EERIE TRAIN OF HEADLIGHTS THAT SNAKED THROUGH THE BACK ROADS OF CLAYFIELD TOWARD ALLEYSAX.
I THOUGHT ABOUT THE REGULAR PEOPLE SLEEPING PEACEFULLY IN THE DARK HOUSES WE WERE PASSING, AND WONDERED WHAT THEY'D HAVE THOUGHT IF THEY'D KNOWN WE WERE PASSING BY.
EFFIE! MARGE! BREAK OPEN THE CHAMPAGNE! ESMERELDUS IS HERE!
WHEN WE ARRIVED, ESMO HIT THE GROUND RUNNING.
ALLEYSAX
TRY TO KEEP YOUR SCREAMIN' DOWN TO THE EAR-SPLITTIN' LEVEL, GIRL.
WE'VE GOT SOME GOOD MUSIC HAPPENIN' INSIDE.
ALLEYSAX WAS CROWDED AND LOUD, BUT THE LIVE JAZZ CUT RIGHT THROUGH THE DIN.
OH, LOOK, TOLAND! OVER THERE IN THE SHADOWS.
WHAT? WHERE?
IT'S ANNA DELLYNE.

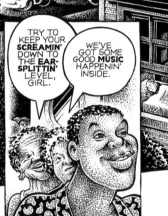

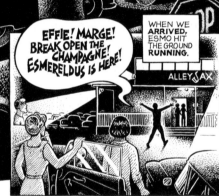

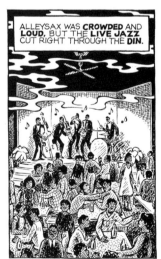

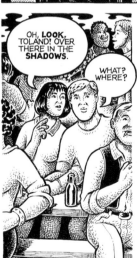

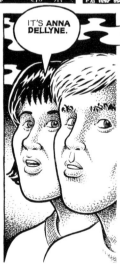

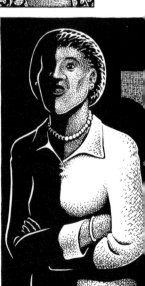

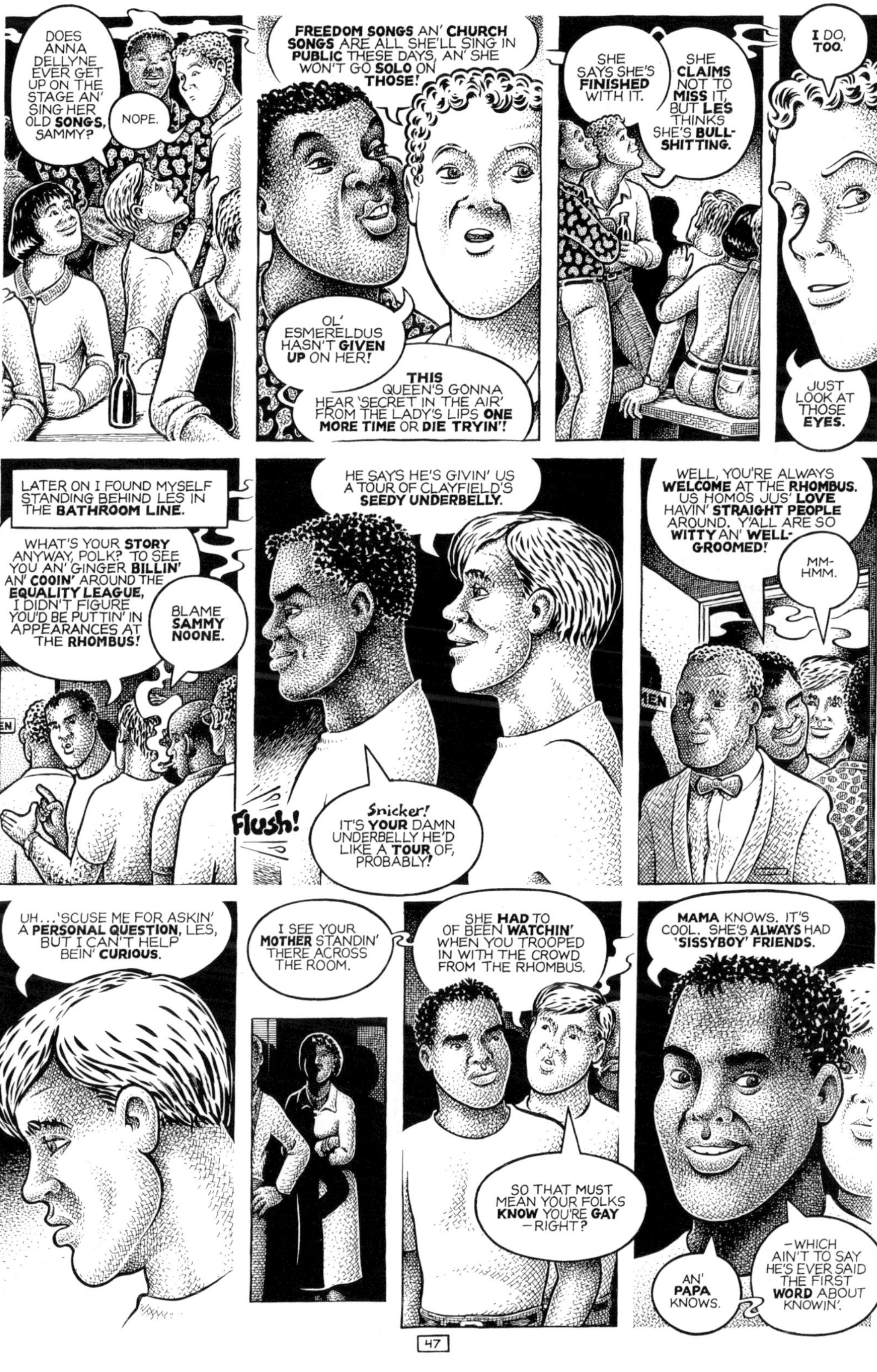

DOES ANNA DELLYNE EVER GET UP ON THE STAGE AN' SING HER OLD SONGS, SAMMY?
NOPE.
FREEDOM SONGS AN' CHURCH SONGS ARE ALL SHE'LL SING IN PUBLIC THESE DAYS, AN' SHE WON'T GO SOLO ON THOSE!
OL' ESMERELDUS HASN'T GIVEN UP ON HER!
THIS QUEEN'S GONNA HEAR 'SECRET IN THE AIR' FROM THE LADY'S LIPS ONE MORE TIME OR DIE TRYIN'!
SHE SAYS SHE'S FINISHED WITH IT.
SHE CLAIMS NOT TO MISS IT, BUT LES THINKS SHE'S BULL-SHITTING.
I DO, TOO.
JUST LOOK AT THOSE EYES.
LATER ON I FOUND MYSELF STANDING BEHIND LES IN THE BATHROOM LINE.
WHAT'S YOUR STORY ANYWAY, POLK? TO SEE YOU AN' GINGER BILLIN' AN' COOIN' AROUND THE EQUALITY LEAGUE, I DIDN'T FIGURE YOU'D BE PUTTIN' IN APPEARANCES AT THE RHOMBUS!
BLAME SAMMY NOONE.
HE SAYS HE'S GIVIN' US A TOUR OF CLAYFIELD'S SEEDY UNDERBELLY.
FLUSH!
Snicker! IT'S YOUR DAMN UNDERBELLY HE'D LIKE A TOUR OF, PROBABLY!
WELL, YOU'RE ALWAYS WELCOME AT THE RHOMBUS. US HOMOS JUS' LOVE HAVIN' STRAIGHT PEOPLE AROUND. Y'ALL ARE SO WITTY AN' WELL-GROOMED!
MM-HMM.
MEN
UH... 'SCUSE ME FOR ASKIN' A PERSONAL QUESTION, LES, BUT I CAN'T HELP BEIN' CURIOUS.
I SEE YOUR MOTHER STANDIN' THERE ACROSS THE ROOM.
SHE HAD TO OF BEEN WATCHIN' WHEN YOU TROOPED IN WITH THE CROWD FROM THE RHOMBUS.
SO THAT MUST MEAN YOUR FOLKS KNOW YOU'RE GAY —RIGHT?
MAMA KNOWS. IT'S COOL. SHE'S ALWAYS HAD 'SISSYBOY' FRIENDS.
AN' PAPA KNOWS.
—WHICH AIN'T TO SAY HE'S EVER SAID THE FIRST WORD ABOUT KNOWIN'.

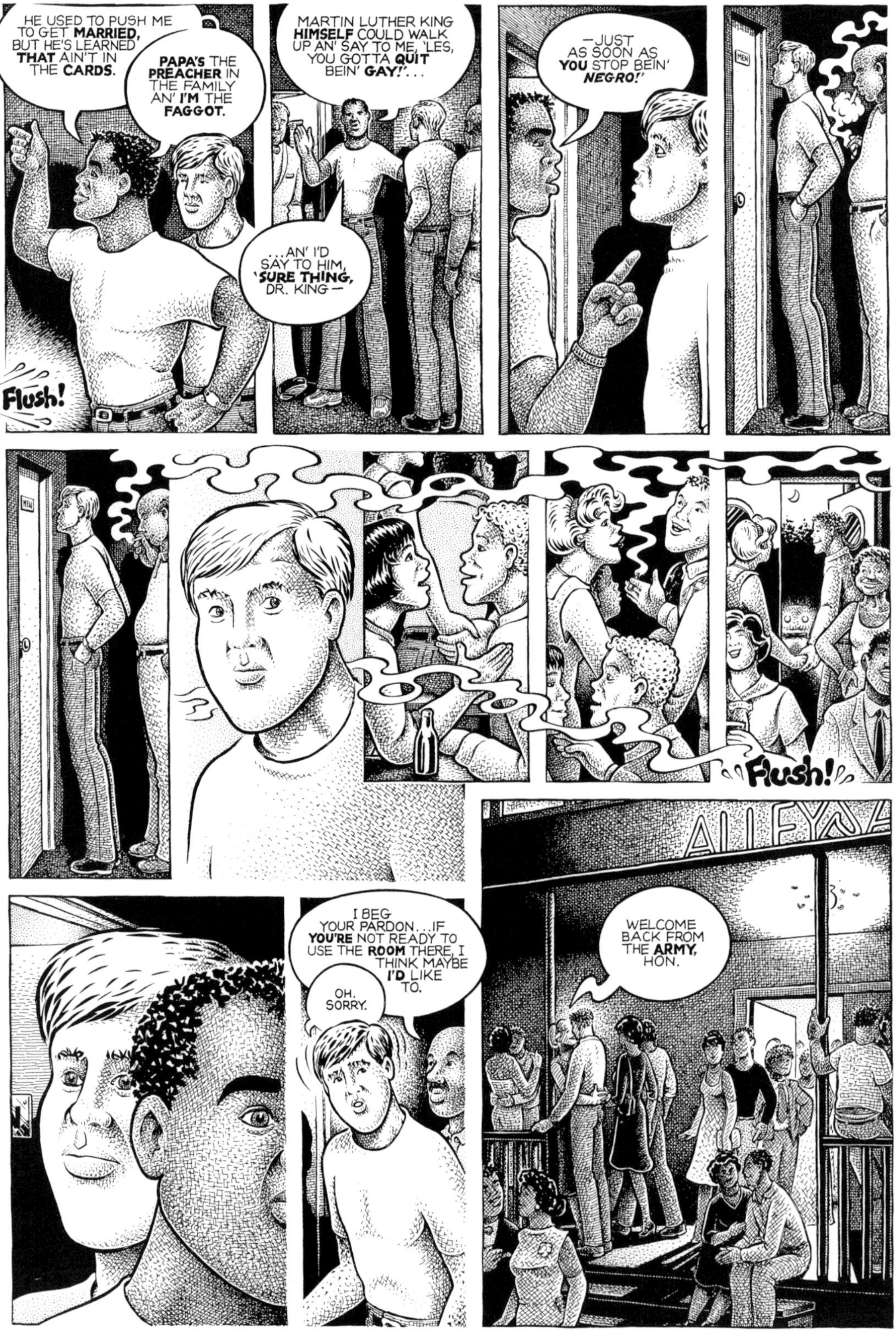

HE USED TO PUSH ME TO GET **MARRIED,** BUT HE'S LEARNED **THAT** AIN'T IN THE **CARDS**.
PAPA'S THE **PREACHER** IN THE FAMILY AN' **I'M** THE **FAGGOT**.
Flush!
MARTIN LUTHER KING **HIMSELF** COULD WALK UP AN' SAY TO ME, 'LES, YOU GOTTA **QUIT** BEIN' **GAY!'**...
...AN' I'D SAY TO HIM, '**SURE THING,** DR. KING—
—JUST AS SOON AS **YOU** STOP BEIN' ***NEGRO!'***
MEN
MEN
Flush!
I BEG YOUR PARDON...IF **YOU'RE** NOT READY TO USE THE **ROOM** THERE, I THINK MAYBE **I'D** LIKE TO.
OH. SORRY.
WELCOME BACK FROM THE **ARMY,** HON.

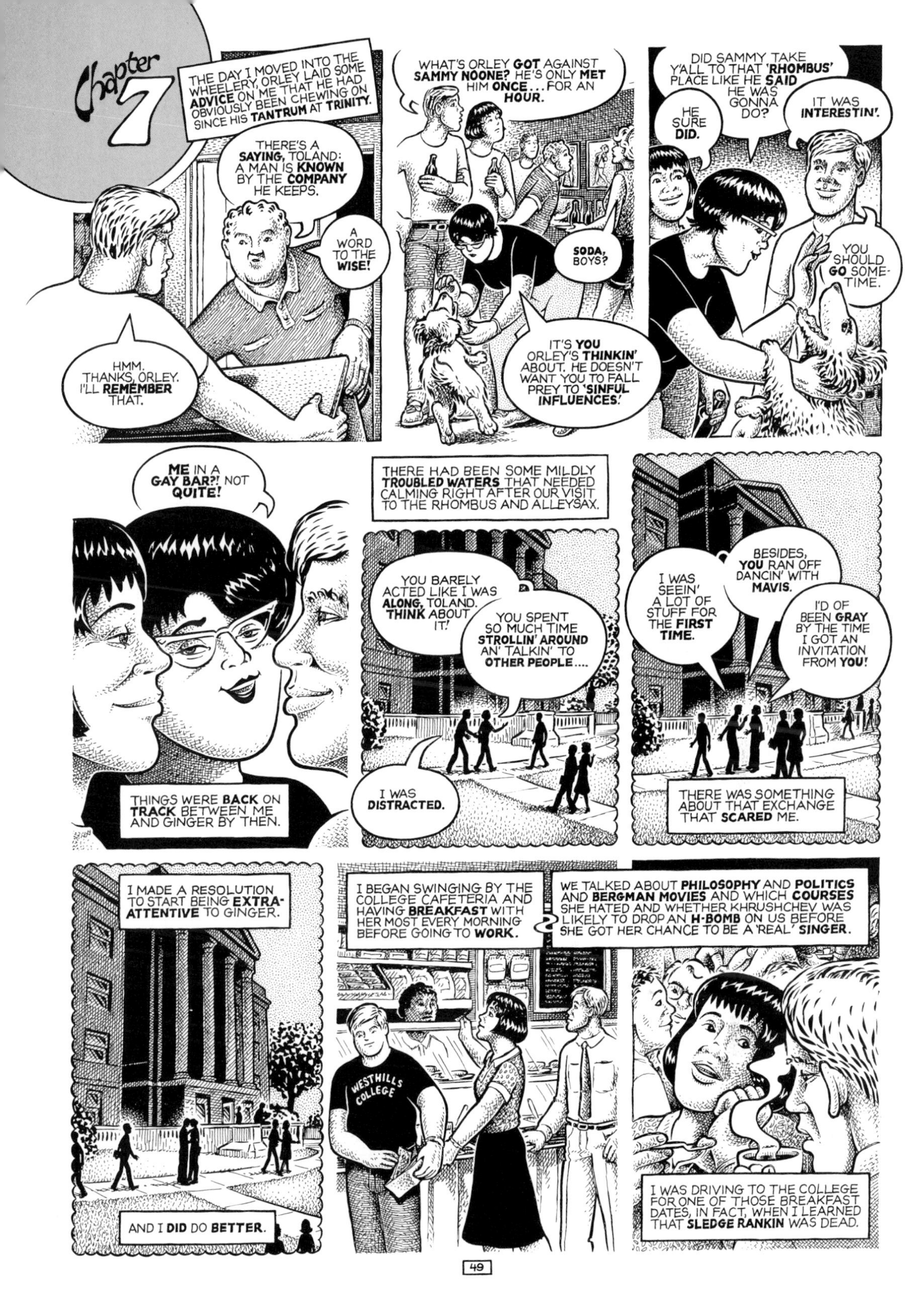
Chapter 7
THE DAY I MOVED INTO THE WHEELERY, ORLEY LAID SOME ADVICE ON ME THAT HE HAD OBVIOUSLY BEEN CHEWING ON SINCE HIS TANTRUM AT TRINITY.
THERE'S A SAYING, TOLAND: A MAN IS KNOWN BY THE COMPANY HE KEEPS.
A WORD TO THE WISE!
HMM. THANKS, ORLEY. I'LL REMEMBER THAT.
WHAT'S ORLEY GOT AGAINST SAMMY NOONE? HE'S ONLY MET HIM ONCE... FOR AN HOUR.
SODA, BOYS?
IT'S YOU ORLEY'S THINKIN' ABOUT. HE DOESN'T WANT YOU TO FALL PREY TO 'SINFUL INFLUENCES.'
DID SAMMY TAKE Y'ALL TO THAT 'RHOMBUS' PLACE LIKE HE SAID HE WAS GONNA DO?
HE SURE DID.
IT WAS INTERESTIN'.
YOU SHOULD GO SOMETIME.
ME IN A GAY BAR?! NOT QUITE!
THINGS WERE BACK ON TRACK BETWEEN ME AND GINGER BY THEN.
THERE HAD BEEN SOME MILDLY TROUBLED WATERS THAT NEEDED CALMING RIGHT AFTER OUR VISIT TO THE RHOMBUS AND ALLEYSAX.
YOU BARELY ACTED LIKE I WAS ALONG, TOLAND. THINK ABOUT IT!
YOU SPENT SO MUCH TIME STROLLIN' AROUND AN' TALKIN' TO OTHER PEOPLE....
I WAS DISTRACTED.
I WAS SEEIN' A LOT OF STUFF FOR THE FIRST TIME.
BESIDES, YOU RAN OFF DANCIN' WITH MAVIS.
I'D OF BEEN GRAY BY THE TIME I GOT AN INVITATION FROM YOU!
THERE WAS SOMETHING ABOUT THAT EXCHANGE THAT SCARED ME.
I MADE A RESOLUTION TO START BEING EXTRA-ATTENTIVE TO GINGER.
AND I DID DO BETTER.
I BEGAN SWINGING BY THE COLLEGE CAFETERIA AND HAVING BREAKFAST WITH HER MOST EVERY MORNING BEFORE GOING TO WORK.
WE TALKED ABOUT PHILOSOPHY AND POLITICS AND BERGMAN MOVIES AND WHICH COURSES SHE HATED AND WHETHER KHRUSHCHEV WAS LIKELY TO DROP AN H-BOMB ON US BEFORE SHE GOT HER CHANCE TO BE A 'REAL' SINGER.
WESTHILLS COLLEGE
I WAS DRIVING TO THE COLLEGE FOR ONE OF THOSE BREAKFAST DATES, IN FACT, WHEN I LEARNED THAT SLEDGE RANKIN WAS DEAD.

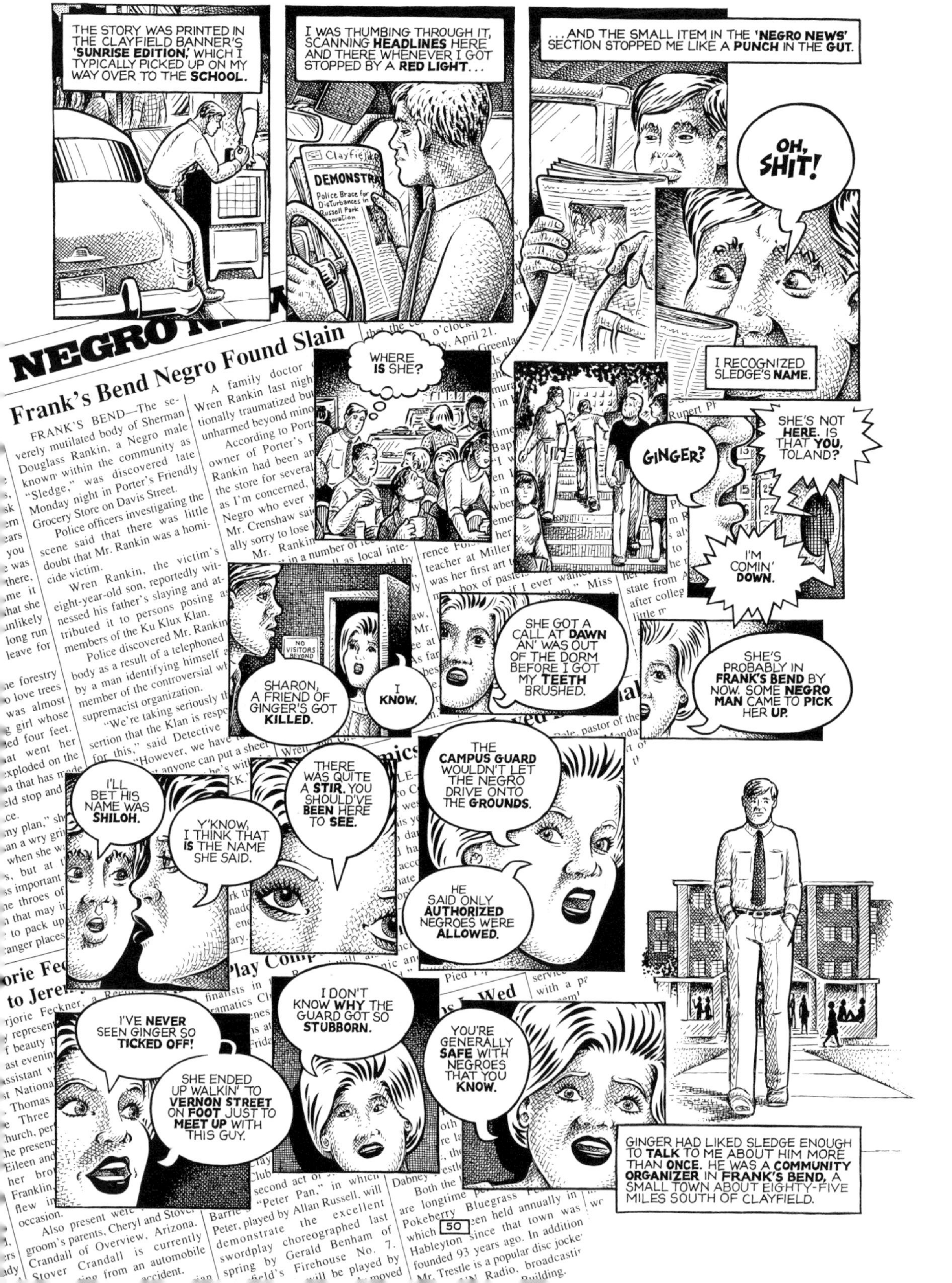
THE STORY WAS PRINTED IN THE CLAYFIELD BANNER'S 'SUNRISE EDITION,' WHICH I TYPICALLY PICKED UP ON MY WAY OVER TO THE SCHOOL.
I WAS THUMBING THROUGH IT, SCANNING HEADLINES HERE AND THERE WHENEVER I GOT STOPPED BY A RED LIGHT...
Clayfield
DEMONSTRA
Police Brace for Disturbances in Russell Park
...AND THE SMALL ITEM IN THE 'NEGRO NEWS' SECTION STOPPED ME LIKE A PUNCH IN THE GUT.
OH, SHIT!
I RECOGNIZED SLEDGE'S NAME.
NEGRO
Frank's Bend Negro Found Slain
WHERE IS SHE?
GINGER?
SHE'S NOT HERE. IS THAT YOU, TOLAND?
I'M COMIN' DOWN.
NO VISITORS BEYOND
SHARON, A FRIEND OF GINGER'S GOT KILLED.
I KNOW.
SHE GOT A CALL AT DAWN AN' WAS OUT OF THE DORM BEFORE I GOT MY TEETH BRUSHED.
SHE'S PROBABLY IN FRANK'S BEND BY NOW. SOME NEGRO MAN CAME TO PICK HER UP.
I'LL BET HIS NAME WAS SHILOH.
Y'KNOW, I THINK THAT IS THE NAME SHE SAID.
THERE WAS QUITE A STIR. YOU SHOULD'VE BEEN HERE TO SEE.
THE CAMPUS GUARD WOULDN'T LET THE NEGRO DRIVE ONTO THE GROUNDS.
HE SAID ONLY AUTHORIZED NEGROES WERE ALLOWED.
I'VE NEVER SEEN GINGER SO TICKED OFF!
SHE ENDED UP WALKIN' TO VERNON STREET ON FOOT JUST TO MEET UP WITH THIS GUY.
I DON'T KNOW WHY THE GUARD GOT SO STUBBORN.
YOU'RE GENERALLY SAFE WITH NEGROES THAT YOU KNOW.
GINGER HAD LIKED SLEDGE ENOUGH TO TALK TO ME ABOUT HIM MORE THAN ONCE. HE WAS A COMMUNITY ORGANIZER IN FRANK'S BEND, A SMALL TOWN ABOUT EIGHTY-FIVE MILES SOUTH OF CLAYFIELD.

THAT AREA WAS **KLAN COUNTRY**, FOR SURE!

OFFICIALS MADE **DISAPPROVING NOISES** ABOUT THE PERIODIC **LYNCHINGS**, BUT NO WHITE PERSON HAD **EVER** BEEN INDICTED FOR THE MURDER OF SOMEONE **BLACK**.

GINGER LIKED TO TELL HOW SLEDGE HAD DRIVEN TO CLAYFIELD AND PRACTICALLY **KIDNAPPED** SHILOH AND HER TO GET THEM TO PERFORM AT A **RALLY** FOR SOME **PAPER MILL WORKERS** WHO WERE ON **STRIKE**.

...Oh, you can't scare me! I'm stickin' with the union...

AFTERWARDS THEY'D GONE BACK TO SLEDGE'S **HOME** FOR A **CHICKEN DINNER** TOPPED OFF WITH **BLACKBERRY COBBLER**.

WREN, SHOW SHILOH AN' GINGER THAT **MAGIC TRICK** YOU DO WITH THE **PENNIES** AN' THE PEOPLE'S **EARS**....

IT WAS A VISIT THAT LEFT EVERYBODY FEELING LIKE THEY'D ALL BEEN **REARED** IN THE SAME **CRADLE**, ACCORDING TO GINGER.

I WAS **UPSET** ABOUT SLEDGE BEING KILLED, BUT THERE WASN'T ANYTHING I COULD FIGURE OUT TO **DO** BUT GO ON TO **WORK** AND HOPE TO HEAR FROM GINGER **EVENTUALLY**.

YOUR **GIRLFRIEND'S** ON THE HORN **LONG-DISTANCE**, POLK.

WILL YOU BE GOIN' STRAIGHT **HOME** FROM **WORK** TONIGHT? SHILOH AN' I WILL BE LEAVIN' **FRANK'S BEND** SOON, AN' WE WERE CONSIDERIN' STOPPIN' BY THE **WHEELERY**.

I'VE HAD TO BE **STRONG** ALL DAY FOR SLEDGE'S **FAMILY** AN' I'M GOIN' **CRAZY** FOR A **CRY**.

MY SHOULDER'LL BE **WAITIN'** FOR YOU.

NOW **SOME** FELLAS WOULD'VE HAD THE GOOD SENSE TO LEAVE IT **THERE**—BUT NOT **ME**!

I WAS SLIGHTLY **BOTHERED**, TO BE HONEST, THAT IT WAS **SHILOH** SHE'D HOOKED UP WITH IN HER TIME OF GRIEF INSTEAD OF **ME**.

IN THE LATE AFTERNOON, SHE **CALLED**.

WHEN I GOT HOME TO THE WHEELERY, SHILOH'S **CAR** WAS ALREADY IN THE **DRIVEWAY**. RILEY AND **LOCO** WERE ON THE FRONT PORCH LOOKING **TENSE**.

WHAT'S WITH THE **GUN**?

I WISH YOU COULD'VE **PHONED** ME THIS MORNIN' BEFORE YOU LEFT. IT WAS **WEIRD** GETTIN' TO THE CAFETERIA AN' YOU NOT **BEIN'** THERE.

I **APOLOGIZE**, TOLAND. I'LL TRY TO BE MORE **CONSIDERATE** OF YOU THE NEXT TIME SOMEBODY I LOVE GETS MURDERED.

I'LL SEE YOU **LATER**.
click!

I LOVE YOU.

OPEN **MOUTH**; INSERT **FOOT**!

HONEY, I DIDN'T **MEAN** THAT THE WAY IT~

I SPENT A **LOVELY** COUPLE OF HOURS **KICKING** MYSELF UNTIL MY SHIFT WAS OVER AND I COULD **LEAVE**.

51

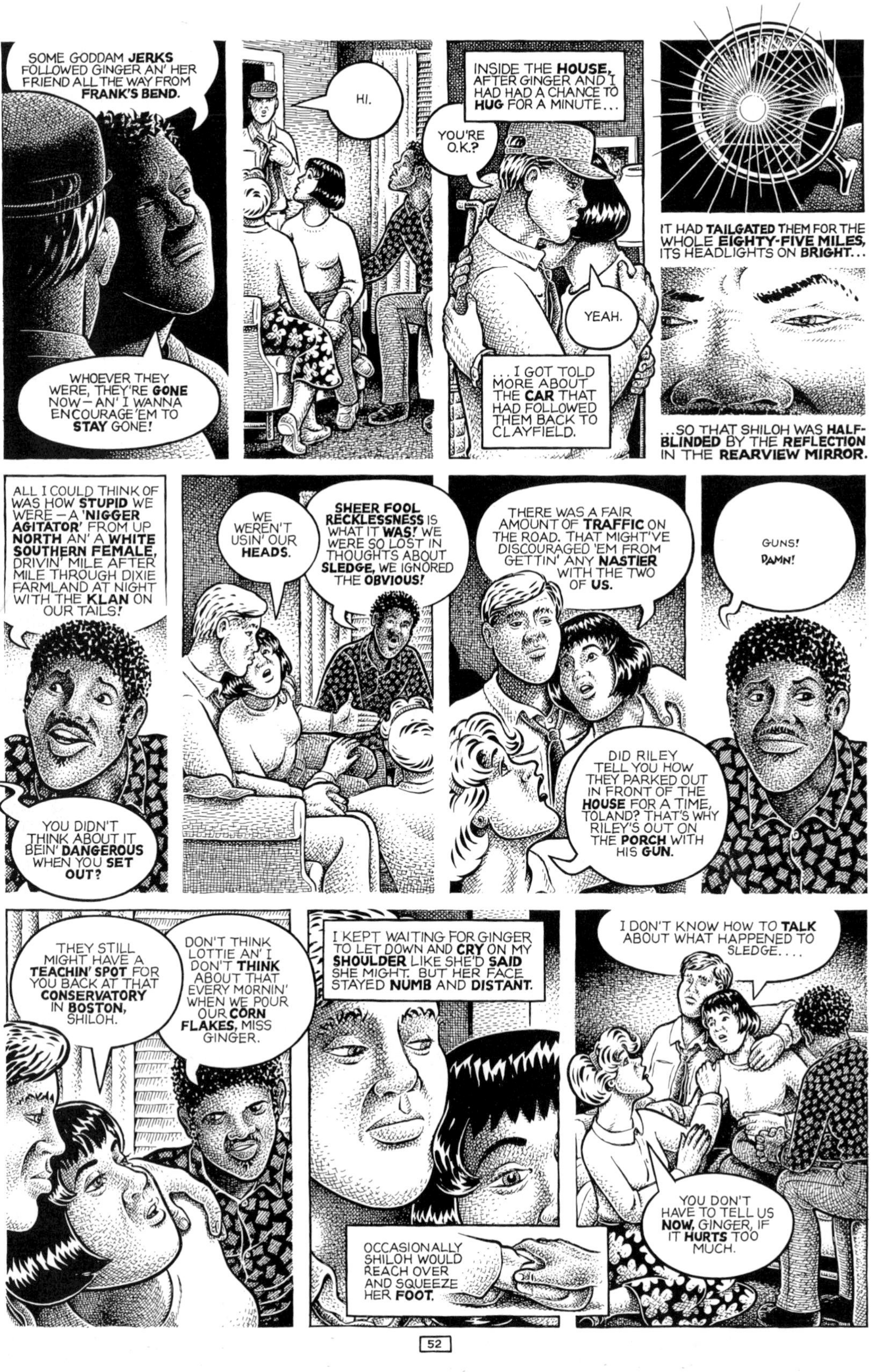

SOME GODDAM JERKS FOLLOWED GINGER AN' HER FRIEND ALL THE WAY FROM FRANK'S BEND.
WHOEVER THEY WERE, THEY'RE GONE NOW—AN' I WANNA ENCOURAGE 'EM TO STAY GONE!
HI.
INSIDE THE HOUSE, AFTER GINGER AND I HAD HAD A CHANCE TO HUG FOR A MINUTE...
YOU'RE O.K.?
YEAH.
...I GOT TOLD MORE ABOUT THE CAR THAT HAD FOLLOWED THEM BACK TO CLAYFIELD.
IT HAD TAILGATED THEM FOR THE WHOLE EIGHTY-FIVE MILES, ITS HEADLIGHTS ON BRIGHT...
...SO THAT SHILOH WAS HALF-BLINDED BY THE REFLECTION IN THE REARVIEW MIRROR.
ALL I COULD THINK OF WAS HOW STUPID WE WERE—A 'NIGGER AGITATOR' FROM UP NORTH AN' A WHITE SOUTHERN FEMALE, DRIVIN' MILE AFTER MILE THROUGH DIXIE FARMLAND AT NIGHT WITH THE KLAN ON OUR TAILS!
YOU DIDN'T THINK ABOUT IT BEIN' DANGEROUS WHEN YOU SET OUT?
WE WEREN'T USIN' OUR HEADS.
SHEER FOOL RECKLESSNESS IS WHAT IT WAS! WE WERE SO LOST IN THOUGHTS ABOUT SLEDGE, WE IGNORED THE OBVIOUS!
THERE WAS A FAIR AMOUNT OF TRAFFIC ON THE ROAD. THAT MIGHT'VE DISCOURAGED 'EM FROM GETTIN' ANY NASTIER WITH THE TWO OF US.
DID RILEY TELL YOU HOW THEY PARKED OUT IN FRONT OF THE HOUSE FOR A TIME, TOLAND? THAT'S WHY RILEY'S OUT ON THE PORCH WITH HIS GUN.
GUNS! DAMN!
THEY STILL MIGHT HAVE A TEACHIN' SPOT FOR YOU BACK AT THAT CONSERVATORY IN BOSTON, SHILOH.
DON'T THINK LOTTIE AN' I DON'T THINK ABOUT THAT EVERY MORNIN' WHEN WE POUR OUR CORN FLAKES, MISS GINGER.
I KEPT WAITING FOR GINGER TO LET DOWN AND CRY ON MY SHOULDER LIKE SHE'D SAID SHE MIGHT. BUT HER FACE STAYED NUMB AND DISTANT.
OCCASIONALLY SHILOH WOULD REACH OVER AND SQUEEZE HER FOOT.
I DON'T KNOW HOW TO TALK ABOUT WHAT HAPPENED TO SLEDGE....
YOU DON'T HAVE TO TELL US NOW, GINGER, IF IT HURTS TOO MUCH.

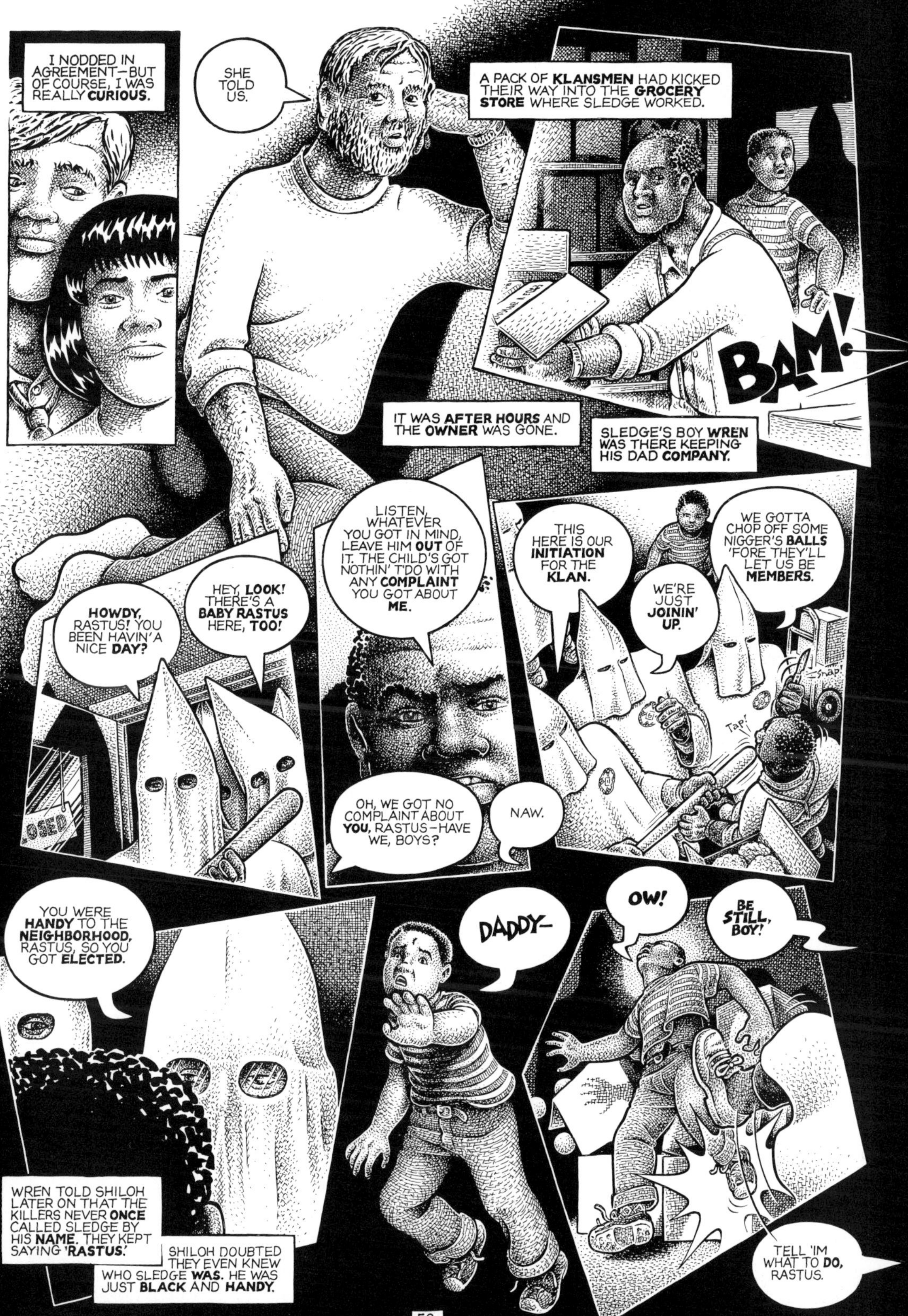

I NODDED IN AGREEMENT—BUT OF COURSE, I WAS REALLY CURIOUS.
SHE TOLD US.
A PACK OF KLANSMEN HAD KICKED THEIR WAY INTO THE GROCERY STORE WHERE SLEDGE WORKED.
BAM!
IT WAS AFTER HOURS AND THE OWNER WAS GONE.
SLEDGE'S BOY WREN WAS THERE KEEPING HIS DAD COMPANY.
HOWDY, RASTUS! YOU BEEN HAVIN' A NICE DAY?
HEY, LOOK! THERE'S A BABY RASTUS HERE, TOO!
LISTEN, WHATEVER YOU GOT IN MIND, LEAVE HIM OUT OF IT. THE CHILD'S GOT NOTHIN' T'DO WITH ANY COMPLAINT YOU GOT ABOUT ME.
OH, WE GOT NO COMPLAINT ABOUT YOU, RASTUS—HAVE WE, BOYS?
NAW.
THIS HERE IS OUR INITIATION FOR THE KLAN.
WE'RE JUST JOININ' UP.
WE GOTTA CHOP OFF SOME NIGGER'S BALLS 'FORE THEY'LL LET US BE MEMBERS.
Snap!
Tap!
YOU WERE HANDY TO THE NEIGHBORHOOD, RASTUS, SO YOU GOT ELECTED.
WREN TOLD SHILOH LATER ON THAT THE KILLERS NEVER ONCE CALLED SLEDGE BY HIS NAME. THEY KEPT SAYING 'RASTUS.'
SHILOH DOUBTED THEY EVEN KNEW WHO SLEDGE WAS. HE WAS JUST BLACK AND HANDY.
DADDY—
OW!
BE STILL, BOY!
TELL 'IM WHAT TO DO, RASTUS.

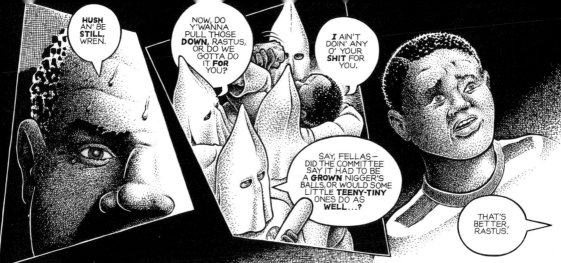

HUSH AN' BE **STILL**, WREN.

NOW, DO Y'WANNA PULL THOSE **DOWN**, RASTUS, OR DO WE GOTTA DO IT **FOR** YOU?

I AIN'T DOIN' ANY O' YOUR **SHIT** FOR YOU.

SAY, FELLAS— DID THE COMMITTEE SAY IT HAD TO BE A **GROWN** NIGGER'S BALLS, OR WOULD SOME LITTLE **TEENY-TINY** ONES DO AS **WELL**...?

THAT'S **BETTER**, RASTUS.

WELL... I GUESS I CAN'T SPEND THE WHOLE **NIGHT** ON THE PORCH!

SHOULD WE CALL THE **POLICE** AN' REPORT HOW YOU AN' GINGER WERE BEIN' **FOLLOWED**, SHILOH?

ALL THEY HAD TO DO WAS PUT A LITTLE **MILEAGE** ON THEIR **CAR** AN' THEY'VE GOT US HAULIN' OUT THE **GUNS!**

SURE **THING**, MAVIS! I'LL BET KEEPIN' THE LIKES OF **US** OUTA **HARM'S WAY** IS RIGHT UP THERE AT THE **TOP** OF SUTTON CHOPPER'S **PRIORITY LIST!**

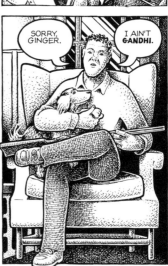

SORRY, GINGER.

I AIN'T **GANDHI.**

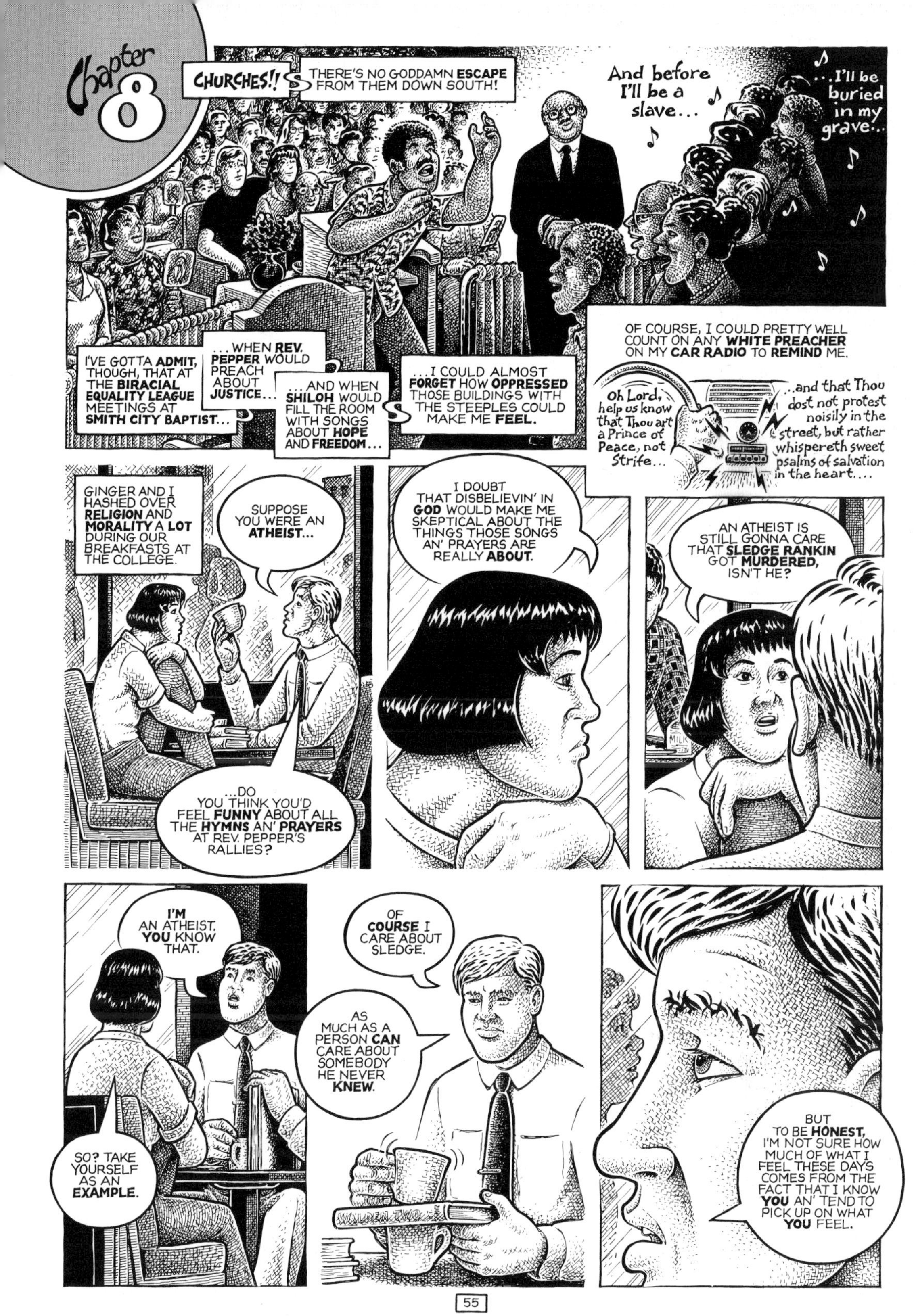
Chapter 8
CHURCHES!!
THERE'S NO GODDAMN ESCAPE FROM THEM DOWN SOUTH!
And before I'll be a slave...
...I'll be buried in my grave...
I'VE GOTTA ADMIT, THOUGH, THAT AT THE BIRACIAL EQUALITY LEAGUE MEETINGS AT SMITH CITY BAPTIST...
...WHEN REV. PEPPER WOULD PREACH ABOUT JUSTICE...
...AND WHEN SHILOH WOULD FILL THE ROOM WITH SONGS ABOUT HOPE AND FREEDOM...
...I COULD ALMOST FORGET HOW OPPRESSED THOSE BUILDINGS WITH THE STEEPLES COULD MAKE ME FEEL.
OF COURSE, I COULD PRETTY WELL COUNT ON ANY WHITE PREACHER ON MY CAR RADIO TO REMIND ME.
Oh Lord, help us know that Thou art a Prince of Peace, not Strife...
...and that Thou dost not protest noisily in the street, but rather whispereth sweet psalms of salvation in the heart....
GINGER AND I HASHED OVER RELIGION AND MORALITY A LOT DURING OUR BREAKFASTS AT THE COLLEGE.
SUPPOSE YOU WERE AN ATHEIST...
...DO YOU THINK YOU'D FEEL FUNNY ABOUT ALL THE HYMNS AN' PRAYERS AT REV. PEPPER'S RALLIES?
I DOUBT THAT DISBELIEVIN' IN GOD WOULD MAKE ME SKEPTICAL ABOUT THE THINGS THOSE SONGS AN' PRAYERS ARE REALLY ABOUT.
AN ATHEIST IS STILL GONNA CARE THAT SLEDGE RANKIN GOT MURDERED, ISN'T HE?
MILK
I'M AN ATHEIST. YOU KNOW THAT.
SO? TAKE YOURSELF AS AN EXAMPLE.
OF COURSE I CARE ABOUT SLEDGE.
AS MUCH AS A PERSON CAN CARE ABOUT SOMEBODY HE NEVER KNEW.
WALDEN TWO
BUT TO BE HONEST, I'M NOT SURE HOW MUCH OF WHAT I FEEL THESE DAYS COMES FROM THE FACT THAT I KNOW YOU AN' TEND TO PICK UP ON WHAT YOU FEEL.

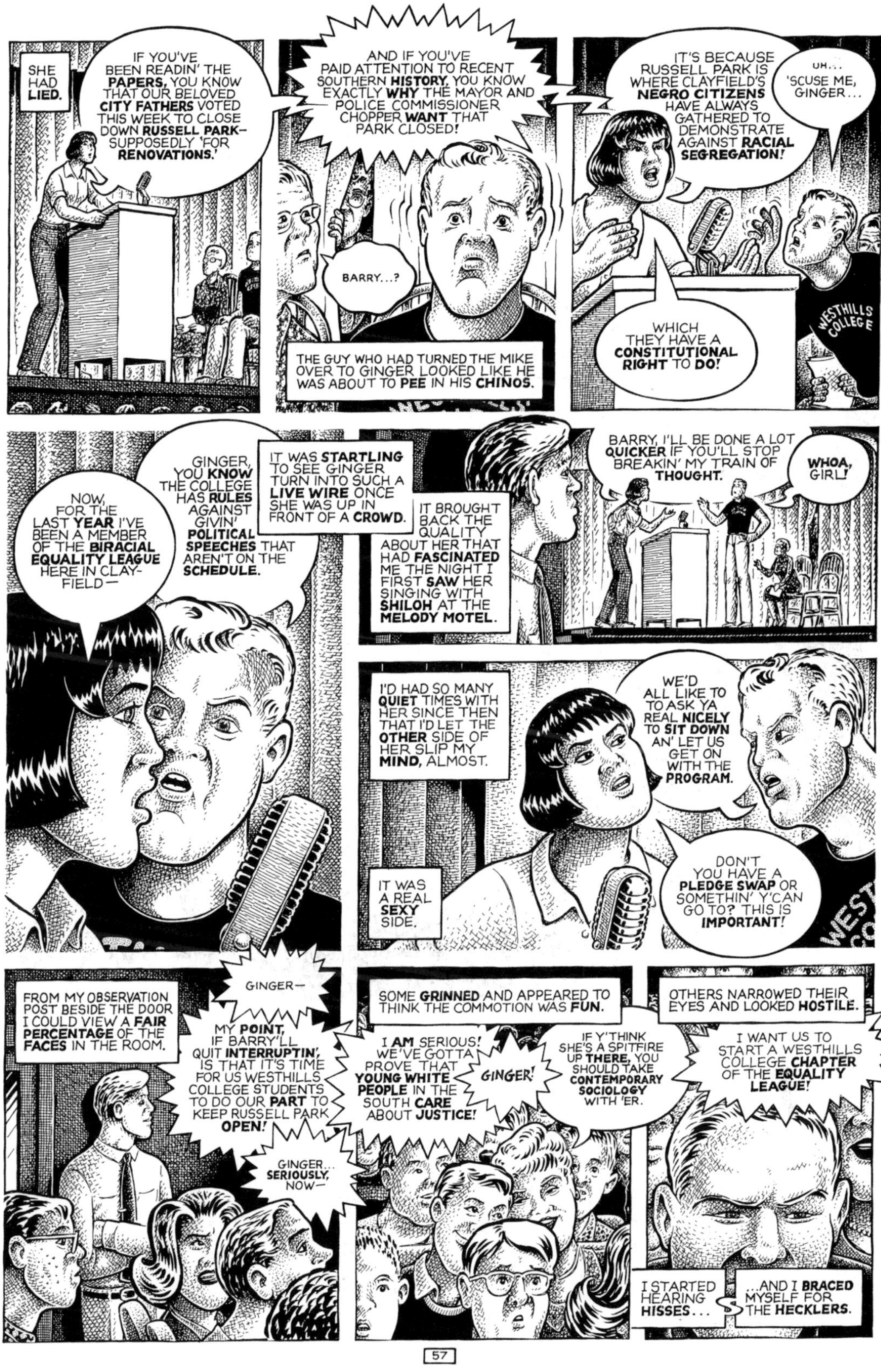
SHE HAD LIED.
IF YOU'VE BEEN READIN' THE PAPERS, YOU KNOW THAT OUR BELOVED CITY FATHERS VOTED THIS WEEK TO CLOSE DOWN RUSSELL PARK– SUPPOSEDLY 'FOR RENOVATIONS.'
AND IF YOU'VE PAID ATTENTION TO RECENT SOUTHERN HISTORY, YOU KNOW EXACTLY WHY THE MAYOR AND POLICE COMMISSIONER CHOPPER WANT THAT PARK CLOSED!
BARRY...?
THE GUY WHO HAD TURNED THE MIKE OVER TO GINGER LOOKED LIKE HE WAS ABOUT TO PEE IN HIS CHINOS.
IT'S BECAUSE RUSSELL PARK IS WHERE CLAYFIELD'S NEGRO CITIZENS HAVE ALWAYS GATHERED TO DEMONSTRATE AGAINST RACIAL SEGREGATION!
UH... 'SCUSE ME, GINGER...
WHICH THEY HAVE A CONSTITUTIONAL RIGHT TO DO!
WESTHILLS COLLEGE
NOW, FOR THE LAST YEAR I'VE BEEN A MEMBER OF THE BIRACIAL EQUALITY LEAGUE HERE IN CLAY-FIELD—
GINGER, YOU KNOW THE COLLEGE HAS RULES AGAINST GIVIN' POLITICAL SPEECHES THAT AREN'T ON THE SCHEDULE.
IT WAS STARTLING TO SEE GINGER TURN INTO SUCH A LIVE WIRE ONCE SHE WAS UP IN FRONT OF A CROWD.
IT BROUGHT BACK THE QUALITY ABOUT HER THAT HAD FASCINATED ME THE NIGHT I FIRST SAW HER SINGING WITH SHILOH AT THE MELODY MOTEL.
BARRY, I'LL BE DONE A LOT QUICKER IF YOU'LL STOP BREAKIN' MY TRAIN OF THOUGHT.
WHOA, GIRL!
I'D HAD SO MANY QUIET TIMES WITH HER SINCE THEN THAT I'D LET THE OTHER SIDE OF HER SLIP MY MIND, ALMOST.
WE'D ALL LIKE TO ASK YA REAL NICELY TO SIT DOWN AN' LET US GET ON WITH THE PROGRAM.
IT WAS A REAL SEXY SIDE.
DON'T YOU HAVE A PLEDGE SWAP OR SOMETHIN' Y'CAN GO TO? THIS IS IMPORTANT!
FROM MY OBSERVATION POST BESIDE THE DOOR I COULD VIEW A FAIR PERCENTAGE OF THE FACES IN THE ROOM.
GINGER—
MY POINT, IF BARRY'LL QUIT INTERRUPTIN', IS THAT IT'S TIME FOR US WESTHILLS COLLEGE STUDENTS TO DO OUR PART TO KEEP RUSSELL PARK OPEN!
GINGER... SERIOUSLY, NOW—
SOME GRINNED AND APPEARED TO THINK THE COMMOTION WAS FUN.
I AM SERIOUS! WE'VE GOTTA PROVE THAT YOUNG WHITE PEOPLE IN THE SOUTH CARE ABOUT JUSTICE!
GINGER!
IF Y'THINK SHE'S A SPITFIRE UP THERE, YOU SHOULD TAKE CONTEMPORARY SOCIOLOGY WITH 'ER.
OTHERS NARROWED THEIR EYES AND LOOKED HOSTILE.
I WANT US TO START A WESTHILLS COLLEGE CHAPTER OF THE EQUALITY LEAGUE!
I STARTED HEARING HISSES...
...AND I BRACED MYSELF FOR THE HECKLERS.

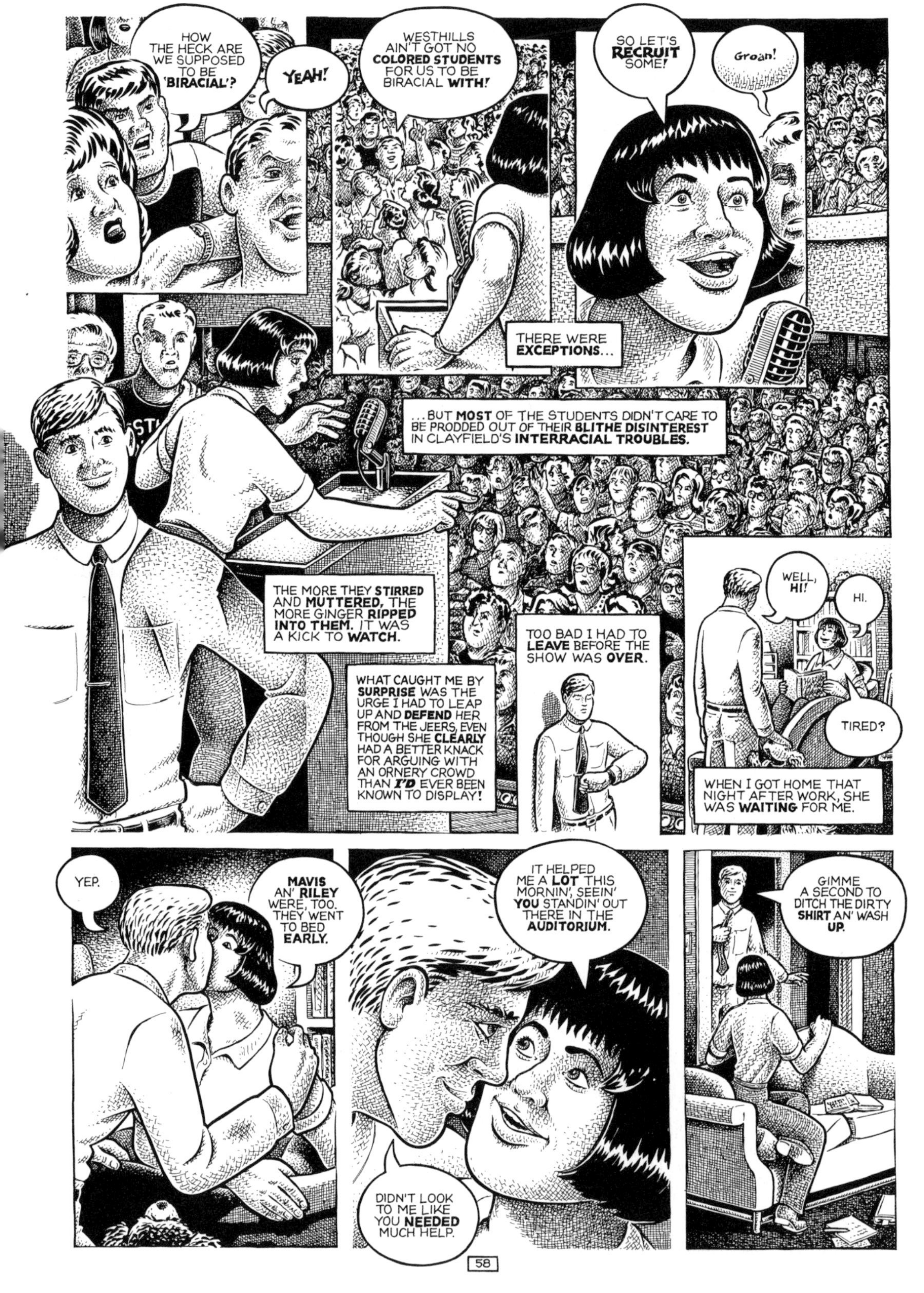

HOW THE HECK ARE WE SUPPOSED TO BE 'BIRACIAL'?
YEAH!
WESTHILLS AIN'T GOT NO COLORED STUDENTS FOR US TO BE BIRACIAL WITH!
SO LET'S RECRUIT SOME!
Groan!
THERE WERE EXCEPTIONS...
...BUT MOST OF THE STUDENTS DIDN'T CARE TO BE PRODDED OUT OF THEIR BLITHE DISINTEREST IN CLAYFIELD'S INTERRACIAL TROUBLES.
THE MORE THEY STIRRED AND MUTTERED, THE MORE GINGER RIPPED INTO THEM. IT WAS A KICK TO WATCH.
WHAT CAUGHT ME BY SURPRISE WAS THE URGE I HAD TO LEAP UP AND DEFEND HER FROM THE JEERS, EVEN THOUGH SHE CLEARLY HAD A BETTER KNACK FOR ARGUING WITH AN ORNERY CROWD THAN I'D EVER BEEN KNOWN TO DISPLAY!
TOO BAD I HAD TO LEAVE BEFORE THE SHOW WAS OVER.
WELL, HI!
HI.
TIRED?
WHEN I GOT HOME THAT NIGHT AFTER WORK, SHE WAS WAITING FOR ME.
YEP.
MAVIS AN' RILEY WERE, TOO. THEY WENT TO BED EARLY.
IT HELPED ME A LOT THIS MORNIN', SEEIN' YOU STANDIN' OUT THERE IN THE AUDITORIUM.
DIDN'T LOOK TO ME LIKE YOU NEEDED MUCH HELP.
GIMME A SECOND TO DITCH THE DIRTY SHIRT AN' WASH UP.

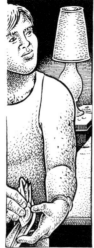

WINE?

ALL MY **INSTINCTS** WERE TELLING ME THAT GINGER FELT THE SAME WAY **I** DID.

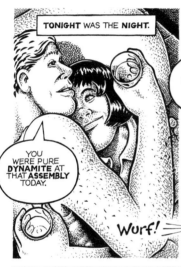

TONIGHT WAS THE **NIGHT.**

YOU WERE PURE **DYNAMITE** AT THAT **ASSEMBLY** TODAY.

Wurf!

DID YOU GET ANY OF YOUR **FELLOW STUDENTS** SIGNED UP FOR THE **EQUALITY LEAGUE?**

A FEW SAID THEY **WISHED** THEY COULD HELP, BUT THEY'RE **SCARED.**

Whimper!

THERE'S PRESSURE ON THE SCHOOL TO **SUSPEND** ANY-BODY WHO GETS INVOLVED IN **SOCIAL UNREST!**

I'D LIKELY BE LONG GONE **MYSELF** IF THE DEAN'S **COUSIN** WASN'T A **BUSINESS PARTNER** OF MY **DAD'S** UP IN **OHIO.**

AREN'T COLLEGE STUDENTS SUPPOSED TO HAVE FREEDOM OF **SPEECH** AN' FREEDOM OF **ASSEMBLY** AN'—

TOLAND, THIS IS THE **SOUTH!** WHERE DO YOU THINK YOU **ARE,** ANY-WAY— IN **AMERICA?!**

POLITICAL TALK. NOT SO **EROTIC.**

IT CAN BE **TOUGH** TO SWITCH GEARS.

WINE HELPS.

BY THE WAY...

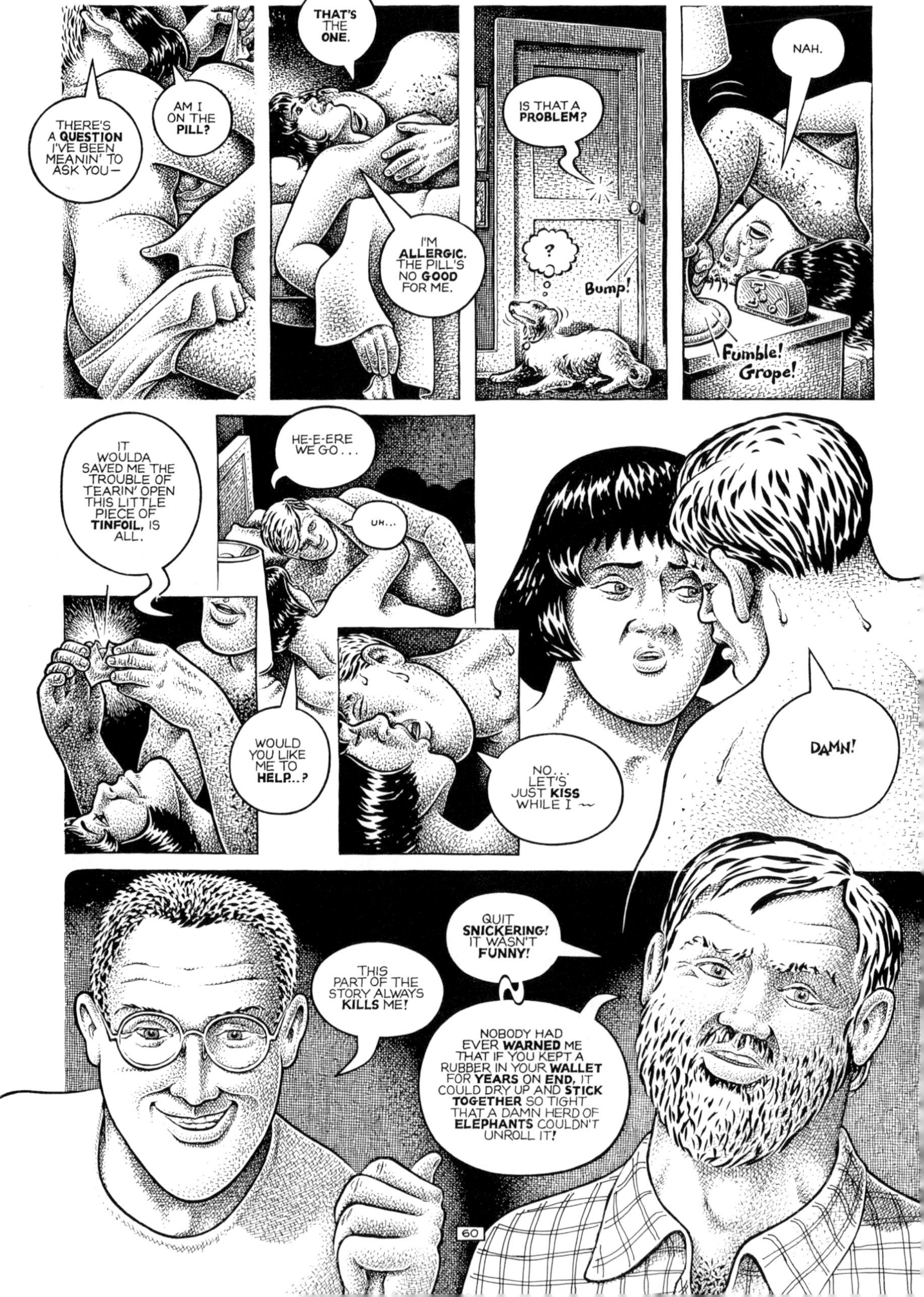
THERE'S A QUESTION I'VE BEEN MEANIN' TO ASK YOU—
AM I ON THE PILL?
THAT'S THE ONE.
I'M ALLERGIC. THE PILL'S NO GOOD FOR ME.
IS THAT A PROBLEM?
?
Bump!
NAH.
Fumble! Grope!
IT WOULDA SAVED ME THE TROUBLE OF TEARIN' OPEN THIS LITTLE PIECE OF TINFOIL, IS ALL.
HE-E-ERE WE GO...
UH...
WOULD YOU LIKE ME TO HELP...?
NO... LET'S JUST KISS WHILE I ~
DAMN!
THIS PART OF THE STORY ALWAYS KILLS ME!
QUIT SNICKERING! IT WASN'T FUNNY!
NOBODY HAD EVER WARNED ME THAT IF YOU KEPT A RUBBER IN YOUR WALLET FOR YEARS ON END, IT COULD DRY UP AND STICK TOGETHER SO TIGHT THAT A DAMN HERD OF ELEPHANTS COULDN'T UNROLL IT!

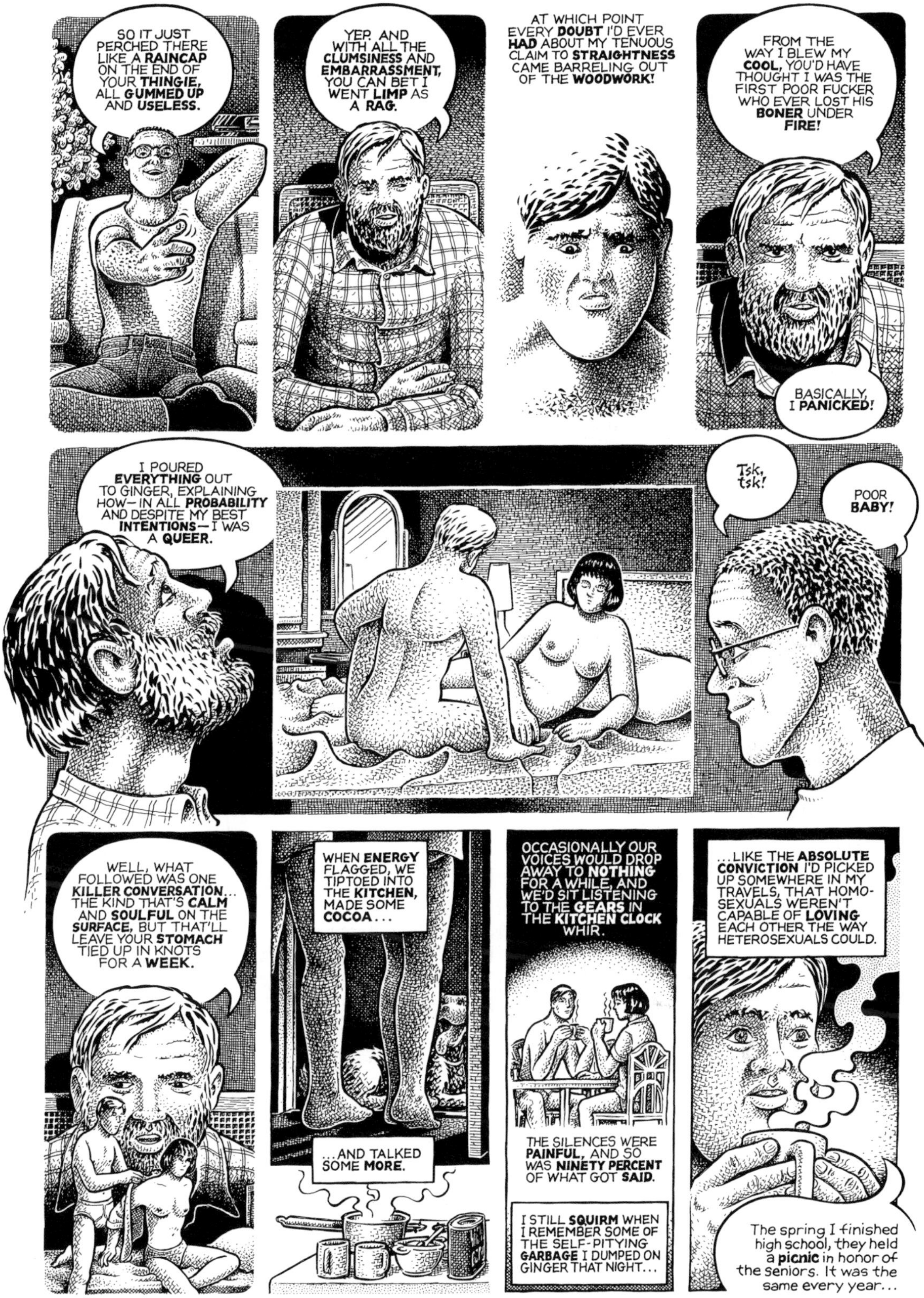

SO IT JUST PERCHED THERE LIKE A RAINCAP ON THE END OF YOUR THINGIE, ALL GUMMED UP AND USELESS.
YEP. AND WITH ALL THE CLUMSINESS AND EMBARRASSMENT, YOU CAN BET I WENT LIMP AS A RAG.
AT WHICH POINT EVERY DOUBT I'D EVER HAD ABOUT MY TENUOUS CLAIM TO STRAIGHTNESS CAME BARRELING OUT OF THE WOODWORK!
FROM THE WAY I BLEW MY COOL, YOU'D HAVE THOUGHT I WAS THE FIRST POOR FUCKER WHO EVER LOST HIS BONER UNDER FIRE!
BASICALLY, I PANICKED!
I POURED EVERYTHING OUT TO GINGER, EXPLAINING HOW—IN ALL PROBABILITY AND DESPITE MY BEST INTENTIONS—I WAS A QUEER.
Tsk, tsk!
POOR BABY!
WELL, WHAT FOLLOWED WAS ONE KILLER CONVERSATION... THE KIND THAT'S CALM AND SOULFUL ON THE SURFACE, BUT THAT'LL LEAVE YOUR STOMACH TIED UP IN KNOTS FOR A WEEK.
WHEN ENERGY FLAGGED, WE TIPTOED INTO THE KITCHEN, MADE SOME COCOA...
...AND TALKED SOME MORE.
OCCASIONALLY OUR VOICES WOULD DROP AWAY TO NOTHING FOR A WHILE, AND WE'D SIT LISTENING TO THE GEARS IN THE KITCHEN CLOCK WHIR.
THE SILENCES WERE PAINFUL, AND SO WAS NINETY PERCENT OF WHAT GOT SAID.
I STILL SQUIRM WHEN I REMEMBER SOME OF THE SELF-PITYING GARBAGE I DUMPED ON GINGER THAT NIGHT...
...LIKE THE ABSOLUTE CONVICTION I'D PICKED UP SOMEWHERE IN MY TRAVELS, THAT HOMO-SEXUALS WEREN'T CAPABLE OF LOVING EACH OTHER THE WAY HETEROSEXUALS COULD.
The spring I finished high school, they held a picnic in honor of the seniors. It was the same every year...

Half the class, it seemed, was **paired off**: boy, girl, boy, girl....

Some of 'em were in **love**, or **felt** like they were.

A fair number knew they'd be **separated** soon, what with **college** or goin' into the **military**.

They sat around on the **grass**, some of 'em holdin' **hands**, a few practically **neckin'** right there in front of **every**body.

The chaperons were careful to see that nothin' got out of **hand**, but even **so**, they kept castin' **tender, indulgent glances** at all the young couples...

...Like it was so fuckin' **wonderful** that the **plan** of **nature** was bein' **fulfilled** by these **sweet, straight** teenagers, all **moon-eyed** an' **horny**...

...An' I felt like **shit**, 'cause I knew in my **gut** —as much as I worked at not puttin' anything into **words**— that I'd **never** be part of that **picture**.

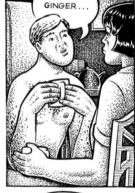
GINGER...

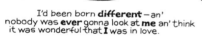
I'd been born **different**—an' nobody was **ever** gonna look at **me** an' think it was wonderful that **I** was in love.

WOULD YA MIND NOT **TELLIN'** ANY OF OUR FRIENDS ABOUT ME? IT'D JUST **COMPLICATE** AN' **CONFUSE** THINGS.

Y'SEE, I **DEFINITELY** PLAN ON BEIN' **STRAIGHT** IN THE **LONG RUN**.

I THINK, IF I'M **DETERMINED** TO, I CAN **DO** IT.

I'VE BEEN DOIN' PRETTY **GOOD**. O.K.—I SCREWED UP **TONIGHT**, BUT, IN GENERAL, I'VE REALLY BEEN FEELIN' LIKE I WAS IN **LOVE** WITH YOU.

TOLAND, YOU NEED TO **THINK** THINGS **THROUGH**.

I MEAN, I **AM** IN LOVE WITH YOU.

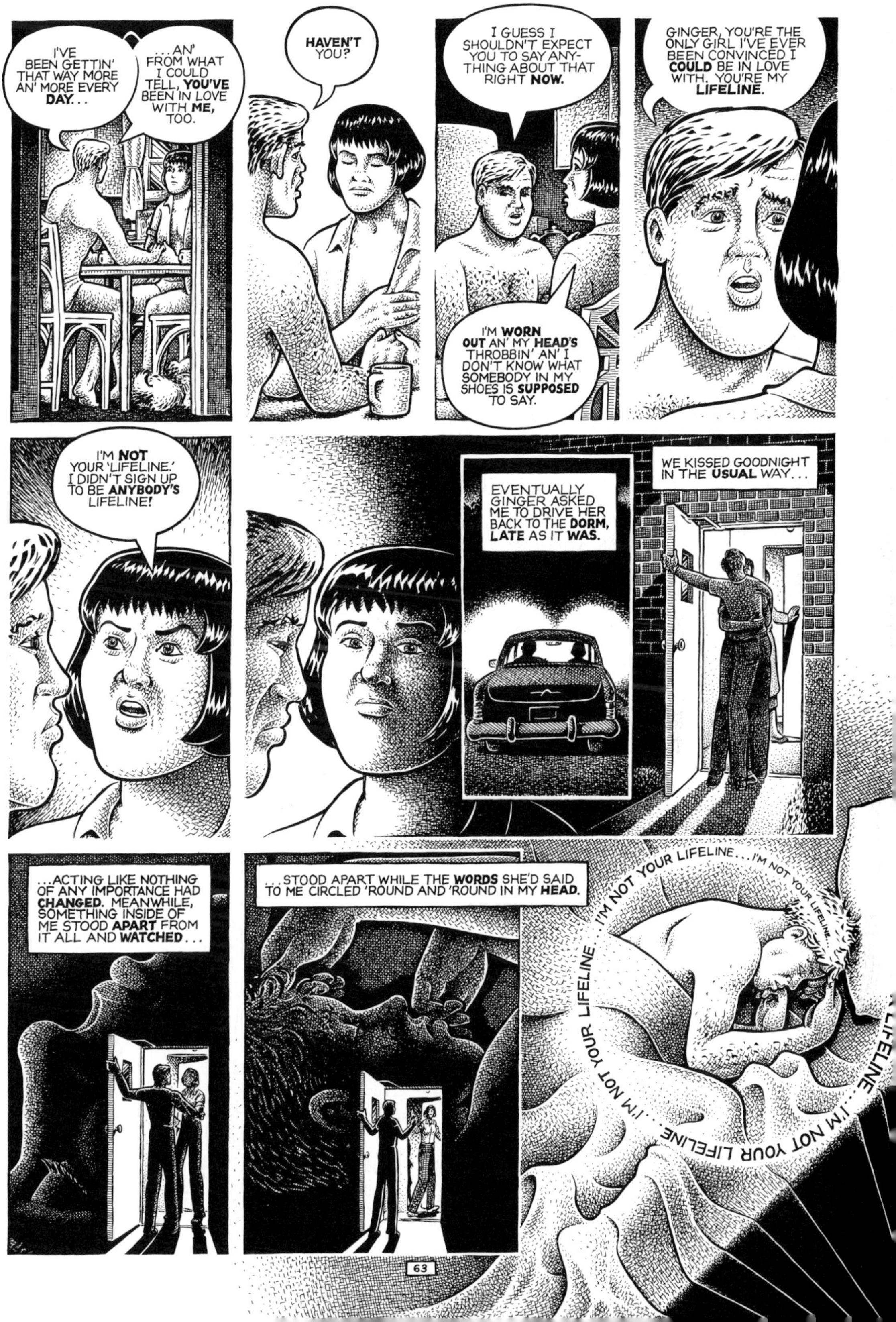

I'VE BEEN GETTIN' THAT WAY MORE AN' MORE EVERY DAY...
...AN' FROM WHAT I COULD TELL, YOU'VE BEEN IN LOVE WITH ME, TOO.
HAVEN'T YOU?
I GUESS I SHOULDN'T EXPECT YOU TO SAY ANY-THING ABOUT THAT RIGHT NOW.
I'M WORN OUT AN' MY HEAD'S THROBBIN' AN' I DON'T KNOW WHAT SOMEBODY IN MY SHOES IS SUPPOSED TO SAY.
GINGER, YOU'RE THE ONLY GIRL I'VE EVER BEEN CONVINCED I COULD BE IN LOVE WITH. YOU'RE MY LIFELINE.
I'M NOT YOUR 'LIFELINE.' I DIDN'T SIGN UP TO BE ANYBODY'S LIFELINE!
EVENTUALLY GINGER ASKED ME TO DRIVE HER BACK TO THE DORM, LATE AS IT WAS.
WE KISSED GOODNIGHT IN THE USUAL WAY...
...ACTING LIKE NOTHING OF ANY IMPORTANCE HAD CHANGED. MEANWHILE, SOMETHING INSIDE OF ME STOOD APART FROM IT ALL AND WATCHED...
...STOOD APART WHILE THE WORDS SHE'D SAID TO ME CIRCLED 'ROUND AND 'ROUND IN MY HEAD.
I'M NOT YOUR LIFELINE... I'M NOT YOUR LIFELINE... I'M NOT YOUR LIFELINE... I'M NOT YOUR LIFELINE... I'M NOT YOUR LIFELINE... I'M NOT YOUR LIFELINE

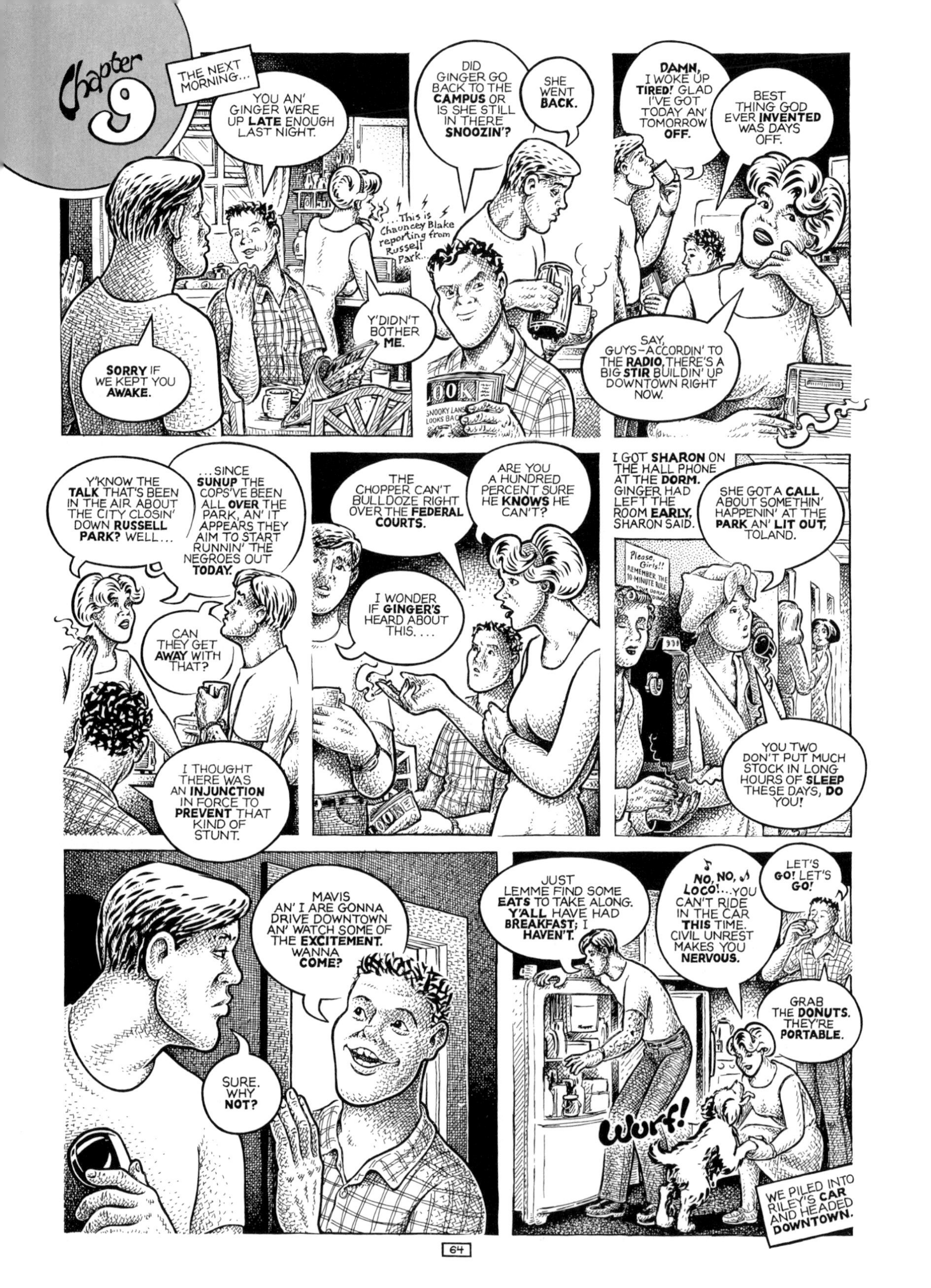
Chapter 9
THE NEXT MORNING...
YOU AN' GINGER WERE UP LATE ENOUGH LAST NIGHT.
SORRY IF WE KEPT YOU AWAKE.
...This is Chauncey Blake reporting from Russell Park...
Y'DIDN'T BOTHER ME.
DID GINGER GO BACK TO THE CAMPUS OR IS SHE STILL IN THERE SNOOZIN'?
SHE WENT BACK.
LOOK
SNOOKY LANS LOOKS BAC
DAMN, I WOKE UP TIRED! GLAD I'VE GOT TODAY AN' TOMORROW OFF.
BEST THING GOD EVER INVENTED WAS DAYS OFF.
SAY, GUYS—ACCORDIN' TO THE RADIO, THERE'S A BIG STIR BUILDIN' UP DOWNTOWN RIGHT NOW.
Y'KNOW THE TALK THAT'S BEEN IN THE AIR ABOUT THE CITY CLOSIN' DOWN RUSSELL PARK? WELL...
...SINCE SUNUP THE COPS'VE BEEN ALL OVER THE PARK, AN' IT APPEARS THEY AIM TO START RUNNIN' THE NEGROES OUT TODAY.
CAN THEY GET AWAY WITH THAT?
I THOUGHT THERE WAS AN INJUNCTION IN FORCE TO PREVENT THAT KIND OF STUNT.
THE CHOPPER CAN'T BULLDOZE RIGHT OVER THE FEDERAL COURTS.
ARE YOU A HUNDRED PERCENT SURE HE KNOWS HE CAN'T?
I WONDER IF GINGER'S HEARD ABOUT THIS....
I GOT SHARON ON THE HALL PHONE AT THE DORM. GINGER HAD LEFT THE ROOM EARLY, SHARON SAID.
SHE GOT A CALL ABOUT SOMETHIN' HAPPENIN' AT THE PARK AN' LIT OUT, TOLAND.
Please, Girls!! REMEMBER THE 10-MINUTE RULE
YOU TWO DON'T PUT MUCH STOCK IN LONG HOURS OF SLEEP THESE DAYS, DO YOU!
MAVIS AN' I ARE GONNA DRIVE DOWNTOWN AN' WATCH SOME OF THE EXCITEMENT. WANNA COME?
SURE. WHY NOT?
JUST LEMME FIND SOME EATS TO TAKE ALONG. Y'ALL HAVE HAD BREAKFAST; I HAVEN'T.
NO, NO, LOCO!...YOU CAN'T RIDE IN THE CAR THIS TIME. CIVIL UNREST MAKES YOU NERVOUS.
LET'S GO! LET'S GO!
GRAB THE DONUTS. THEY'RE PORTABLE.
Wurf!
WE PILED INTO RILEY'S CAR AND HEADED DOWNTOWN.

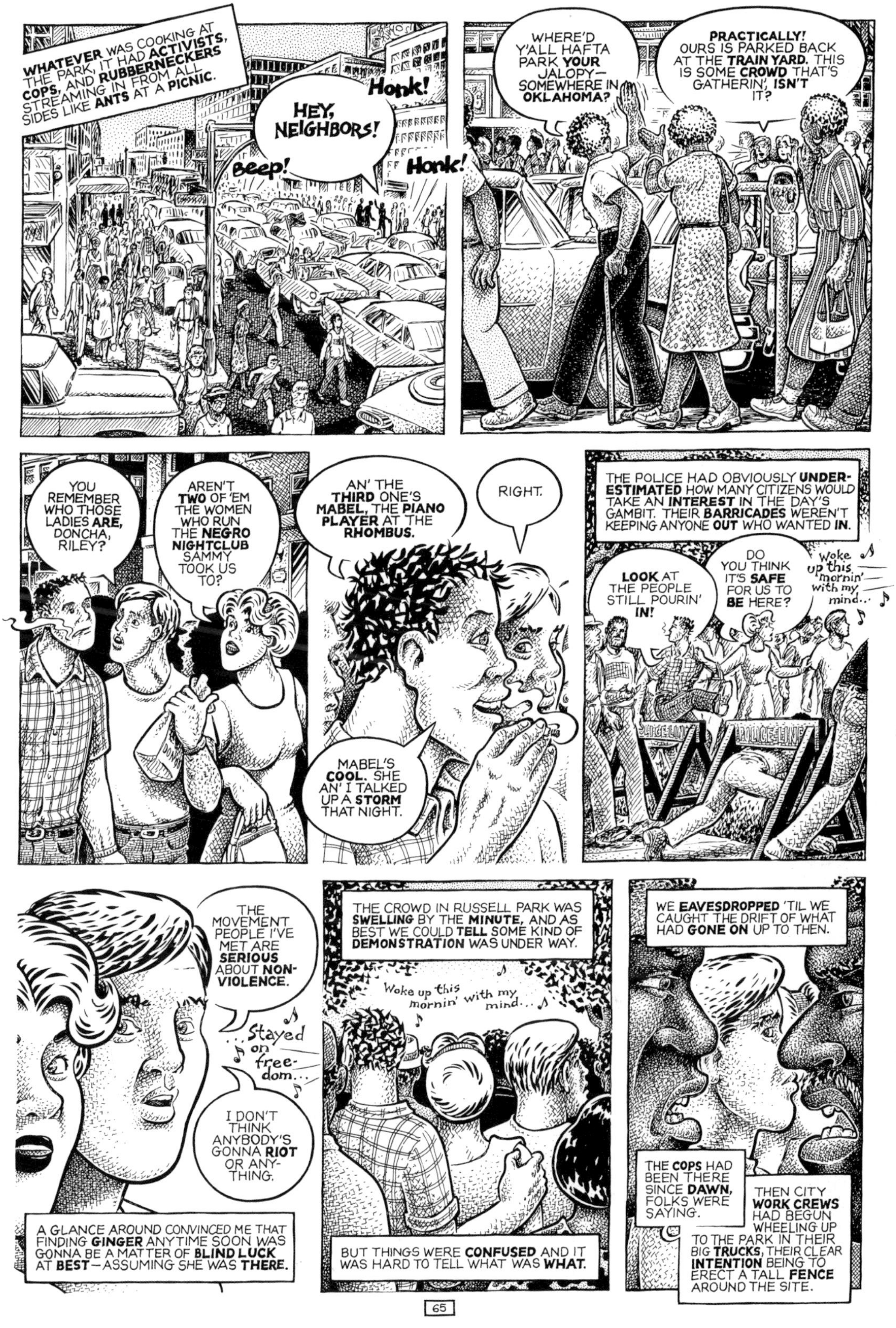
WHATEVER WAS COOKING AT THE PARK, IT HAD ACTIVISTS, COPS, AND RUBBERNECKERS STREAMING IN FROM ALL SIDES LIKE ANTS AT A PICNIC.
Honk!
HEY, NEIGHBORS!
Beep!
Honk!
WHERE'D Y'ALL HAFTA PARK YOUR JALOPY— SOMEWHERE IN OKLAHOMA?
PRACTICALLY! OURS IS PARKED BACK AT THE TRAIN YARD. THIS IS SOME CROWD THAT'S GATHERIN', ISN'T IT?
YOU REMEMBER WHO THOSE LADIES ARE, DONCHA, RILEY?
AREN'T TWO OF 'EM THE WOMEN WHO RUN THE NEGRO NIGHTCLUB SAMMY TOOK US TO?
AN' THE THIRD ONE'S MABEL, THE PIANO PLAYER AT THE RHOMBUS.
RIGHT.
MABEL'S COOL. SHE AN' I TALKED UP A STORM THAT NIGHT.
THE POLICE HAD OBVIOUSLY UNDERESTIMATED HOW MANY CITIZENS WOULD TAKE AN INTEREST IN THE DAY'S GAMBIT. THEIR BARRICADES WEREN'T KEEPING ANYONE OUT WHO WANTED IN.
LOOK AT THE PEOPLE STILL POURIN' IN!
DO YOU THINK IT'S SAFE FOR US TO BE HERE?
Woke up this mornin' with my mind...
POLICE LINE
THE MOVEMENT PEOPLE I'VE MET ARE SERIOUS ABOUT NON-VIOLENCE.
...Stayed on free-dom...
I DON'T THINK ANYBODY'S GONNA RIOT OR ANYTHING.
A GLANCE AROUND CONVINCED ME THAT FINDING GINGER ANYTIME SOON WAS GONNA BE A MATTER OF BLIND LUCK AT BEST—ASSUMING SHE WAS THERE.
THE CROWD IN RUSSELL PARK WAS SWELLING BY THE MINUTE, AND AS BEST WE COULD TELL SOME KIND OF DEMONSTRATION WAS UNDER WAY.
Woke up this mornin' with my mind...
BUT THINGS WERE CONFUSED AND IT WAS HARD TO TELL WHAT WAS WHAT.
WE EAVESDROPPED 'TIL WE CAUGHT THE DRIFT OF WHAT HAD GONE ON UP TO THEN.
THE COPS HAD BEEN THERE SINCE DAWN, FOLKS WERE SAYING.
THEN CITY WORK CREWS HAD BEGUN WHEELING UP TO THE PARK IN THEIR BIG TRUCKS, THEIR CLEAR INTENTION BEING TO ERECT A TALL FENCE AROUND THE SITE.

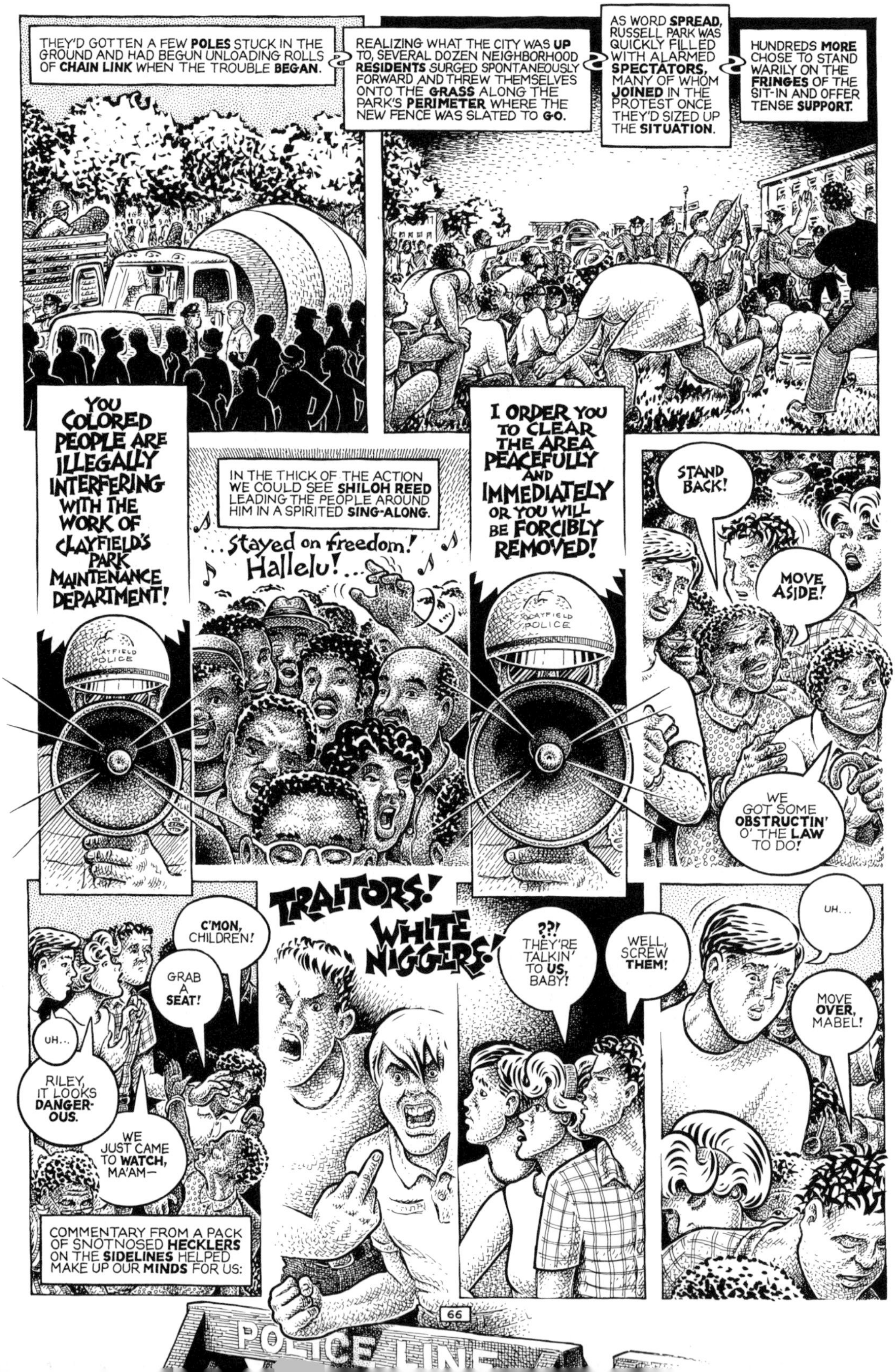
THEY'D GOTTEN A FEW POLES STUCK IN THE GROUND AND HAD BEGUN UNLOADING ROLLS OF CHAIN LINK WHEN THE TROUBLE BEGAN.
REALIZING WHAT THE CITY WAS UP TO, SEVERAL DOZEN NEIGHBORHOOD RESIDENTS SURGED SPONTANEOUSLY FORWARD AND THREW THEMSELVES ONTO THE GRASS ALONG THE PARK'S PERIMETER WHERE THE NEW FENCE WAS SLATED TO GO.
AS WORD SPREAD, RUSSELL PARK WAS QUICKLY FILLED WITH ALARMED SPECTATORS, MANY OF WHOM JOINED IN THE PROTEST ONCE THEY'D SIZED UP THE SITUATION.
HUNDREDS MORE CHOSE TO STAND WARILY ON THE FRINGES OF THE SIT-IN AND OFFER TENSE SUPPORT.
YOU COLORED PEOPLE ARE ILLEGALLY INTERFERING WITH THE WORK OF CLAYFIELD'S PARK MAINTENANCE DEPARTMENT!
CLAYFIELD POLICE
IN THE THICK OF THE ACTION WE COULD SEE SHILOH REED LEADING THE PEOPLE AROUND HIM IN A SPIRITED SING-ALONG.
...Stayed on freedom! Hallelu!...
I ORDER YOU TO CLEAR THE AREA PEACEFULLY AND IMMEDIATELY OR YOU WILL BE FORCIBLY REMOVED!
CLAYFIELD POLICE
STAND BACK!
MOVE ASIDE!
WE GOT SOME OBSTRUCTIN' O' THE LAW TO DO!
C'MON, CHILDREN!
GRAB A SEAT!
UH...
RILEY, IT LOOKS DANGER-OUS.
WE JUST CAME TO WATCH, MA'AM—
COMMENTARY FROM A PACK OF SNOTNOSED HECKLERS ON THE SIDELINES HELPED MAKE UP OUR MINDS FOR US:
TRAITORS!
WHITE NIGGERS!
??! THEY'RE TALKIN' TO US, BABY!
WELL, SCREW THEM!
UH...
MOVE OVER, MABEL!
POLICE LIN

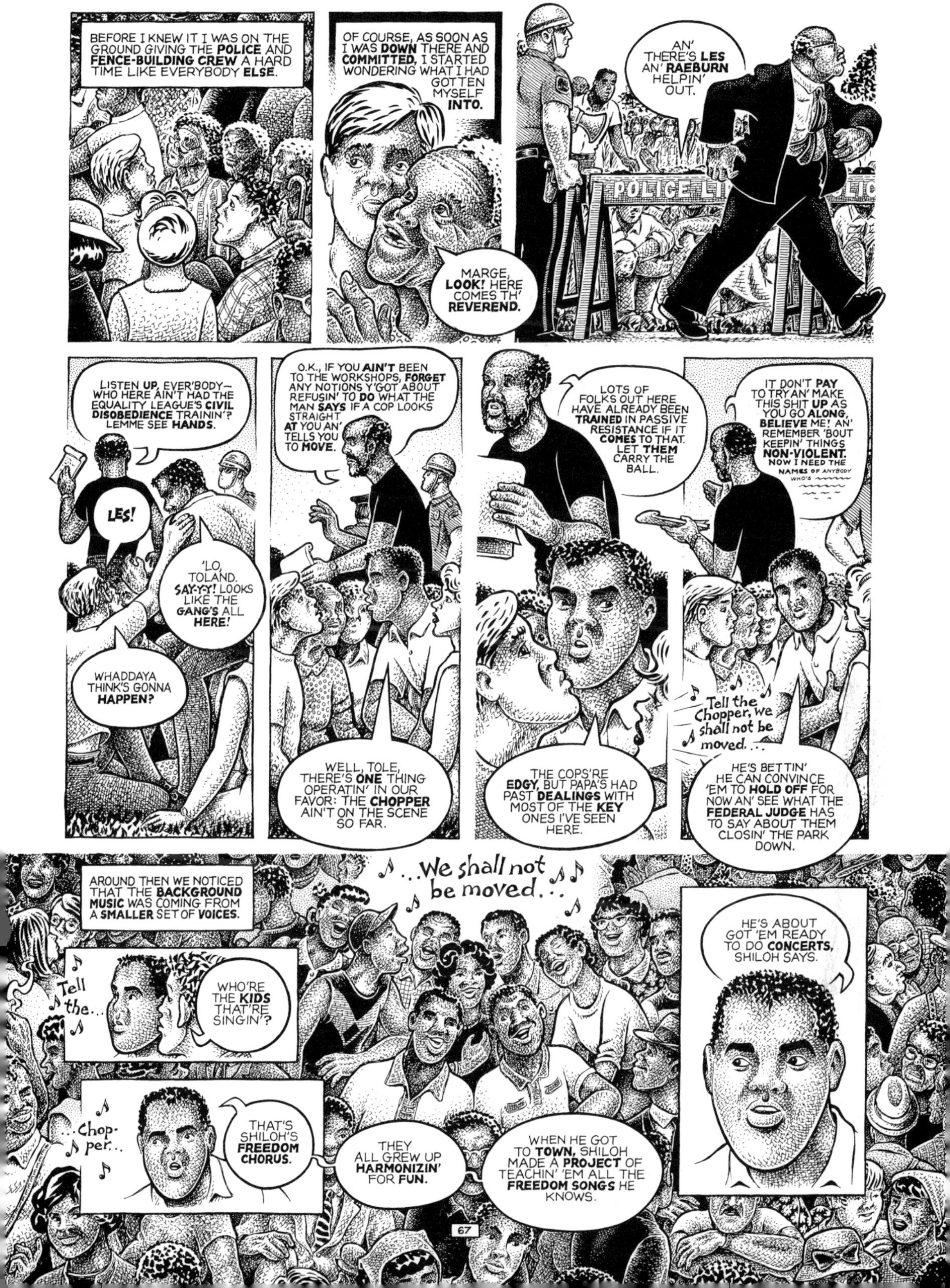
BEFORE I KNEW IT I WAS ON THE GROUND GIVING THE POLICE AND FENCE-BUILDING CREW A HARD TIME LIKE EVERYBODY ELSE.
OF COURSE, AS SOON AS I WAS DOWN THERE AND COMMITTED, I STARTED WONDERING WHAT I HAD GOTTEN MYSELF INTO.
MARGE, LOOK! HERE COMES TH' REVEREND.
AN' THERE'S LES AN' RAEBURN HELPIN' OUT.
POLICE LI
LISTEN UP, EVER'BODY— WHO HERE AIN'T HAD THE EQUALITY LEAGUE'S CIVIL DISOBEDIENCE TRAININ'? LEMME SEE HANDS.
LES!
'LO, TOLAND. SAY-Y-Y! LOOKS LIKE THE GANG'S ALL HERE!
WHADDAYA THINK'S GONNA HAPPEN?
O.K., IF YOU AIN'T BEEN TO THE WORKSHOPS, FORGET ANY NOTIONS Y'GOT ABOUT REFUSIN' TO DO WHAT THE MAN SAYS IF A COP LOOKS STRAIGHT AT YOU AN' TELLS YOU TO MOVE.
WELL, TOLE, THERE'S ONE THING OPERATIN' IN OUR FAVOR: THE CHOPPER AIN'T ON THE SCENE SO FAR.
LOTS OF FOLKS OUT HERE HAVE ALREADY BEEN TRAINED IN PASSIVE RESISTANCE IF IT COMES TO THAT. LET THEM CARRY THE BALL.
THE COPS'RE EDGY, BUT PAPA'S HAD PAST DEALINGS WITH MOST OF THE KEY ONES I'VE SEEN HERE.
IT DON'T PAY TO TRY AN' MAKE THIS SHIT UP AS YOU GO ALONG, BELIEVE ME! AN' REMEMBER 'BOUT KEEPIN' THINGS NON-VIOLENT. NOW I NEED THE NAMES OF ANYBODY WHO'S
Tell the Chopper, we shall not be moved. . .
HE'S BETTIN' HE CAN CONVINCE 'EM TO HOLD OFF FOR NOW AN' SEE WHAT THE FEDERAL JUDGE HAS TO SAY ABOUT THEM CLOSIN' THE PARK DOWN.
AROUND THEN WE NOTICED THAT THE BACKGROUND MUSIC WAS COMING FROM A SMALLER SET OF VOICES.
. . .We shall not be moved. . .
Tell the. . .
WHO'RE THE KIDS THAT'RE SINGIN'?
. . Chop-per. .
THAT'S SHILOH'S FREEDOM CHORUS.
THEY ALL GREW UP HARMONIZIN' FOR FUN.
WHEN HE GOT TO TOWN, SHILOH MADE A PROJECT OF TEACHIN' 'EM ALL THE FREEDOM SONGS HE KNOWS.
HE'S ABOUT GOT 'EM READY TO DO CONCERTS, SHILOH SAYS.

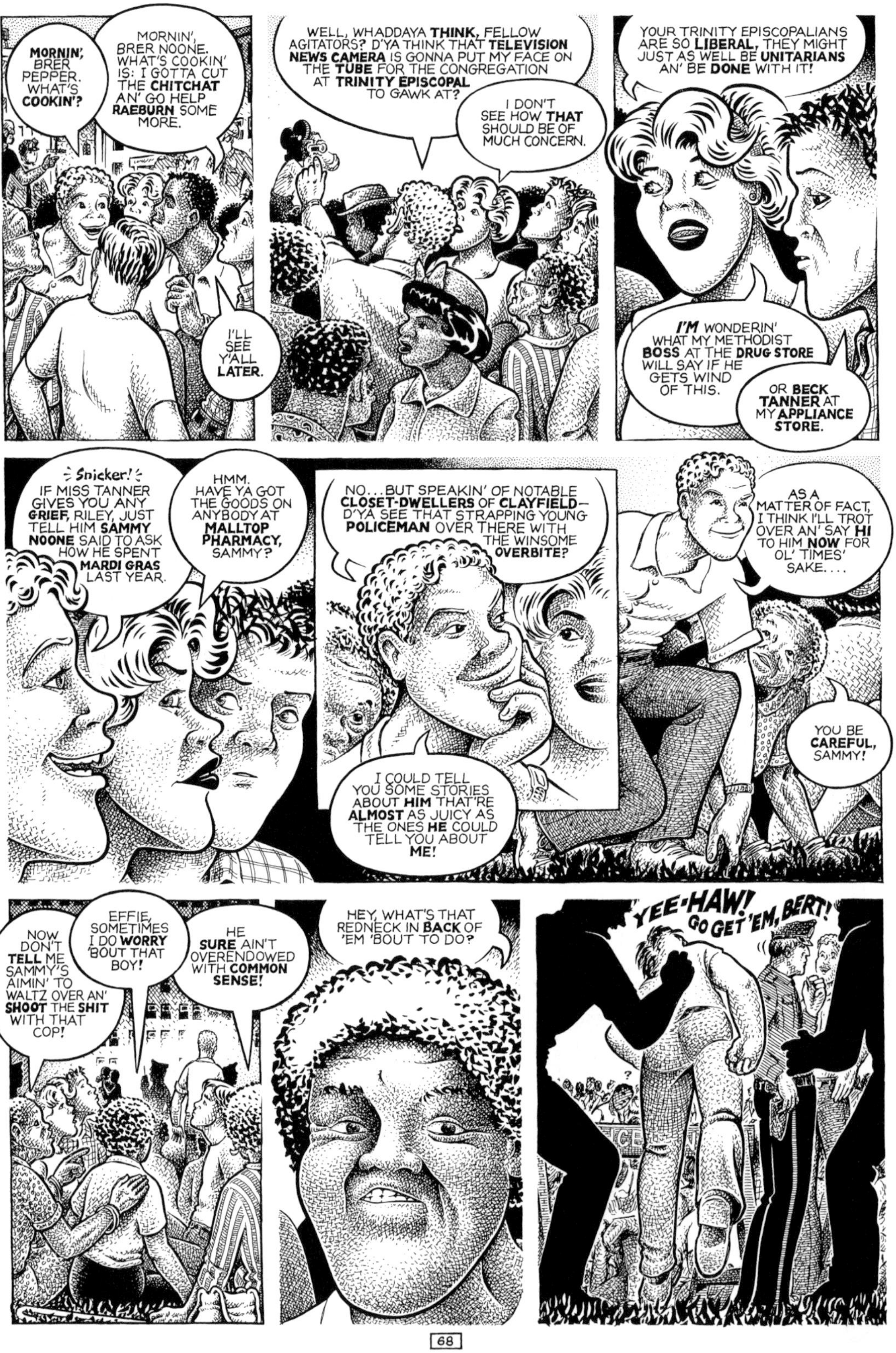
MORNIN', BRER PEPPER. WHAT'S COOKIN'?
MORNIN', BRER NOONE. WHAT'S COOKIN' IS: I GOTTA CUT THE CHITCHAT AN' GO HELP RAEBURN SOME MORE.
I'LL SEE Y'ALL LATER.
WELL, WHADDAYA THINK, FELLOW AGITATORS? D'YA THINK THAT TELEVISION NEWS CAMERA IS GONNA PUT MY FACE ON THE TUBE FOR THE CONGREGATION AT TRINITY EPISCOPAL TO GAWK AT?
I DON'T SEE HOW THAT SHOULD BE OF MUCH CONCERN.
YOUR TRINITY EPISCOPALIANS ARE SO LIBERAL, THEY MIGHT JUST AS WELL BE UNITARIANS AN' BE DONE WITH IT!
I'M WONDERIN' WHAT MY METHODIST BOSS AT THE DRUG STORE WILL SAY IF HE GETS WIND OF THIS.
OR BECK TANNER AT MY APPLIANCE STORE.
Snicker!
IF MISS TANNER GIVES YOU ANY GRIEF, RILEY, JUST TELL HIM SAMMY NOONE SAID TO ASK HOW HE SPENT MARDI GRAS LAST YEAR.
HMM. HAVE YA GOT THE GOODS ON ANYBODY AT MALLTOP PHARMACY, SAMMY?
NO... BUT SPEAKIN' OF NOTABLE CLOSET-DWELLERS OF CLAYFIELD— D'YA SEE THAT STRAPPING YOUNG POLICEMAN OVER THERE WITH THE WINSOME OVERBITE?
I COULD TELL YOU SOME STORIES ABOUT HIM THAT'RE ALMOST AS JUICY AS THE ONES HE COULD TELL YOU ABOUT ME!
AS A MATTER OF FACT, I THINK I'LL TROT OVER AN' SAY HI TO HIM NOW FOR OL' TIMES' SAKE....
YOU BE CAREFUL, SAMMY!
NOW DON'T TELL ME SAMMY'S AIMIN' TO WALTZ OVER AN' SHOOT THE SHIT WITH THAT COP!
EFFIE, SOMETIMES I DO WORRY 'BOUT THAT BOY!
HE SURE AIN'T OVERENDOWED WITH COMMON SENSE!
HEY, WHAT'S THAT REDNECK IN BACK OF 'EM 'BOUT TO DO?
YEE-HAW! GO GET 'EM, BERT!

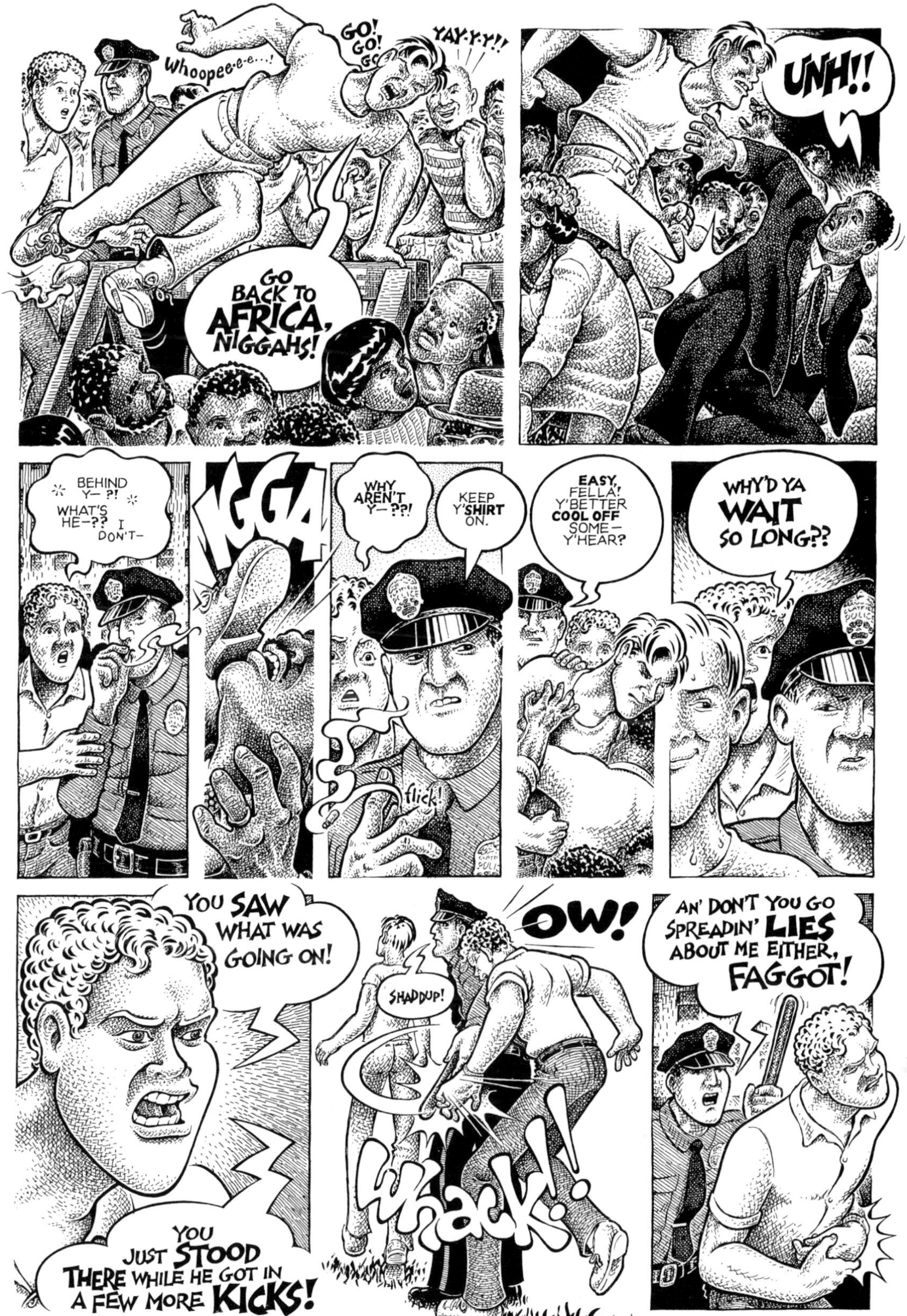
Whoopee-e-e...!
GO! GO! GO
YAY-Y-Y!!
GO BACK TO AFRICA, NIGGAHS!
UNH!!
BEHIND Y— ?! WHAT'S HE—?? I DON'T—
WHY AREN'T Y— ??!
KEEP Y'SHIRT ON.
flick!
EASY, FELLA! Y'BETTER COOL OFF SOME— Y'HEAR?
WHY'D YA WAIT SO LONG??
YOU SAW WHAT WAS GOING ON!
YOU JUST STOOD THERE WHILE HE GOT IN A FEW MORE KICKS!
OW!
SHADDUP!
WHACK!!
AN' DON'T YOU GO SPREADIN' LIES ABOUT ME EITHER, FAGGOT!

ARE YOU **ALL** RIGHT, SAMMY?

Groan! THE BASTARD HIT MY **HAND!** AN' HE **KNOWS** HOW I EARN MY **LIVIN'!**

DAMN COP BETTER NOT SWING AT **ME** OR I'LL KNOCK HIS BUTT CLEAR TO **BILOXI!**

DON'T TALK LIKE **THAT**, MABEL! **THAT** AIN'T THE **SPIRIT!**

Y'WANNA GO TO A **DOCTOR**, PAL?

DON'T WANNA GO **ANYWHERE** RIGHT NOW. JUST LEMME BE **STILL** HERE 'TIL IT STOPS **THROBBIN'**.

IF ASKED, I'D HAVE TOLD YOU A **RIOT** WAS GONNA BREAK OUT ONCE THE **KICKING** STARTED. BUT SOMEHOW **TEMPERS** GOT **HELD.**

COME MID-AFTERNOON, OUR ASSES WERE STILL RIGHT **THERE** ON THE **GRASS.**

IT WAS A HELL OF A WAY TO SPEND A **SATURDAY.**

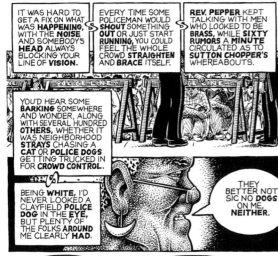

IT WAS HARD TO GET A FIX ON WHAT WAS **HAPPENING**, WITH THE **NOISE** AND SOMEBODY'S **HEAD** ALWAYS BLOCKING YOUR LINE OF **VISION.**

EVERY TIME SOME POLICEMAN WOULD **SHOUT** SOMETHING **OUT** OR JUST START **RUNNING**, YOU COULD FEEL THE WHOLE CROWD **STRAIGHTEN** AND **BRACE** ITSELF.

REV. PEPPER KEPT TALKING WITH MEN WHO LOOKED TO BE **BRASS**, WHILE **SIXTY** RUMORS A **MINUTE** CIRCULATED AS TO **SUTTON CHOPPER'S** WHEREABOUTS.

YOU'D HEAR SOME **BARKING** SOMEWHERE AND WONDER, ALONG WITH SEVERAL HUNDRED **OTHERS**, WHETHER IT WAS NEIGHBORHOOD **STRAYS** CHASING A **CAT** OR **POLICE DOGS** GETTING TRUCKED IN FOR **CROWD CONTROL.**

BEING **WHITE**, I'D NEVER LOOKED A CLAYFIELD **POLICE DOG** IN THE **EYE**, BUT PLENTY OF THE FOLKS **AROUND** ME CLEARLY **HAD.**

THEY BETTER NOT SIC NO **DOGS** ON ME, NEITHER.

'COONS WARE!

AND THERE, TO GRATE ON **EVERYBODY'S** NERVES, WERE CARS FULL OF COCKY WHITE **TEENAGERS** THAT KEPT CIRCLING THE BLOCK WITH **REBEL FLAGS** FLAPPING FROM THEIR **RADIO ANTENNAS.**

MABEL, DO YOUR **EYES** FOR MAVIS AN' TOLAND.

AW, **HELL**, RILEY... I CAN'T JUST DO MY EYES AT THE DROP OF A **HAT**. I'VE GOTTA BE IN THE **MOOD.**

C'MON, **YOU** CAN DO IT. I WANT 'EM TO HEAR YOUR **'CRAZY NIGGER'** STORY.

LORD! YOU BEEN TELLIN' THAT STORY **AGAIN**, SISTER?

WELL... O.K.

YOU **ASKED** FOR IT.

HERE GOES.

YIKES!

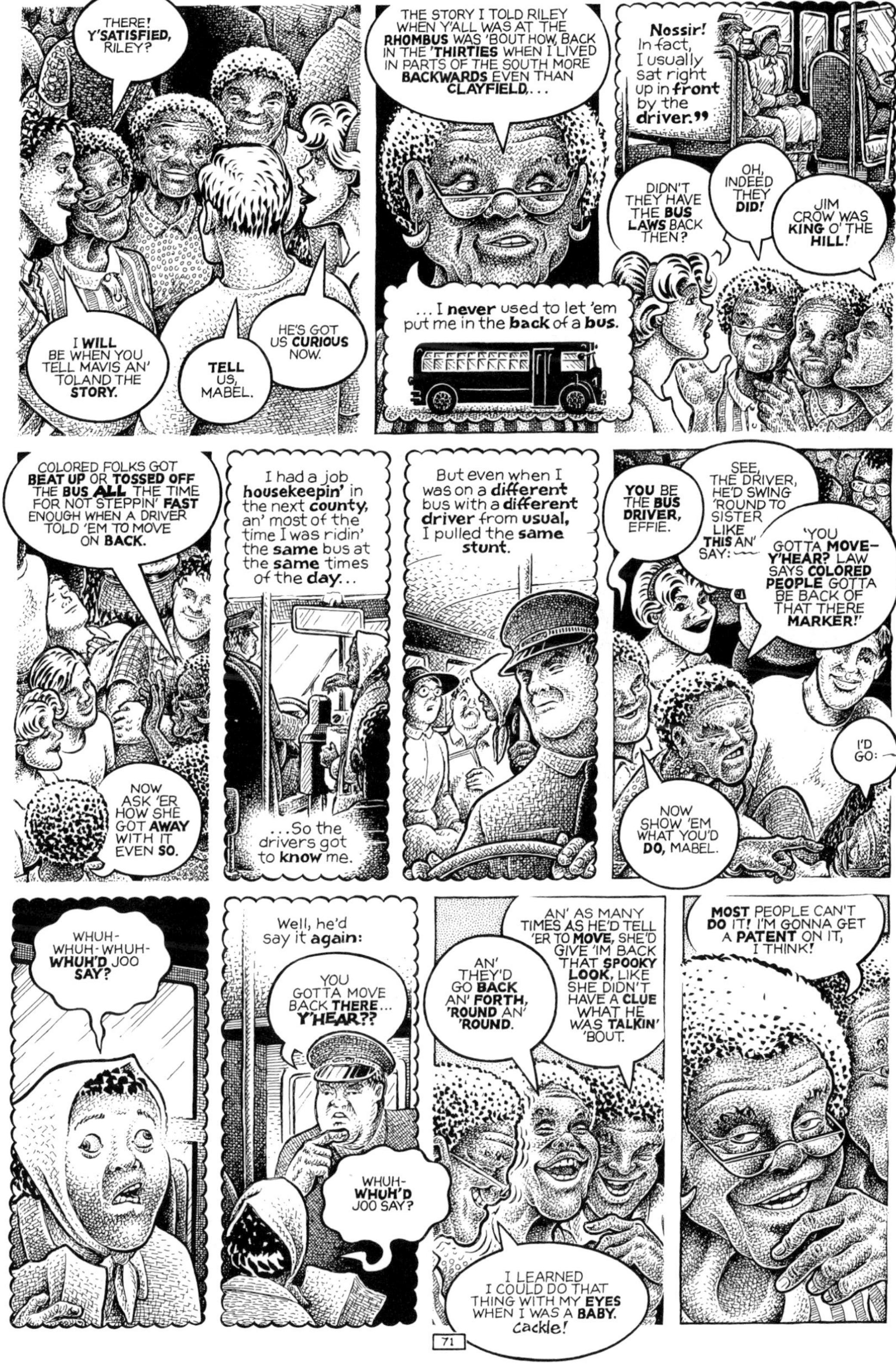
THERE! Y'SATISFIED, RILEY?
I WILL BE WHEN YOU TELL MAVIS AN' TOLAND THE STORY.
TELL US, MABEL.
HE'S GOT US CURIOUS NOW.
THE STORY I TOLD RILEY WHEN Y'ALL WAS AT THE RHOMBUS WAS 'BOUT HOW, BACK IN THE 'THIRTIES WHEN I LIVED IN PARTS OF THE SOUTH MORE BACKWARDS EVEN THAN CLAYFIELD...
...I never used to let 'em put me in the back of a bus.
Nossir! In fact, I usually sat right up in front by the driver."
DIDN'T THEY HAVE THE BUS LAWS BACK THEN?
OH, INDEED THEY DID!
JIM CROW WAS KING O' THE HILL!
COLORED FOLKS GOT BEAT UP OR TOSSED OFF THE BUS ALL THE TIME FOR NOT STEPPIN' FAST ENOUGH WHEN A DRIVER TOLD 'EM TO MOVE ON BACK.
NOW ASK 'ER HOW SHE GOT AWAY WITH IT EVEN SO.
I had a job housekeepin' in the next county, an' most of the time I was ridin' the same bus at the same times of the day...
...So the drivers got to know me.
But even when I was on a different bus with a different driver from usual, I pulled the same stunt.
YOU BE THE BUS DRIVER, EFFIE.
SEE, THE DRIVER, HE'D SWING 'ROUND TO SISTER LIKE THIS AN' SAY:
'YOU GOTTA MOVE— Y'HEAR? LAW SAYS COLORED PEOPLE GOTTA BE BACK OF THAT THERE MARKER!'
I'D GO:
NOW SHOW 'EM WHAT YOU'D DO, MABEL.
WHUH-WHUH-WHUH-WHUH'D JOO SAY?
Well, he'd say it again:
YOU GOTTA MOVE BACK THERE... Y'HEAR??
WHUH-WHUH'D JOO SAY?
AN' AS MANY TIMES AS HE'D TELL 'ER TO MOVE, SHE'D GIVE 'IM BACK THAT SPOOKY LOOK, LIKE SHE DIDN'T HAVE A CLUE WHAT HE WAS TALKIN' 'BOUT.
AN' THEY'D GO BACK AN' FORTH, 'ROUND AN' 'ROUND.
I LEARNED I COULD DO THAT THING WITH MY EYES WHEN I WAS A BABY. Cackle!
MOST PEOPLE CAN'T DO IT! I'M GONNA GET A PATENT ON IT, I THINK!

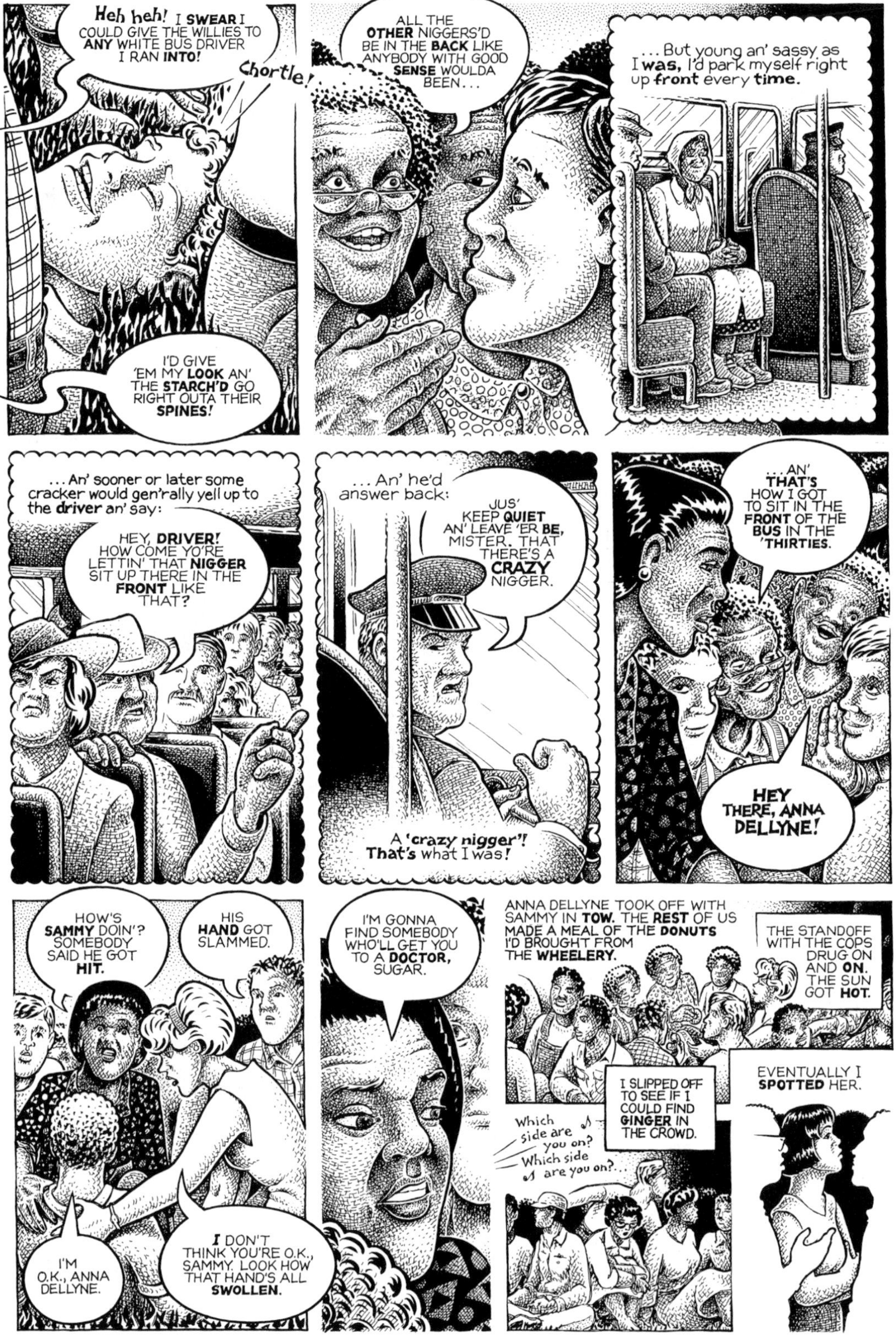
Heh heh! I SWEAR I COULD GIVE THE WILLIES TO ANY WHITE BUS DRIVER I RAN INTO!
Chortle!
I'D GIVE 'EM MY LOOK AN' THE STARCH'D GO RIGHT OUTA THEIR SPINES!
ALL THE OTHER NIGGERS'D BE IN THE BACK LIKE ANYBODY WITH GOOD SENSE WOULDA BEEN...
... But young an' sassy as I was, I'd park myself right up front every time.
... An' sooner or later some cracker would gen'rally yell up to the driver an' say:
HEY, DRIVER! HOW COME YO'RE LETTIN' THAT NIGGER SIT UP THERE IN THE FRONT LIKE THAT?
... An' he'd answer back:
JUS' KEEP QUIET AN' LEAVE 'ER BE, MISTER. THAT THERE'S A CRAZY NIGGER.
A 'crazy nigger'! That's what I was!
... AN' THAT'S HOW I GOT TO SIT IN THE FRONT OF THE BUS IN THE 'THIRTIES.
HEY THERE, ANNA DELLYNE!
HOW'S SAMMY DOIN'? SOMEBODY SAID HE GOT HIT.
HIS HAND GOT SLAMMED.
I'M O.K., ANNA DELLYNE.
I DON'T THINK YOU'RE O.K., SAMMY. LOOK HOW THAT HAND'S ALL SWOLLEN.
I'M GONNA FIND SOMEBODY WHO'LL GET YOU TO A DOCTOR, SUGAR.
ANNA DELLYNE TOOK OFF WITH SAMMY IN TOW. THE REST OF US MADE A MEAL OF THE DONUTS I'D BROUGHT FROM THE WHEELERY.
THE STANDOFF WITH THE COPS DRUG ON AND ON. THE SUN GOT HOT.
I SLIPPED OFF TO SEE IF I COULD FIND GINGER IN THE CROWD.
Which side are you on? Which side are you on?...
EVENTUALLY I SPOTTED HER.

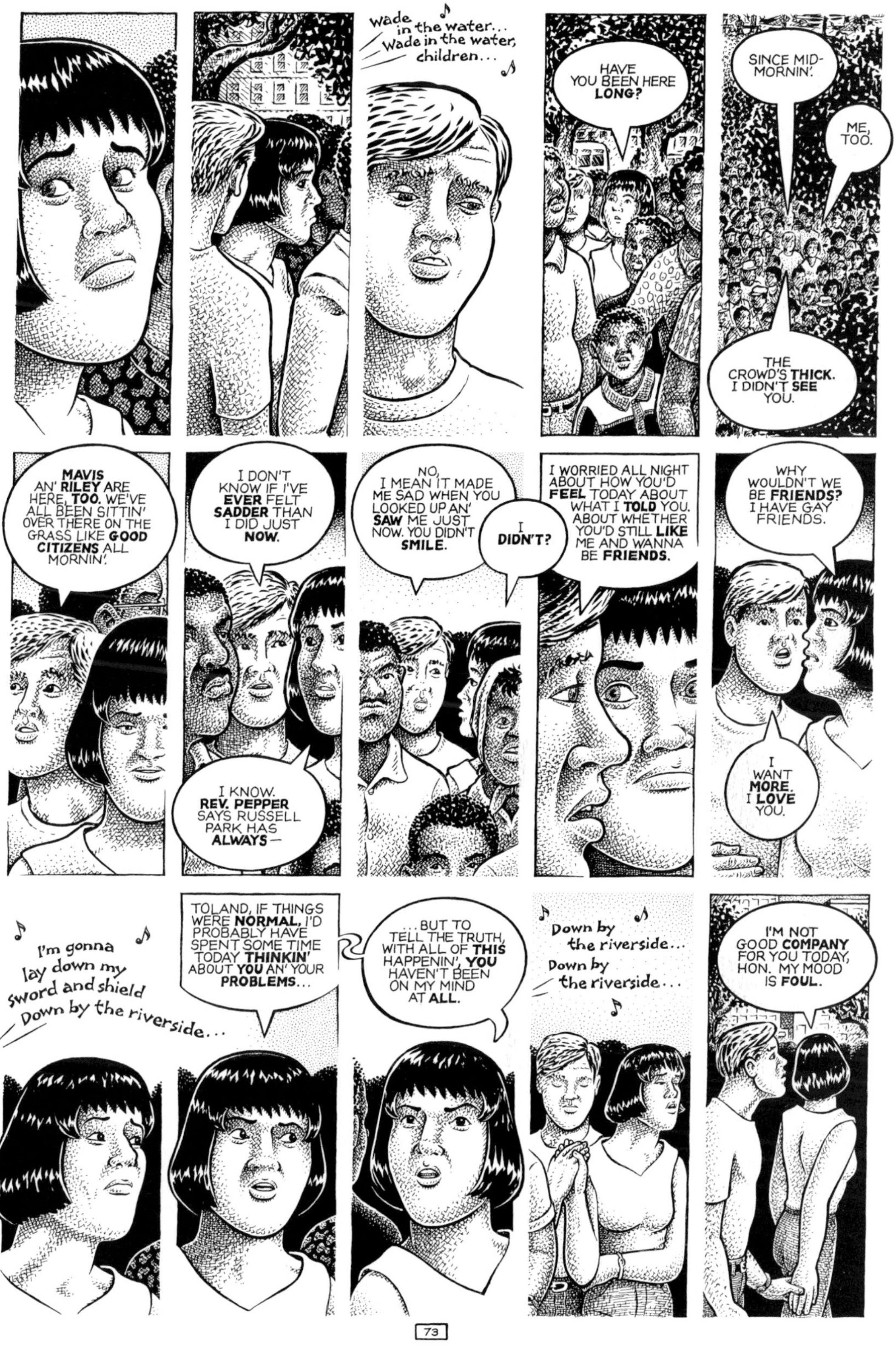

Wade in the water... Wade in the water, children...
HAVE YOU BEEN HERE LONG?
SINCE MID-MORNIN'.
ME, TOO.
THE CROWD'S THICK. I DIDN'T SEE YOU.
MAVIS AN' RILEY ARE HERE, TOO. WE'VE ALL BEEN SITTIN' OVER THERE ON THE GRASS LIKE GOOD CITIZENS ALL MORNIN'.
I DON'T KNOW IF I'VE EVER FELT SADDER THAN I DID JUST NOW.
I KNOW. REV. PEPPER SAYS RUSSELL PARK HAS ALWAYS—
NO, I MEAN IT MADE ME SAD WHEN YOU LOOKED UP AN' SAW ME JUST NOW. YOU DIDN'T SMILE.
I DIDN'T?
I WORRIED ALL NIGHT ABOUT HOW YOU'D FEEL TODAY ABOUT WHAT I TOLD YOU. ABOUT WHETHER YOU'D STILL LIKE ME AND WANNA BE FRIENDS.
WHY WOULDN'T WE BE FRIENDS? I HAVE GAY FRIENDS.
I WANT MORE. I LOVE YOU.
I'm gonna lay down my sword and shield Down by the riverside...
TOLAND, IF THINGS WERE NORMAL, I'D PROBABLY HAVE SPENT SOME TIME TODAY THINKIN' ABOUT YOU AN' YOUR PROBLEMS...
...BUT TO TELL THE TRUTH, WITH ALL OF THIS HAPPENIN', YOU HAVEN'T BEEN ON MY MIND AT ALL.
Down by the riverside... Down by the riverside...
I'M NOT GOOD COMPANY FOR YOU TODAY, HON. MY MOOD IS FOUL.

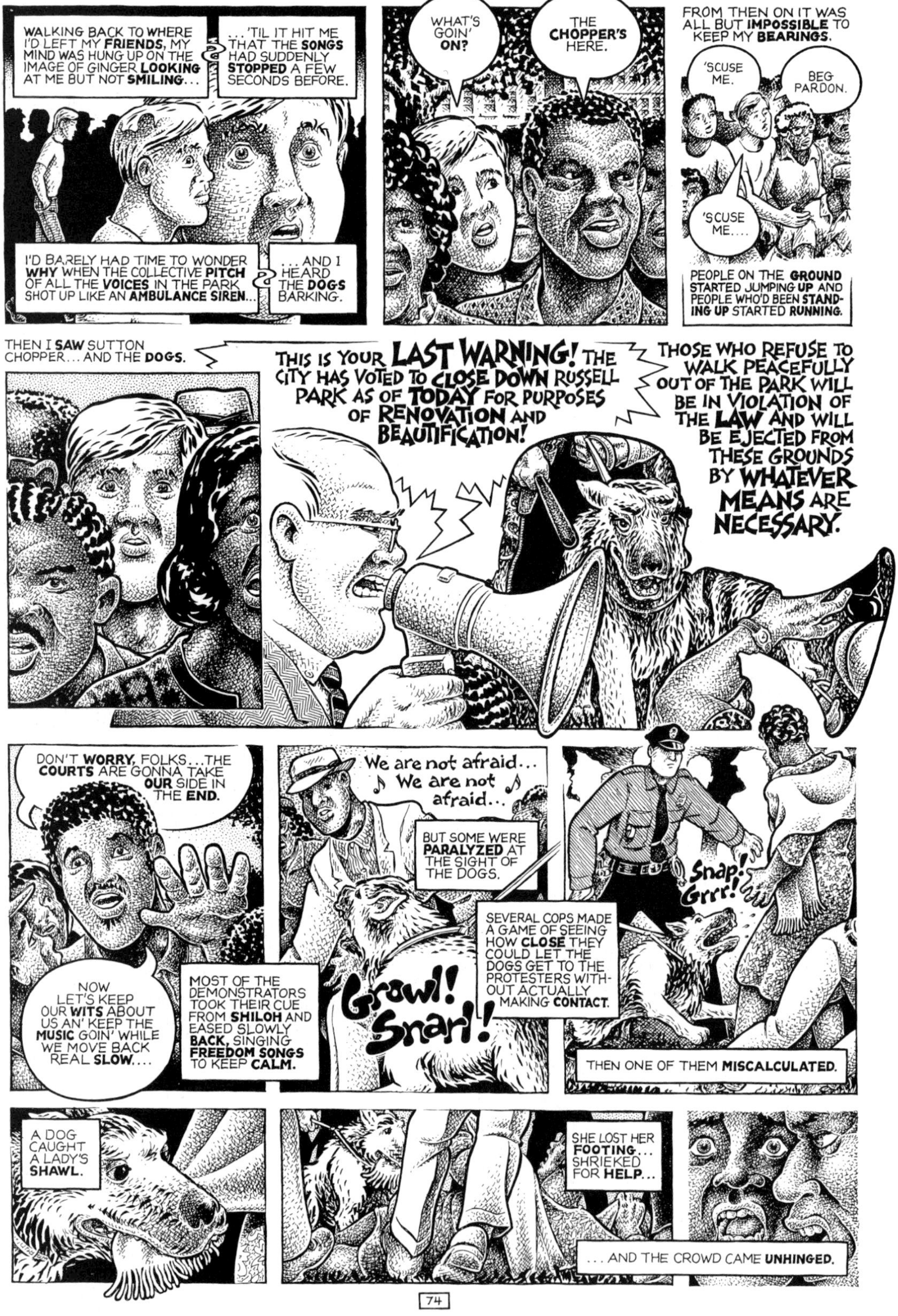

WALKING BACK TO WHERE I'D LEFT MY FRIENDS, MY MIND WAS HUNG UP ON THE IMAGE OF GINGER LOOKING AT ME BUT NOT SMILING...
...'TIL IT HIT ME THAT THE SONGS HAD SUDDENLY STOPPED A FEW SECONDS BEFORE.
I'D BARELY HAD TIME TO WONDER WHY WHEN THE COLLECTIVE PITCH OF ALL THE VOICES IN THE PARK SHOT UP LIKE AN AMBULANCE SIREN...
...AND I HEARD THE DOGS BARKING.
WHAT'S GOIN' ON?
THE CHOPPER'S HERE.
FROM THEN ON IT WAS ALL BUT IMPOSSIBLE TO KEEP MY BEARINGS.
'SCUSE ME.
BEG PARDON.
'SCUSE ME....
PEOPLE ON THE GROUND STARTED JUMPING UP AND PEOPLE WHO'D BEEN STANDING UP STARTED RUNNING.
THEN I SAW SUTTON CHOPPER... AND THE DOGS.
THIS IS YOUR LAST WARNING! THE CITY HAS VOTED TO CLOSE DOWN RUSSELL PARK AS OF TODAY FOR PURPOSES OF RENOVATION AND BEAUTIFICATION!
THOSE WHO REFUSE TO WALK PEACEFULLY OUT OF THE PARK WILL BE IN VIOLATION OF THE LAW AND WILL BE EJECTED FROM THESE GROUNDS BY WHATEVER MEANS ARE NECESSARY.
DON'T WORRY, FOLKS...THE COURTS ARE GONNA TAKE OUR SIDE IN THE END.
NOW LET'S KEEP OUR WITS ABOUT US AN' KEEP THE MUSIC GOIN' WHILE WE MOVE BACK REAL SLOW....
MOST OF THE DEMONSTRATORS TOOK THEIR CUE FROM SHILOH AND EASED SLOWLY BACK, SINGING FREEDOM SONGS TO KEEP CALM.
We are not afraid... ♪ We are not ♪ afraid...
BUT SOME WERE PARALYZED AT THE SIGHT OF THE DOGS.
Growl! Snarl!
SEVERAL COPS MADE A GAME OF SEEING HOW CLOSE THEY COULD LET THE DOGS GET TO THE PROTESTERS WITHOUT ACTUALLY MAKING CONTACT.
Snap! Grrr!
THEN ONE OF THEM MISCALCULATED.
A DOG CAUGHT A LADY'S SHAWL.
SHE LOST HER FOOTING... SHRIEKED FOR HELP...
...AND THE CROWD CAME UNHINGED.

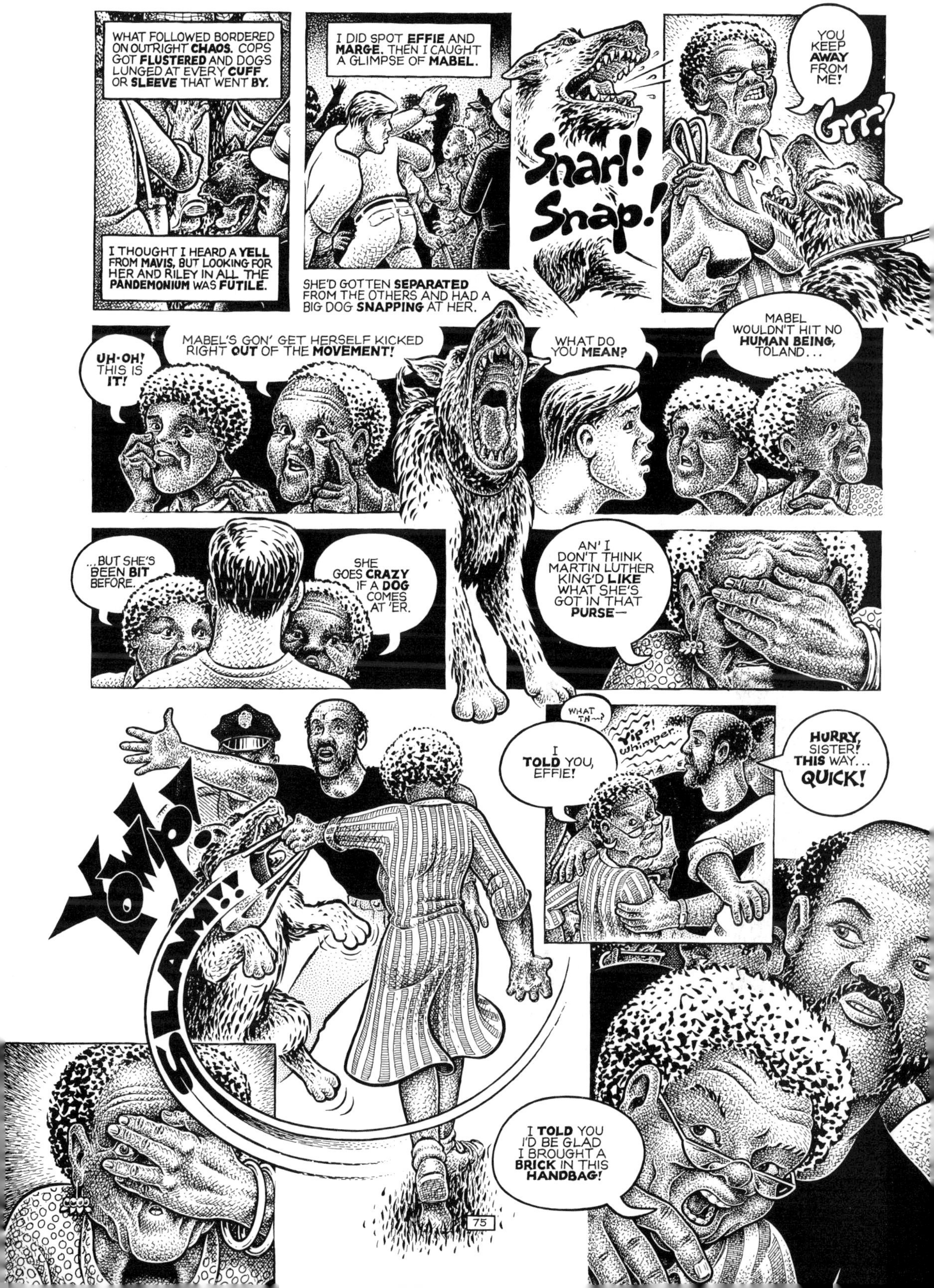

WHAT FOLLOWED BORDERED ON OUTRIGHT CHAOS. COPS GOT FLUSTERED AND DOGS LUNGED AT EVERY CUFF OR SLEEVE THAT WENT BY.
I THOUGHT I HEARD A YELL FROM MAVIS, BUT LOOKING FOR HER AND RILEY IN ALL THE PANDEMONIUM WAS FUTILE.
I DID SPOT EFFIE AND MARGE. THEN I CAUGHT A GLIMPSE OF MABEL.
SHE'D GOTTEN SEPARATED FROM THE OTHERS AND HAD A BIG DOG SNAPPING AT HER.
Snarl! Snap!
YOU KEEP AWAY FROM ME!
Grr?
UH-OH! THIS IS IT!
MABEL'S GON' GET HERSELF KICKED RIGHT OUT OF THE MOVEMENT!
WHAT DO YOU MEAN?
MABEL WOULDN'T HIT NO HUMAN BEING, TOLAND...
...BUT SHE'S BEEN BIT BEFORE.
SHE GOES CRAZY IF A DOG COMES AT 'ER.
AN' I DON'T THINK MARTIN LUTHER KING'D LIKE WHAT SHE'S GOT IN THAT PURSE—
WHOMP!!
SLAM!!
WHAT TH—?
Yip?! whimper...
I TOLD YOU, EFFIE!
HURRY, SISTER! THIS WAY... QUICK!
I TOLD YOU I'D BE GLAD I BROUGHT A BRICK IN THIS HANDBAG!

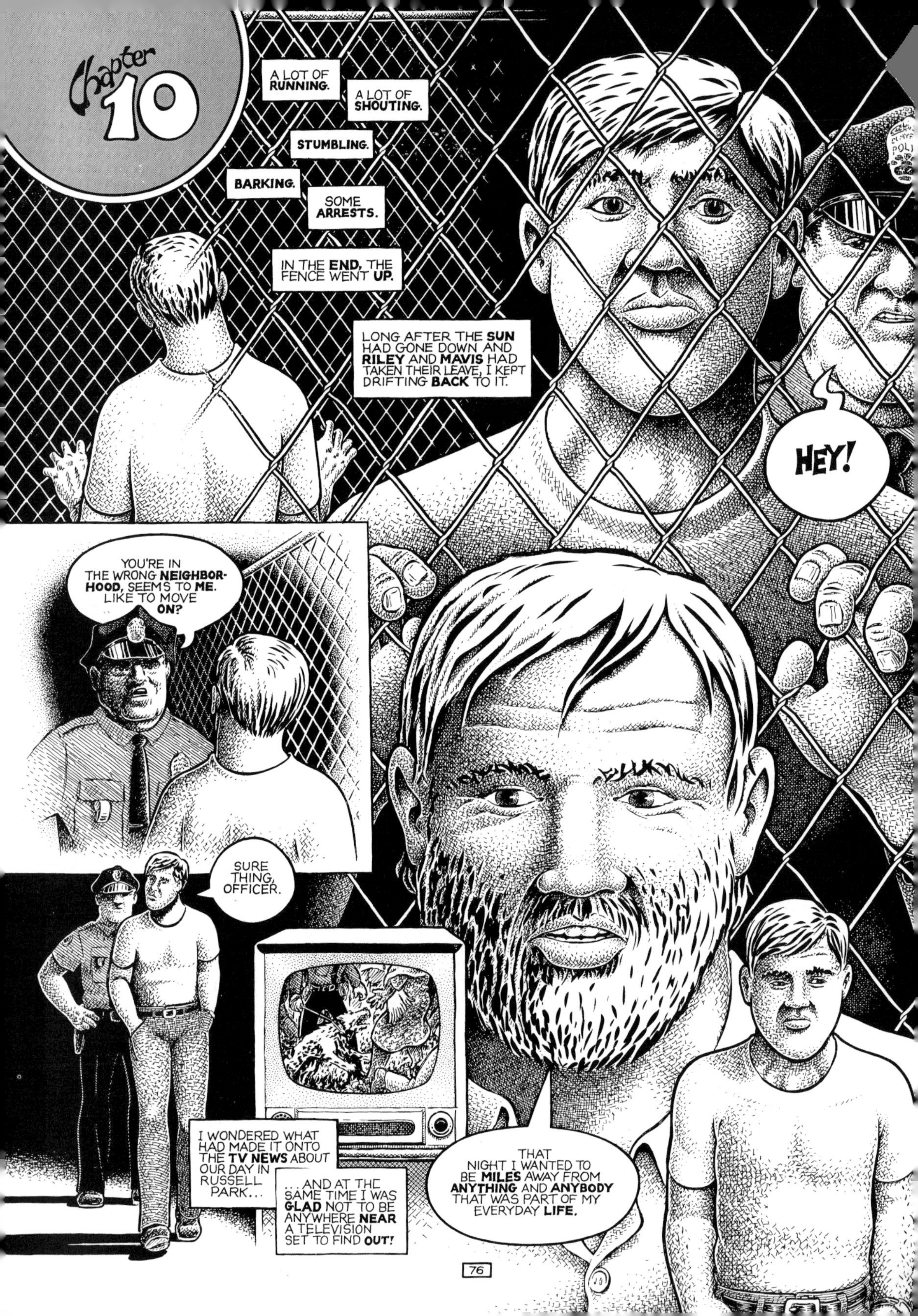
Chapter 10
A LOT OF RUNNING.
A LOT OF SHOUTING.
STUMBLING.
BARKING.
SOME ARRESTS.
IN THE END, THE FENCE WENT UP.
LONG AFTER THE SUN HAD GONE DOWN AND RILEY AND MAVIS HAD TAKEN THEIR LEAVE, I KEPT DRIFTING BACK TO IT.
HEY!
YOU'RE IN THE WRONG NEIGHBOR-HOOD, SEEMS TO ME. LIKE TO MOVE ON?
SURE THING, OFFICER.
I WONDERED WHAT HAD MADE IT ONTO THE TV NEWS ABOUT OUR DAY IN RUSSELL PARK...
...AND AT THE SAME TIME I WAS GLAD NOT TO BE ANYWHERE NEAR A TELEVISION SET TO FIND OUT!
THAT NIGHT I WANTED TO BE MILES AWAY FROM ANYTHING AND ANYBODY THAT WAS PART OF MY EVERYDAY LIFE.

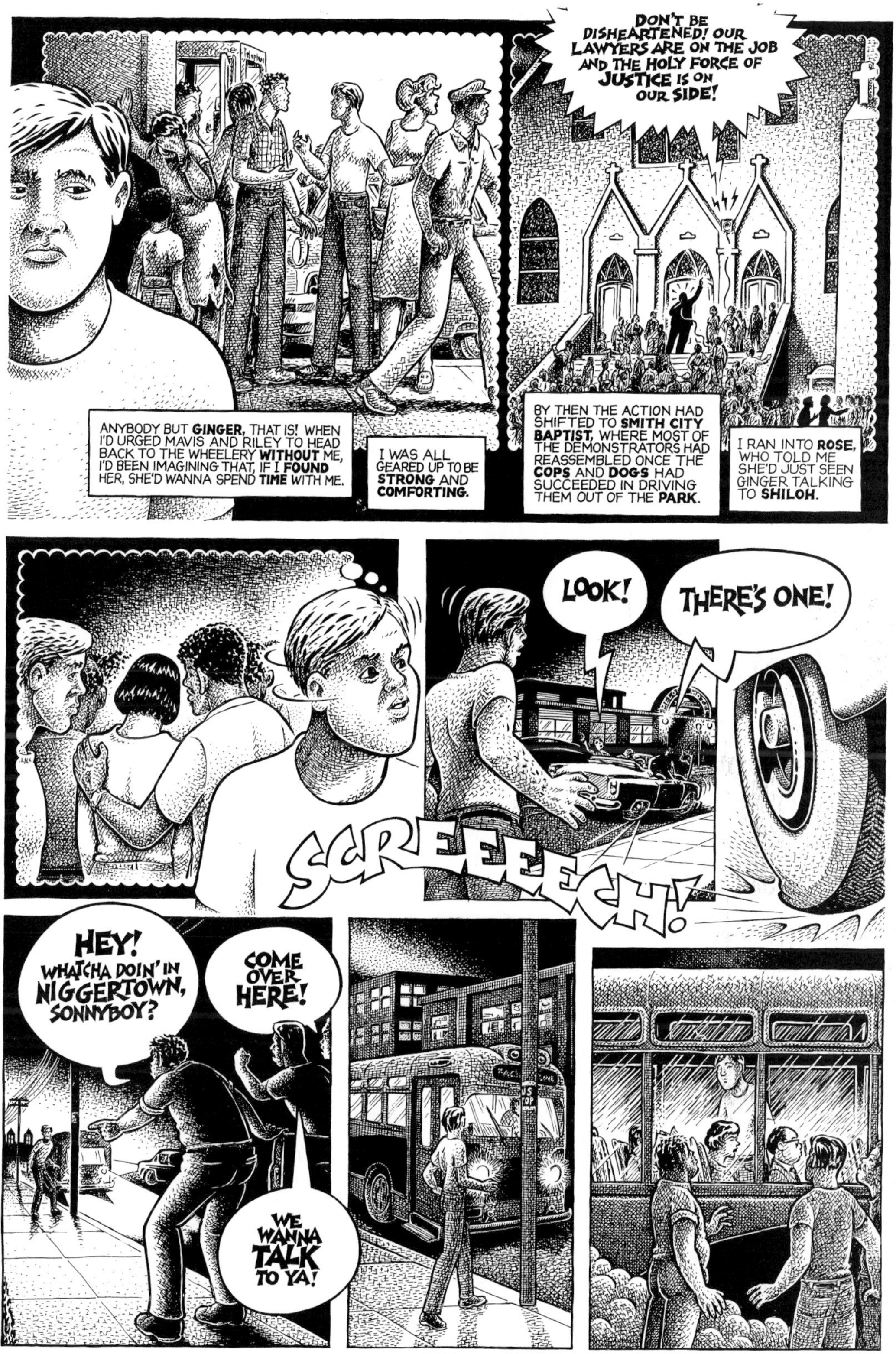
ANYBODY BUT GINGER, THAT IS! WHEN I'D URGED MAVIS AND RILEY TO HEAD BACK TO THE WHEELERY WITHOUT ME, I'D BEEN IMAGINING THAT, IF I FOUND HER, SHE'D WANNA SPEND TIME WITH ME.
I WAS ALL GEARED UP TO BE STRONG AND COMFORTING.
DON'T BE DISHEARTENED! OUR LAWYERS ARE ON THE JOB AND THE HOLY FORCE OF JUSTICE IS ON OUR SIDE!
BY THEN THE ACTION HAD SHIFTED TO SMITH CITY BAPTIST, WHERE MOST OF THE DEMONSTRATORS HAD REASSEMBLED ONCE THE COPS AND DOGS HAD SUCCEEDED IN DRIVING THEM OUT OF THE PARK.
I RAN INTO ROSE, WHO TOLD ME SHE'D JUST SEEN GINGER TALKING TO SHILOH.
LOOK!
THERE'S ONE!
SCREEEECH!
HEY! WHATCHA DOIN' IN NIGGERTOWN, SONNYBOY?
COME OVER HERE!
WE WANNA TALK TO YA!

WHEN I GOT ON THE BUS, MY **INTENTION** WAS TO TRANSFER AT EIGHTEENTH STREET TO THE **COLLEGE LINE,** WHICH WOULD HAVE TAKEN ME DIRECTLY OUT TO THE **WHEELERY.**

BUT I NEVER **TRANSFERRED.**

INSTEAD I RODE ON TO **NINTH STREET.**

YOU HAVEN'T EATEN A **BURGER** UNTIL YOU'VE EATEN A **DONBURGER**

DON'S DINER

DON'S BLACKBERRY COBBLER FAMOUS THROUGHOUT THE SOUTH

COME AGAIN! YOU'RE ALWAYS WELCOME AT **DON'S DINER**

WE RESERVE THE RIGHT TO REFUSE SERVICE TO ANYONE AT THE DISCRETION OF THE MANAGER

DID YOU KNOW ABOUT THESE **DIXIE PATRIOTS** BEIN' STACKED THERE BY THE DOOR?

OH, **THOSE** THINGS! AREN'T THEY **AWFUL?**

SOME MAN **INSISTS** ON COMIN' AN' PUTTIN' **PILES** OF THOSE PAPERS OUT FRONT. MY **BOSS** LETS HIM DO IT. NOBODY ASKS **ME!**

THE PEOPLE THAT PUT THAT OUT **SAY** THEY'RE **CHRISTIANS,** BUT I DON'T THINK THEY **ACT** VERY CHRISTIAN... DO **YOU?**

THEY **SAY** THINGS ABOUT PEOPLE THAT DON'T SEEM CHRISTIAN TO **ME** AT ALL!

OF COURSE, I **DO** THINK THEY HAVE A **POINT** WHEN THEY SAY IT'S PROBABLY THE **COMMUNISTS** WHO'RE CONVINCIN' THE NEGROES THAT THEY'RE SO **DISSATISFIED.**

BUT IT'S THE UGLY **WAY** THEY SAY IT!

UHN-UH!!

IT'S **WAY** TOO UNCHRISTIAN FOR **ME!**

AFTER MY **MEAL...**

I STOOD, THEN STOOD SOME **MORE.** THEN FINALLY I WENT **IN.**

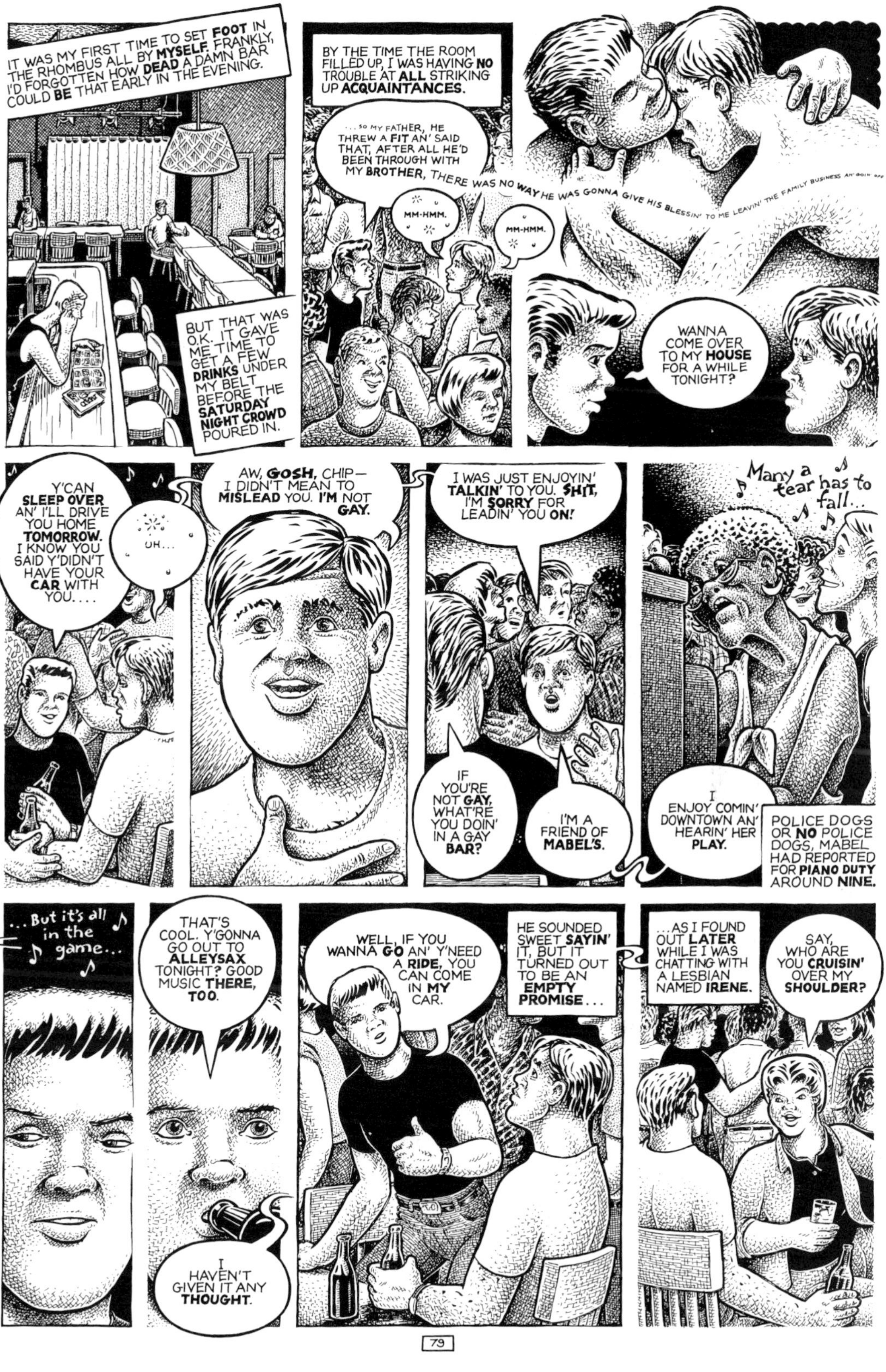
IT WAS MY FIRST TIME TO SET FOOT IN THE RHOMBUS ALL BY MYSELF. FRANKLY, I'D FORGOTTEN HOW DEAD A DAMN BAR COULD BE THAT EARLY IN THE EVENING.
BUT THAT WAS O.K. IT GAVE ME TIME TO GET A FEW DRINKS UNDER MY BELT BEFORE THE SATURDAY NIGHT CROWD POURED IN.
BY THE TIME THE ROOM FILLED UP, I WAS HAVING NO TROUBLE AT ALL STRIKING UP ACQUAINTANCES.
. . . SO MY FATHER, HE THREW A FIT AN' SAID THAT, AFTER ALL HE'D BEEN THROUGH WITH MY BROTHER, THERE WAS NO WAY HE WAS GONNA GIVE HIS BLESSIN' TO ME LEAVIN' THE FAMILY BUSINESS AN' GOIN' OFF
MM-HMM.
MM-HMM.
WANNA COME OVER TO MY HOUSE FOR A WHILE TONIGHT?
Y'CAN SLEEP OVER AN' I'LL DRIVE YOU HOME TOMORROW. I KNOW YOU SAID Y'DIDN'T HAVE YOUR CAR WITH YOU. . . .
UH . . .
AW, GOSH, CHIP— I DIDN'T MEAN TO MISLEAD YOU. I'M NOT GAY.
I WAS JUST ENJOYIN' TALKIN' TO YOU. SHIT, I'M SORRY FOR LEADIN' YOU ON!
IF YOU'RE NOT GAY, WHAT'RE YOU DOIN' IN A GAY BAR?
I'M A FRIEND OF MABEL'S.
Many a tear has to fall . . .
I ENJOY COMIN' DOWNTOWN AN' HEARIN' HER PLAY.
POLICE DOGS OR NO POLICE DOGS, MABEL HAD REPORTED FOR PIANO DUTY AROUND NINE.
. . . But it's all in the game . . .
THAT'S COOL. Y'GONNA GO OUT TO ALLEYSAX TONIGHT? GOOD MUSIC THERE, TOO.
I HAVEN'T GIVEN IT ANY THOUGHT.
WELL, IF YOU WANNA GO AN' Y'NEED A RIDE, YOU CAN COME IN MY CAR.
HE SOUNDED SWEET SAYIN' IT, BUT IT TURNED OUT TO BE AN EMPTY PROMISE . . .
. . . AS I FOUND OUT LATER WHILE I WAS CHATTING WITH A LESBIAN NAMED IRENE.
SAY, WHO ARE YOU CRUISIN' OVER MY SHOULDER?

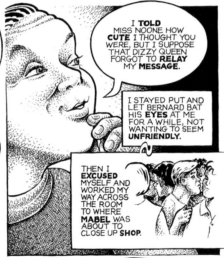

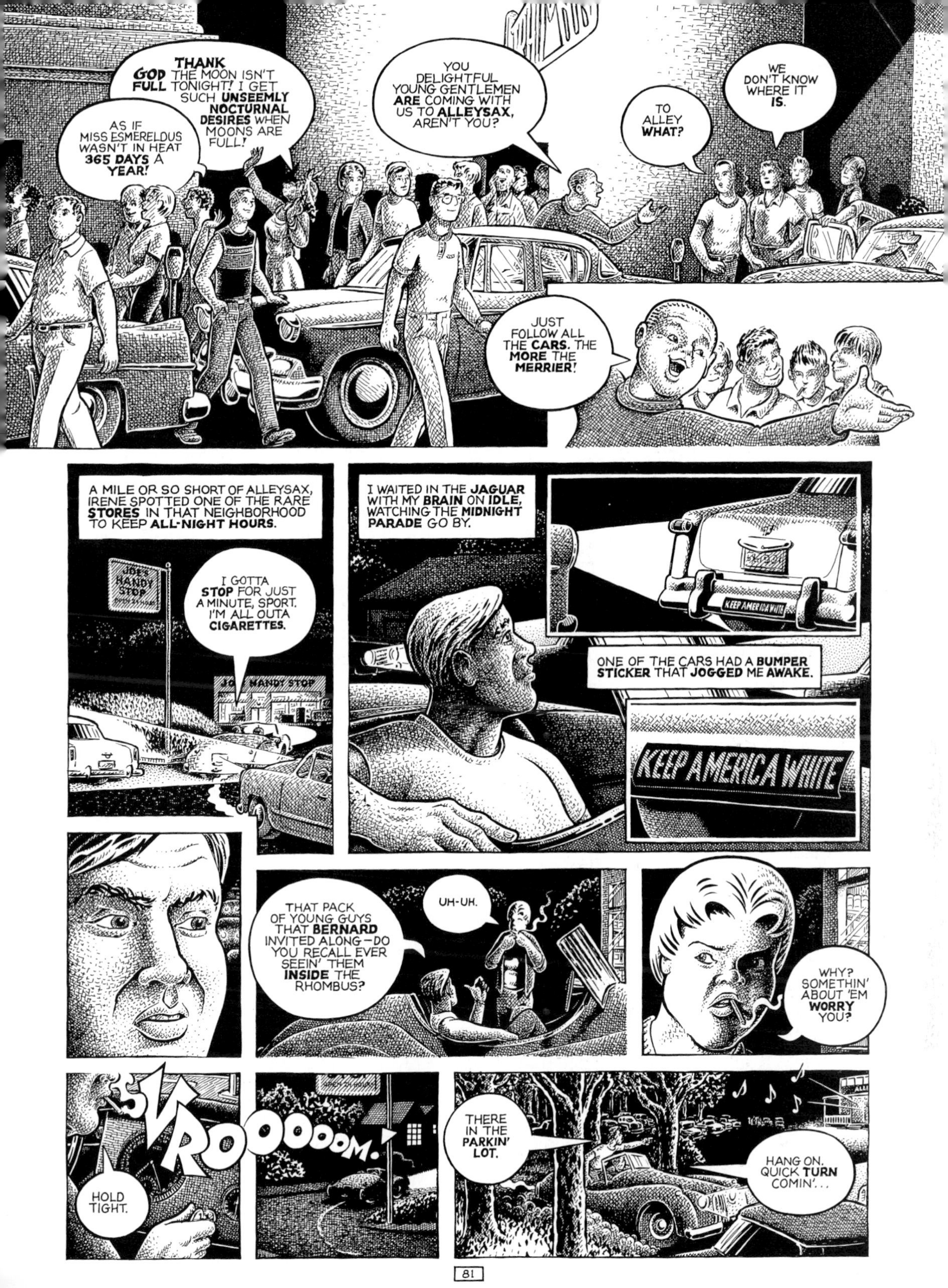
THANK GOD THE MOON ISN'T FULL TONIGHT! I GET SUCH UNSEEMLY NOCTURNAL DESIRES WHEN MOONS ARE FULL!
AS IF MISS ESMERELDUS WASN'T IN HEAT 365 DAYS A YEAR!
YOU DELIGHTFUL YOUNG GENTLEMEN ARE COMING WITH US TO ALLEYSAX, AREN'T YOU?
TO ALLEY WHAT?
WE DON'T KNOW WHERE IT IS.
JUST FOLLOW ALL THE CARS. THE MORE THE MERRIER!
A MILE OR SO SHORT OF ALLEYSAX, IRENE SPOTTED ONE OF THE RARE STORES IN THAT NEIGHBORHOOD TO KEEP ALL-NIGHT HOURS.
JOE'S HANDY STOP
I GOTTA STOP FOR JUST A MINUTE, SPORT. I'M ALL OUTA CIGARETTES.
I WAITED IN THE JAGUAR WITH MY BRAIN ON IDLE, WATCHING THE MIDNIGHT PARADE GO BY.
KEEP AMERICA WHITE
ONE OF THE CARS HAD A BUMPER STICKER THAT JOGGED ME AWAKE.
KEEP AMERICA WHITE
THAT PACK OF YOUNG GUYS THAT BERNARD INVITED ALONG—DO YOU RECALL EVER SEEIN' THEM INSIDE THE RHOMBUS?
UH-UH.
WHY? SOMETHIN' ABOUT 'EM WORRY YOU?
SVROOOOOOM!
HOLD TIGHT.
THERE IN THE PARKIN' LOT.
HANG ON. QUICK TURN COMIN'...

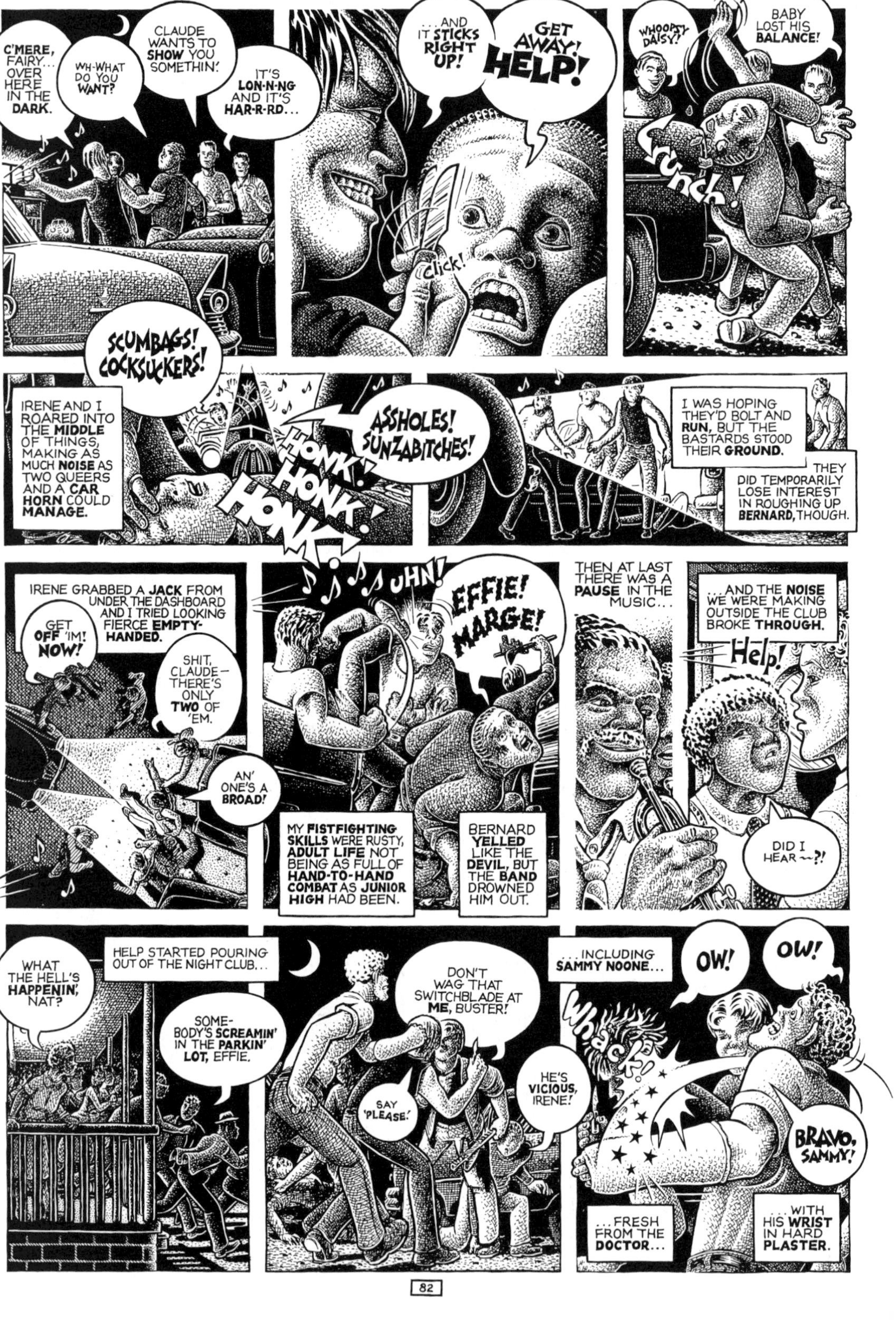
C'MERE, FAIRY... OVER HERE IN THE DARK.
WH-WHAT DO YOU WANT?
CLAUDE WANTS TO SHOW YOU SOMETHIN'.
IT'S LON-N-NG AND IT'S HAR-R-RD...
...AND IT STICKS RIGHT UP!
GET AWAY! HELP!
CLICK!
WHOOPSY DAISY!
BABY LOST HIS BALANCE!
SCUMBAGS! COCKSUCKERS!
IRENE AND I ROARED INTO THE MIDDLE OF THINGS, MAKING AS MUCH NOISE AS TWO QUEERS AND A CAR HORN COULD MANAGE.
ASSHOLES! SUNZABITCHES!
HONK! HONK! HONK! HONK!
I WAS HOPING THEY'D BOLT AND RUN, BUT THE BASTARDS STOOD THEIR GROUND.
THEY DID TEMPORARILY LOSE INTEREST IN ROUGHING UP BERNARD, THOUGH.
IRENE GRABBED A JACK FROM UNDER THE DASHBOARD AND I TRIED LOOKING FIERCE EMPTY-HANDED.
GET OFF 'IM! NOW!
SHIT, CLAUDE— THERE'S ONLY TWO OF 'EM.
AN' ONE'S A BROAD!
UHN!
EFFIE! MARGE!
MY FISTFIGHTING SKILLS WERE RUSTY, ADULT LIFE NOT BEING AS FULL OF HAND-TO-HAND COMBAT AS JUNIOR HIGH HAD BEEN.
BERNARD YELLED LIKE THE DEVIL, BUT THE BAND DROWNED HIM OUT.
THEN AT LAST THERE WAS A PAUSE IN THE MUSIC...
...AND THE NOISE WE WERE MAKING OUTSIDE THE CLUB BROKE THROUGH.
Help!
DID I HEAR ~~?!
WHAT THE HELL'S HAPPENIN', NAT?
HELP STARTED POURING OUT OF THE NIGHT CLUB...
SOME-BODY'S SCREAMIN' IN THE PARKIN' LOT, EFFIE.
DON'T WAG THAT SWITCHBLADE AT ME, BUSTER!
SAY 'PLEASE.'
HE'S VICIOUS, IRENE!
...INCLUDING SAMMY NOONE...
OW!
OW!
Whack!
...FRESH FROM THE DOCTOR...
...WITH HIS WRIST IN HARD PLASTER.
BRAVO, SAMMY!

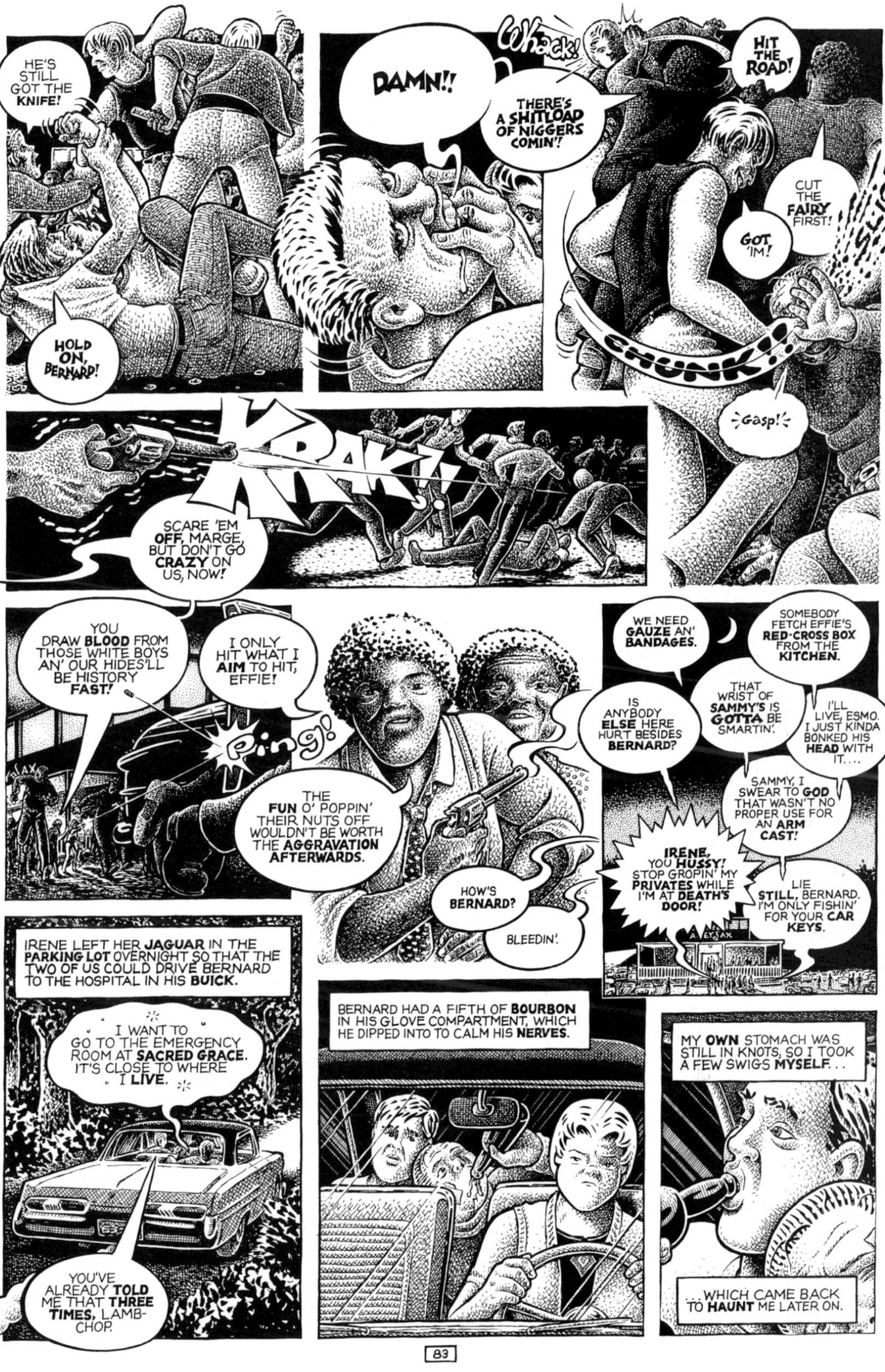
HE'S STILL GOT THE KNIFE!
HOLD ON, BERNARD!
DAMN!!
WHACK!
THERE'S A SHITLOAD OF NIGGERS COMIN'!
HIT THE ROAD!
CUT THE FAIRY FIRST!
GOT 'IM!
SLICE!!
CHUNK!!
Gasp!
KRAK!!
SCARE 'EM OFF, MARGE, BUT DON'T GO CRAZY ON US, NOW!
YOU DRAW BLOOD FROM THOSE WHITE BOYS AN' OUR HIDES'LL BE HISTORY FAST!
I ONLY HIT WHAT I AIM TO HIT, EFFIE!
PING!
THE FUN O' POPPIN' THEIR NUTS OFF WOULDN'T BE WORTH THE AGGRAVATION AFTERWARDS.
HOW'S BERNARD?
BLEEDIN'.
WE NEED GAUZE AN' BANDAGES.
SOMEBODY FETCH EFFIE'S RED-CROSS BOX FROM THE KITCHEN.
IS ANYBODY ELSE HERE HURT BESIDES BERNARD?
THAT WRIST OF SAMMY'S IS GOTTA BE SMARTIN'.
I'LL LIVE, ESMO. I JUST KINDA BONKED HIS HEAD WITH IT....
SAMMY, I SWEAR TO GOD THAT WASN'T NO PROPER USE FOR AN ARM CAST!
IRENE, YOU HUSSY! STOP GROPIN' MY PRIVATES WHILE I'M AT DEATH'S DOOR!
LIE STILL, BERNARD. I'M ONLY FISHIN' FOR YOUR CAR KEYS.
IRENE LEFT HER JAGUAR IN THE PARKING LOT OVERNIGHT SO THAT THE TWO OF US COULD DRIVE BERNARD TO THE HOSPITAL IN HIS BUICK.
I WANT TO GO TO THE EMERGENCY ROOM AT SACRED GRACE. IT'S CLOSE TO WHERE I LIVE.
YOU'VE ALREADY TOLD ME THAT THREE TIMES, LAMB-CHOP.
BERNARD HAD A FIFTH OF BOURBON IN HIS GLOVE COMPARTMENT, WHICH HE DIPPED INTO TO CALM HIS NERVES.
MY OWN STOMACH WAS STILL IN KNOTS, SO I TOOK A FEW SWIGS MYSELF...
...WHICH CAME BACK TO HAUNT ME LATER ON.

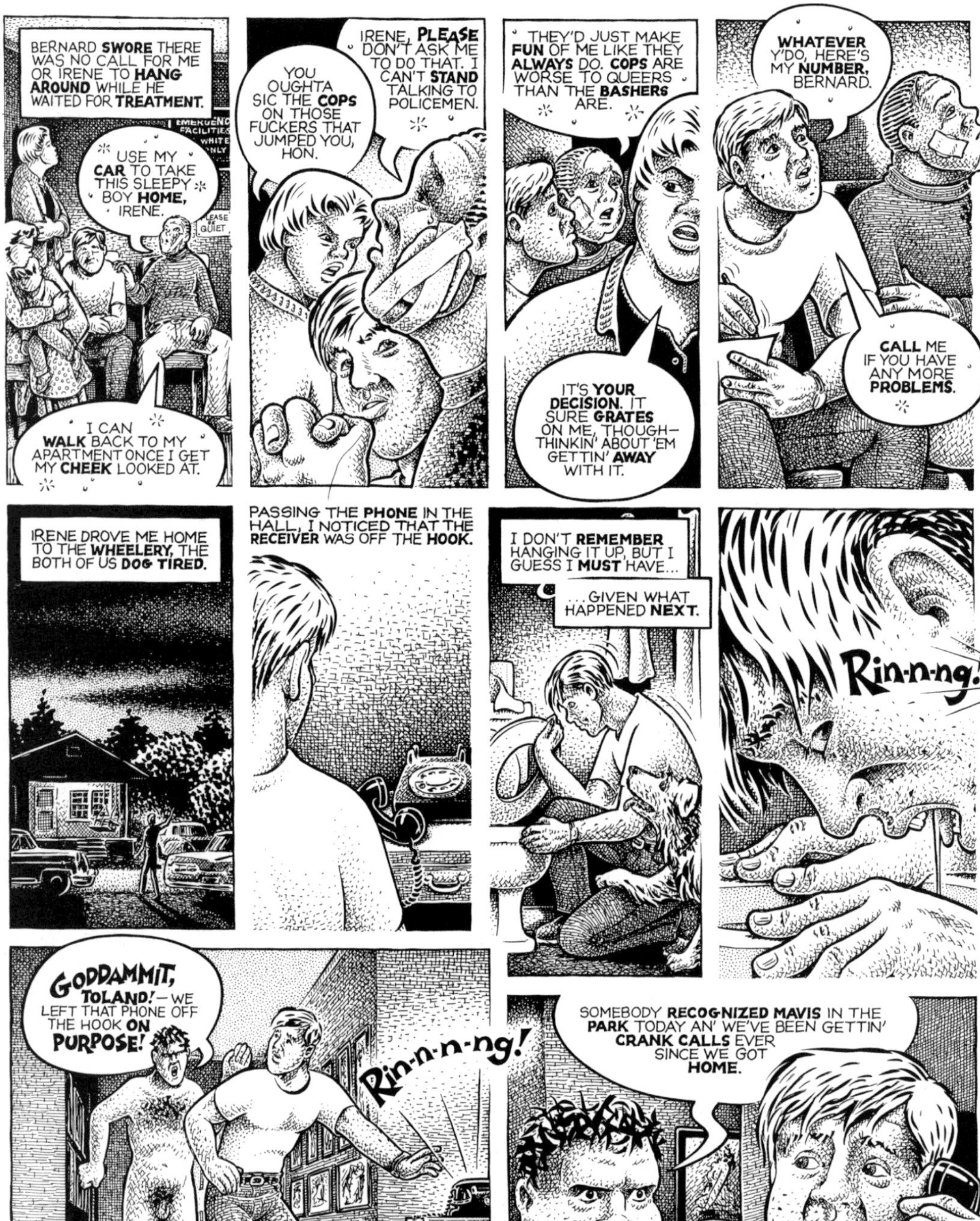

BERNARD **SWORE** THERE WAS NO CALL FOR ME OR IRENE TO **HANG AROUND** WHILE HE WAITED FOR **TREATMENT.**
USE MY **CAR** TO TAKE THIS SLEEPY BOY **HOME,** IRENE.
I CAN **WALK** BACK TO MY APARTMENT ONCE I GET MY **CHEEK** LOOKED AT.
YOU OUGHTA SIC THE **COPS** ON THOSE FUCKERS THAT JUMPED YOU, HON.
IRENE, **PLEASE** DON'T ASK ME TO DO THAT. I CAN'T **STAND** TALKING TO POLICEMEN.
THEY'D JUST MAKE **FUN** OF ME LIKE THEY **ALWAYS** DO. **COPS** ARE WORSE TO QUEERS THAN THE **BASHERS** ARE.
IT'S **YOUR DECISION.** IT SURE **GRATES** ON ME, THOUGH— THINKIN' ABOUT 'EM GETTIN' **AWAY** WITH IT.
WHATEVER Y'DO, HERE'S MY **NUMBER,** BERNARD.
CALL ME IF YOU HAVE ANY MORE **PROBLEMS.**
IRENE DROVE ME HOME TO THE **WHEELERY,** THE BOTH OF US **DOG TIRED.**
PASSING THE **PHONE** IN THE HALL, I NOTICED THAT THE **RECEIVER** WAS OFF THE **HOOK.**
I DON'T **REMEMBER** HANGING IT UP, BUT I GUESS I **MUST** HAVE...
...GIVEN WHAT HAPPENED **NEXT.**
Rin-n-ng!
GODDAMMIT, TOLAND!—WE LEFT THAT PHONE OFF THE HOOK **ON PURPOSE!**
Rin-n-n-ng!
SOMEBODY **RECOGNIZED MAVIS** IN THE **PARK** TODAY AN' WE'VE BEEN GETTIN' **CRANK CALLS** EVER SINCE WE GOT **HOME.**
HELLO..?
WITH **RILEY** YELLING IN **ONE** OF MY EARS, I HAD **BERNARD** HALF-HYSTERICAL IN THE **OTHER.**
TOLAND, YOU'VE GOT TO COME HELP ME!

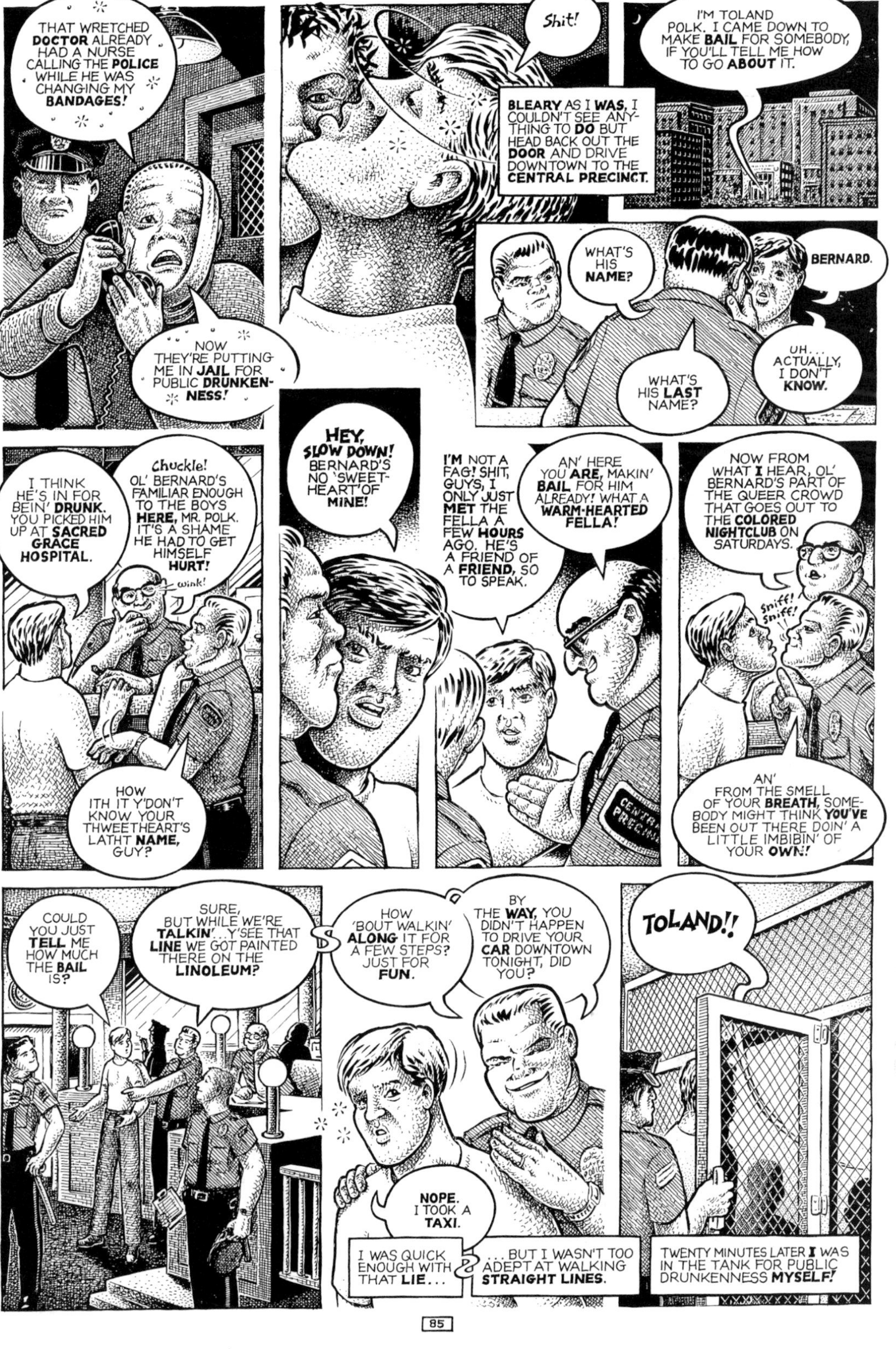
THAT WRETCHED DOCTOR ALREADY HAD A NURSE CALLING THE POLICE WHILE HE WAS CHANGING MY BANDAGES!
NOW THEY'RE PUTTING ME IN JAIL FOR PUBLIC DRUNKENNESS!
Shit!
BLEARY AS I WAS, I COULDN'T SEE ANYTHING TO DO BUT HEAD BACK OUT THE DOOR AND DRIVE DOWNTOWN TO THE CENTRAL PRECINCT.
I'M TOLAND POLK. I CAME DOWN TO MAKE BAIL FOR SOMEBODY, IF YOU'LL TELL ME HOW TO GO ABOUT IT.
WHAT'S HIS NAME?
BERNARD.
WHAT'S HIS LAST NAME?
UH... ACTUALLY, I DON'T KNOW.
I THINK HE'S IN FOR BEIN' DRUNK. YOU PICKED HIM UP AT SACRED GRACE HOSPITAL.
Chuckle! OL' BERNARD'S FAMILIAR ENOUGH TO THE BOYS HERE, MR. POLK. IT'S A SHAME HE HAD TO GET HIMSELF HURT!
wink!
HOW ITH IT Y'DON'T KNOW YOUR THWEETHEART'S LATHT NAME, GUY?
HEY, SLOW DOWN! BERNARD'S NO 'SWEETHEART' OF MINE!
I'M NOT A FAG! SHIT, GUYS, I ONLY JUST MET THE FELLA A FEW HOURS AGO. HE'S A FRIEND OF A FRIEND, SO TO SPEAK.
AN' HERE YOU ARE, MAKIN' BAIL FOR HIM ALREADY! WHAT A WARM-HEARTED FELLA!
CENTRAL PRECINCT
NOW FROM WHAT I HEAR, OL' BERNARD'S PART OF THE QUEER CROWD THAT GOES OUT TO THE COLORED NIGHTCLUB ON SATURDAYS.
Sniff! Sniff!
AN' FROM THE SMELL OF YOUR BREATH, SOMEBODY MIGHT THINK YOU'VE BEEN OUT THERE DOIN' A LITTLE IMBIBIN' OF YOUR OWN!
COULD YOU JUST TELL ME HOW MUCH THE BAIL IS?
SURE, BUT WHILE WE'RE TALKIN'... Y'SEE THAT LINE WE GOT PAINTED THERE ON THE LINOLEUM?
HOW 'BOUT WALKIN' ALONG IT FOR A FEW STEPS? JUST FOR FUN.
BY THE WAY, YOU DIDN'T HAPPEN TO DRIVE YOUR CAR DOWNTOWN TONIGHT, DID YOU?
NOPE. I TOOK A TAXI.
I WAS QUICK ENOUGH WITH THAT LIE...
...BUT I WASN'T TOO ADEPT AT WALKING STRAIGHT LINES.
TOLAND!!
TWENTY MINUTES LATER I WAS IN THE TANK FOR PUBLIC DRUNKENNESS MYSELF!

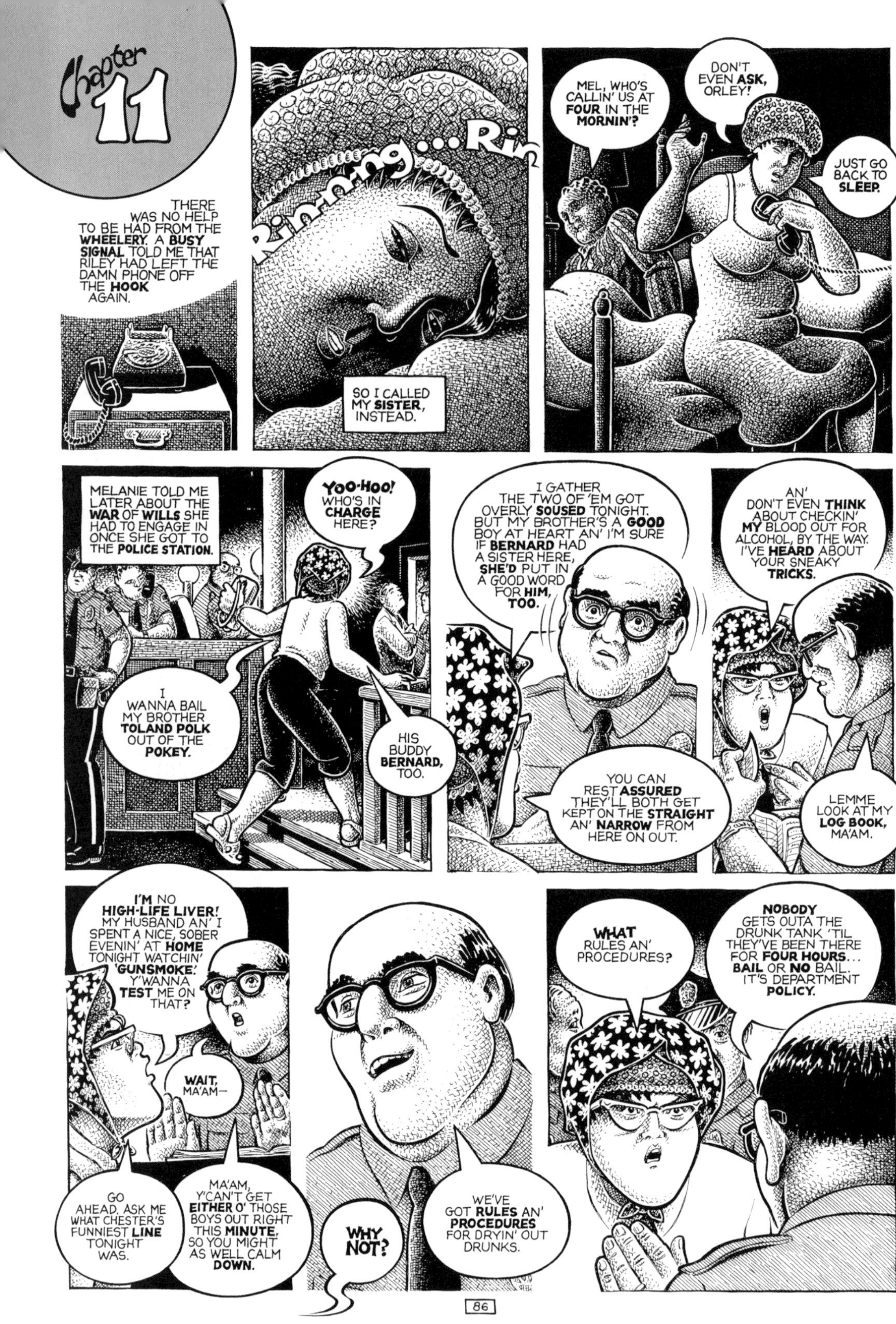
Chapter 11
THERE WAS NO HELP TO BE HAD FROM THE WHEELERY. A BUSY SIGNAL TOLD ME THAT RILEY HAD LEFT THE DAMN PHONE OFF THE HOOK AGAIN.
Rinnng...Rin
SO I CALLED MY SISTER, INSTEAD.
MEL, WHO'S CALLIN' US AT FOUR IN THE MORNIN'?
DON'T EVEN ASK, ORLEY!
JUST GO BACK TO SLEEP.
MELANIE TOLD ME LATER ABOUT THE WAR OF WILLS SHE HAD TO ENGAGE IN ONCE SHE GOT TO THE POLICE STATION.
YOO-HOO! WHO'S IN CHARGE HERE?
I WANNA BAIL MY BROTHER TOLAND POLK OUT OF THE POKEY.
HIS BUDDY BERNARD, TOO.
I GATHER THE TWO OF 'EM GOT OVERLY SOUSED TONIGHT. BUT MY BROTHER'S A GOOD BOY AT HEART AN' I'M SURE IF BERNARD HAD A SISTER HERE, SHE'D PUT IN A GOOD WORD FOR HIM, TOO.
YOU CAN REST ASSURED THEY'LL BOTH GET KEPT ON THE STRAIGHT AN' NARROW FROM HERE ON OUT.
AN' DON'T EVEN THINK ABOUT CHECKIN' MY BLOOD OUT FOR ALCOHOL, BY THE WAY. I'VE HEARD ABOUT YOUR SNEAKY TRICKS.
LEMME LOOK AT MY LOG BOOK, MA'AM.
I'M NO HIGH-LIFE LIVER! MY HUSBAND AN' I SPENT A NICE, SOBER EVENIN' AT HOME TONIGHT WATCHIN' 'GUNSMOKE.' Y'WANNA TEST ME ON THAT?
WAIT, MA'AM—
GO AHEAD. ASK ME WHAT CHESTER'S FUNNIEST LINE TONIGHT WAS.
MA'AM, Y'CAN'T GET EITHER O' THOSE BOYS OUT RIGHT THIS MINUTE, SO YOU MIGHT AS WELL CALM DOWN.
WHY NOT?
WE'VE GOT RULES AN' PROCEDURES FOR DRYIN' OUT DRUNKS.
WHAT RULES AN' PROCEDURES?
NOBODY GETS OUTA THE DRUNK TANK 'TIL THEY'VE BEEN THERE FOR FOUR HOURS... BAIL OR NO BAIL. IT'S DEPARTMENT POLICY.

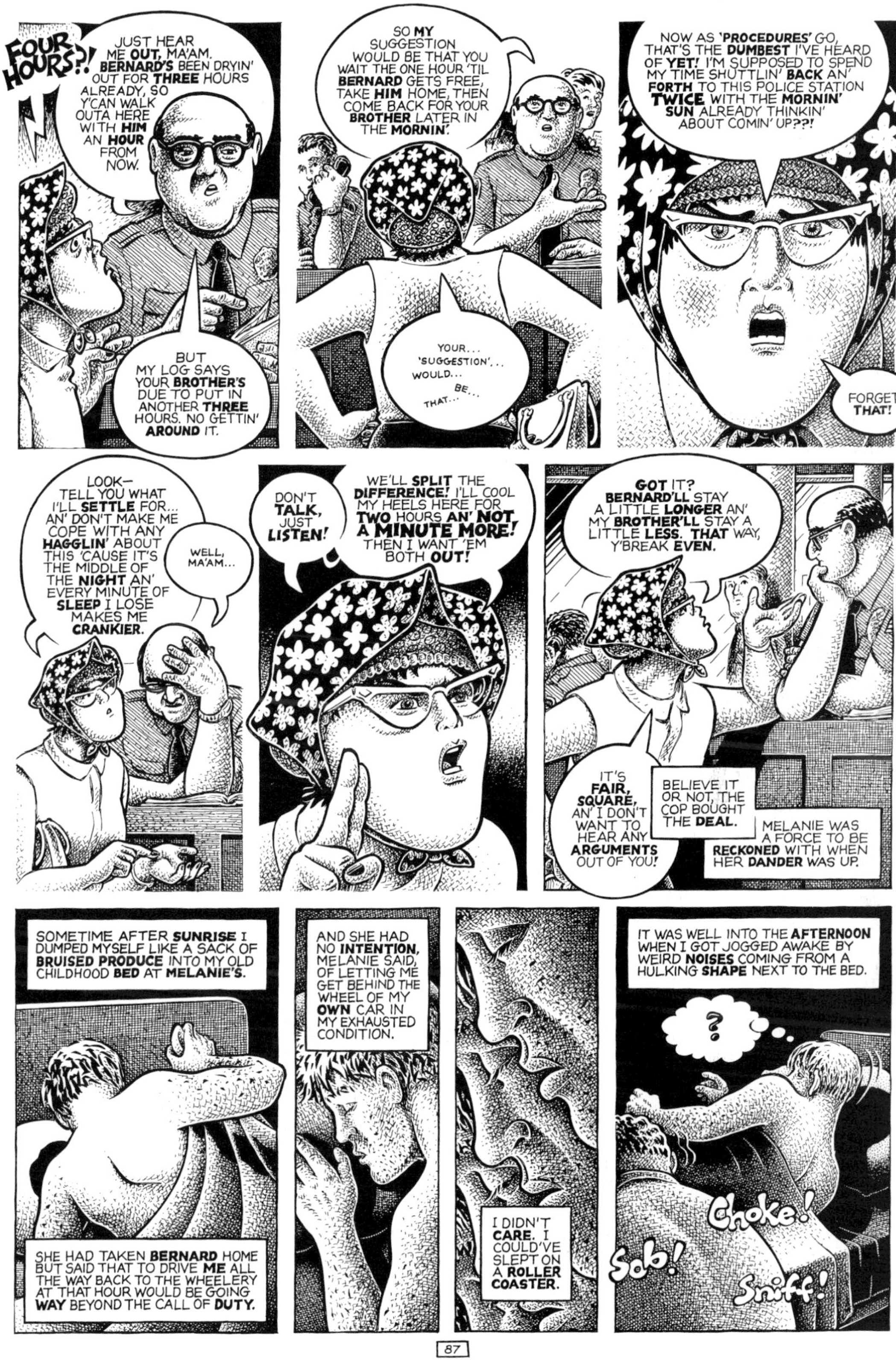
FOUR HOURS?!
JUST HEAR ME OUT, MA'AM. BERNARD'S BEEN DRYIN' OUT FOR THREE HOURS ALREADY, SO Y'CAN WALK OUTA HERE WITH HIM AN HOUR FROM NOW.
BUT MY LOG SAYS YOUR BROTHER'S DUE TO PUT IN ANOTHER THREE HOURS. NO GETTIN' AROUND IT.
SO MY SUGGESTION WOULD BE THAT YOU WAIT THE ONE HOUR 'TIL BERNARD GETS FREE, TAKE HIM HOME, THEN COME BACK FOR YOUR BROTHER LATER IN THE MORNIN'.
YOUR... 'SUGGESTION'... WOULD... BE... THAT...
NOW AS 'PROCEDURES' GO, THAT'S THE DUMBEST I'VE HEARD OF YET! I'M SUPPOSED TO SPEND MY TIME SHUTTLIN' BACK AN' FORTH TO THIS POLICE STATION TWICE WITH THE MORNIN' SUN ALREADY THINKIN' ABOUT COMIN' UP??!
FORGET THAT!
LOOK— TELL YOU WHAT I'LL SETTLE FOR... AN' DON'T MAKE ME COPE WITH ANY HAGGLIN' ABOUT THIS 'CAUSE IT'S THE MIDDLE OF THE NIGHT AN' EVERY MINUTE OF SLEEP I LOSE MAKES ME CRANKIER.
WELL, MA'AM...
DON'T TALK, JUST LISTEN!
WE'LL SPLIT THE DIFFERENCE! I'LL COOL MY HEELS HERE FOR TWO HOURS AN' NOT A MINUTE MORE! THEN I WANT 'EM BOTH OUT!
GOT IT? BERNARD'LL STAY A LITTLE LONGER AN' MY BROTHER'LL STAY A LITTLE LESS. THAT WAY, Y'BREAK EVEN.
IT'S FAIR, SQUARE, AN' I DON'T WANT TO HEAR ANY ARGUMENTS OUT OF YOU!
BELIEVE IT OR NOT, THE COP BOUGHT THE DEAL.
MELANIE WAS A FORCE TO BE RECKONED WITH WHEN HER DANDER WAS UP.
SOMETIME AFTER SUNRISE I DUMPED MYSELF LIKE A SACK OF BRUISED PRODUCE INTO MY OLD CHILDHOOD BED AT MELANIE'S.
SHE HAD TAKEN BERNARD HOME BUT SAID THAT TO DRIVE ME ALL THE WAY BACK TO THE WHEELERY AT THAT HOUR WOULD BE GOING WAY BEYOND THE CALL OF DUTY.
AND SHE HAD NO INTENTION, MELANIE SAID, OF LETTING ME GET BEHIND THE WHEEL OF MY OWN CAR IN MY EXHAUSTED CONDITION.
I DIDN'T CARE. I COULD'VE SLEPT ON A ROLLER COASTER.
IT WAS WELL INTO THE AFTERNOON WHEN I GOT JOGGED AWAKE BY WEIRD NOISES COMING FROM A HULKING SHAPE NEXT TO THE BED.
?
Choke!
Sob!
Sniff!

ORLEY??

I'M **SORRY**, TOLAND. ~sniff!~

I SHOULDN'T OF BEEN **IN** HERE WITH YOU **ASLEEP**.

I WAS **INTENDIN'** TO SAY A LITTLE BEDSIDE **PRAYER** ...BUT THEN I JUST STARTED **CRYIN'**.

ORLEY, WHAT'VE **YOU** GOT TO FRET ABOUT? **I'M** THE ONE WITH THE **HANGOVER**!

THAT'S RIGHT, PAL. BE **FLIP**. NEVER ACT LIKE THERE MIGHT BE ANYTHING OF **IMPORTANCE** GOIN' ON IN THE MIND OF A DUMB OL' GUY THAT **LOVES** YOU.

YOU'RE SOMETHIN' **ELSE** TO WAKE **UP** TO... THAT'S FOR **SURE**!

HEY!... ORL!... WHAT'S **BUGGIN'** YOU?

THE **PATH** YOU'RE SHOWIN' SIGNS OF HEADIN' DOWN.

DRINKIN' IN **BARS**...HANGIN' AROUND WITH PEOPLE THAT GET **ARRESTED**...

...IT COULD END UP WITH YOU GOIN' TO **HELL**.

OH, I KNOW YOU'RE THE **LAST** PERSON WHO'D TAKE **THAT** RISK TO HEART. YOU THINK THAT HELL'S SOME **IMAGINARY CONCEPT**!

BUT HELL IS **REAL**. IT'S AN **ACTUAL PLACE** IN THE **UNIVERSE**.

I DON'T WANT YOU TO FIND THAT OUT THE **HARD** WAY. BUT IF YOU DON'T TAKE A CAREFUL **LOOK** AT THE **LIFE** YOU'RE LEADIN'.

PLEASE, TOLAND... **THINK** ABOUT WHAT MIGHT BE IN **STORE** FOR YOU.

HORRIBLE **TORTURE** THAT'LL LAST FOR **EVER** AND **EVER**. THERE'LL BE NO **END** TO IT, TOLAND. NO **RELIEF** FROM THE **AGONY**.

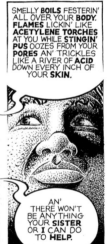

SMELLY **BOILS** FESTERIN' ALL OVER YOUR **BODY**. FLAMES LICKIN' LIKE **ACETYLENE TORCHES** AT YOU WHILE **STINGIN' PUS** OOZES FROM YOUR **PORES** AN' TRICKLES LIKE A RIVER OF **ACID** DOWN EVERY INCH OF YOUR **SKIN**.

AN' THERE WON'T BE ANYTHING YOUR **SISTER** OR **I** CAN DO TO **HELP**.

WE'LL BE IN **HEAVEN**, LORD WILLIN'! BUT IT'S HARD TO SEE HOW WE CAN BE VERY **HAPPY** THERE, KNOWIN' YOU'RE IN THE PIT **SUFFERIN'**.

YOU'VE **GOT** TO BE HAPPY IN **HEAVEN**, ORLEY. HOUSE **RULES**!

FLIPPANCY!... FLIPPANCY!...

CUT RIGHT INTO MY **HEART** WITH YOUR FLIPPANCY!

NOTHIN' LEFT FOR ME TO **DO** BUT PRAY FOR YOU A HUNDRED TIMES **HARDER**, JUST TO MAKE UP FOR THE **BLINDNESS** THAT WON'T LET YOU PRAY FOR **YOUR-SELF**.

I'LL TELL MELANIE YOU'RE **AWAKE**. I'VE GOT SOME **WEEDS** TO PULL IN THE YARD.

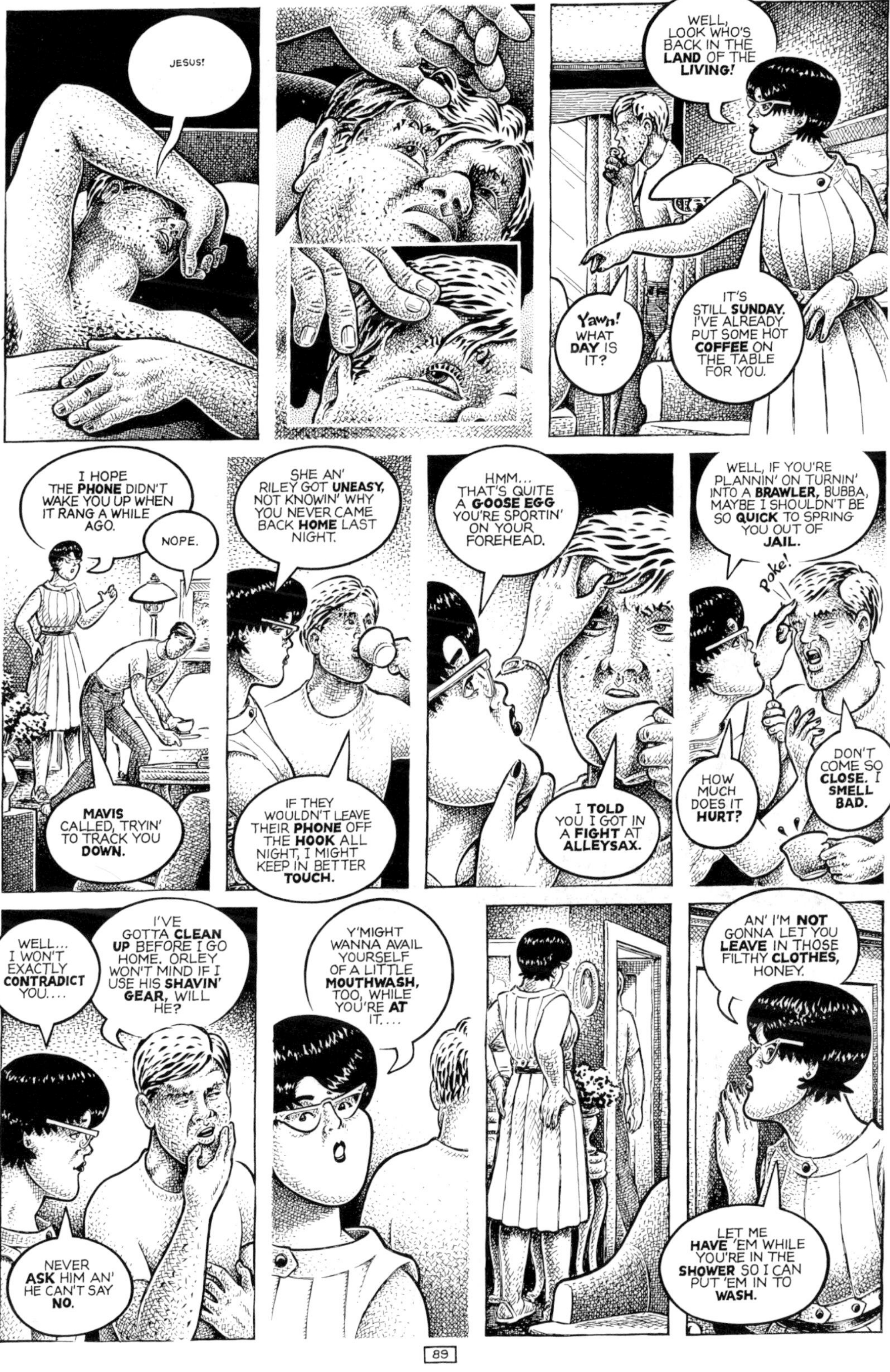
JESUS!
WELL, LOOK WHO'S BACK IN THE LAND OF THE LIVING!
Yawn! WHAT DAY IS IT?
IT'S STILL SUNDAY. I'VE ALREADY PUT SOME HOT COFFEE ON THE TABLE FOR YOU.
I HOPE THE PHONE DIDN'T WAKE YOU UP WHEN IT RANG A WHILE AGO.
NOPE.
MAVIS CALLED, TRYIN' TO TRACK YOU DOWN.
SHE AN' RILEY GOT UNEASY, NOT KNOWIN' WHY YOU NEVER CAME BACK HOME LAST NIGHT.
IF THEY WOULDN'T LEAVE THEIR PHONE OFF THE HOOK ALL NIGHT, I MIGHT KEEP IN BETTER TOUCH.
HMM... THAT'S QUITE A GOOSE EGG YOU'RE SPORTIN' ON YOUR FOREHEAD.
I TOLD YOU I GOT IN A FIGHT AT ALLEYSAX.
WELL, IF YOU'RE PLANNIN' ON TURNIN' INTO A BRAWLER, BUBBA, MAYBE I SHOULDN'T BE SO QUICK TO SPRING YOU OUT OF JAIL.
Poke!
HOW MUCH DOES IT HURT?
DON'T COME SO CLOSE. I SMELL BAD.
WELL... I WON'T EXACTLY CONTRADICT YOU....
I'VE GOTTA CLEAN UP BEFORE I GO HOME. ORLEY WON'T MIND IF I USE HIS SHAVIN' GEAR, WILL HE?
NEVER ASK HIM AN' HE CAN'T SAY NO.
Y'MIGHT WANNA AVAIL YOURSELF OF A LITTLE MOUTHWASH, TOO, WHILE YOU'RE AT IT....
AN' I'M NOT GONNA LET YOU LEAVE IN THOSE FILTHY CLOTHES, HONEY.
LET ME HAVE 'EM WHILE YOU'RE IN THE SHOWER SO I CAN PUT 'EM IN TO WASH.

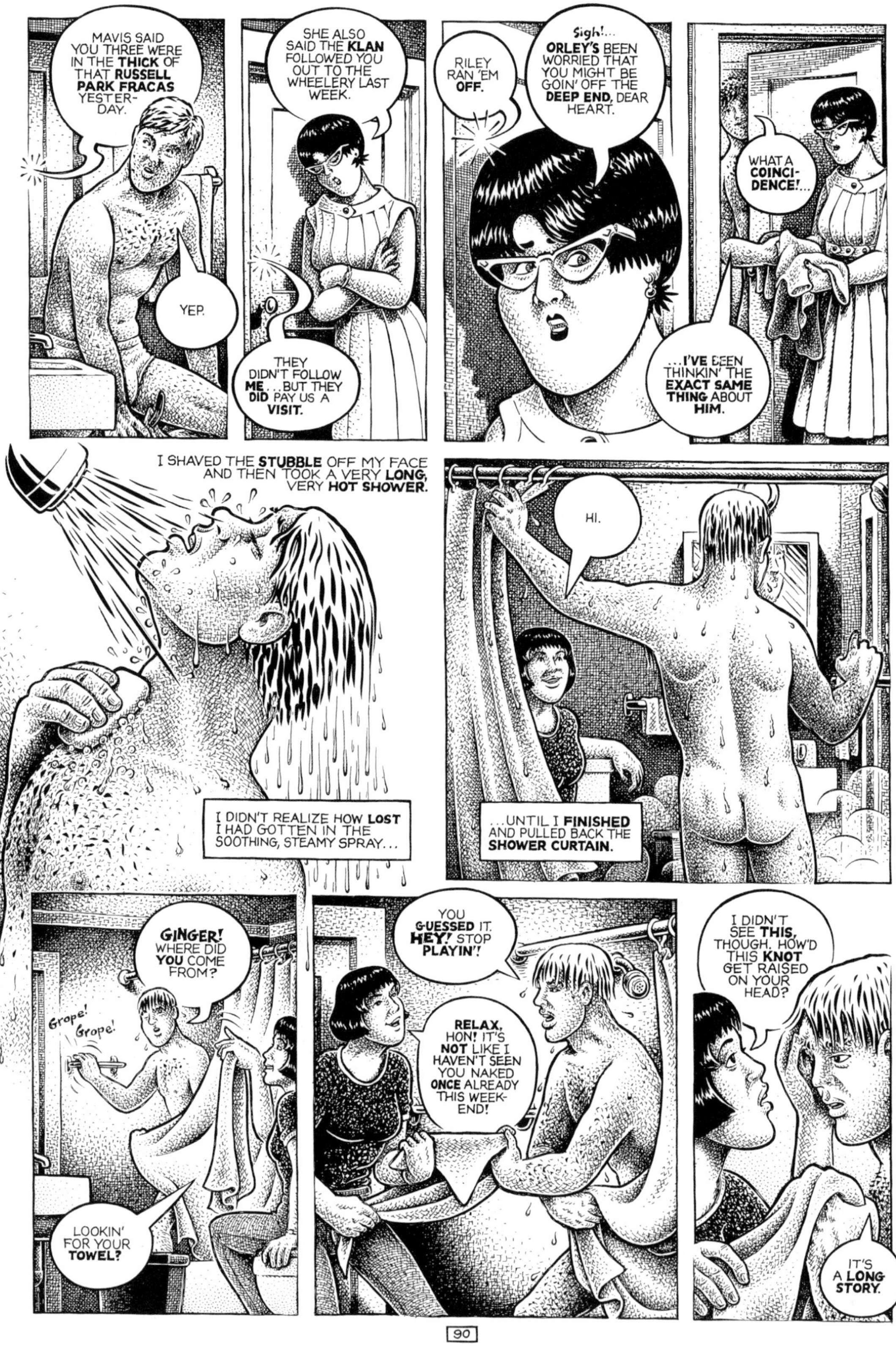

MAVIS SAID YOU THREE WERE IN THE **THICK** OF THAT **RUSSELL PARK FRACAS** YESTER-DAY.
YEP.
SHE ALSO SAID THE **KLAN** FOLLOWED YOU OUT TO THE WHEELERY LAST WEEK.
THEY DIDN'T FOLLOW **ME**... BUT THEY **DID** PAY US A **VISIT**.
RILEY RAN 'EM **OFF**.
Sigh!... **ORLEY'S** BEEN WORRIED THAT YOU MIGHT BE GOIN' OFF THE **DEEP END**, DEAR HEART.
WHAT A **COINCI-DENCE!**...
...**I'VE** BEEN THINKIN' THE **EXACT SAME THING** ABOUT **HIM**.
I SHAVED THE **STUBBLE** OFF MY FACE AND THEN TOOK A VERY **LONG**, VERY **HOT SHOWER**.
I DIDN'T REALIZE HOW **LOST** I HAD GOTTEN IN THE SOOTHING, STEAMY SPRAY...
...UNTIL I **FINISHED** AND PULLED BACK THE **SHOWER CURTAIN**.
HI.
GINGER! WHERE DID **YOU** COME FROM?
Grope! Grope!
LOOKIN' FOR YOUR **TOWEL?**
YOU **GUESSED** IT. **HEY!** STOP **PLAYIN'!**
RELAX, HON! IT'S **NOT** LIKE I HAVEN'T SEEN YOU NAKED **ONCE** ALREADY THIS WEEK-END!
I DIDN'T SEE **THIS**, THOUGH. HOW'D THIS **KNOT** GET RAISED ON YOUR HEAD?
IT'S A **LONG STORY**.

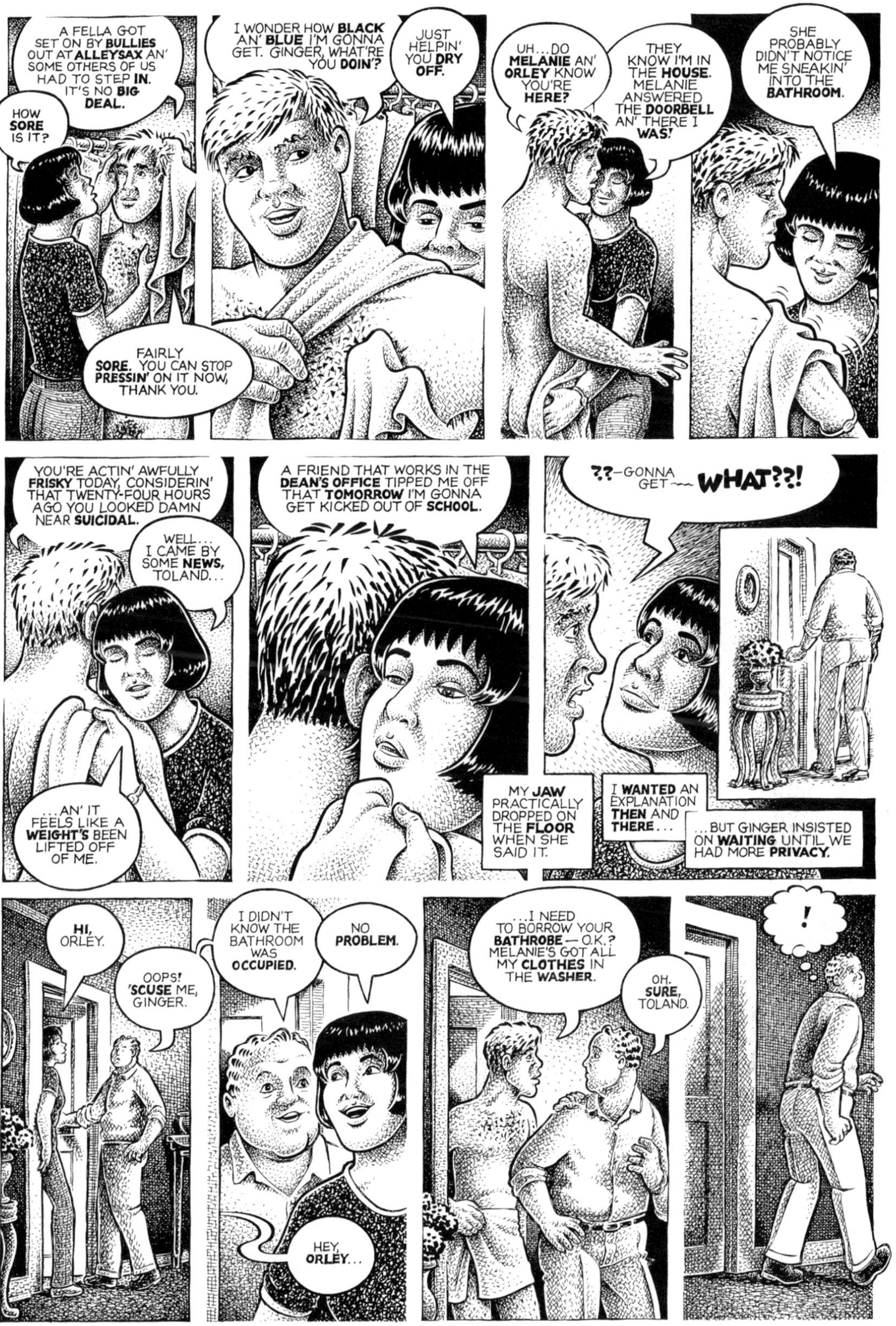
A FELLA GOT SET ON BY BULLIES OUT AT ALLEYSAX AN' SOME OTHERS OF US HAD TO STEP IN. IT'S NO BIG DEAL.
HOW SORE IS IT?
FAIRLY SORE. YOU CAN STOP PRESSIN' ON IT NOW, THANK YOU.
I WONDER HOW BLACK AN' BLUE I'M GONNA GET. GINGER, WHAT'RE YOU DOIN'?
JUST HELPIN' YOU DRY OFF.
UH...DO MELANIE AN' ORLEY KNOW YOU'RE HERE?
THEY KNOW I'M IN THE HOUSE. MELANIE ANSWERED THE DOORBELL AN' THERE I WAS!
SHE PROBABLY DIDN'T NOTICE ME SNEAKIN' INTO THE BATHROOM.
YOU'RE ACTIN' AWFULLY FRISKY TODAY, CONSIDERIN' THAT TWENTY-FOUR HOURS AGO YOU LOOKED DAMN NEAR SUICIDAL.
WELL... I CAME BY SOME NEWS, TOLAND...
...AN' IT FEELS LIKE A WEIGHT'S BEEN LIFTED OFF OF ME.
A FRIEND THAT WORKS IN THE DEAN'S OFFICE TIPPED ME OFF THAT TOMORROW I'M GONNA GET KICKED OUT OF SCHOOL.
??–GONNA GET~~ WHAT??!
MY JAW PRACTICALLY DROPPED ON THE FLOOR WHEN SHE SAID IT.
I WANTED AN EXPLANATION THEN AND THERE...
...BUT GINGER INSISTED ON WAITING UNTIL WE HAD MORE PRIVACY.
HI, ORLEY.
OOPS! 'SCUSE ME, GINGER.
I DIDN'T KNOW THE BATHROOM WAS OCCUPIED.
NO PROBLEM.
HEY, ORLEY...
...I NEED TO BORROW YOUR BATHROBE — O.K.? MELANIE'S GOT ALL MY CLOTHES IN THE WASHER.
OH. SURE, TOLAND.
!

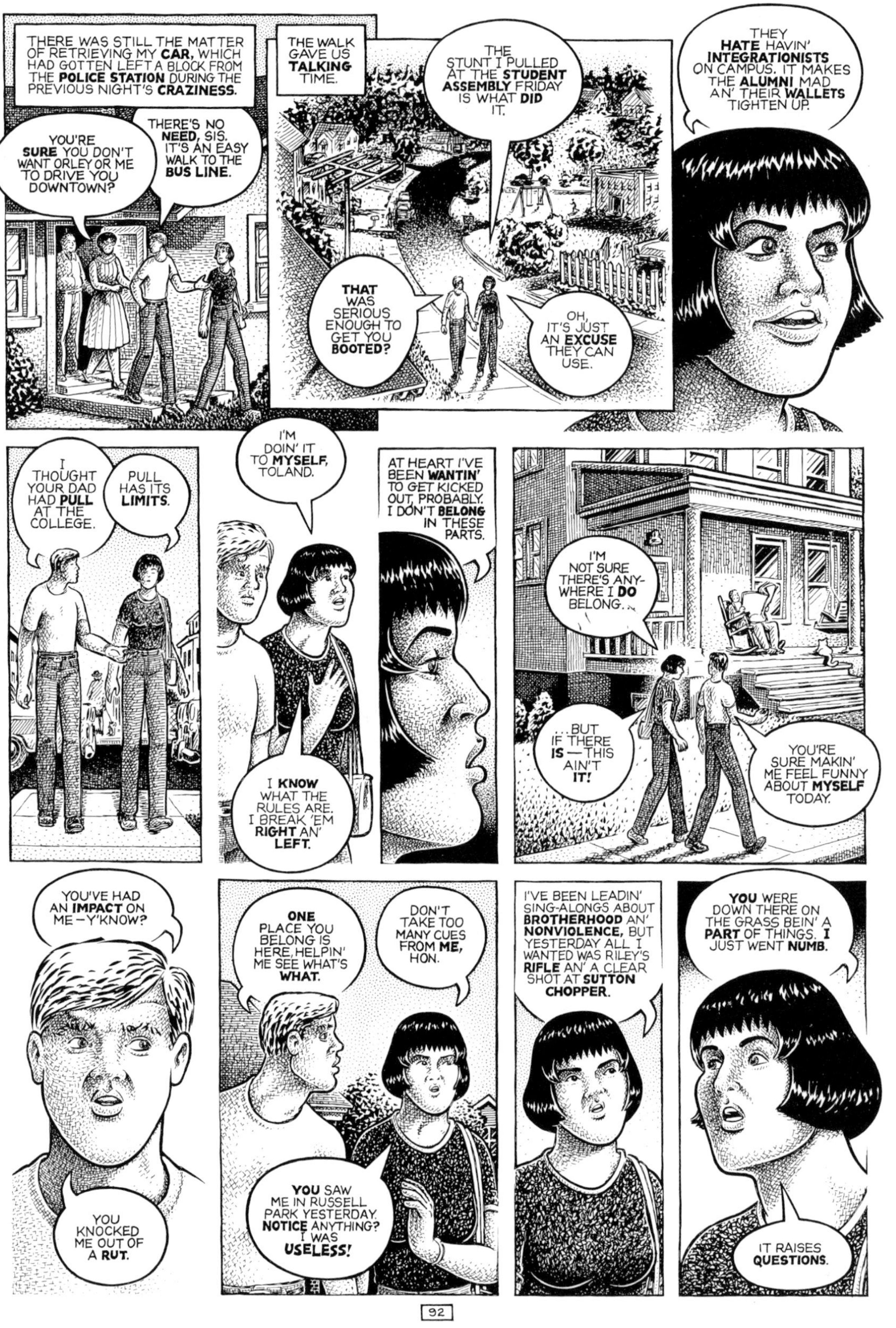

THERE WAS STILL THE MATTER OF RETRIEVING MY **CAR**, WHICH HAD GOTTEN LEFT A BLOCK FROM THE **POLICE STATION** DURING THE PREVIOUS NIGHT'S **CRAZINESS**.
YOU'RE **SURE** YOU DON'T WANT ORLEY OR ME TO DRIVE YOU DOWNTOWN?
THERE'S NO **NEED**, SIS. IT'S AN EASY WALK TO THE **BUS LINE**.
THE WALK GAVE US **TALKING** TIME.
THE STUNT I PULLED AT THE **STUDENT ASSEMBLY** FRIDAY IS WHAT **DID** IT.
THAT WAS SERIOUS ENOUGH TO GET YOU **BOOTED?**
OH, IT'S JUST AN **EXCUSE** THEY CAN USE.
THEY **HATE** HAVIN' **INTEGRATIONISTS** ON CAMPUS. IT MAKES THE **ALUMNI** MAD AN' THEIR **WALLETS** TIGHTEN UP.
I THOUGHT YOUR DAD HAD **PULL** AT THE COLLEGE.
PULL HAS ITS **LIMITS**.
I'M DOIN' IT TO **MYSELF**, TOLAND.
I **KNOW** WHAT THE RULES ARE. I BREAK 'EM **RIGHT** AN' **LEFT**.
AT HEART I'VE BEEN **WANTIN'** TO GET KICKED OUT, PROBABLY. I DON'T **BELONG** IN THESE PARTS.
I'M NOT SURE THERE'S ANY-WHERE I **DO** BELONG...
...BUT IF THERE **IS** — THIS AIN'T **IT!**
YOU'RE SURE MAKIN' ME FEEL FUNNY ABOUT **MYSELF** TODAY.
YOU'VE HAD AN **IMPACT** ON ME — Y'KNOW?
YOU KNOCKED ME OUT OF A **RUT**.
ONE PLACE YOU BELONG IS HERE, HELPIN' ME SEE WHAT'S **WHAT**.
DON'T TAKE TOO MANY CUES FROM **ME**, HON.
YOU SAW ME IN RUSSELL PARK YESTERDAY. **NOTICE** ANYTHING? I WAS **USELESS!**
I'VE BEEN LEADIN' SING-ALONGS ABOUT **BROTHERHOOD** AN' **NONVIOLENCE**, BUT YESTERDAY WAS ALL I WANTED WAS RILEY'S **RIFLE** AN' A CLEAR SHOT AT **SUTTON CHOPPER**.
YOU WERE DOWN THERE ON THE GRASS BEIN' A **PART** OF THINGS. **I** JUST WENT **NUMB**.
IT RAISES **QUESTIONS**.

YOU DID SEEM **UPSET**. I SAW YOU LATER ON AT THE **CHURCH**, GETTIN' SOME COMFORT FROM **SHILOH**.

YOU **SAW** US? WE DIDN'T SEE **YOU**.

YOU SHOULD'VE COME **OVER**.

I DIDN'T WANNA **INTRUDE**.

ARE YOU **JEALOUS** OF SHILOH?

NO. NOT AT **ALL.**

BUT I WISH I COULD BUY A **BOTTLE** OF WHATEVER PEOPLE LIKE SHILOH HAVE.

LOOK HOW HE'S **CHEERED** YOU **UP!**

I'M NOT **CHEERFUL.** I'M **ADRIFT.**

THERE'S A CERTAIN **GIDDINESS** IN THAT.

WHAT'LL YOU **DO** WITH YOURSELF IF YOU DO GET KICKED OUT OF WESTHILLS?

GO BACK TO **AKRON**, I GUESS.

DO YOU **HAFTA** LEAVE TOWN...?

I'LL HAVE SOME **FENCES** TO MEND WITH MY **FOLKS.**

AT TIMES LIKE THAT, THEY TEND TO WANT ME AT **CLOSE RANGE.**

I'M **CONFUSED. I** THOUGHT THE LAST FEW MONTHS WERE WHAT YOU'D CALL **HAPPY** TIMES FOR THE TWO OF US.

BUT NOW YOU'RE ACTIN' PLEASED AS **PUNCH** AT THE THOUGHT OF LEAVIN' CLAYFIELD AN' ME **BEHIND.**

ANY CHANCE THE **RELIEF** YOU'RE FEELIN' COMES FROM SHEDDIN' A BOYFRIEND THAT'S GONE **QUEER** ON YOU?

GOD DAMN IT, TOLAND!

EVERYTHING THAT GOES ON INSIDE OF ME DOESN'T HAVE TO DO WITH **YOU!** QUITE A **LOT** GOES ON THAT DOESN'T HAVE **ANYTHING** TO DO WITH YOU AT **ALL!**

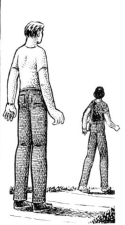

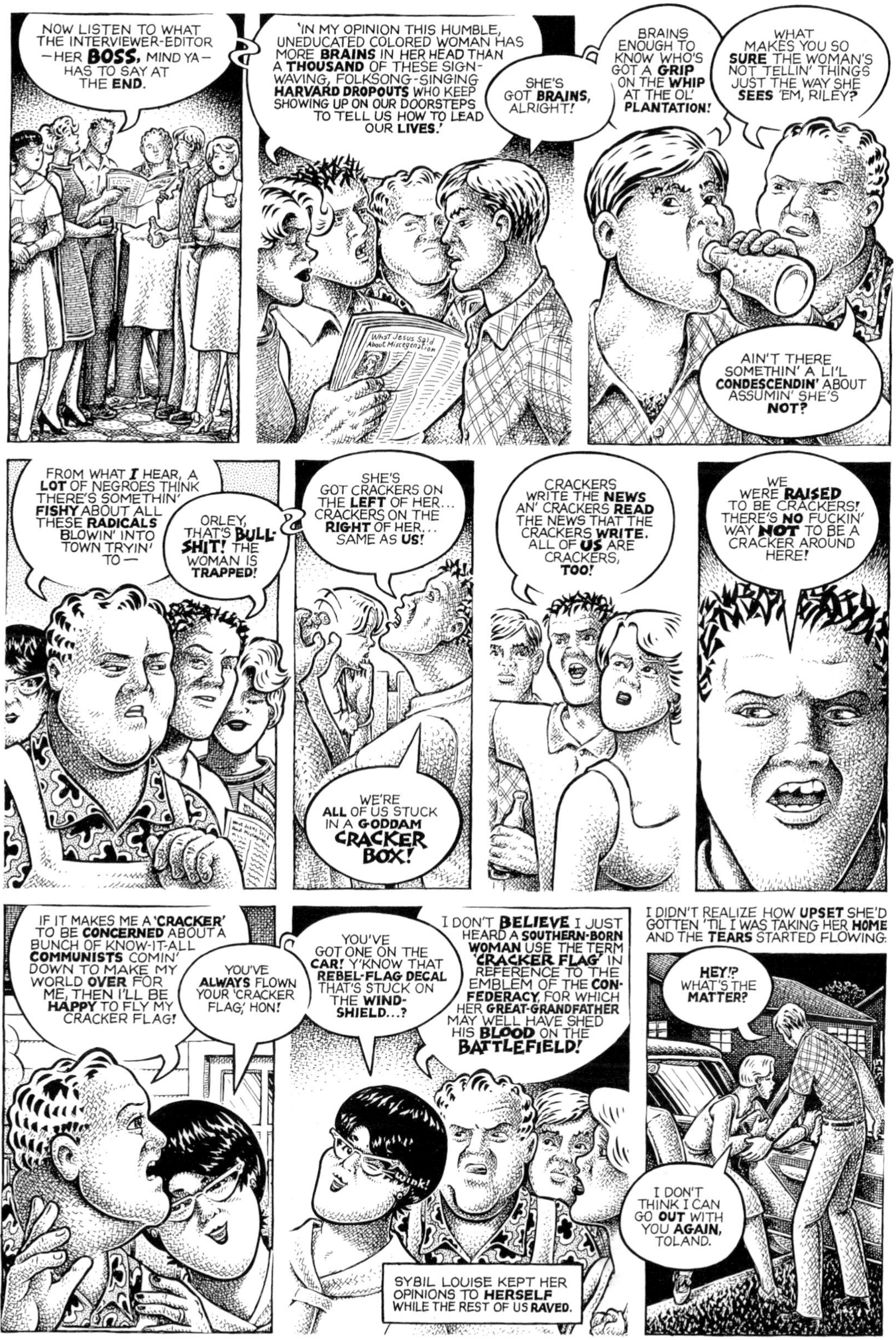

NOW LISTEN TO WHAT THE INTERVIEWER-EDITOR —HER BOSS, MIND YA— HAS TO SAY AT THE END.
'IN MY OPINION THIS HUMBLE, UNEDUCATED COLORED WOMAN HAS MORE BRAINS IN HER HEAD THAN A THOUSAND OF THESE SIGN-WAVING, FOLKSONG-SINGING HARVARD DROPOUTS WHO KEEP SHOWING UP ON OUR DOORSTEPS TO TELL US HOW TO LEAD OUR LIVES.'
What Jesus Said About Miscegenation
SHE'S GOT BRAINS, ALRIGHT!
BRAINS ENOUGH TO KNOW WHO'S GOT A GRIP ON THE WHIP AT THE OL' PLANTATION!
WHAT MAKES YOU SO SURE THE WOMAN'S NOT TELLIN' THINGS JUST THE WAY SHE SEES 'EM, RILEY?
AIN'T THERE SOMETHIN' A LI'L CONDESCENDIN' ABOUT ASSUMIN' SHE'S NOT?
FROM WHAT I HEAR, A LOT OF NEGROES THINK THERE'S SOMETHIN' FISHY ABOUT ALL THESE RADICALS BLOWIN' INTO TOWN TRYIN' TO—
ORLEY, THAT'S BULL-SHIT! THE WOMAN IS TRAPPED!
SHE'S GOT CRACKERS ON THE LEFT OF HER... CRACKERS ON THE RIGHT OF HER... SAME AS US!
WE'RE ALL OF US STUCK IN A GODDAM CRACKER BOX!
CRACKERS WRITE THE NEWS AN' CRACKERS READ THE NEWS THAT THE CRACKERS WRITE. ALL OF US ARE CRACKERS, TOO!
WE WERE RAISED TO BE CRACKERS! THERE'S NO FUCKIN' WAY NOT TO BE A CRACKER AROUND HERE!
IF IT MAKES ME A 'CRACKER' TO BE CONCERNED ABOUT A BUNCH OF KNOW-IT-ALL COMMUNISTS COMIN' DOWN TO MAKE MY WORLD OVER FOR ME, THEN I'LL BE HAPPY TO FLY MY CRACKER FLAG!
YOU'VE ALWAYS FLOWN YOUR 'CRACKER FLAG,' HON!
YOU'VE GOT ONE ON THE CAR! Y'KNOW THAT REBEL-FLAG DECAL THAT'S STUCK ON THE WIND-SHIELD...?
I DON'T BELIEVE I JUST HEARD A SOUTHERN-BORN WOMAN USE THE TERM 'CRACKER FLAG' IN REFERENCE TO THE EMBLEM OF THE CON-FEDERACY, FOR WHICH HER GREAT-GRANDFATHER MAY WELL HAVE SHED HIS BLOOD ON THE BATTLEFIELD!
SYBIL LOUISE KEPT HER OPINIONS TO HERSELF WHILE THE REST OF US RAVED.
I DIDN'T REALIZE HOW UPSET SHE'D GOTTEN 'TIL I WAS TAKING HER HOME AND THE TEARS STARTED FLOWING.
HEY!? WHAT'S THE MATTER?
I DON'T THINK I CAN GO OUT WITH YOU AGAIN, TOLAND.

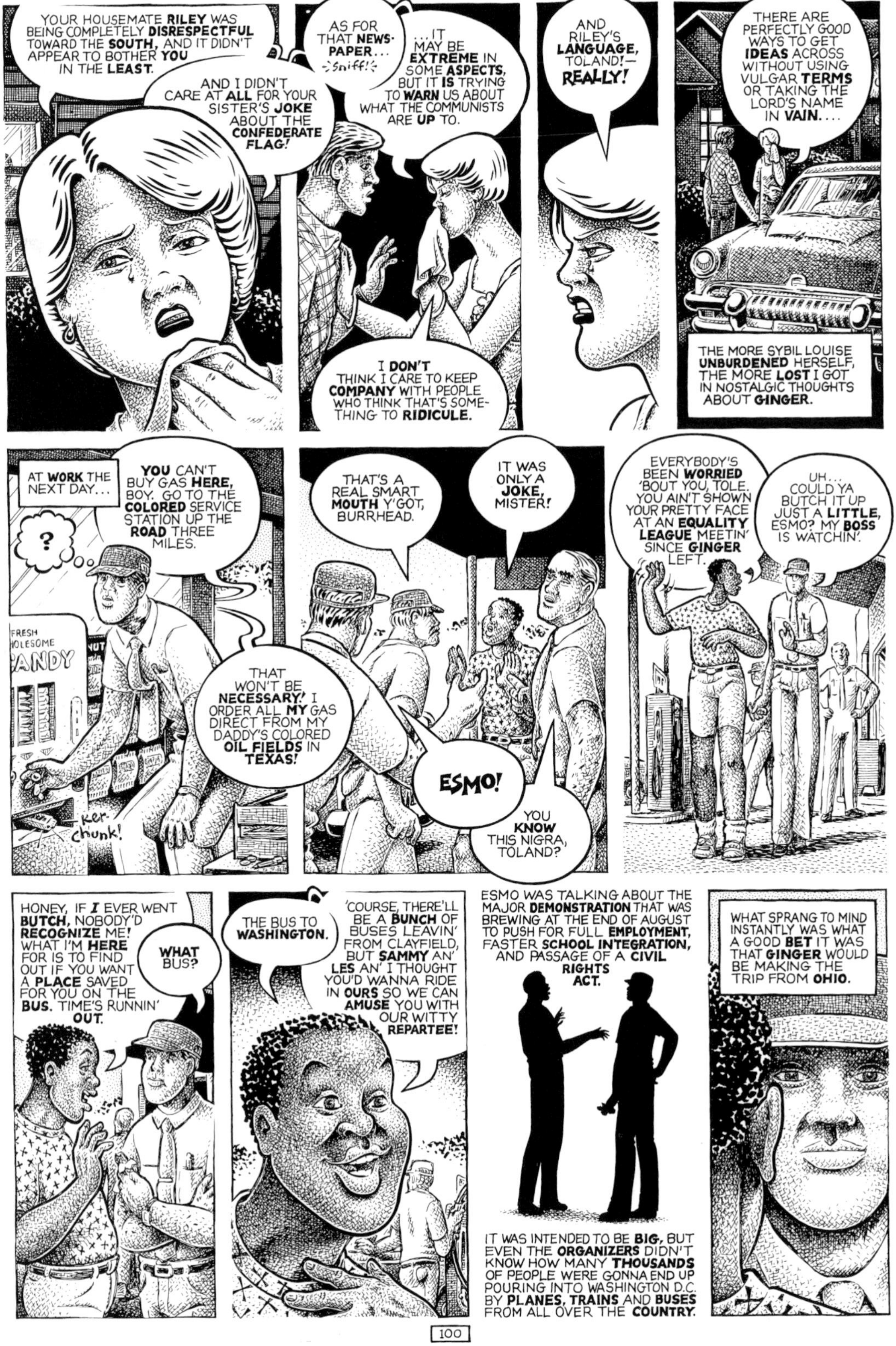
YOUR HOUSEMATE RILEY WAS BEING COMPLETELY DISRESPECTFUL TOWARD THE SOUTH, AND IT DIDN'T APPEAR TO BOTHER YOU IN THE LEAST.
AND I DIDN'T CARE AT ALL FOR YOUR SISTER'S JOKE ABOUT THE CONFEDERATE FLAG!
AS FOR THAT NEWS-PAPER... -Sniff!-
...IT MAY BE EXTREME IN SOME ASPECTS, BUT IT IS TRYING TO WARN US ABOUT WHAT THE COMMUNISTS ARE UP TO.
I DON'T THINK I CARE TO KEEP COMPANY WITH PEOPLE WHO THINK THAT'S SOME-THING TO RIDICULE.
AND RILEY'S LANGUAGE, TOLAND!— REALLY!
THERE ARE PERFECTLY GOOD WAYS TO GET IDEAS ACROSS WITHOUT USING VULGAR TERMS OR TAKING THE LORD'S NAME IN VAIN....
THE MORE SYBIL LOUISE UNBURDENED HERSELF, THE MORE LOST I GOT IN NOSTALGIC THOUGHTS ABOUT GINGER.
AT WORK THE NEXT DAY...
YOU CAN'T BUY GAS HERE, BOY. GO TO THE COLORED SERVICE STATION UP THE ROAD THREE MILES.
?
FRESH WHOLESOME CANDY
Ker-chunk!
THAT'S A REAL SMART MOUTH Y'GOT, BURRHEAD.
IT WAS ONLY A JOKE, MISTER!
THAT WON'T BE NECESSARY! I ORDER ALL MY GAS DIRECT FROM MY DADDY'S COLORED OIL FIELDS IN TEXAS!
ESMO!
YOU KNOW THIS NIGRA, TOLAND?
EVERYBODY'S BEEN WORRIED 'BOUT YOU, TOLE. YOU AIN'T SHOWN YOUR PRETTY FACE AT AN EQUALITY LEAGUE MEETIN' SINCE GINGER LEFT.
UH... COULD YA BUTCH IT UP JUST A LITTLE, ESMO? MY BOSS IS WATCHIN'.
HONEY, IF I EVER WENT BUTCH, NOBODY'D RECOGNIZE ME! WHAT I'M HERE FOR IS TO FIND OUT IF YOU WANT A PLACE SAVED FOR YOU ON THE BUS. TIME'S RUNNIN' OUT.
WHAT BUS?
THE BUS TO WASHINGTON.
'COURSE, THERE'LL BE A BUNCH OF BUSES LEAVIN' FROM CLAYFIELD, BUT SAMMY AN' LES AN' I THOUGHT YOU'D WANNA RIDE IN OURS SO WE CAN AMUSE YOU WITH OUR WITTY REPARTEE!
ESMO WAS TALKING ABOUT THE MAJOR DEMONSTRATION THAT WAS BREWING AT THE END OF AUGUST TO PUSH FOR FULL EMPLOYMENT, FASTER SCHOOL INTEGRATION, AND PASSAGE OF A CIVIL RIGHTS ACT.
IT WAS INTENDED TO BE BIG, BUT EVEN THE ORGANIZERS DIDN'T KNOW HOW MANY THOUSANDS OF PEOPLE WERE GONNA END UP POURING INTO WASHINGTON D.C. BY PLANES, TRAINS AND BUSES FROM ALL OVER THE COUNTRY.
WHAT SPRANG TO MIND INSTANTLY WAS WHAT A GOOD BET IT WAS THAT GINGER WOULD BE MAKING THE TRIP FROM OHIO.

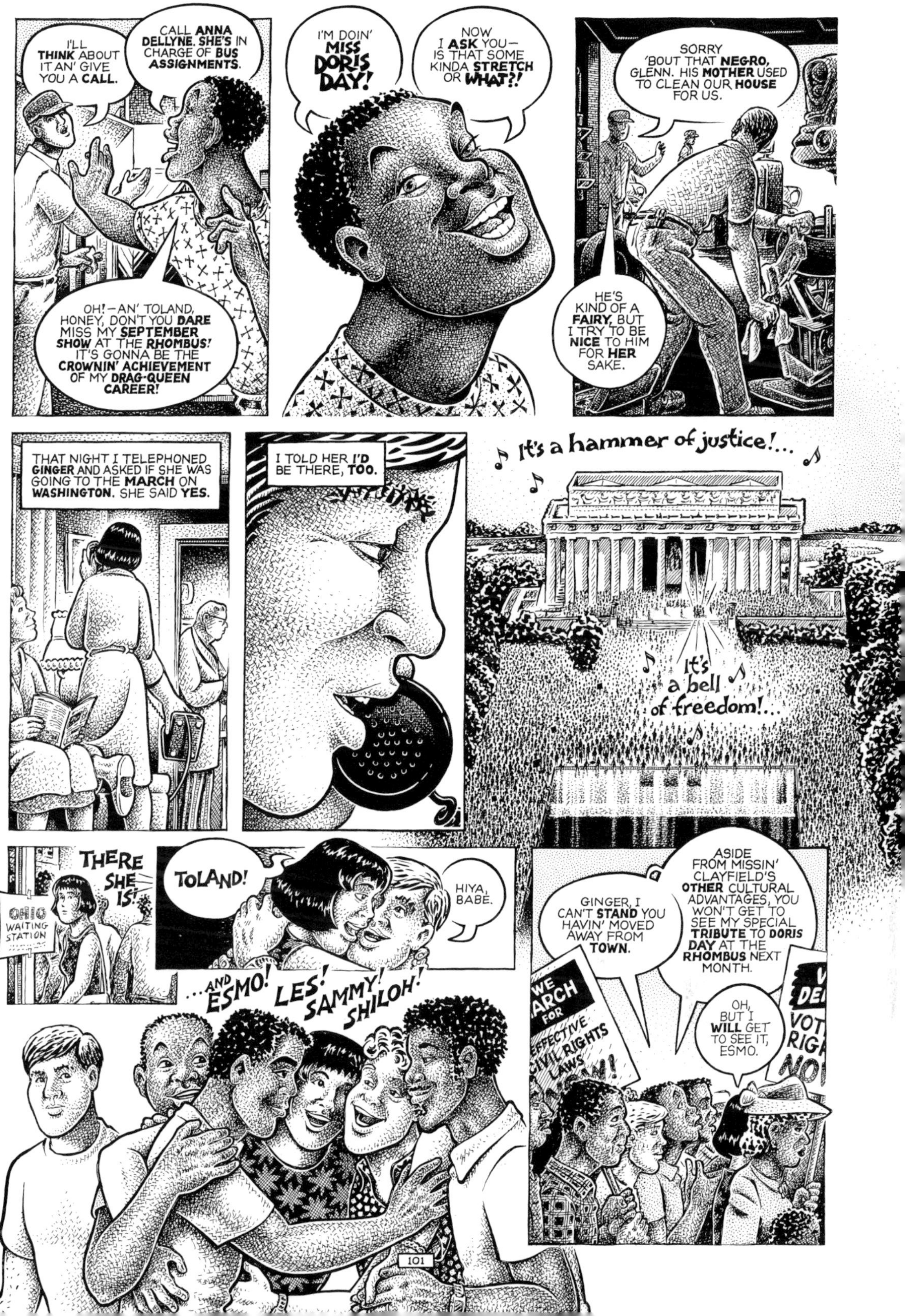
I'LL THINK ABOUT IT AN' GIVE YOU A CALL.
CALL ANNA DELLYNE. SHE'S IN CHARGE OF BUS ASSIGNMENTS.
OH!—AN' TOLAND, HONEY, DON'T YOU DARE MISS MY SEPTEMBER SHOW AT THE RHOMBUS! IT'S GONNA BE THE CROWNIN' ACHIEVEMENT OF MY DRAG-QUEEN CAREER!
I'M DOIN' MISS DORIS DAY!
NOW I ASK YOU— IS THAT SOME KINDA STRETCH OR WHAT?!
SORRY 'BOUT THAT NEGRO, GLENN. HIS MOTHER USED TO CLEAN OUR HOUSE FOR US.
HE'S KIND OF A FAIRY, BUT I TRY TO BE NICE TO HIM FOR HER SAKE.
THAT NIGHT I TELEPHONED GINGER AND ASKED IF SHE WAS GOING TO THE MARCH ON WASHINGTON. SHE SAID YES.
I TOLD HER I'D BE THERE, TOO.
It's a hammer of justice!...
It's a bell of freedom!...
OHIO WAITING STATION
THERE SHE IS!
TOLAND!
HIYA, BABE.
...AND ESMO! LES! SAMMY! SHILOH!
GINGER, I CAN'T STAND YOU HAVIN' MOVED AWAY FROM TOWN.
ASIDE FROM MISSIN' CLAYFIELD'S OTHER CULTURAL ADVANTAGES, YOU WON'T GET TO SEE MY SPECIAL TRIBUTE TO DORIS DAY AT THE RHOMBUS NEXT MONTH.
OH, BUT I WILL GET TO SEE IT, ESMO.
WE MARCH FOR EFFECTIVE CIVIL RIGHTS LAWS

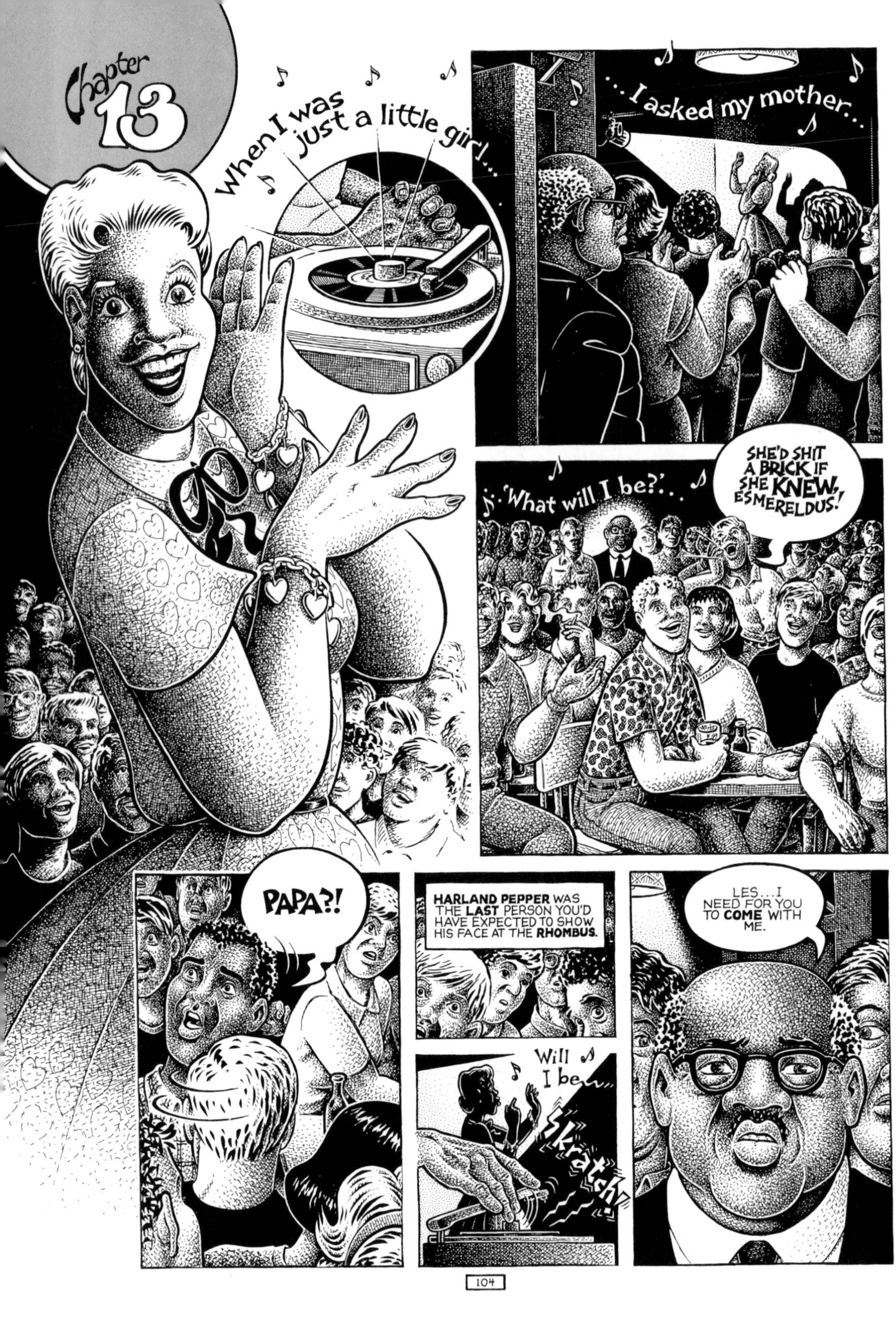
Chapter 13
When I was just a little girl...
...I asked my mother...
'What will I be?'...
SHE'D SHIT A BRICK IF SHE KNEW, ESMERELDUS!
PAPA?!
HARLAND PEPPER WAS THE LAST PERSON YOU'D HAVE EXPECTED TO SHOW HIS FACE AT THE RHOMBUS.
Will I be...
Skratch
LES... I NEED FOR YOU TO COME WITH ME.

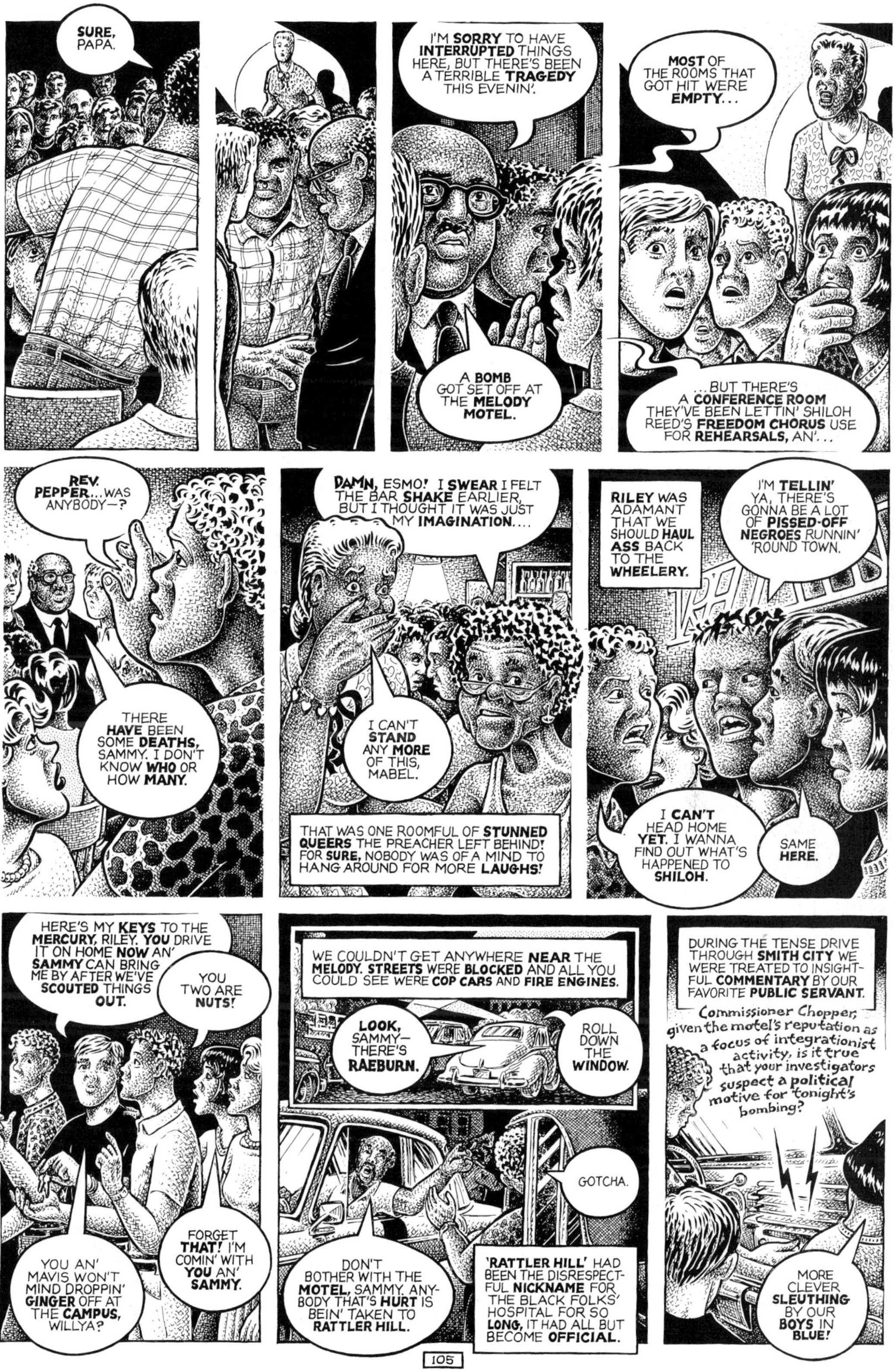
SURE, PAPA.
I'M SORRY TO HAVE INTERRUPTED THINGS HERE, BUT THERE'S BEEN A TERRIBLE TRAGEDY THIS EVENIN'.
A BOMB GOT SET OFF AT THE MELODY MOTEL.
MOST OF THE ROOMS THAT GOT HIT WERE EMPTY...
...BUT THERE'S A CONFERENCE ROOM THEY'VE BEEN LETTIN' SHILOH REED'S FREEDOM CHORUS USE FOR REHEARSALS, AN'...
REV. PEPPER...WAS ANYBODY—?
THERE HAVE BEEN SOME DEATHS, SAMMY. I DON'T KNOW WHO OR HOW MANY.
DAMN, ESMO! I SWEAR I FELT THE BAR SHAKE EARLIER, BUT I THOUGHT IT WAS JUST MY IMAGINATION....
I CAN'T STAND ANY MORE OF THIS, MABEL.
THAT WAS ONE ROOMFUL OF STUNNED QUEERS THE PREACHER LEFT BEHIND! FOR SURE, NOBODY WAS OF A MIND TO HANG AROUND FOR MORE LAUGHS!
RILEY WAS ADAMANT THAT WE SHOULD HAUL ASS BACK TO THE WHEELERY.
I'M TELLIN' YA, THERE'S GONNA BE A LOT OF PISSED-OFF NEGROES RUNNIN' 'ROUND TOWN.
I CAN'T HEAD HOME YET. I WANNA FIND OUT WHAT'S HAPPENED TO SHILOH.
SAME HERE.
HERE'S MY KEYS TO THE MERCURY, RILEY. YOU DRIVE IT ON HOME NOW AN' SAMMY CAN BRING ME BY AFTER WE'VE SCOUTED THINGS OUT.
YOU TWO ARE NUTS!
YOU AN' MAVIS WON'T MIND DROPPIN' GINGER OFF AT THE CAMPUS, WILLYA?
FORGET THAT! I'M COMIN' WITH YOU AN' SAMMY.
WE COULDN'T GET ANYWHERE NEAR THE MELODY. STREETS WERE BLOCKED AND ALL YOU COULD SEE WERE COP CARS AND FIRE ENGINES.
LOOK, SAMMY— THERE'S RAEBURN.
ROLL DOWN THE WINDOW.
GOTCHA.
DON'T BOTHER WITH THE MOTEL, SAMMY. ANYBODY THAT'S HURT IS BEIN' TAKEN TO RATTLER HILL.
'RATTLER HILL' HAD BEEN THE DISRESPECTFUL NICKNAME FOR THE BLACK FOLKS' HOSPITAL FOR SO LONG, IT HAD ALL BUT BECOME OFFICIAL.
DURING THE TENSE DRIVE THROUGH SMITH CITY WE WERE TREATED TO INSIGHTFUL COMMENTARY BY OUR FAVORITE PUBLIC SERVANT.
Commissioner Chopper, given the motel's reputation as a focus of integrationist activity, is it true that your investigators suspect a political motive for 'tonight's bombing?
MORE CLEVER SLEUTHING BY OUR BOYS IN BLUE!

WHILE THE THREE OF US **LISTENED** AND **GLOWERED**, I GOT LOST IN CONTEMPLATION OF THE **MUSCLES** THAT WERE FLEXING IN SAMMY'S **JAW**.

That's right, Bill... And as shocked as we all are by this deplorable crime, I'm obliged to point out that those sweet children would be alive right now were it not for the inflammatory street demonstrations we've all been subjected to by local malcontents as well as Communistic outside agitators...

EVEN WITH HIS FACE **HIDDEN**, IT WAS CLEAR HIS **BLOOD** WAS **BOILING**.

AT RATTLER HILL WE HAD TO WEAVE PAST **NEWS CREWS** FROM THE LOCAL **TELEVISION STATIONS**.

JEROME RADLER HILL MEMORIAL HOSPITAL FOR NEGROES

THEY WEREN'T BEING ALLOWED **INSIDE**, BUT THAT WASN'T STOPPING THEM FROM ANGLING FOR DRAMATIC FOOTAGE IN THE **PARKING LOT**.

WE SQUEEZED INTO A LOBBY THAT WAS **PACKED** WITH **FRIENDS** AND **RELATIVES** OF THE BOMB VICTIMS.

HARLAND PEPPER WAS A **SIGHT** TO **BEHOLD** AS HE DASHED BACK AND FORTH TENDING TO **FIFTEEN EMOTIONAL CRISES** A MINUTE.

LES STAYED AT HIS DADDY'S **BECK** AND **CALL**. I WAS **IMPRESSED** AT HOW A **PARTYBOY** FROM THE **RHOMBUS** COULD TURN INTO A PERFECT **PREACHER'S KID** AT THE FLICK OF A **SWITCH**.

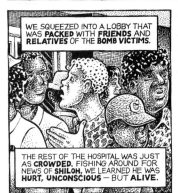

THE REST OF THE HOSPITAL WAS JUST AS **CROWDED**. FISHING AROUND FOR NEWS OF **SHILOH**, WE LEARNED HE WAS **HURT, UNCONSCIOUS** — BUT **ALIVE**.

GINGER NOTICED ANNA DELLYNE COMFORTING A **GAUNT YOUNG WOMAN** IN THE **CORNER**. WE WALKED **OVER**.

GINGER HUGGED LOTTIE AND ANNA DELLYNE AND THE THREE FEMALES WENT INTO AN INTIMATE **WHISPERING** MODE. **I FELT EXTRANEOUS**.

I WANDERED AROUND, WISHING I HAD SOMEBODY TO **TALK** TO.

I SAW PLENTY OF FAMILIAR **FACES** FROM THE **EQUALITY LEAGUE**. THERE WEREN'T **MANY**, HOWEVER, THAT I'D EVER BOTHERED TO STRIKE UP A REAL **FRIENDSHIP** WITH.

IT WAS SHILOH'S WIFE **LOTTIE**, WHOM I'D NEVER **MET**.

IT WAS PROBABLY COMMON **KNOWLEDGE** HOW FAR **GONE** SHE WAS FROM **CANCER**, BUT NOBODY HAD EVER BROUGHT UP THE SUBJECT TO **ME**.

SAMMY GOT **ANTSY** AND **PEELED OFF** FROM THE GROUP. AFTER EXPRESSING MY **CONCERN** TO LOTTIE, I DID, **TOO**.

AND **NOW** SEEMED AN AWKWARD TIME TO SET ABOUT ICE-BREAKING!

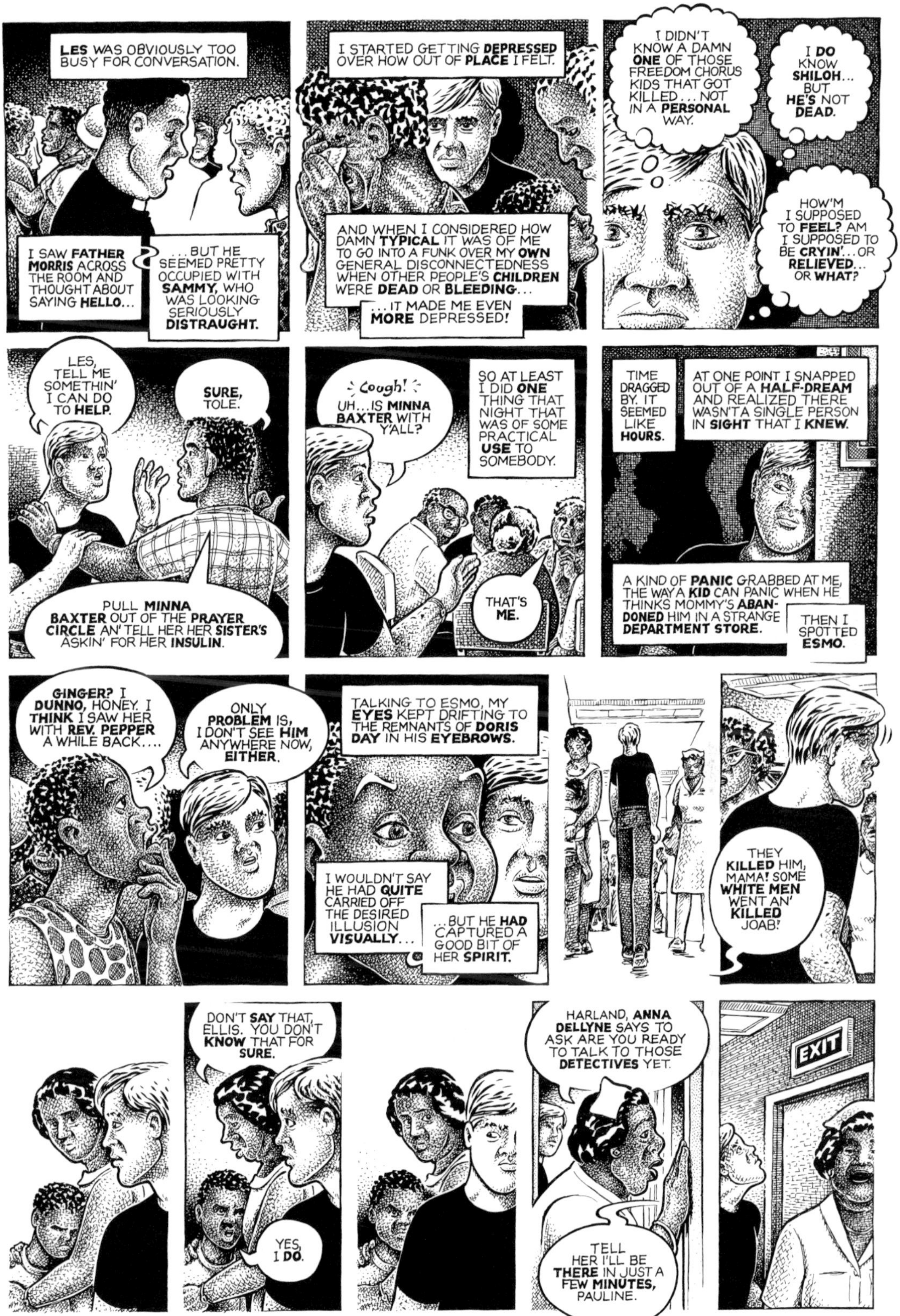
LES WAS OBVIOUSLY TOO BUSY FOR CONVERSATION.
I SAW FATHER MORRIS ACROSS THE ROOM AND THOUGHT ABOUT SAYING HELLO...
...BUT HE SEEMED PRETTY OCCUPIED WITH SAMMY, WHO WAS LOOKING SERIOUSLY DISTRAUGHT.
I STARTED GETTING DEPRESSED OVER HOW OUT OF PLACE I FELT.
AND WHEN I CONSIDERED HOW DAMN TYPICAL IT WAS OF ME TO GO INTO A FUNK OVER MY OWN GENERAL DISCONNECTEDNESS WHEN OTHER PEOPLE'S CHILDREN WERE DEAD OR BLEEDING...
...IT MADE ME EVEN MORE DEPRESSED!
I DIDN'T KNOW A DAMN ONE OF THOSE FREEDOM CHORUS KIDS THAT GOT KILLED... NOT IN A PERSONAL WAY.
I DO KNOW SHILOH... BUT HE'S NOT DEAD.
HOW'M I SUPPOSED TO FEEL? AM I SUPPOSED TO BE CRYIN'... OR RELIEVED... OR WHAT?
LES, TELL ME SOMETHIN' I CAN DO TO HELP.
SURE, TOLE.
PULL MINNA BAXTER OUT OF THE PRAYER CIRCLE AN' TELL HER HER SISTER'S ASKIN' FOR HER INSULIN.
Cough!
UH... IS MINNA BAXTER WITH Y'ALL?
SO AT LEAST I DID ONE THING THAT NIGHT THAT WAS OF SOME PRACTICAL USE TO SOMEBODY.
THAT'S ME.
TIME DRAGGED BY. IT SEEMED LIKE HOURS.
AT ONE POINT I SNAPPED OUT OF A HALF-DREAM AND REALIZED THERE WASN'T A SINGLE PERSON IN SIGHT THAT I KNEW.
A KIND OF PANIC GRABBED AT ME, THE WAY A KID CAN PANIC WHEN HE THINKS MOMMY'S ABANDONED HIM IN A STRANGE DEPARTMENT STORE.
THEN I SPOTTED ESMO.
GINGER? I DUNNO, HONEY. I THINK I SAW HER WITH REV. PEPPER A WHILE BACK....
ONLY PROBLEM IS, I DON'T SEE HIM ANYWHERE NOW, EITHER.
TALKING TO ESMO, MY EYES KEPT DRIFTING TO THE REMNANTS OF DORIS DAY IN HIS EYEBROWS.
I WOULDN'T SAY HE HAD QUITE CARRIED OFF THE DESIRED ILLUSION VISUALLY...
...BUT HE HAD CAPTURED A GOOD BIT OF HER SPIRIT.
THEY KILLED HIM, MAMA! SOME WHITE MEN WENT AN' KILLED JOAB!
DON'T SAY THAT, ELLIS. YOU DON'T KNOW THAT FOR SURE.
YES, I DO.
HARLAND, ANNA DELLYNE SAYS TO ASK ARE YOU READY TO TALK TO THOSE DETECTIVES YET.
TELL HER I'LL BE THERE IN JUST A FEW MINUTES, PAULINE.
EXIT

♪ ...Deep in my heart, I do believe... ♪ ♪ ♪

AS THE **CASKETS** WERE BROUGHT DOWN THE STEEP STONE STEPS, **FAMILIES** FOLLOWED AND THE **SCREAMS** AND **CRYING** GOT **LOUD**.

THEN, ONCE THE **DOORS** ON THE **HEARSES** HAD CLICKED SHUT...

...THE MOURNERS SWAYED AND SANG 'WE SHALL **OVERCOME**.'

BUT NOT **ME**. I COULDN'T GET THE **WORDS** TO **COME**.

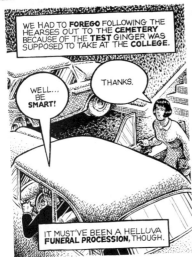

WE HAD TO **FOREGO** FOLLOWING THE HEARSES OUT TO THE **CEMETERY** BECAUSE OF THE **TEST** GINGER WAS SUPPOSED TO TAKE AT THE **COLLEGE**.

WELL... BE **SMART!**

THANKS.

IT MUST'VE BEEN A HELLUVA **FUNERAL PROCESSION,** THOUGH.

AFTER DROPPING GINGER OFF I DROVE BACK TO **GLENN'S GULF & TUNE-UP**.

ARE YA **SURE** YA WANNA SHOW YER FACE IN THERE AGAIN, SLICK?

I THOUGHT THAT GLENN MIGHT HAVE **RECONSIDERED** SINCE OUR **ARGUMENT**.

GLENN—

BE ON YOUR **WAY**, SON. I'M **NOT** LETTIN' **MY BUSINESS** GET BURNED DOWN ON ACCOUNT OF **YOUR** POLITICS.

NO SUCH **LUCK**.

I SAT ON THE BANK OF A NEARBY **CREEK** FOR A WHILE AND TRIED TO **SORT** THINGS **OUT**.

THEN I REALIZED WHERE I NEEDED TO **BE**.

GINGER, MEANWHILE, WASN'T IN THE BEST FRAME OF **MIND** TO BE QUIZZED ABOUT **NATHANIEL HAWTHORNE**.

FINISHED **ALREADY**, MISS RAINES...?

PLOP!

SHE WALKED TO THE CAMPUS **CAFETERIA**.

IT WAS WHERE YOU REFLEXIVELY **WENT** AT THAT TIME OF DAY.

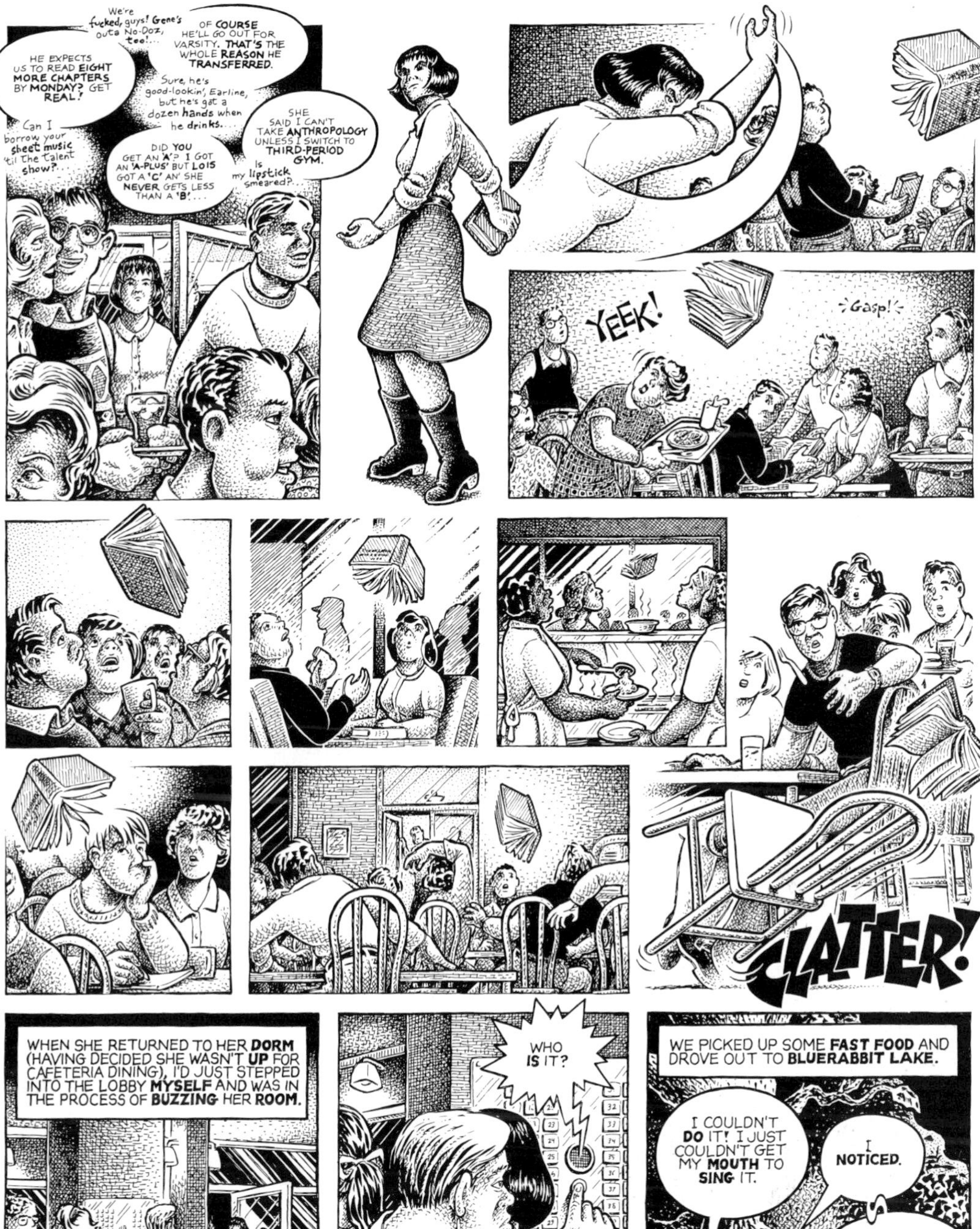
HE EXPECTS US TO READ EIGHT MORE CHAPTERS BY MONDAY? GET REAL!
We're fucked, guys! Gene's outa No-Doz, too!...
OF COURSE HE'LL GO OUT FOR VARSITY. THAT'S THE WHOLE REASON HE TRANSFERRED.
Sure, he's good-lookin', Earline, but he's got a dozen hands when he drinks...
Can I borrow your sheet music 'til the talent show?...
DID YOU GET AN 'A'? I GOT AN 'A-PLUS' BUT LOIS GOT A 'C' AN' SHE NEVER GETS LESS THAN A 'B'...
SHE SAID I CAN'T TAKE ANTHROPOLOGY UNLESS I SWITCH TO THIRD-PERIOD GYM.
Is my lipstick smeared?...
YEEK!
Gasp!
CLATTER!
WHEN SHE RETURNED TO HER DORM (HAVING DECIDED SHE WASN'T UP FOR CAFETERIA DINING), I'D JUST STEPPED INTO THE LOBBY MYSELF AND WAS IN THE PROCESS OF BUZZING HER ROOM.
WHO IS IT?
NEVER MIND, SHARON. FALSE ALARM.
WE PICKED UP SOME FAST FOOD AND DROVE OUT TO BLUERABBIT LAKE.
I COULDN'T DO IT! I JUST COULDN'T GET MY MOUTH TO SING IT.
I NOTICED.
I WONDERED WHAT WAS GOIN' ON INSIDE YOUR HEAD.

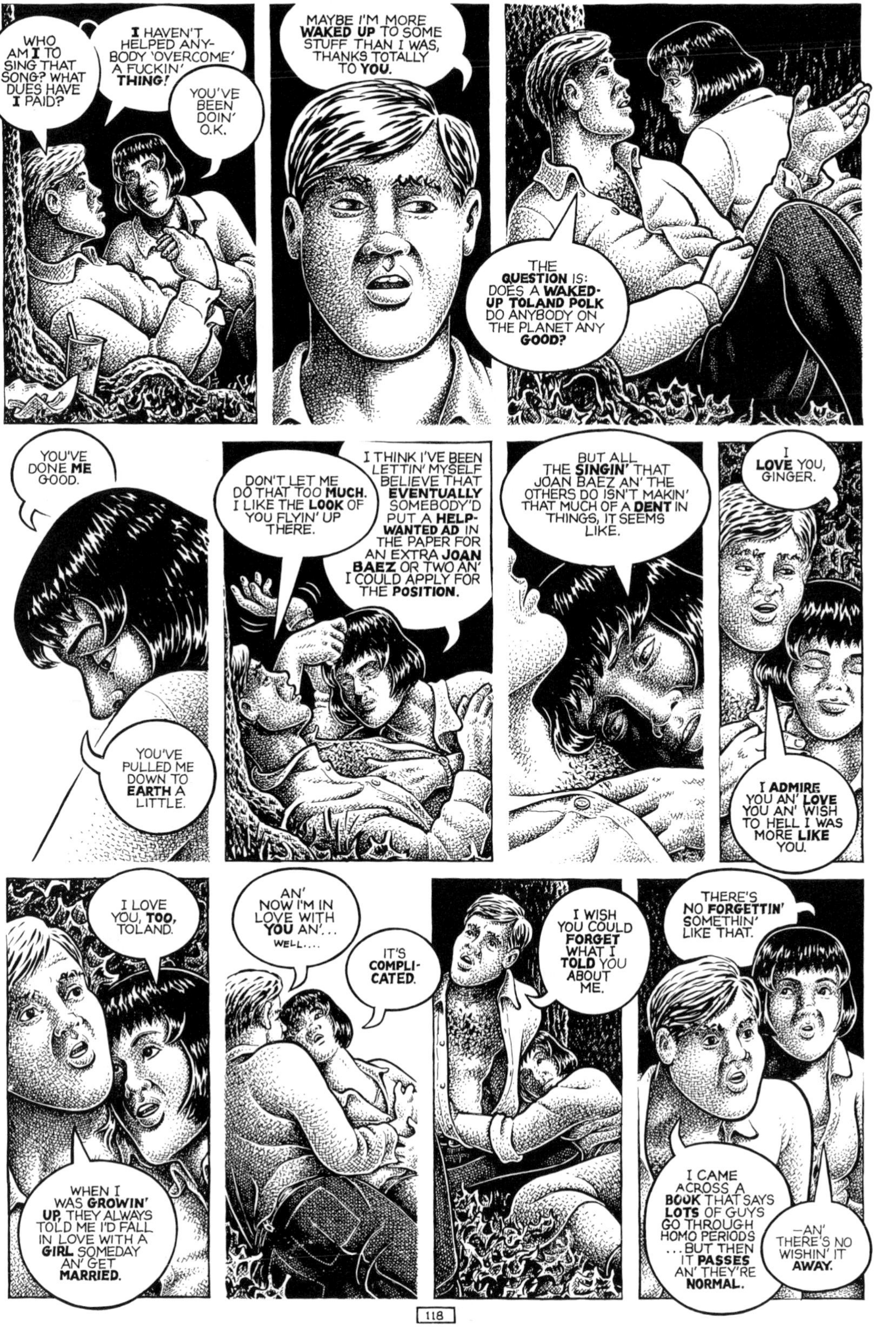

WHO AM I TO SING THAT SONG? WHAT DUES HAVE I PAID?
I HAVEN'T HELPED ANYBODY 'OVERCOME' A FUCKIN' THING!
YOU'VE BEEN DOIN' O.K.
MAYBE I'M MORE WAKED UP TO SOME STUFF THAN I WAS, THANKS TOTALLY TO YOU.
THE QUESTION IS: DOES A WAKED-UP TOLAND POLK DO ANYBODY ON THE PLANET ANY GOOD?
YOU'VE DONE ME GOOD.
YOU'VE PULLED ME DOWN TO EARTH A LITTLE.
DON'T LET ME DO THAT TOO MUCH. I LIKE THE LOOK OF YOU FLYIN' UP THERE.
I THINK I'VE BEEN LETTIN' MYSELF BELIEVE THAT EVENTUALLY SOMEBODY'D PUT A HELP-WANTED AD IN THE PAPER FOR AN EXTRA JOAN BAEZ OR TWO AN' I COULD APPLY FOR THE POSITION.
BUT ALL THE SINGIN' THAT JOAN BAEZ AN' THE OTHERS DO ISN'T MAKIN' THAT MUCH OF A DENT IN THINGS, IT SEEMS LIKE.
I LOVE YOU, GINGER.
I ADMIRE YOU AN' LOVE YOU AN' WISH TO HELL I WAS MORE LIKE YOU.
I LOVE YOU, TOO, TOLAND.
WHEN I WAS GROWIN' UP, THEY ALWAYS TOLD ME I'D FALL IN LOVE WITH A GIRL SOMEDAY AN' GET MARRIED.
AN' NOW I'M IN LOVE WITH YOU AN'... WELL....
IT'S COMPLICATED.
I WISH YOU COULD FORGET WHAT I TOLD YOU ABOUT ME.
THERE'S NO FORGETTIN' SOMETHIN' LIKE THAT.
I CAME ACROSS A BOOK THAT SAYS LOTS OF GUYS GO THROUGH HOMO PERIODS ...BUT THEN IT PASSES AN' THEY'RE NORMAL.
—AN' THERE'S NO WISHIN' IT AWAY.

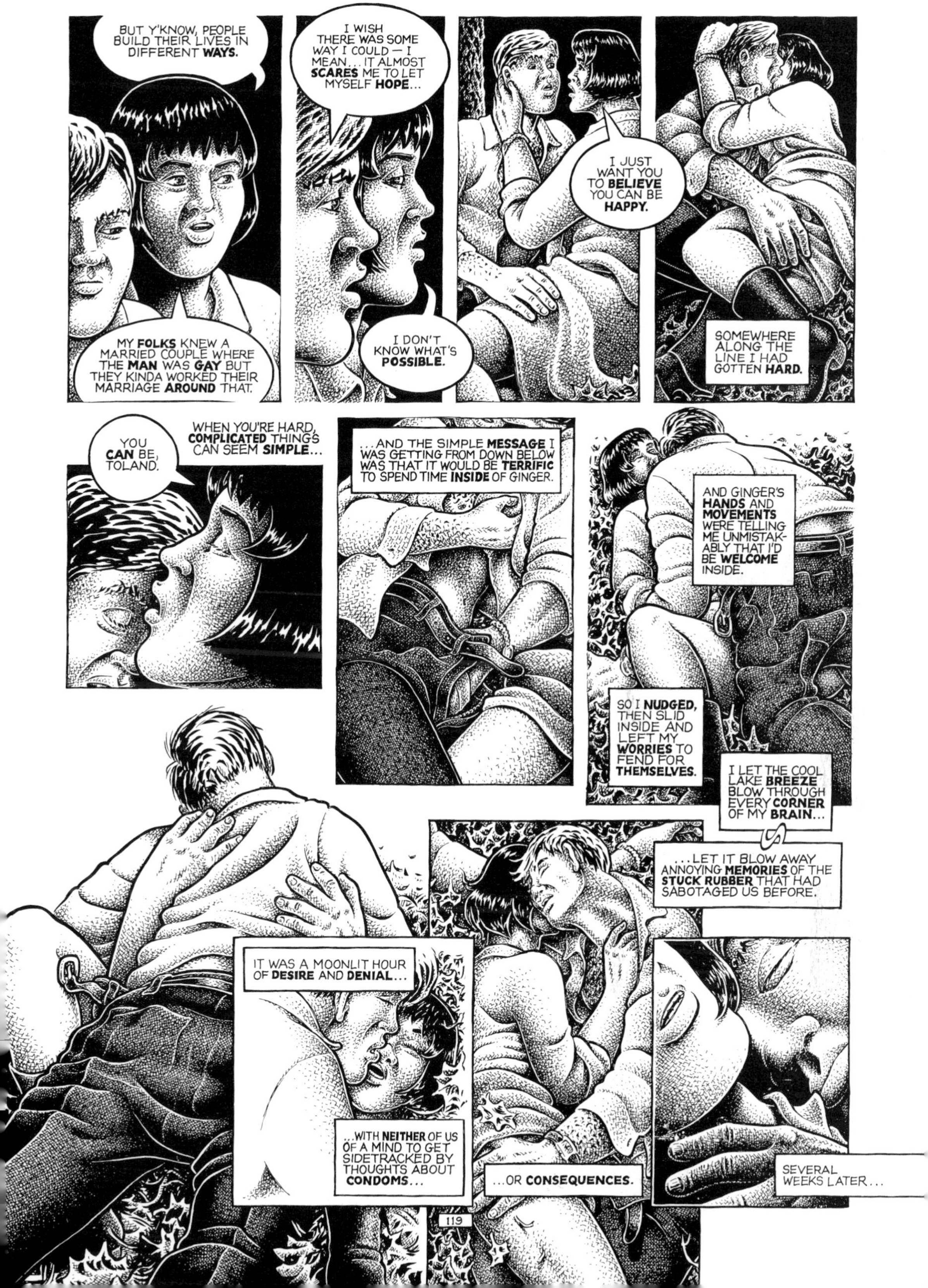

BUT Y'KNOW, PEOPLE BUILD THEIR LIVES IN DIFFERENT WAYS.
MY FOLKS KNEW A MARRIED COUPLE WHERE THE MAN WAS GAY BUT THEY KINDA WORKED THEIR MARRIAGE AROUND THAT.
I WISH THERE WAS SOME WAY I COULD — I MEAN... IT ALMOST SCARES ME TO LET MYSELF HOPE...
I DON'T KNOW WHAT'S POSSIBLE.
I JUST WANT YOU TO BELIEVE YOU CAN BE HAPPY.
SOMEWHERE ALONG THE LINE I HAD GOTTEN HARD.
YOU CAN BE, TOLAND.
WHEN YOU'RE HARD, COMPLICATED THINGS CAN SEEM SIMPLE...
...AND THE SIMPLE MESSAGE I WAS GETTING FROM DOWN BELOW WAS THAT IT WOULD BE TERRIFIC TO SPEND TIME INSIDE OF GINGER.
AND GINGER'S HANDS AND MOVEMENTS WERE TELLING ME UNMISTAKABLY THAT I'D BE WELCOME INSIDE.
SO I NUDGED, THEN SLID INSIDE AND LEFT MY WORRIES TO FEND FOR THEMSELVES.
I LET THE COOL LAKE BREEZE BLOW THROUGH EVERY CORNER OF MY BRAIN...
...LET IT BLOW AWAY ANNOYING MEMORIES OF THE STUCK RUBBER THAT HAD SABOTAGED US BEFORE.
IT WAS A MOONLIT HOUR OF DESIRE AND DENIAL...
...WITH NEITHER OF US OF A MIND TO GET SIDETRACKED BY THOUGHTS ABOUT CONDOMS...
...OR CONSEQUENCES.
SEVERAL WEEKS LATER...

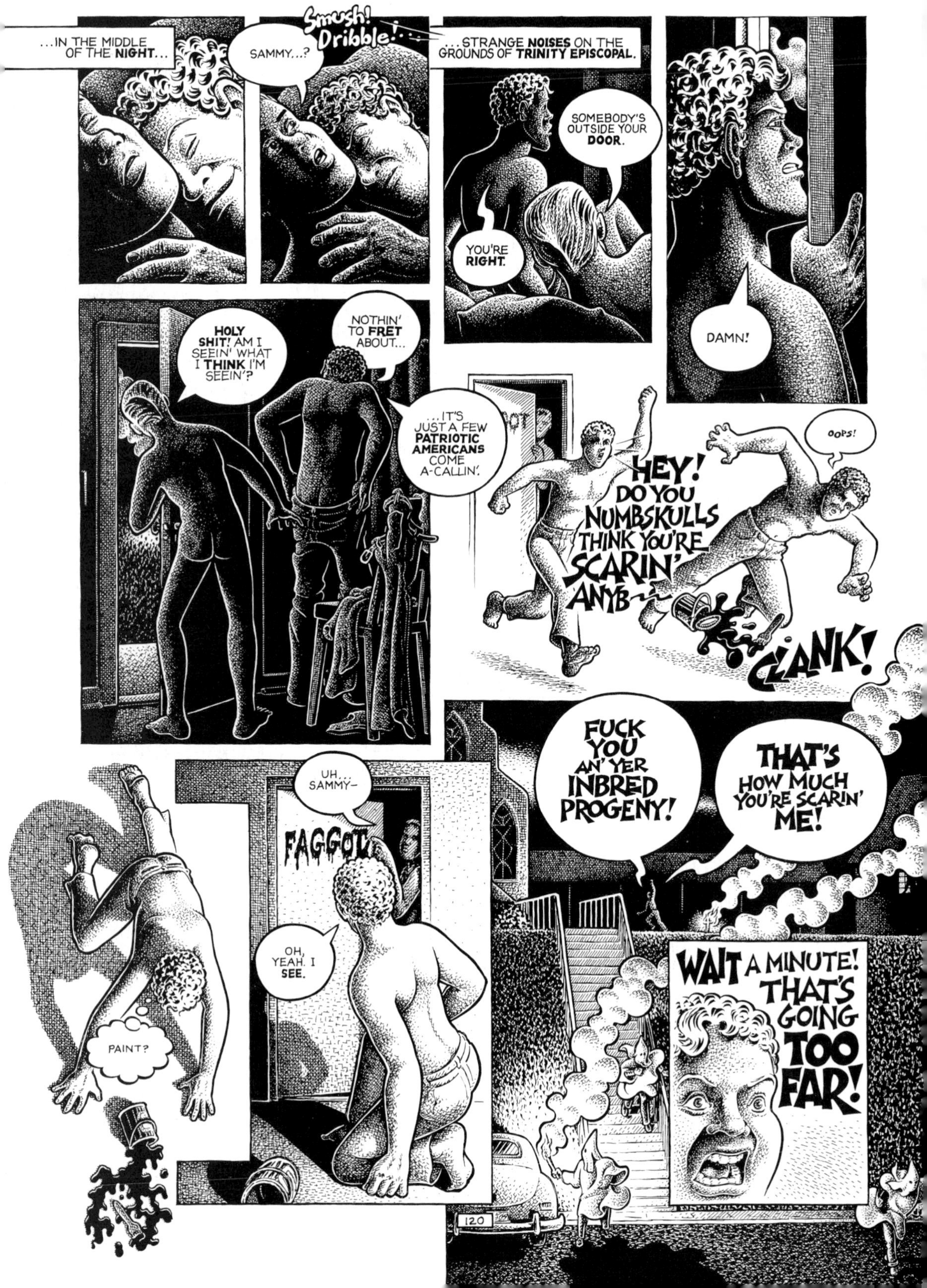
...IN THE MIDDLE OF THE NIGHT...
SAMMY...?
Smush! Dribble!
...STRANGE NOISES ON THE GROUNDS OF TRINITY EPISCOPAL.
SOMEBODY'S OUTSIDE YOUR DOOR.
YOU'RE RIGHT.
DAMN!
HOLY SHIT! AM I SEEIN' WHAT I THINK I'M SEEIN'?
NOTHIN' TO FRET ABOUT...
...IT'S JUST A FEW PATRIOTIC AMERICANS COME A-CALLIN'.
HEY! DO YOU NUMBSKULLS THINK YOU'RE SCARIN' ANYB
OOPS!
CLANK!
PAINT?
UH... SAMMY—
FAGGOT
OH, YEAH. I SEE.
FUCK YOU AN' YER INBRED PROGENY!
THAT'S HOW MUCH YOU'RE SCARIN' ME!
WAIT A MINUTE! THAT'S GOING TOO FAR!

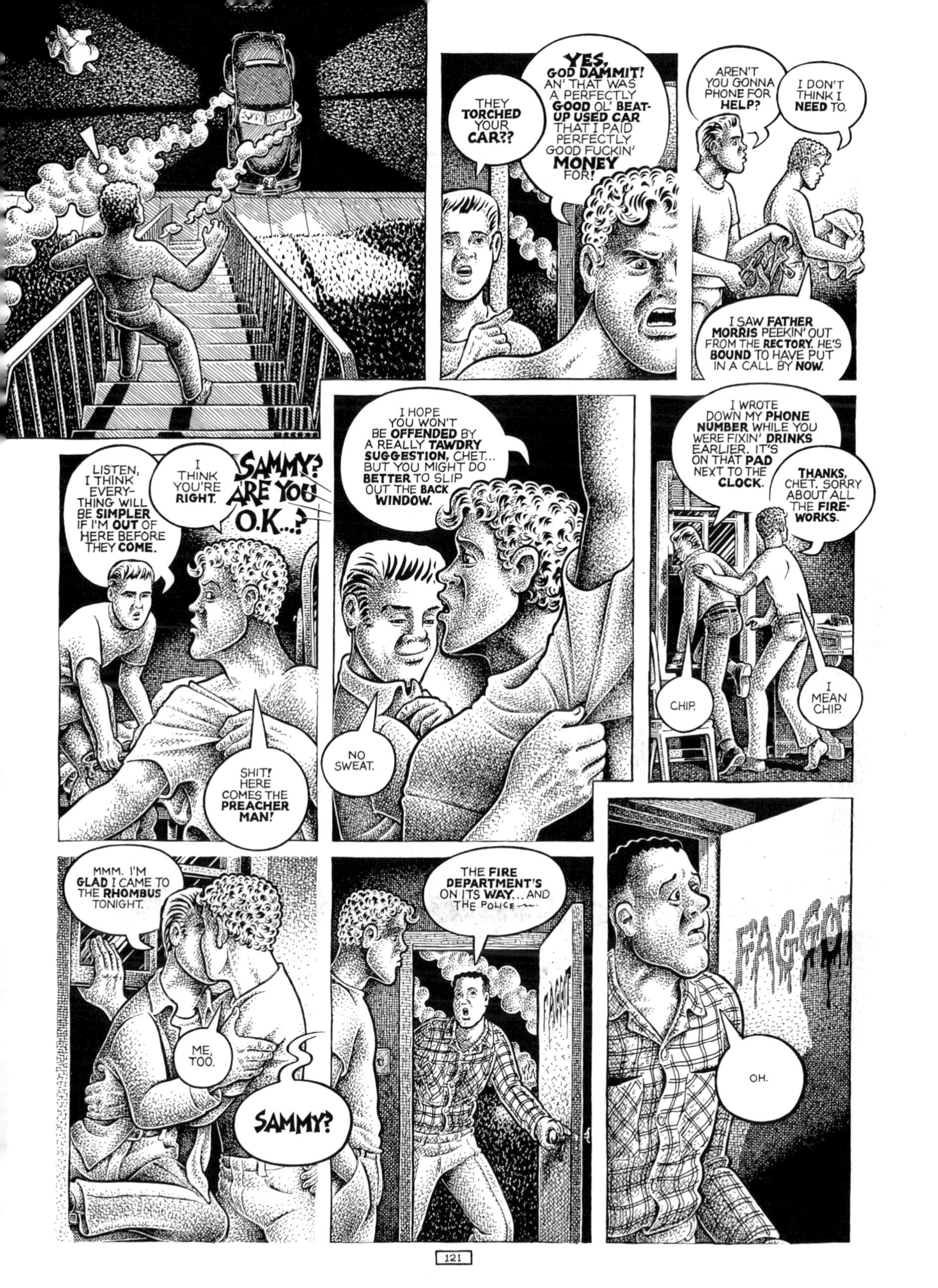
!
THEY TORCHED YOUR CAR??
YES, GOD DAMMIT! AN' THAT WAS A PERFECTLY GOOD OL' BEAT-UP USED CAR THAT I PAID PERFECTLY GOOD FUCKIN' MONEY FOR!
AREN'T YOU GONNA PHONE FOR HELP?
I DON'T THINK I NEED TO.
I SAW FATHER MORRIS PEEKIN' OUT FROM THE RECTORY. HE'S BOUND TO HAVE PUT IN A CALL BY NOW.
LISTEN, I THINK EVERY-THING WILL BE SIMPLER IF I'M OUT OF HERE BEFORE THEY COME.
I THINK YOU'RE RIGHT.
SAMMY? ARE YOU O.K...?
SHIT! HERE COMES THE PREACHER MAN!
I HOPE YOU WON'T BE OFFENDED BY A REALLY TAWDRY SUGGESTION, CHET... BUT YOU MIGHT DO BETTER TO SLIP OUT THE BACK WINDOW.
NO SWEAT.
I WROTE DOWN MY PHONE NUMBER WHILE YOU WERE FIXIN' DRINKS EARLIER. IT'S ON THAT PAD NEXT TO THE CLOCK.
THANKS, CHET. SORRY ABOUT ALL THE FIRE-WORKS.
CHIP.
I MEAN CHIP.
MMM. I'M GLAD I CAME TO THE RHOMBUS TONIGHT.
ME, TOO.
SAMMY?
THE FIRE DEPARTMENT'S ON ITS WAY... AND THE POLICE—
FAGGOT
OH.

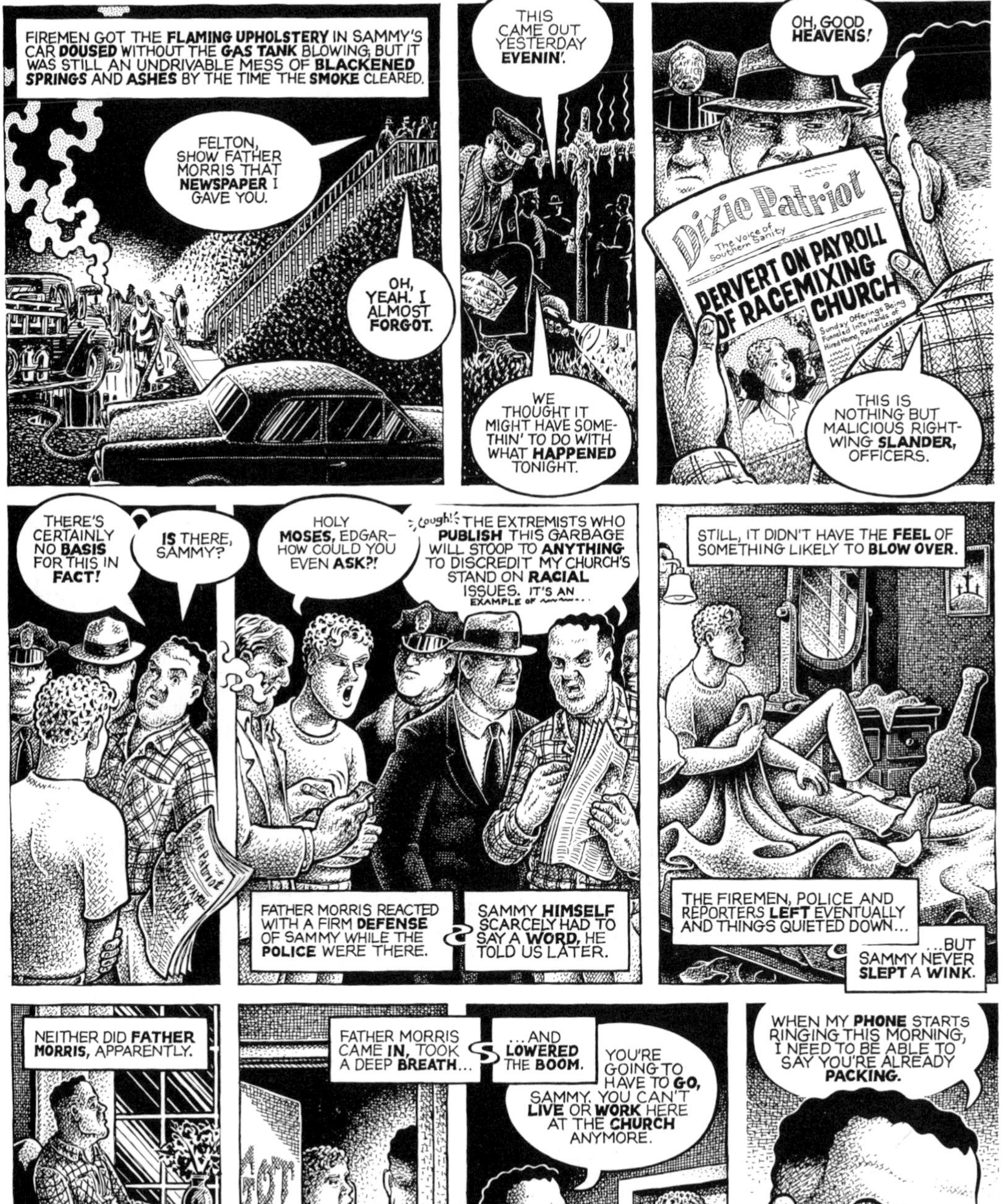
FIREMEN GOT THE **FLAMING UPHOLSTERY** IN SAMMY'S CAR **DOUSED** WITHOUT THE **GAS TANK** BLOWING, BUT IT WAS STILL AN UNDRIVABLE MESS OF **BLACKENED SPRINGS** AND **ASHES** BY THE TIME THE **SMOKE** CLEARED.
FELTON, SHOW FATHER MORRIS THAT **NEWSPAPER** I GAVE YOU.
OH, YEAH. I ALMOST **FORGOT**.
THIS CAME OUT YESTERDAY **EVENIN'**.
WE THOUGHT IT MIGHT HAVE SOMETHIN' TO DO WITH WHAT **HAPPENED** TONIGHT.
OH, GOOD **HEAVENS!**
Dixie Patriot
The Voice of Southern Sanity
PERVERT ON PAYROLL OF RACEMIXING CHURCH
THIS IS NOTHING BUT MALICIOUS RIGHT-WING **SLANDER,** OFFICERS.
THERE'S CERTAINLY NO **BASIS** FOR THIS IN **FACT!**
IS THERE, SAMMY?
HOLY **MOSES,** EDGAR– HOW COULD YOU EVEN **ASK?!**
cough!
THE EXTREMISTS WHO **PUBLISH** THIS GARBAGE WILL STOOP TO **ANYTHING** TO DISCREDIT MY CHURCH'S STAND ON **RACIAL** ISSUES. IT'S AN EXAMPLE OF
FATHER MORRIS REACTED WITH A FIRM **DEFENSE** OF SAMMY WHILE THE **POLICE** WERE THERE.
SAMMY **HIMSELF** SCARCELY HAD TO SAY A **WORD,** HE TOLD US LATER.
STILL, IT DIDN'T HAVE THE **FEEL** OF SOMETHING LIKELY TO **BLOW OVER.**
THE FIREMEN, POLICE AND REPORTERS **LEFT** EVENTUALLY AND THINGS QUIETED DOWN...
...BUT SAMMY NEVER **SLEPT** A **WINK.**
NEITHER DID **FATHER MORRIS**, APPARENTLY.
AROUND **DAWN** HE SHOWED BACK UP AT SAMMY'S **DOOR.**
SAMMY! WAKE **UP!** LET ME **IN!**
Knock, Knock!
WHO'S **SLEEPIN'?**
FATHER MORRIS CAME **IN,** TOOK A DEEP **BREATH**...
...AND **LOWERED** THE **BOOM.**
YOU'RE GOING TO HAVE TO **GO,** SAMMY. YOU CAN'T **LIVE** OR **WORK** HERE AT THE **CHURCH** ANYMORE.
WHEN MY **PHONE** STARTS RINGING THIS MORNING, I NEED TO BE ABLE TO SAY YOU'RE ALREADY **PACKING.**

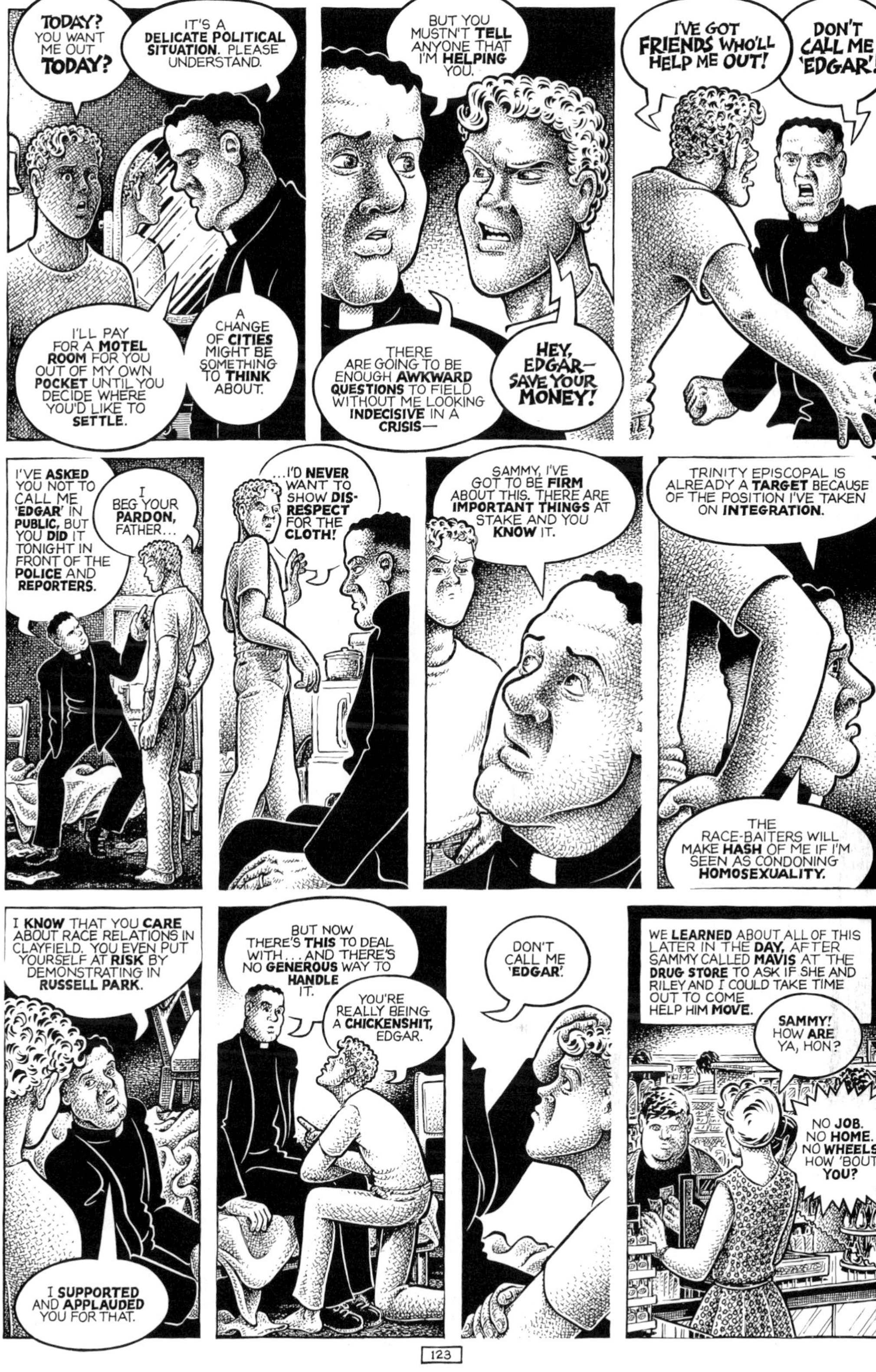
TODAY? YOU WANT ME OUT TODAY?
IT'S A DELICATE POLITICAL SITUATION. PLEASE UNDERSTAND.
I'LL PAY FOR A MOTEL ROOM FOR YOU OUT OF MY OWN POCKET UNTIL YOU DECIDE WHERE YOU'D LIKE TO SETTLE.
A CHANGE OF CITIES MIGHT BE SOMETHING TO THINK ABOUT.
BUT YOU MUSTN'T TELL ANYONE THAT I'M HELPING YOU.
THERE ARE GOING TO BE ENOUGH AWKWARD QUESTIONS TO FIELD WITHOUT ME LOOKING INDECISIVE IN A CRISIS—
HEY, EDGAR— SAVE YOUR MONEY!
I'VE GOT FRIENDS WHO'LL HELP ME OUT!
DON'T CALL ME 'EDGAR'!
I'VE ASKED YOU NOT TO CALL ME 'EDGAR' IN PUBLIC, BUT YOU DID IT TONIGHT IN FRONT OF THE POLICE AND REPORTERS.
I BEG YOUR PARDON, FATHER...
...I'D NEVER WANT TO SHOW DIS-RESPECT FOR THE CLOTH!
SAMMY, I'VE GOT TO BE FIRM ABOUT THIS. THERE ARE IMPORTANT THINGS AT STAKE AND YOU KNOW IT.
TRINITY EPISCOPAL IS ALREADY A TARGET BECAUSE OF THE POSITION I'VE TAKEN ON INTEGRATION.
THE RACE-BAITERS WILL MAKE HASH OF ME IF I'M SEEN AS CONDONING HOMOSEXUALITY.
I KNOW THAT YOU CARE ABOUT RACE RELATIONS IN CLAYFIELD. YOU EVEN PUT YOURSELF AT RISK BY DEMONSTRATING IN RUSSELL PARK.
I SUPPORTED AND APPLAUDED YOU FOR THAT.
BUT NOW THERE'S THIS TO DEAL WITH... AND THERE'S NO GENEROUS WAY TO HANDLE IT.
YOU'RE REALLY BEING A CHICKENSHIT, EDGAR.
DON'T CALL ME 'EDGAR'.
WE LEARNED ABOUT ALL OF THIS LATER IN THE DAY, AFTER SAMMY CALLED MAVIS AT THE DRUG STORE TO ASK IF SHE AND RILEY AND I COULD TAKE TIME OUT TO COME HELP HIM MOVE.
SAMMY! HOW ARE YA, HON?
NO JOB. NO HOME. NO WHEELS. HOW 'BOUT YOU?

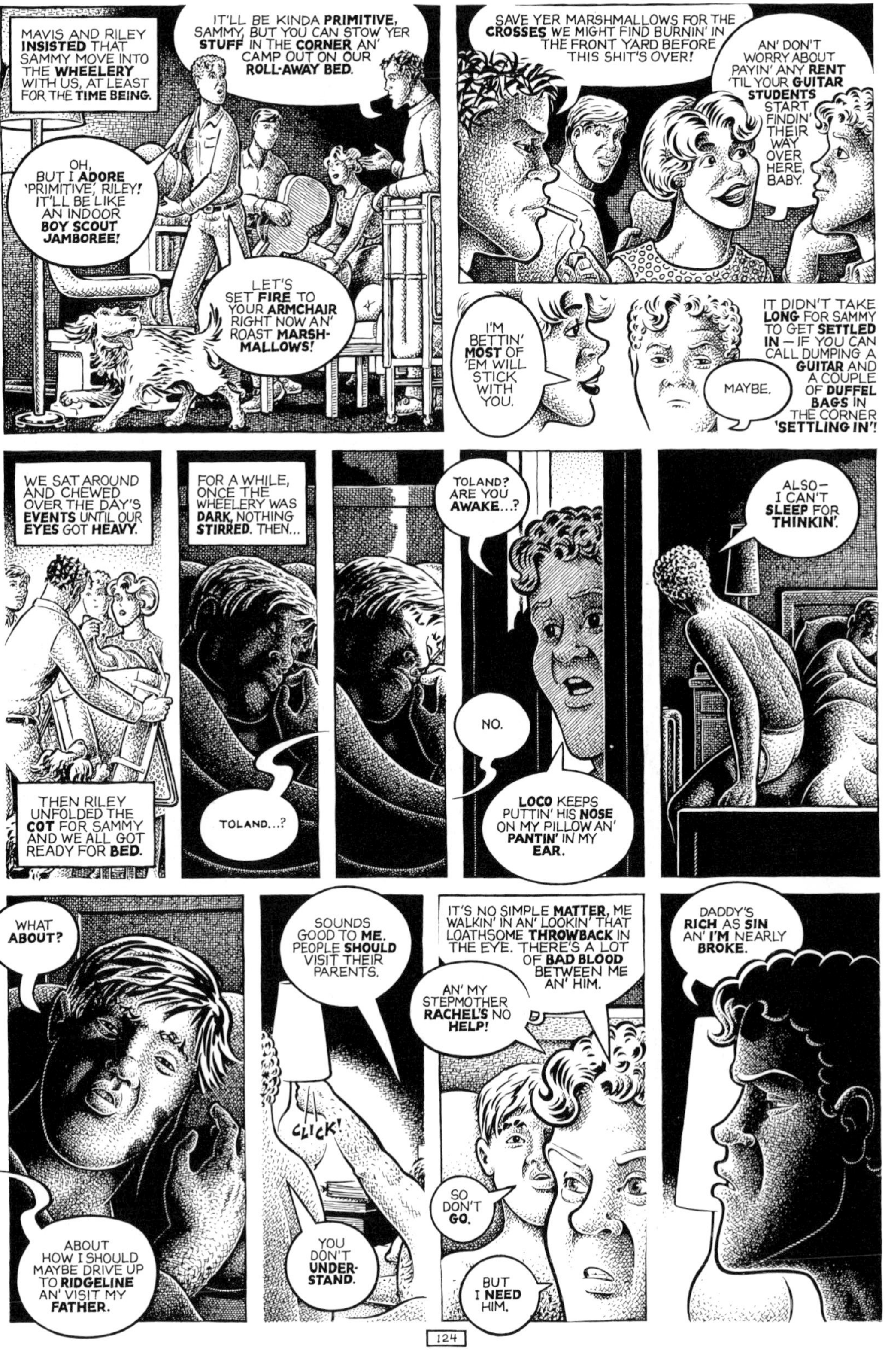
MAVIS AND RILEY **INSISTED** THAT SAMMY MOVE INTO THE **WHEELERY** WITH US, AT LEAST FOR THE **TIME BEING**.
IT'LL BE KINDA **PRIMITIVE**, SAMMY, BUT YOU CAN STOW YER **STUFF** IN THE **CORNER** AN' CAMP OUT ON OUR **ROLL-AWAY BED**.
OH, BUT I **ADORE** 'PRIMITIVE', RILEY! IT'LL BE LIKE AN INDOOR **BOY SCOUT JAMBOREE!**
LET'S SET **FIRE** TO YOUR **ARMCHAIR** RIGHT NOW AN' ROAST **MARSH-MALLOWS!**
SAVE YER MARSHMALLOWS FOR THE **CROSSES** WE MIGHT FIND BURNIN' IN THE FRONT YARD BEFORE THIS SHIT'S OVER!
AN' DON'T WORRY ABOUT PAYIN' ANY **RENT** 'TIL YOUR **GUITAR STUDENTS** START FINDIN' THEIR WAY OVER HERE, BABY.
I'M BETTIN' **MOST** OF 'EM WILL STICK WITH YOU.
MAYBE.
IT DIDN'T TAKE **LONG** FOR SAMMY TO GET **SETTLED IN** — IF *YOU* CAN CALL DUMPING A **GUITAR** AND A COUPLE OF **DUFFEL BAGS** IN THE CORNER **'SETTLING IN'**!
WE SAT AROUND AND CHEWED OVER THE DAY'S **EVENTS** UNTIL OUR **EYES** GOT **HEAVY**.
THEN RILEY UNFOLDED THE **COT** FOR SAMMY AND WE ALL GOT READY FOR **BED**.
FOR A WHILE, ONCE THE WHEELERY WAS **DARK**, NOTHING **STIRRED**. THEN...
TOLAND...?
TOLAND? ARE YOU **AWAKE**...?
NO.
LOCO KEEPS PUTTIN' HIS **NOSE** ON MY PILLOW AN' **PANTIN'** IN MY **EAR**.
ALSO— I CAN'T **SLEEP** FOR **THINKIN'**.
WHAT **ABOUT?**
ABOUT HOW I SHOULD MAYBE DRIVE UP TO **RIDGELINE** AN' VISIT MY **FATHER**.
SOUNDS GOOD TO **ME**. PEOPLE **SHOULD** VISIT THEIR PARENTS.
CLICK!
YOU DON'T **UNDER-STAND**.
IT'S NO SIMPLE **MATTER**, ME WALKIN' IN AN' LOOKIN' THAT LOATHSOME **THROWBACK** IN THE EYE. THERE'S A LOT OF **BAD BLOOD** BETWEEN ME AN' HIM.
AN' MY STEPMOTHER **RACHEL'S** NO **HELP!**
SO DON'T **GO**.
BUT I **NEED** HIM.
DADDY'S **RICH** AS **SIN** AN' **I'M** NEARLY **BROKE**.

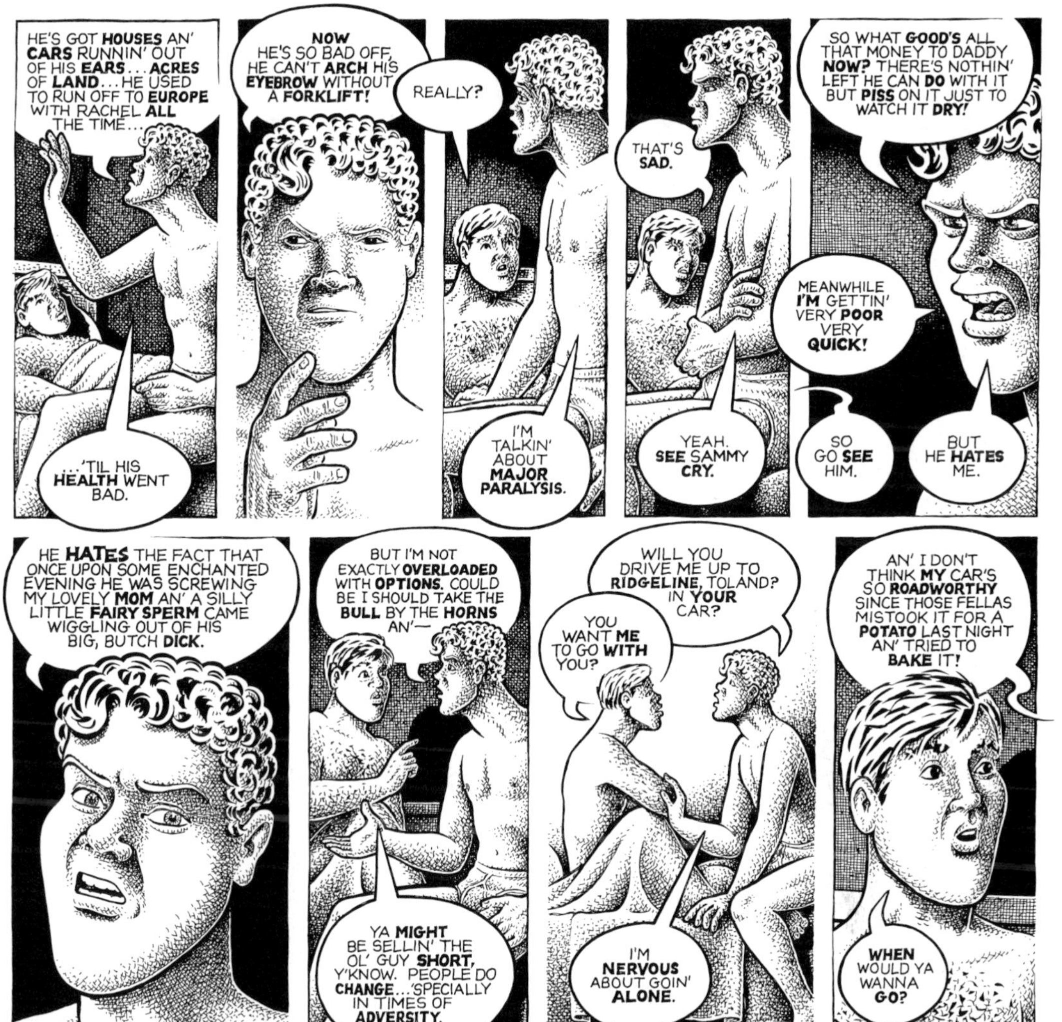
HE'S GOT HOUSES AN' CARS RUNNIN' OUT OF HIS EARS... ACRES OF LAND... HE USED TO RUN OFF TO EUROPE WITH RACHEL ALL THE TIME...
...'TIL HIS HEALTH WENT BAD.
NOW HE'S SO BAD OFF, HE CAN'T ARCH HIS EYEBROW WITHOUT A FORKLIFT!
REALLY?
I'M TALKIN' ABOUT MAJOR PARALYSIS.
THAT'S SAD.
YEAH. SEE SAMMY CRY.
SO WHAT GOOD'S ALL THAT MONEY TO DADDY NOW? THERE'S NOTHIN' LEFT HE CAN DO WITH IT BUT PISS ON IT JUST TO WATCH IT DRY!
MEANWHILE I'M GETTIN' VERY POOR VERY QUICK!
SO GO SEE HIM.
BUT HE HATES ME.
HE HATES THE FACT THAT ONCE UPON SOME ENCHANTED EVENING HE WAS SCREWING MY LOVELY MOM AN' A SILLY LITTLE FAIRY SPERM CAME WIGGLING OUT OF HIS BIG, BUTCH DICK.
BUT I'M NOT EXACTLY OVERLOADED WITH OPTIONS. COULD BE I SHOULD TAKE THE BULL BY THE HORNS AN'—
YA MIGHT BE SELLIN' THE OL' GUY SHORT, Y'KNOW. PEOPLE DO CHANGE...'SPECIALLY IN TIMES OF ADVERSITY.
WILL YOU DRIVE ME UP TO RIDGELINE, TOLAND? IN YOUR CAR?
YOU WANT ME TO GO WITH YOU?
I'M NERVOUS ABOUT GOIN' ALONE.
AN' I DON'T THINK MY CAR'S SO ROADWORTHY SINCE THOSE FELLAS MISTOOK IT FOR A POTATO LAST NIGHT AN' TRIED TO BAKE IT!
WHEN WOULD YA WANNA GO?
I'M NOT SURE. IT'LL TAKE ME A LITTLE WHILE TO BUILD UP MY NERVE.
BUT WE'LL MAKE IT A WEEK-END, FOR SURE, SO IT WON'T INTERFERE WITH YOUR JOB.
WHAT JOB?
OOPS! I KEEP FORGETTIN' YOU'VE SEVERED YOUR TIES WITH THE PETROLEUM INDUSTRY!
HEY, WE'RE BOTH OUT OF WORK AT THE SAME TIME. LET'S START A CLUB!
SERIOUSLY, KID... HOW MUCH OF A BIND DOES IT PUT YOU IN?
OH, I'M O.K. FOR A WHILE....
I'VE STILL GOT SOME SAVINGS FROM MY FOLKS' INSURANCE AN' FROM SELLIN' MELANIE AN' ORLEY MY SHARE OF THE HOUSE.
BUT IF YOU POSTPONE YOUR LI'L FAMILY REUNION TOO LONG, I MIGHT HAFTA TAKE SOME JOB THAT'D KEEP ME FROM—
IT'LL BE SOON. I'VE JUST GOTTA WORK ON WHAT TO SAY.

I'M **SCARED**, TOLAND. I DON'T KNOW WHAT'S GONNA **HAPPEN** TO ME.

I'VE ALWAYS TAKEN **PRIDE** IN MY **CHECKERED HISTORY**, BUT I'VE NEVER GOTTEN MYSELF BRANDED A **PERVERT** ON THE FRONT PAGE OF A **NEWSPAPER** BEFORE!

WHERE'D THAT PHOTO OF YOU **COME** FROM, ANYWAY?

THE **RUSSELL PARK SIT-IN**, AS FAR AS I CAN **TELL**.

MAVIS SAYS I SHOULD POP INTO THE DIXIE PATRIOT **OFFICE** AN' ASK IF THEY'LL SELL ME SOME **EXTRA PRINTS** OF THE PHOTO FOR MY **RELATIVES**!

THE **CLAYFIELD BANNER** IS **ALWAYS** WILLIN' TO DO THAT, Y'KNOW...

...IF THEY **PRINT** YOUR **PICTURE**, YOU CAN ORDER A **COPY**.

IT'S A REGULAR **SERVICE**.

Chuckle! **THAT'D** BE A SIGHT TO SEE!

I CAN JUST **IMAGINE** THOSE DIXIE PATRIOT WEASELS **QUAKIN'** IN THEIR **BOOTS**, WATCHIN' ONE OF THE LOCAL **UNDESIRABLES** THEY'VE FINGERED COME SAUNTERIN' UP THE **DRIVEWAY**!

LOOK, PAL, I'LL DRIVE YOU TO RIDGELINE IF YOU **NEED** ME TO. IT WON'T BE MUCH TROUBLE.

THANKS, TOLAND. YOU'RE A REAL **FRIEND**.

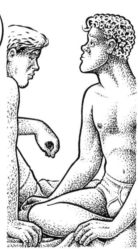

CAN I LIE DOWN **NEXT** TO YOU AN' HOLD **ON** TO YOU FOR JUST A MINUTE?

SAMMY... I WISH YOU WOULDN'T **ASK** THAT.

I'M NOT TALKIN' ABOUT **SEX**.

I JUST WANNA **HOLD ON** TO SOMEBODY FOR **FIVE MINUTES**. I'LL GO AWAY THEN.

THAT'S O.K.— **FORGET** IT.

I JUST REMEMBERED: **LOCO** MIGHT HEAR THE **BEDSPRINGS** CREAKIN' AN' THINK I'M BEIN' **UNFAITHFUL**!

NEVER **TRIFLE** WITH THE AFFECTIONS OF A **CARNIVORE**, IS MY MOTTO!

G'NIGHT.

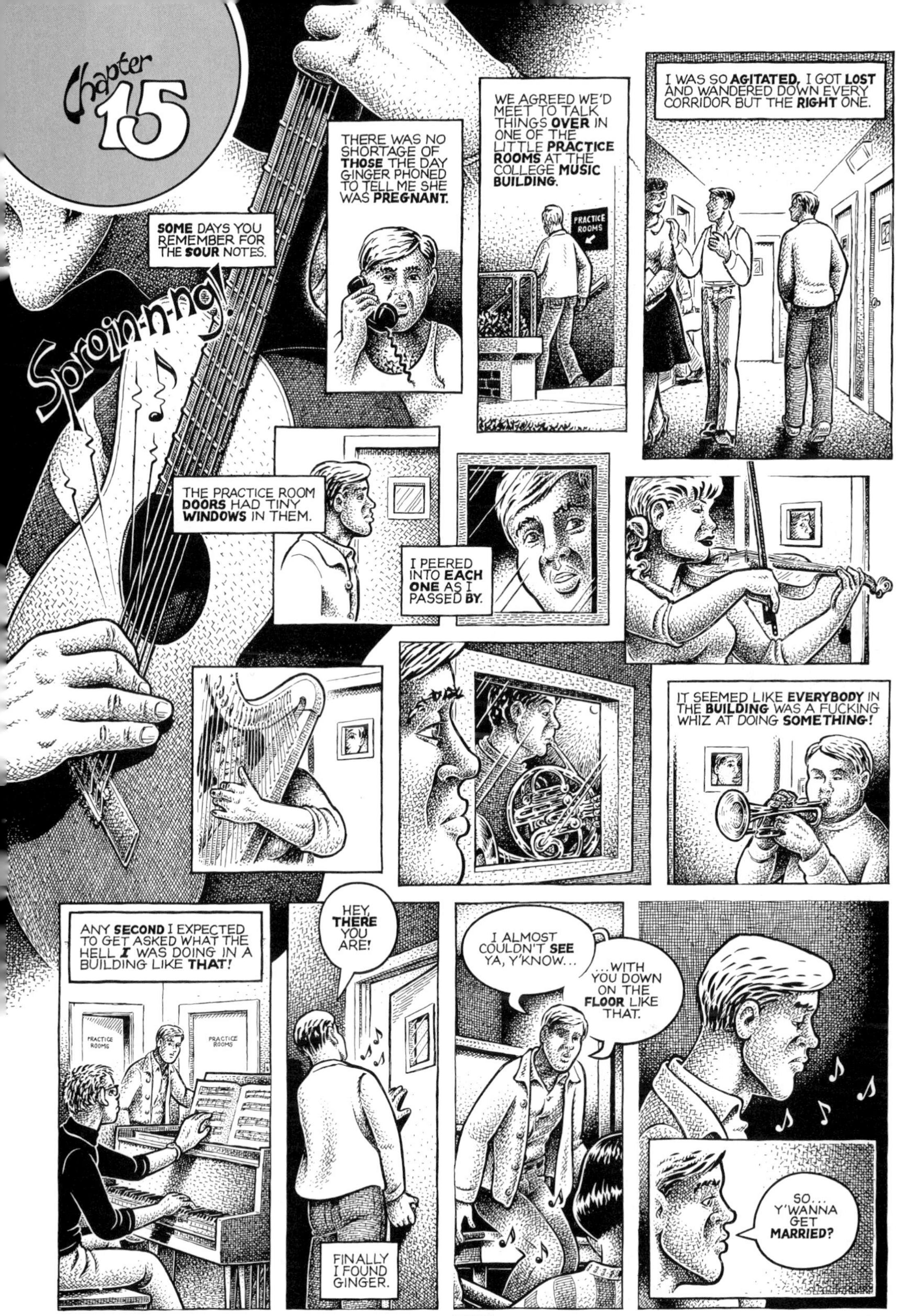
Chapter 15
SOME DAYS YOU REMEMBER FOR THE SOUR NOTES.
Sproin-n-ng!
THERE WAS NO SHORTAGE OF THOSE THE DAY GINGER PHONED TO TELL ME SHE WAS PREGNANT.
WE AGREED WE'D MEET TO TALK THINGS OVER IN ONE OF THE LITTLE PRACTICE ROOMS AT THE COLLEGE MUSIC BUILDING.
PRACTICE ROOMS
I WAS SO AGITATED, I GOT LOST AND WANDERED DOWN EVERY CORRIDOR BUT THE RIGHT ONE.
THE PRACTICE ROOM DOORS HAD TINY WINDOWS IN THEM.
I PEERED INTO EACH ONE AS I PASSED BY.
IT SEEMED LIKE EVERYBODY IN THE BUILDING WAS A FUCKING WHIZ AT DOING SOMETHING!
ANY SECOND I EXPECTED TO GET ASKED WHAT THE HELL I WAS DOING IN A BUILDING LIKE THAT!
PRACTICE ROOMS
PRACTICE ROOMS
HEY, THERE YOU ARE!
FINALLY I FOUND GINGER.
I ALMOST COULDN'T SEE YA, Y'KNOW...
...WITH YOU DOWN ON THE FLOOR LIKE THAT.
SO... Y'WANNA GET MARRIED?

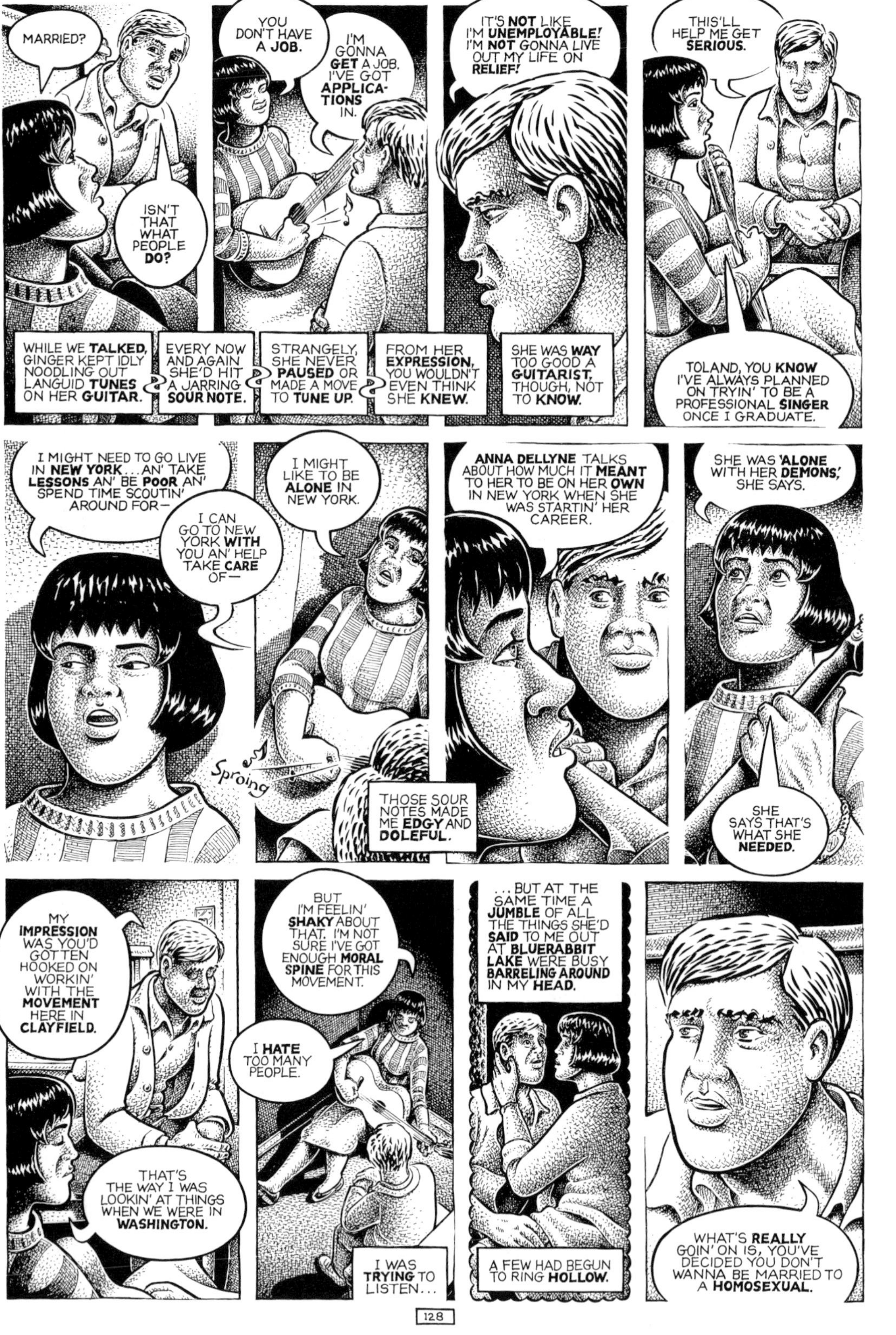

MARRIED?
ISN'T THAT WHAT PEOPLE DO?
YOU DON'T HAVE A JOB.
I'M GONNA GET A JOB. I'VE GOT APPLICATIONS IN.
IT'S NOT LIKE I'M UNEMPLOYABLE! I'M NOT GONNA LIVE OUT MY LIFE ON RELIEF!
THIS'LL HELP ME GET SERIOUS.
WHILE WE TALKED, GINGER KEPT IDLY NOODLING OUT LANGUID TUNES ON HER GUITAR.
EVERY NOW AND AGAIN SHE'D HIT A JARRING SOUR NOTE.
STRANGELY, SHE NEVER PAUSED OR MADE A MOVE TO TUNE UP.
FROM HER EXPRESSION, YOU WOULDN'T EVEN THINK SHE KNEW.
SHE WAS WAY TOO GOOD A GUITARIST, THOUGH, NOT TO KNOW.
TOLAND, YOU KNOW I'VE ALWAYS PLANNED ON TRYIN' TO BE A PROFESSIONAL SINGER ONCE I GRADUATE.
I MIGHT NEED TO GO LIVE IN NEW YORK... AN' TAKE LESSONS AN' BE POOR AN' SPEND TIME SCOUTIN' AROUND FOR—
I CAN GO TO NEW YORK WITH YOU AN' HELP TAKE CARE OF—
I MIGHT LIKE TO BE ALONE IN NEW YORK.
Sproing
THOSE SOUR NOTES MADE ME EDGY AND DOLEFUL.
ANNA DELLYNE TALKS ABOUT HOW MUCH IT MEANT TO HER TO BE ON HER OWN IN NEW YORK WHEN SHE WAS STARTIN' HER CAREER.
SHE WAS 'ALONE WITH HER DEMONS,' SHE SAYS.
SHE SAYS THAT'S WHAT SHE NEEDED.
MY IMPRESSION WAS YOU'D GOTTEN HOOKED ON WORKIN' WITH THE MOVEMENT HERE IN CLAYFIELD.
THAT'S THE WAY I WAS LOOKIN' AT THINGS WHEN WE WERE IN WASHINGTON.
BUT I'M FEELIN' SHAKY ABOUT THAT. I'M NOT SURE I'VE GOT ENOUGH MORAL SPINE FOR THIS MOVEMENT.
I HATE TOO MANY PEOPLE.
I WAS TRYING TO LISTEN...
...BUT AT THE SAME TIME A JUMBLE OF ALL THE THINGS SHE'D SAID TO ME OUT AT BLUERABBIT LAKE WERE BUSY BARRELING AROUND IN MY HEAD.
A FEW HAD BEGUN TO RING HOLLOW.
WHAT'S REALLY GOIN' ON IS, YOU'VE DECIDED YOU DON'T WANNA BE MARRIED TO A HOMOSEXUAL.

TOLAND...

...DO YOU FIND THAT SO **STRANGE**??

SO...LIKE, WHAT AM I SUPPOSED TO **DO**?

WHAT ARE THE **RULES**?

DO I PAY FOR AN **ABORTION**? IS **THAT** WHAT HAPPENS?

ANNA DELLYNE SAYS SHE KNOWS SOMEONE I CAN **TALK** TO... ABOUT THAT.

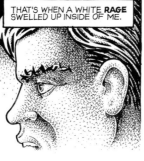

THAT'S WHEN A WHITE **RAGE** SWELLED UP INSIDE OF ME.

SHE'D TALKED IT ALL OVER WITH **ANNA DELLYNE**... ...EVEN **BEFORE** SHE'D SAID ANYTHING TO **ME**!

DO YOU REALLY **WANT** AN ABORTION?

NO.

BUT I WANT MY **LIFE**.

I DON'T WANNA ABORT MY **OWN LIFE**, EITHER.

I DON'T WANNA GET **STUCK**—ALONE OR WITH **YOU**—JUST BARELY SCRAPIN' **BY**... GIVIN' UP ON BEIN' WHO I **WANT** TO BE.

I GOTTA GO **THINK**.

MAYBE IF **YOU** HAD SOMEBODY **YOU** REALLY WANTED TO BE, YOU'D UNDER-STAND.

DRIVING BACK FROM THE WESTHILLS CAMPUS, MY **THOUGHTS** WERE RACING IN EVERY **DIRECTION** AT **ONCE.**

THEN, AS I WAS PASSING **RUSSELL PARK,** I NOTICED **HARLAND PEPPER** STOMPING UP THE STREET TOWARD HIS **CHURCH.**

REV. PEPPER!

DON'T TRY TO **TALK** TO ME **NOW,** TOLAND. I'M **NAIL-SPITTIN'** MAD!

WHAT'S THE **MATTER?**

WE **WON!**

Y'SEE THE CHOPPER'S PRETTY **FENCE** HERE?

ITS DAYS ARE **NUMBERED.**

SO SAID THE **LAW...** AS OF **YESTER-DAY!**

THEN WHY ARE YOU–??...I MEAN, THAT'S **GOOD,** ISN'T IT?

SON, **YOU** KNOW HOW MANY **MONTHS** WE'VE HAD OUR LAWYERS TROOPIN' THROUGH EVERY ROOM OF THE **COURT-HOUSE** SUIN' TO GET THIS FARCICAL **'PARK RENOVATION'** BROUGHT TO AN END.

I'VE LISTENED TO SO MUCH TALK ABOUT **LANDSCAPIN',** I'VE STARTED HAVIN' **DREAMS** ABOUT BULL-DOZERS AN' **BACKHOES!**

SO WE GO THROUGH **FIFTEEN HEARINGS** AN' DO A DANCE WITH **TWO HUNDRED** CITY LAWYERS...

...'TIL WE **FINALLY** GET THE JUDGE TO SAY: NO QUESTION **ABOUT** IT, THE FENCE HAS GOTTA **GO!**

NOW I **ASK** YOU: DO YOU SEE ANY **FENCE** COMIN' DOWN? **I** DON'T! NOR DO I SEE THE FIRST **SIGN** OF ANY **RENOVATION** UNDER WAY.

THE ONLY THING **UNDER WAY** AS WE SPEAK IS MORE **FANCY FOOTWORK** AT CITY HALL! THEY JUST WAVED A **STAY** OF **ENFORCEMENT** AT ME THAT'LL MAKE **SURE** WE DIDDLE AWAY ANOTHER **SIX MONTHS** OR SO PLAYIN' **PING-PONG** WITH **APPEALS!**

I'M TRYIN' TO DO SOMETHIN' ABOUT **RACISM** AN' THEY'VE GOT ME BALLED UP IN GLORIFIED **CHICKEN WIRE!**

IT NEVER **STOPS!** THEY JUST **WEAR YOU DOWN!**

BUT...IT'S ALL **ABSURD!** THEY'RE **STALLIN'!** YOU'LL GET YOUR PARK BACK IN THE **END.**

OH... I **KNOW** WE WILL. I JUST GET SO **FED UP** WITH HAVIN' TO SPEND MY **ENERGY** EVERY DAY THINKIN' ABOUT ALL THIS **CRAP!**

WHEN THE PREACHER HAD GOTTEN ENOUGH OF HIS **FUMING** DONE FOR ME TO DARE CHANGE THE **SUBJECT,** I ASKED HIM IF **ANNA DELLYNE** WAS ANYWHERE AROUND THE CHURCH THAT AFTERNOON.

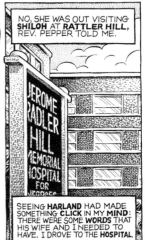

NO, SHE WAS OUT VISITING **SHILOH** AT **RATTLER HILL,** REV. PEPPER TOLD ME.

JEROME RADLER HILL MEMORIAL HOSPITAL FOR NEGROES

SEEING **HARLAND** HAD MADE SOMETHING **CLICK** IN MY **MIND:** THERE WERE SOME **WORDS** THAT HIS WIFE AND I NEEDED TO HAVE. I DROVE TO THE **HOSPITAL.**

WHEN I GOT OFF THE **ELEVATOR** I NOTICED THAT A WHOLE BUNCH OF **NURSES** WERE HOVERING EXCITEDLY AROUND THE DOOR TO **SHILOH'S** ROOM.

THEY **SHUSHED** ME AS I WALKED **OVER** TO THEM.

THEN I SAW **WHY.**

ANNA DELLYNE WAS SITTING ON THE EDGE OF SHILOH'S **BED,** LOVINGLY SINGING ONE OF HER OLD-TIME **SONGS** FOR HIM.

♪ You may try forgetting me, but you will not succeed... Your soul is under lock and key... ♪

HIS **EYES** WERE **CLOSED.** WHO COULD TELL IF HE WAS EVEN **HEARING** HER?

THE AUDIENCE IN THE **DOORWAY,** THOUGH, WAS TOTALLY **RAPT.**

♪ ...And it will not be freed...You'll always be a part of me... ♪

HER VOICE WAS **SOFT.** IT WASN'T LIKE SHE WAS ON A **STAGE...**

...BUT MY **IMAGINATION** GAVE HER A **MICROPHONE** TO SING INTO, AND SHILOH'S **ROOM** TURNED INTO A SMOKY HARLEM **NIGHTSPOT** FROM **DECADES** BEFORE.

WHAT KIND OF A DIFFERENT **LIFE** WOULD I HAVE BEEN LIVING, I WONDERED, IF I COULD'VE **BEEN** THERE, BACK THEN, TO **HEAR** HER?

♪ ...Forever in the heart of me...You may have left me before... ♪

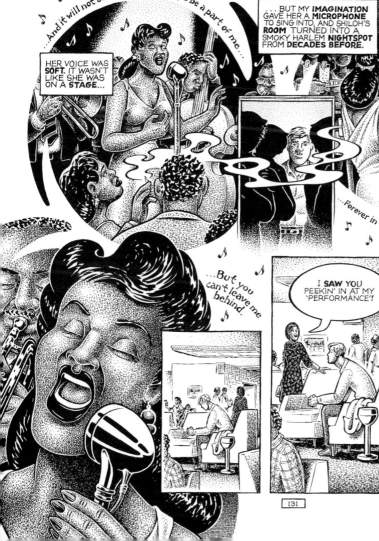

...But you can't leave me behind!

I **SAW** YOU PEEKIN' IN AT MY 'PERFORMANCE'!

I SHOULD GET MYSELF LAID UP IN HERE SOMETIME. MAYBE YOU'LL COME AND SING THOSE OLD SONGS FOR *ME!*

DO ME A **FAVOR** AN' DON'T GET YOUR **HEAD** BASHED IN WITH A **MOTEL WALL** JUST FOR THE PLEASURE OF HEARIN' ME **WAIL!**

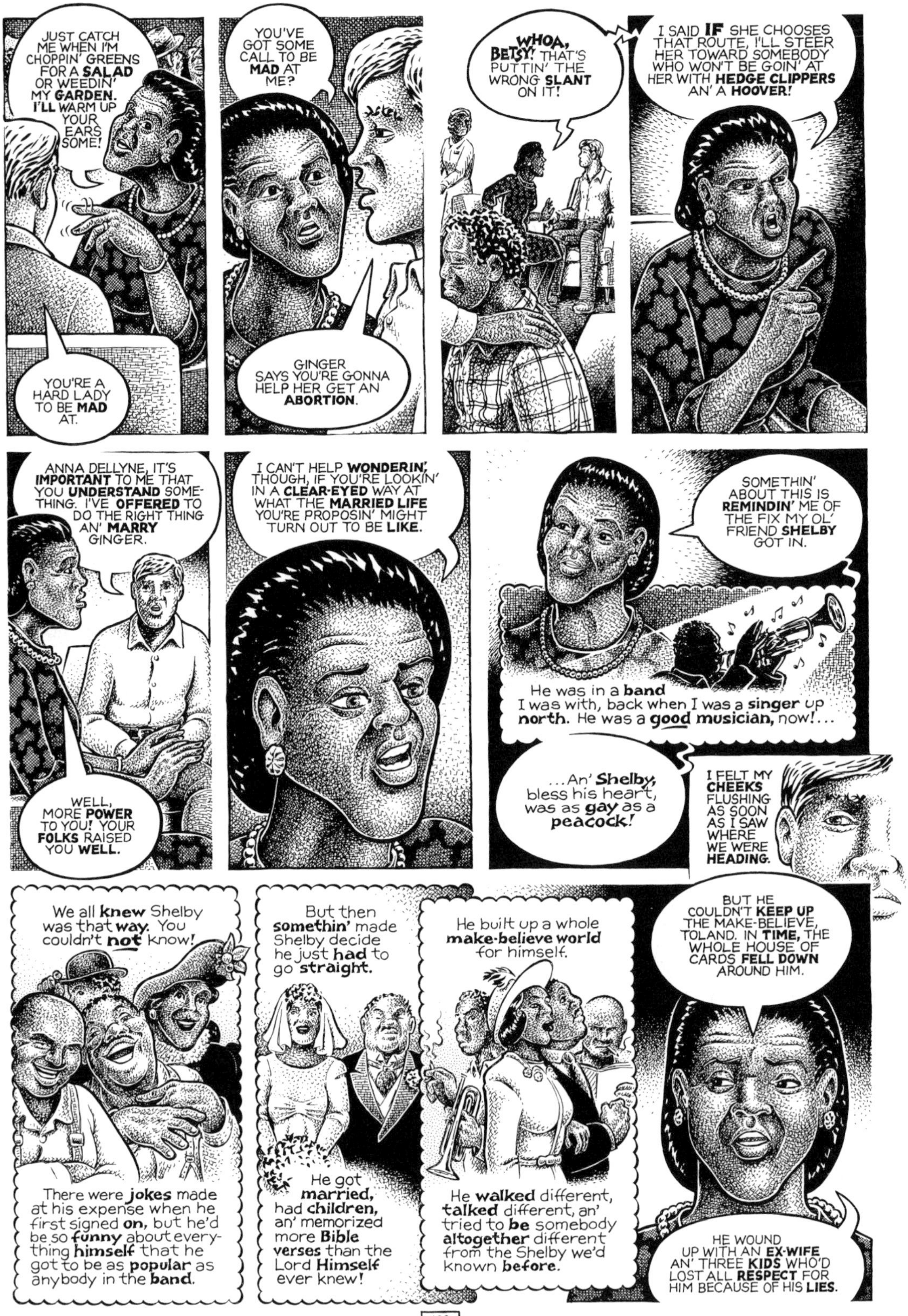
JUST CATCH ME WHEN I'M CHOPPIN' GREENS FOR A SALAD OR WEEDIN' MY GARDEN. I'LL WARM UP YOUR EARS SOME!
YOU'RE A HARD LADY TO BE MAD AT.
YOU'VE GOT SOME CALL TO BE MAD AT ME?
GINGER SAYS YOU'RE GONNA HELP HER GET AN ABORTION.
WHOA, BETSY! THAT'S PUTTIN' THE WRONG SLANT ON IT!
I SAID IF SHE CHOOSES THAT ROUTE, I'LL STEER HER TOWARD SOMEBODY WHO WON'T BE GOIN' AT HER WITH HEDGE CLIPPERS AN' A HOOVER!
ANNA DELLYNE, IT'S IMPORTANT TO ME THAT YOU UNDERSTAND SOMETHING. I'VE OFFERED TO DO THE RIGHT THING AN' MARRY GINGER.
WELL, MORE POWER TO YOU! YOUR FOLKS RAISED YOU WELL.
I CAN'T HELP WONDERIN', THOUGH, IF YOU'RE LOOKIN' IN A CLEAR-EYED WAY AT WHAT THE MARRIED LIFE YOU'RE PROPOSIN' MIGHT TURN OUT TO BE LIKE.
SOMETHIN' ABOUT THIS IS REMINDIN' ME OF THE FIX MY OL' FRIEND SHELBY GOT IN.
He was in a band I was with, back when I was a singer up north. He was a good musician, now!...
...An' Shelby, bless his heart, was as gay as a peacock!
I FELT MY CHEEKS FLUSHING AS SOON AS I SAW WHERE WE WERE HEADING.
We all knew Shelby was that way. You couldn't not know!
There were jokes made at his expense when he first signed on, but he'd be so funny about everything himself that he got to be as popular as anybody in the band.
But then somethin' made Shelby decide he just had to go straight.
He got married, had children, an' memorized more Bible verses than the Lord Himself ever knew!
He built up a whole make-believe world for himself.
He walked different, talked different, an' tried to be somebody altogether different from the Shelby we'd known before.
BUT HE COULDN'T KEEP UP THE MAKE-BELIEVE, TOLAND. IN TIME, THE WHOLE HOUSE OF CARDS FELL DOWN AROUND HIM.
HE WOUND UP WITH AN EX-WIFE AN' THREE KIDS WHO'D LOST ALL RESPECT FOR HIM BECAUSE OF HIS LIES.

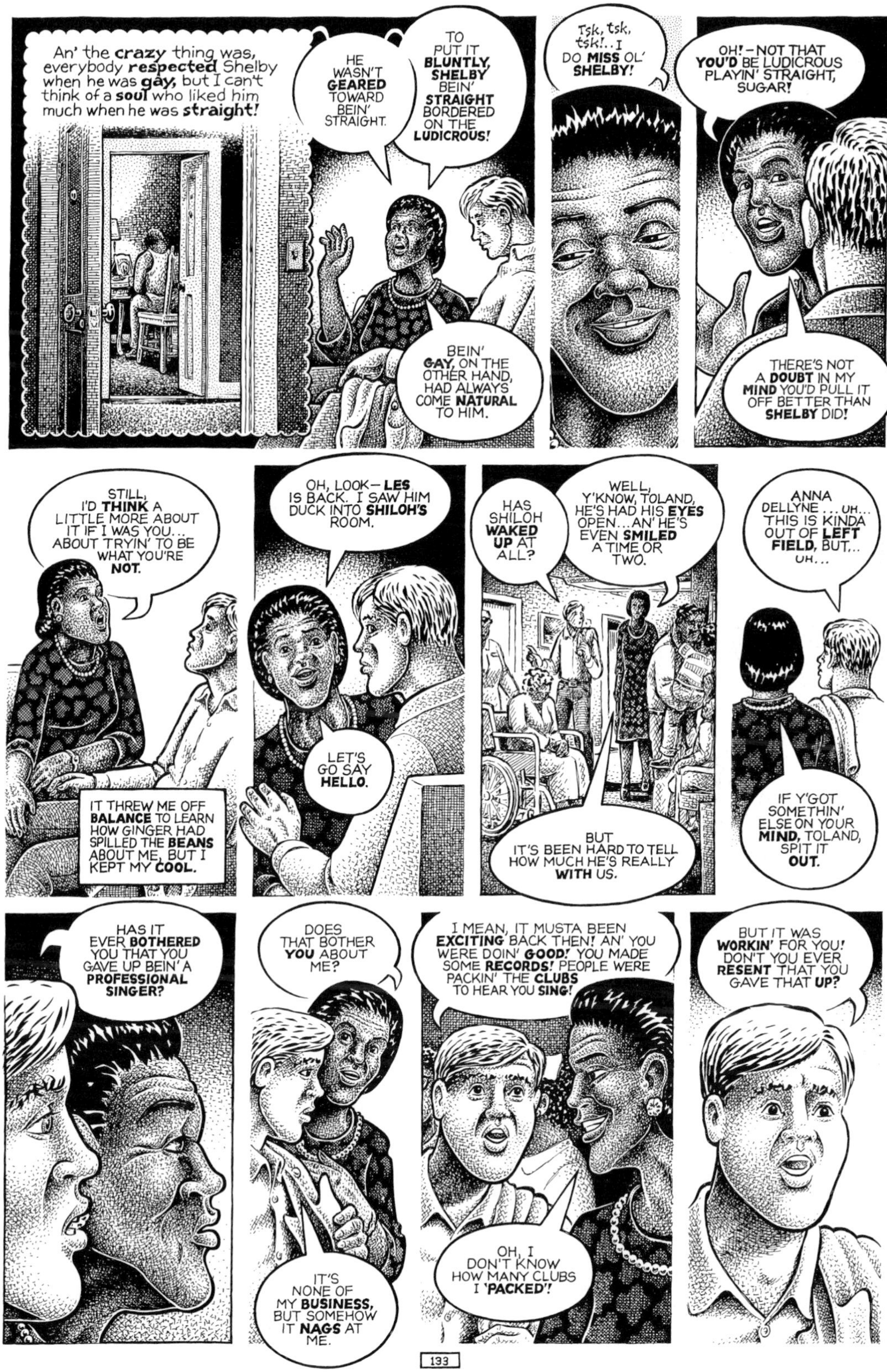
An' the crazy thing was, everybody respected Shelby when he was gay, but I can't think of a soul who liked him much when he was straight!
HE WASN'T GEARED TOWARD BEIN' STRAIGHT.
TO PUT IT BLUNTLY, SHELBY BEIN' STRAIGHT BORDERED ON THE LUDICROUS!
BEIN' GAY, ON THE OTHER HAND, HAD ALWAYS COME NATURAL TO HIM.
Tsk, tsk, tsk!.. I DO MISS OL' SHELBY!
OH! – NOT THAT YOU'D BE LUDICROUS PLAYIN' STRAIGHT, SUGAR!
THERE'S NOT A DOUBT IN MY MIND YOU'D PULL IT OFF BETTER THAN SHELBY DID!
STILL, I'D THINK A LITTLE MORE ABOUT IT IF I WAS YOU... ABOUT TRYIN' TO BE WHAT YOU'RE NOT.
IT THREW ME OFF BALANCE TO LEARN HOW GINGER HAD SPILLED THE BEANS ABOUT ME, BUT I KEPT MY COOL.
OH, LOOK— LES IS BACK. I SAW HIM DUCK INTO SHILOH'S ROOM.
LET'S GO SAY HELLO.
HAS SHILOH WAKED UP AT ALL?
WELL, Y'KNOW, TOLAND, HE'S HAD HIS EYES OPEN... AN' HE'S EVEN SMILED A TIME OR TWO.
BUT IT'S BEEN HARD TO TELL HOW MUCH HE'S REALLY WITH US.
ANNA DELLYNE ... UH... THIS IS KINDA OUT OF LEFT FIELD, BUT... UH...
IF Y'GOT SOMETHIN' ELSE ON YOUR MIND, TOLAND, SPIT IT OUT.
HAS IT EVER BOTHERED YOU THAT YOU GAVE UP BEIN' A PROFESSIONAL SINGER?
DOES THAT BOTHER YOU ABOUT ME?
IT'S NONE OF MY BUSINESS, BUT SOMEHOW IT NAGS AT ME.
I MEAN, IT MUSTA BEEN EXCITING BACK THEN! AN' YOU WERE DOIN' GOOD! YOU MADE SOME RECORDS! PEOPLE WERE PACKIN' THE CLUBS TO HEAR YOU SING!
OH, I DON'T KNOW HOW MANY CLUBS I 'PACKED'!
BUT IT WAS WORKIN' FOR YOU! DON'T YOU EVER RESENT THAT YOU GAVE THAT UP?

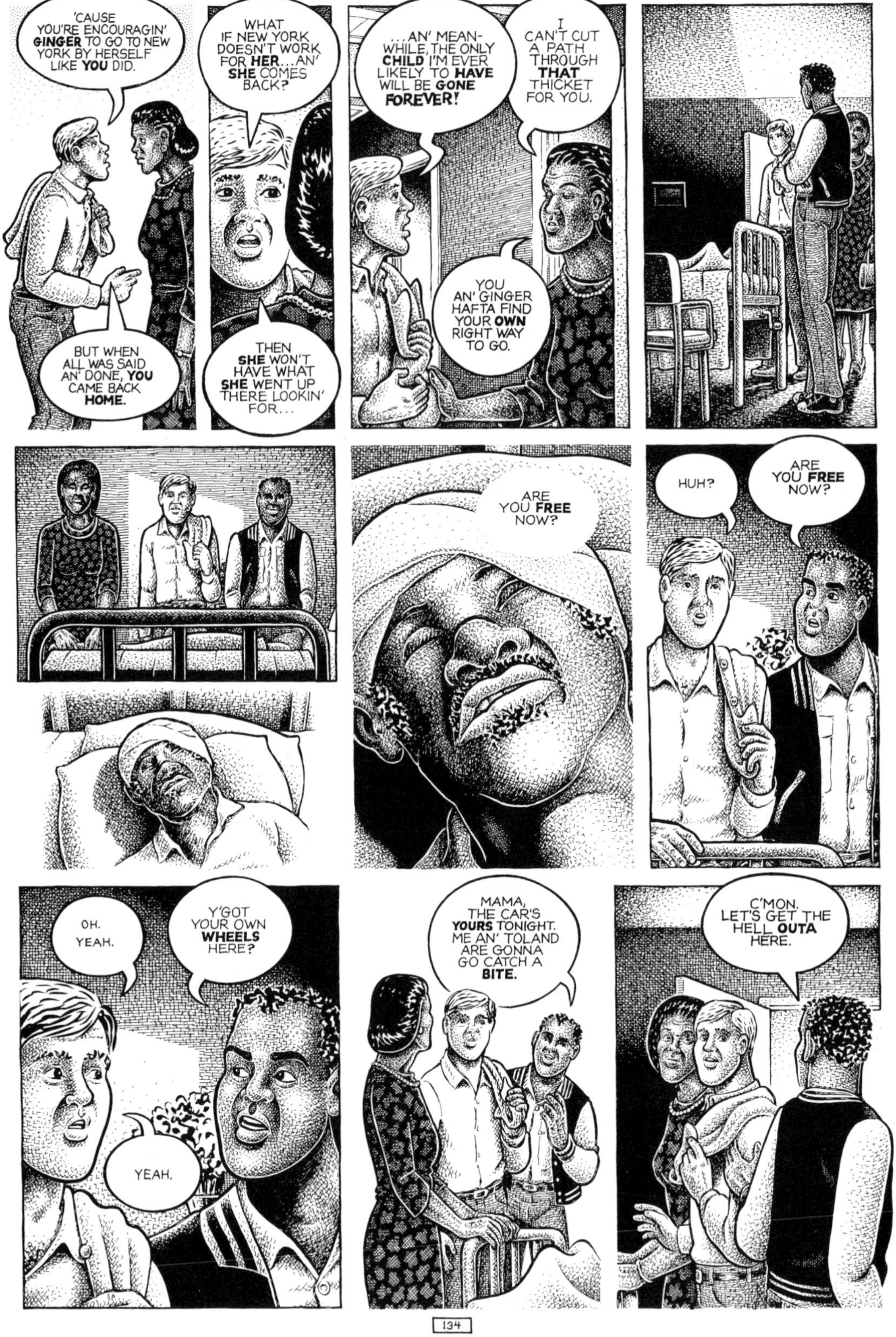
'CAUSE YOU'RE ENCOURAGIN' **GINGER** TO GO TO NEW YORK BY HERSELF LIKE **YOU** DID.
BUT WHEN ALL WAS SAID AN' DONE, **YOU** CAME BACK **HOME.**
WHAT IF NEW YORK DOESN'T WORK FOR **HER**...AN' **SHE** COMES BACK?
THEN **SHE** WON'T HAVE WHAT **SHE** WENT UP THERE LOOKIN' FOR...
...AN' MEAN-WHILE, THE ONLY **CHILD** I'M EVER LIKELY TO **HAVE** WILL BE **GONE FOREVER!**
I CAN'T CUT A PATH THROUGH **THAT** THICKET FOR YOU.
YOU AN' GINGER HAFTA FIND YOUR **OWN** RIGHT WAY TO GO.
ARE YOU **FREE** NOW?
HUH?
ARE YOU **FREE** NOW?
OH. YEAH.
Y'GOT YOUR OWN **WHEELS** HERE?
YEAH.
MAMA, THE CAR'S **YOURS** TONIGHT. ME AN' TOLAND ARE GONNA GO CATCH A **BITE.**
C'MON. LET'S GET THE HELL **OUTA** HERE.

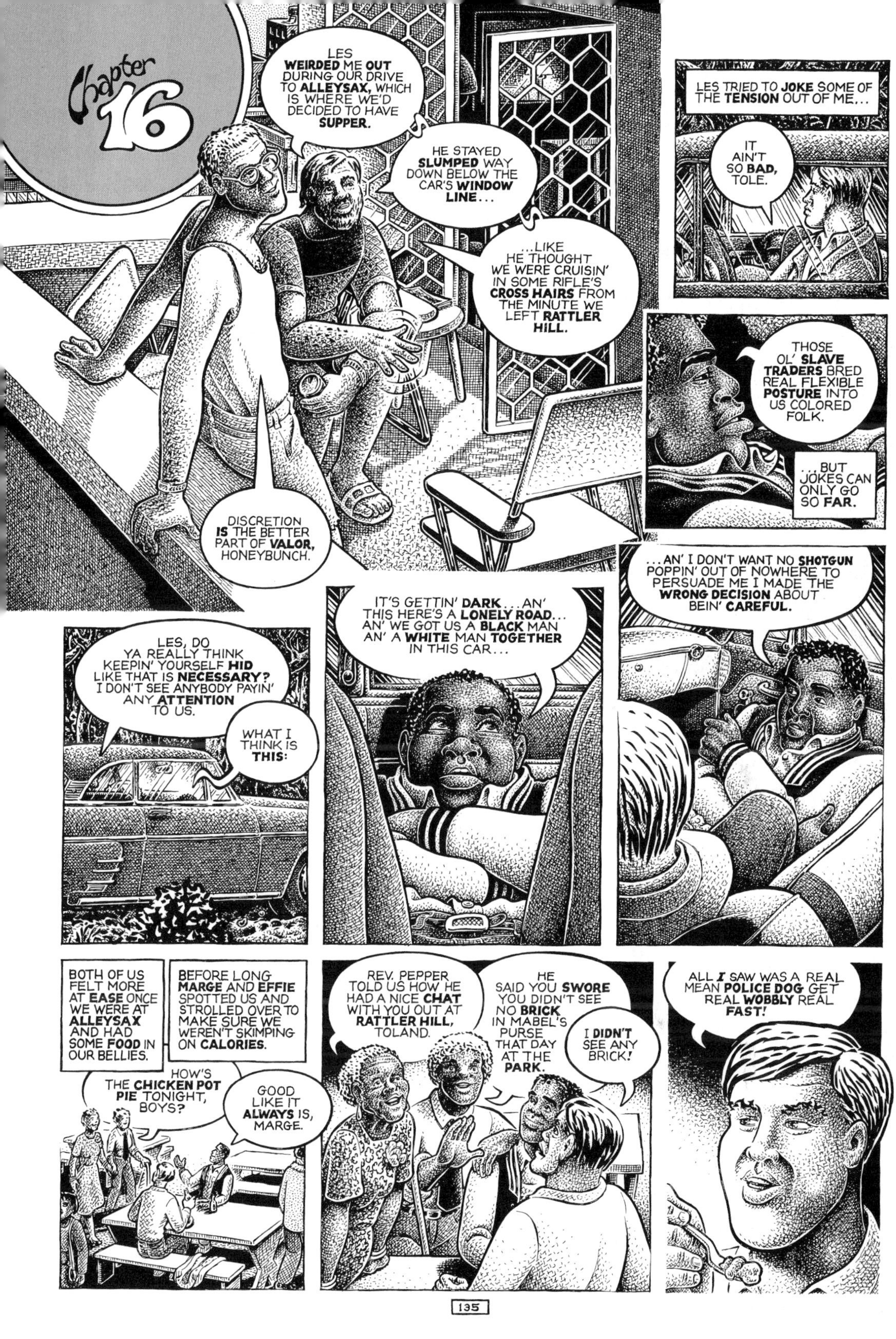
Chapter 16
LES WEIRDED ME OUT DURING OUR DRIVE TO ALLEYSAX, WHICH IS WHERE WE'D DECIDED TO HAVE SUPPER.
HE STAYED SLUMPED WAY DOWN BELOW THE CAR'S WINDOW LINE...
...LIKE HE THOUGHT WE WERE CRUISIN' IN SOME RIFLE'S CROSS HAIRS FROM THE MINUTE WE LEFT RATTLER HILL.
DISCRETION IS THE BETTER PART OF VALOR, HONEYBUNCH.
LES TRIED TO JOKE SOME OF THE TENSION OUT OF ME...
IT AIN'T SO BAD, TOLE.
THOSE OL' SLAVE TRADERS BRED REAL FLEXIBLE POSTURE INTO US COLORED FOLK.
...BUT JOKES CAN ONLY GO SO FAR.
LES, DO YA REALLY THINK KEEPIN' YOURSELF HID LIKE THAT IS NECESSARY? I DON'T SEE ANYBODY PAYIN' ANY ATTENTION TO US.
WHAT I THINK IS THIS:
IT'S GETTIN' DARK... AN' THIS HERE'S A LONELY ROAD... AN' WE GOT US A BLACK MAN AN' A WHITE MAN TOGETHER IN THIS CAR...
...AN' I DON'T WANT NO SHOTGUN POPPIN' OUT OF NOWHERE TO PERSUADE ME I MADE THE WRONG DECISION ABOUT BEIN' CAREFUL.
BOTH OF US FELT MORE AT EASE ONCE WE WERE AT ALLEYSAX AND HAD SOME FOOD IN OUR BELLIES.
BEFORE LONG MARGE AND EFFIE SPOTTED US AND STROLLED OVER TO MAKE SURE WE WEREN'T SKIMPING ON CALORIES.
HOW'S THE CHICKEN POT PIE TONIGHT, BOYS?
GOOD LIKE IT ALWAYS IS, MARGE.
REV. PEPPER TOLD US HOW HE HAD A NICE CHAT WITH YOU OUT AT RATTLER HILL, TOLAND.
HE SAID YOU SWORE YOU DIDN'T SEE NO BRICK IN MABEL'S PURSE THAT DAY AT THE PARK.
I DIDN'T SEE ANY BRICK!
ALL I SAW WAS A REAL MEAN POLICE DOG GET REAL WOBBLY REAL FAST!

WELL, THE PREACHER SAID YOU WERE *O.K.* IN *HIS* BOOK.

HE SAID YOU AN' HIM TALKED *PHILOSOPHY.*

Snort! I'D LIKE TO OF SEEN *THAT!*

I'LL BET THAT WAS A REAL *TWO-WAY* CONVERSATION, WASN'T IT, TOLE!

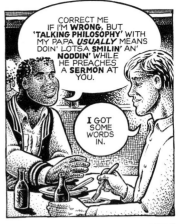

CORRECT ME IF I'M *WRONG,* BUT 'TALKING PHILOSOPHY' WITH MY PAPA *USUALLY* MEANS DOIN' LOTSA *SMILIN'* AN' *NODDIN'* WHILE HE PREACHES A *SERMON* AT YOU.

I GOT SOME WORDS IN.

Y'KNOW, LES, THIS PLACE IS *DIFFERENT* WHEN IT'S *QUIET.* THERE'S ALWAYS BEEN A *BAND* PLAYIN' WHEN I'VE BEEN HERE BEFORE.

Y'GOTTA BE HERE *LATE* AT *NIGHT* TO GET *LIVE* MUSIC.

THERE'S SOME NICE COZY TUNES ON THE *JUKEBOX,* THOUGH.

WHY DON'T I GO PUT ONE OF 'EM *ON* SO YOU AN' ME CAN *DANCE?*

BUT DONCHA THINK I CAN *SEE* WHICH WAY YOUR *EYEBALLS* DRIFT EVERY TIME A HANDSOME *MAN* PASSES BY?

LES...

C'MON. GIVE *IN* A LITTLE. *I* CAN READ YOUR *BEADS.*

DID YOUR *MOTHER* TALK TO YOU ABOUT ME?

MY MOTHER AIN'T SAID A FUCKIN' *WORD* ABOUT YOU.

C'MON, BABY. LET'S DO THE *SCARY* THING.

I'M GONNA GO PUT MY *MONEY* IN THE SLOT. THEN I WANT YOU TO COME *OVER* TO ME.

Give me just one minute...

...of the Love of a Lifetime...

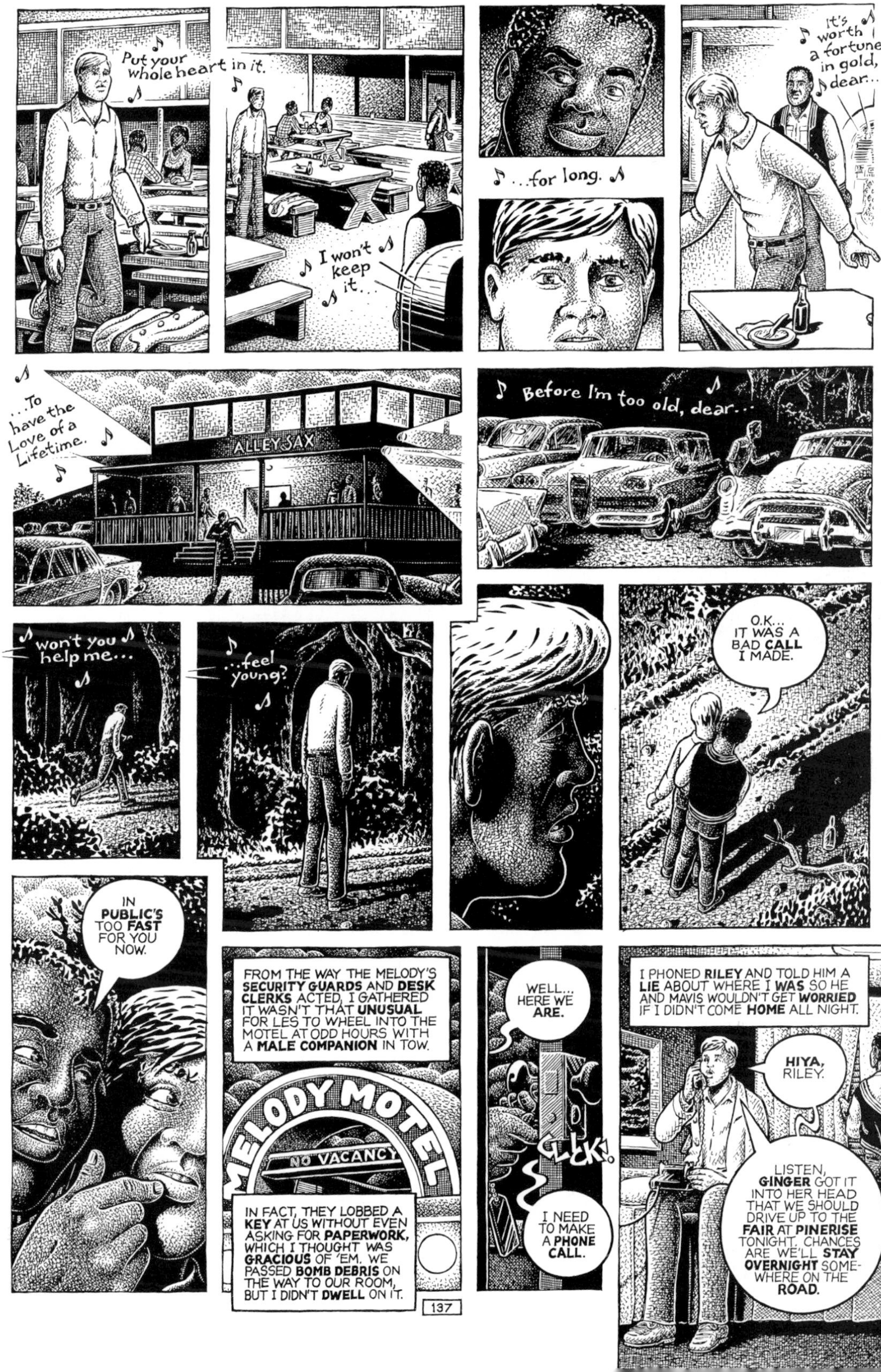

Put your whole heart in it.
I won't keep it...
...for long.
It's worth a fortune in gold, dear...
...To have the Love of a Lifetime.
ALLEY SAX
Before I'm too old, dear...
won't you help me...
...feel young?
O.K... IT WAS A BAD CALL I MADE.
IN PUBLIC'S TOO FAST FOR YOU NOW.
FROM THE WAY THE MELODY'S SECURITY GUARDS AND DESK CLERKS ACTED, I GATHERED IT WASN'T THAT UNUSUAL FOR LES TO WHEEL INTO THE MOTEL AT ODD HOURS WITH A MALE COMPANION IN TOW.
MELODY MOTEL
NO VACANCY
IN FACT, THEY LOBBED A KEY AT US WITHOUT EVEN ASKING FOR PAPERWORK, WHICH I THOUGHT WAS GRACIOUS OF 'EM. WE PASSED BOMB DEBRIS ON THE WAY TO OUR ROOM, BUT I DIDN'T DWELL ON IT.
WELL... HERE WE ARE.
CLICK!
I NEED TO MAKE A PHONE CALL.
I PHONED RILEY AND TOLD HIM A LIE ABOUT WHERE I WAS SO HE AND MAVIS WOULDN'T GET WORRIED IF I DIDN'T COME HOME ALL NIGHT.
HIYA, RILEY.
LISTEN, GINGER GOT IT INTO HER HEAD THAT WE SHOULD DRIVE UP TO THE FAIR AT PINERISE TONIGHT. CHANCES ARE WE'LL STAY OVERNIGHT SOMEWHERE ON THE ROAD.

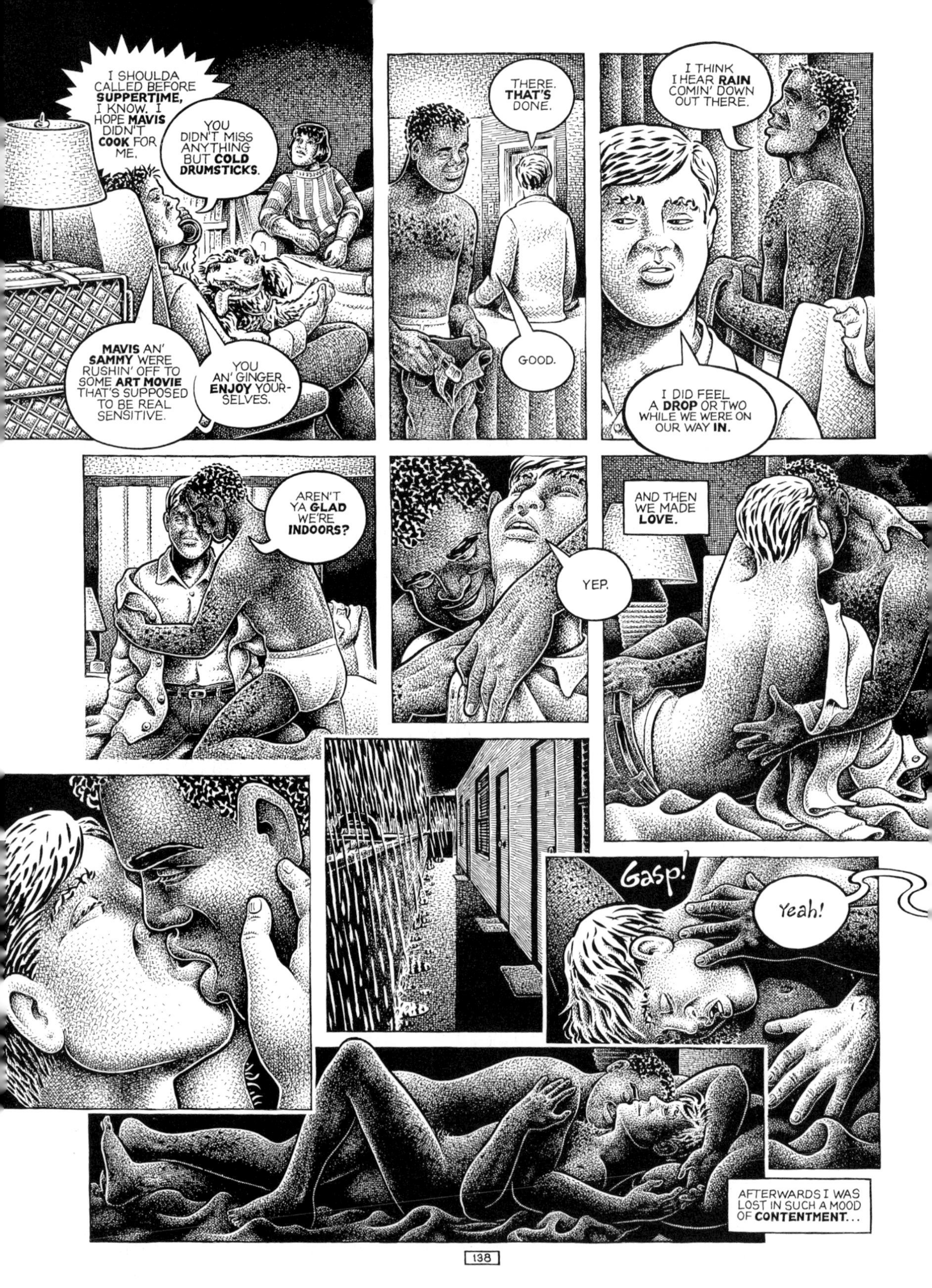

I SHOULDA CALLED BEFORE SUPPERTIME, I KNOW. I HOPE MAVIS DIDN'T COOK FOR ME.
YOU DIDN'T MISS ANYTHING BUT COLD DRUMSTICKS.
MAVIS AN' SAMMY WERE RUSHIN' OFF TO SOME ART MOVIE THAT'S SUPPOSED TO BE REAL SENSITIVE.
YOU AN' GINGER ENJOY YOURSELVES.
THERE. THAT'S DONE.
GOOD.
I THINK I HEAR RAIN COMIN' DOWN OUT THERE.
I DID FEEL A DROP OR TWO WHILE WE WERE ON OUR WAY IN.
AREN'T YA GLAD WE'RE INDOORS?
YEP.
AND THEN WE MADE LOVE.
Gasp!
Yeah!
AFTERWARDS I WAS LOST IN SUCH A MOOD OF CONTENTMENT...

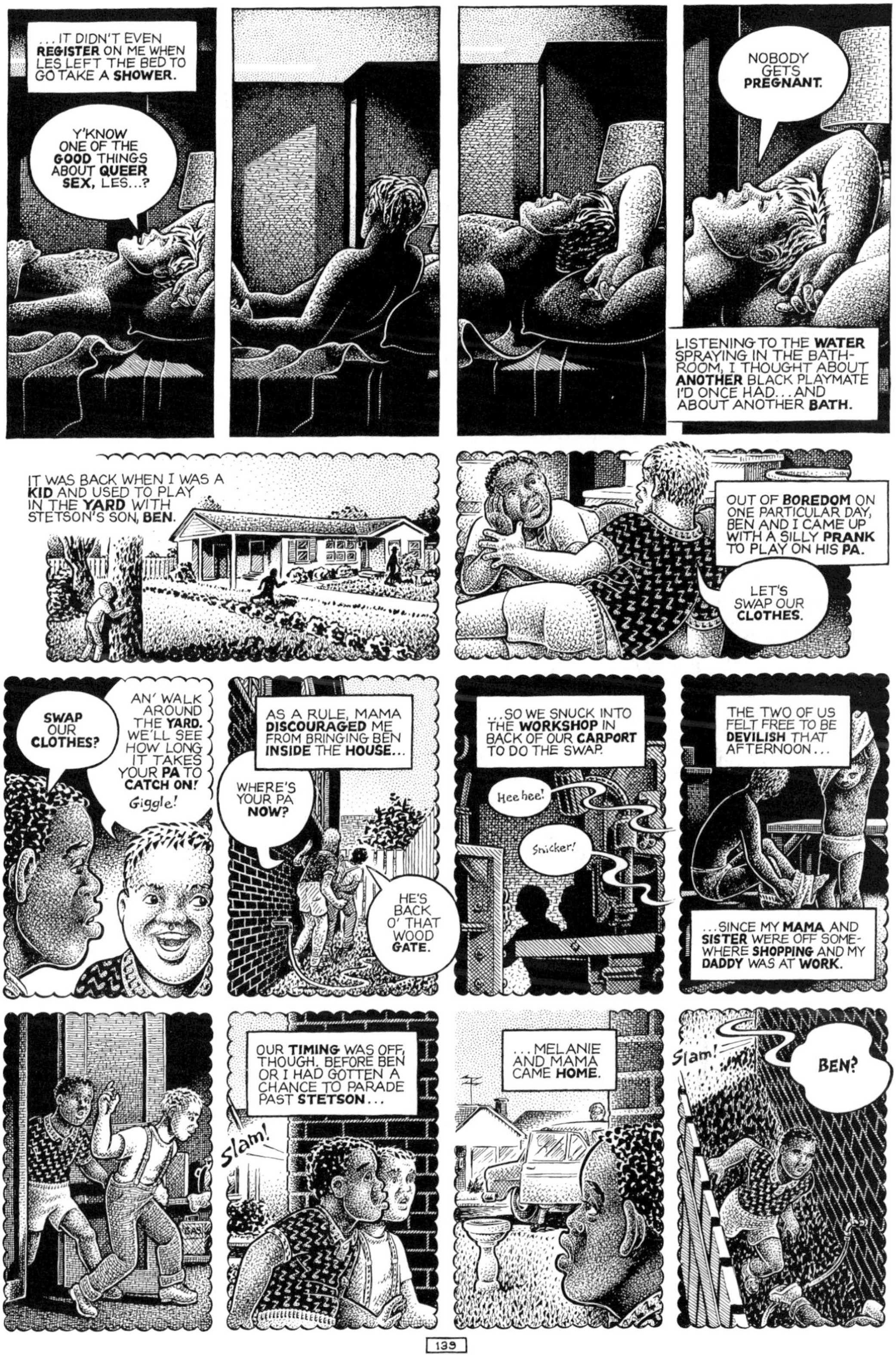
...IT DIDN'T EVEN REGISTER ON ME WHEN LES LEFT THE BED TO GO TAKE A SHOWER.
Y'KNOW ONE OF THE GOOD THINGS ABOUT QUEER SEX, LES...?
NOBODY GETS PREGNANT.
LISTENING TO THE WATER SPRAYING IN THE BATHROOM, I THOUGHT ABOUT ANOTHER BLACK PLAYMATE I'D ONCE HAD... AND ABOUT ANOTHER BATH.
IT WAS BACK WHEN I WAS A KID AND USED TO PLAY IN THE YARD WITH STETSON'S SON, BEN.
OUT OF BOREDOM ON ONE PARTICULAR DAY, BEN AND I CAME UP WITH A SILLY PRANK TO PLAY ON HIS PA.
LET'S SWAP OUR CLOTHES.
SWAP OUR CLOTHES?
AN' WALK AROUND THE YARD. WE'LL SEE HOW LONG IT TAKES YOUR PA TO CATCH ON!
Giggle!
AS A RULE, MAMA DISCOURAGED ME FROM BRINGING BEN INSIDE THE HOUSE...
WHERE'S YOUR PA NOW?
HE'S BACK O' THAT WOOD GATE.
...SO WE SNUCK INTO THE WORKSHOP IN BACK OF OUR CARPORT TO DO THE SWAP.
Hee hee!
Snicker!
THE TWO OF US FELT FREE TO BE DEVILISH THAT AFTERNOON...
...SINCE MY MAMA AND SISTER WERE OFF SOMEWHERE SHOPPING AND MY DADDY WAS AT WORK.
OUR TIMING WAS OFF, THOUGH. BEFORE BEN OR I HAD GOTTEN A CHANCE TO PARADE PAST STETSON...
Slam!
...MELANIE AND MAMA CAME HOME.
Slam!
BEN?

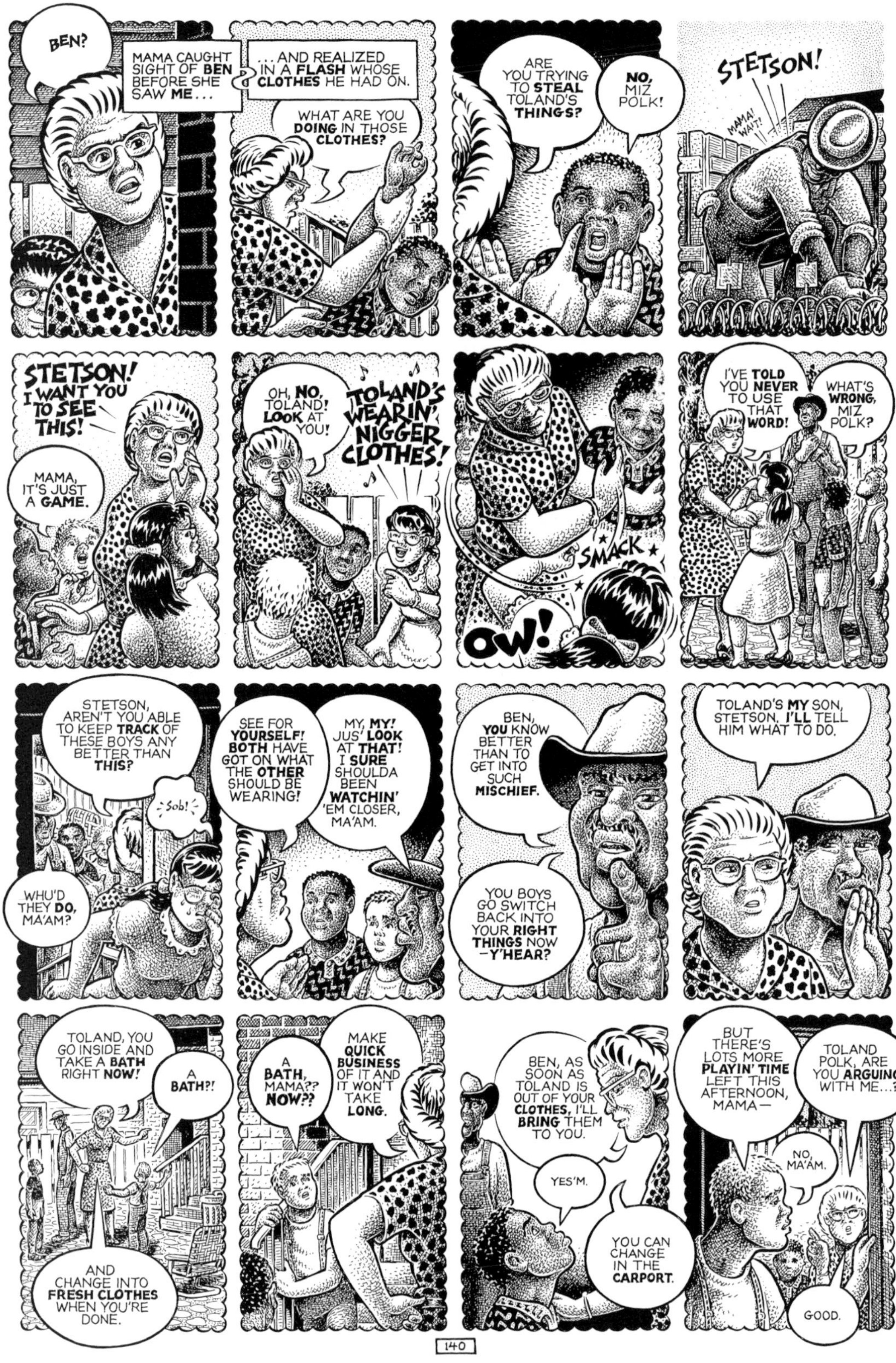
BEN?
MAMA CAUGHT SIGHT OF BEN BEFORE SHE SAW ME...
...AND REALIZED IN A FLASH WHOSE CLOTHES HE HAD ON.
WHAT ARE YOU DOING IN THOSE CLOTHES?
ARE YOU TRYING TO STEAL TOLAND'S THINGS?
NO, MIZ POLK!
STETSON!
MAMA! WAIT!
STETSON! I WANT YOU TO SEE THIS!
MAMA, IT'S JUST A GAME.
OH, NO, TOLAND! LOOK AT YOU!
TOLAND'S WEARIN' NIGGER CLOTHES!
SMACK
OW!
I'VE TOLD YOU NEVER TO USE THAT WORD!
WHAT'S WRONG, MIZ POLK?
STETSON, AREN'T YOU ABLE TO KEEP TRACK OF THESE BOYS ANY BETTER THAN THIS?
Sob!
WHU'D THEY DO, MA'AM?
SEE FOR YOURSELF! BOTH HAVE GOT ON WHAT THE OTHER SHOULD BE WEARING!
MY, MY! JUS' LOOK AT THAT! I SURE SHOULDA BEEN WATCHIN' 'EM CLOSER, MA'AM.
BEN, YOU KNOW BETTER THAN TO GET INTO SUCH MISCHIEF.
YOU BOYS GO SWITCH BACK INTO YOUR RIGHT THINGS NOW —Y'HEAR?
TOLAND'S MY SON, STETSON. I'LL TELL HIM WHAT TO DO.
TOLAND, YOU GO INSIDE AND TAKE A BATH RIGHT NOW!
A BATH?!
AND CHANGE INTO FRESH CLOTHES WHEN YOU'RE DONE.
A BATH, MAMA?? NOW??
MAKE QUICK BUSINESS OF IT AND IT WON'T TAKE LONG.
BEN, AS SOON AS TOLAND IS OUT OF YOUR CLOTHES, I'LL BRING THEM TO YOU.
YES'M.
YOU CAN CHANGE IN THE CARPORT.
BUT THERE'S LOTS MORE PLAYIN' TIME LEFT THIS AFTERNOON, MAMA—
TOLAND POLK, ARE YOU ARGUING WITH ME...?
NO, MA'AM.
GOOD.

SCRUB YOURSELF **GOOD.** **THEN** YOU CAN PLAY WITH BEN SOME MORE.

IT WAS **CONFUSING.**

I COULDN'T SEE WHERE ALL THE **URGENCY** WAS COMING FROM.

WHY DID I HAVE TO TAKE A BATH **THAT** VERY **MINUTE?**

WHY WAS IT SO **IMPORTANT?**

MAMA....

SSSSSSSSSSSSSSSSSSSSS

WELL... LOOK WHO'S **HERE.**

141

LET'S RUB A LITTLE **SOAP** ON THIS WHITE BOY'S SKIN.

Chapter 17

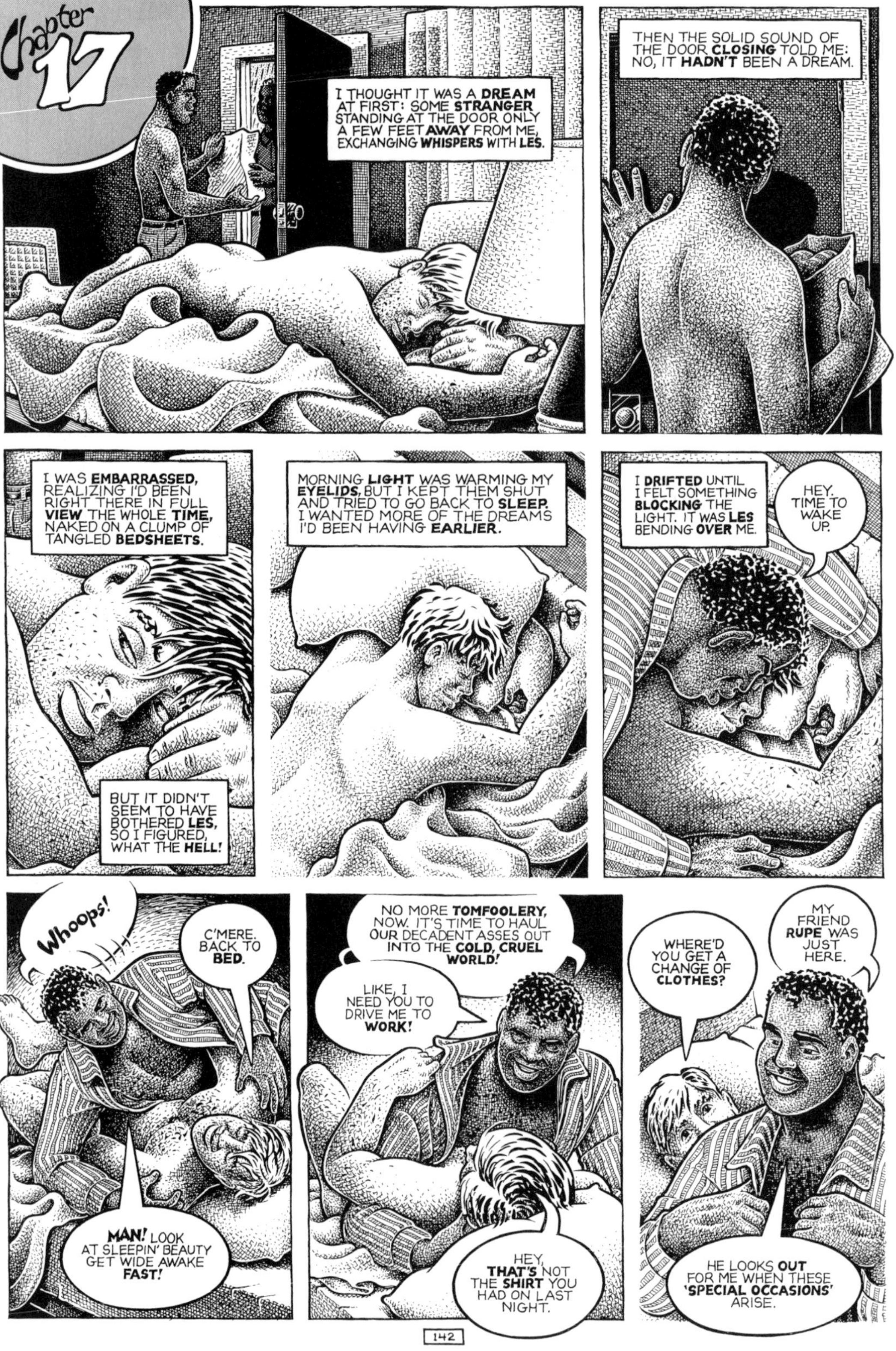

I THOUGHT IT WAS A DREAM AT FIRST: SOME STRANGER STANDING AT THE DOOR ONLY A FEW FEET AWAY FROM ME, EXCHANGING WHISPERS WITH LES.
THEN THE SOLID SOUND OF THE DOOR CLOSING TOLD ME: NO, IT HADN'T BEEN A DREAM.
I WAS EMBARRASSED, REALIZING I'D BEEN RIGHT THERE IN FULL VIEW THE WHOLE TIME, NAKED ON A CLUMP OF TANGLED BEDSHEETS.
BUT IT DIDN'T SEEM TO HAVE BOTHERED LES, SO I FIGURED, WHAT THE HELL!
MORNING LIGHT WAS WARMING MY EYELIDS, BUT I KEPT THEM SHUT AND TRIED TO GO BACK TO SLEEP. I WANTED MORE OF THE DREAMS I'D BEEN HAVING EARLIER.
I DRIFTED UNTIL I FELT SOMETHING BLOCKING THE LIGHT. IT WAS LES BENDING OVER ME.
HEY. TIME TO WAKE UP.
Whoops!
C'MERE. BACK TO BED.
MAN! LOOK AT SLEEPIN' BEAUTY GET WIDE AWAKE FAST!
NO MORE TOMFOOLERY, NOW. IT'S TIME TO HAUL OUR DECADENT ASSES OUT INTO THE COLD, CRUEL WORLD!
LIKE, I NEED YOU TO DRIVE ME TO WORK!
HEY, THAT'S NOT THE SHIRT YOU HAD ON LAST NIGHT.
WHERE'D YOU GET A CHANGE OF CLOTHES?
MY FRIEND RUPE WAS JUST HERE.
HE LOOKS OUT FOR ME WHEN THESE 'SPECIAL OCCASIONS' ARISE.

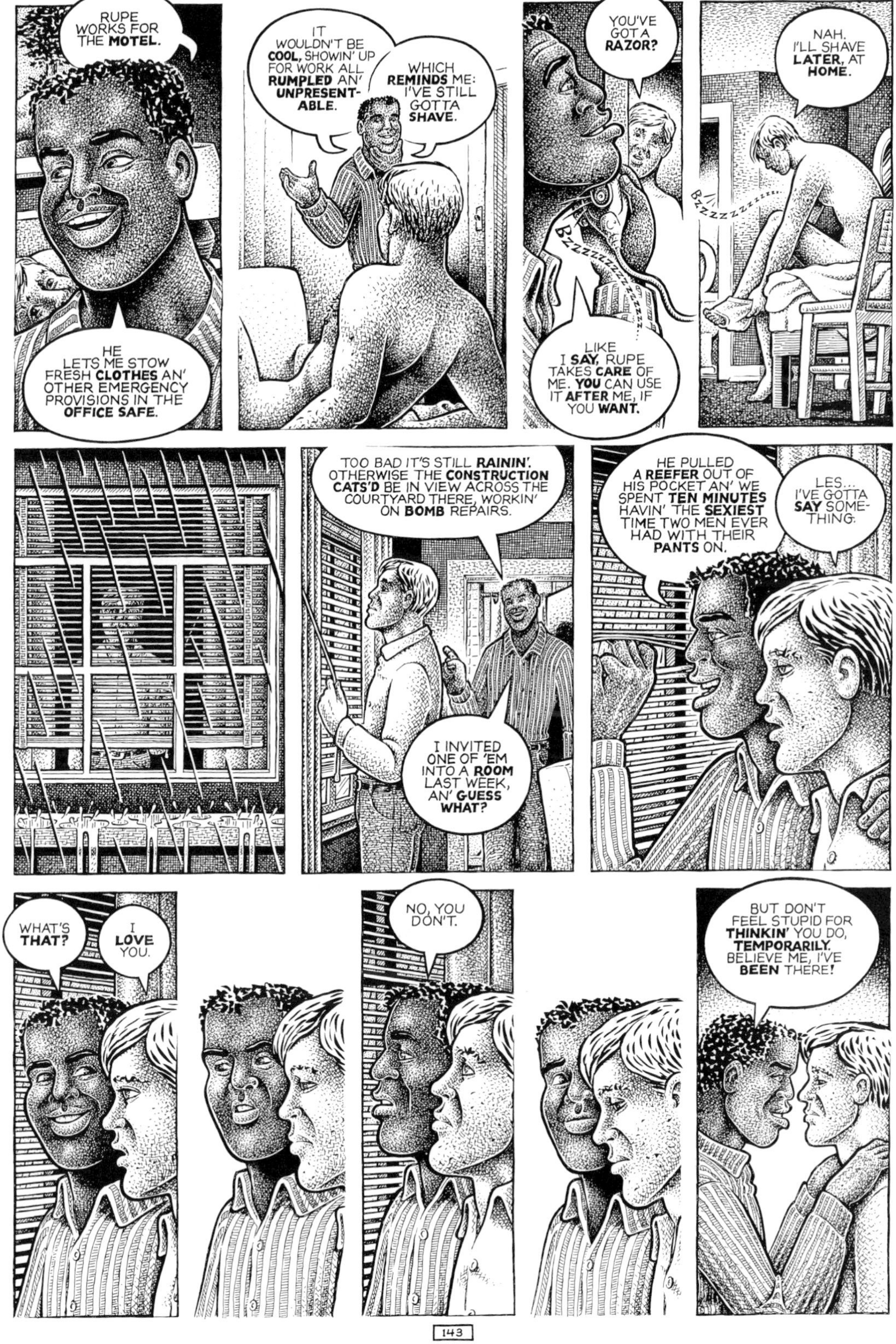

RUPE WORKS FOR THE MOTEL.
HE LETS ME STOW FRESH CLOTHES AN' OTHER EMERGENCY PROVISIONS IN THE OFFICE SAFE.
IT WOULDN'T BE COOL, SHOWIN' UP FOR WORK ALL RUMPLED AN' UNPRESENT-ABLE.
WHICH REMINDS ME: I'VE STILL GOTTA SHAVE.
YOU'VE GOT A RAZOR?
BZZZZZZZZZZZZZZZZ...
LIKE I SAY, RUPE TAKES CARE OF ME. YOU CAN USE IT AFTER ME, IF YOU WANT.
NAH. I'LL SHAVE LATER, AT HOME.
BZZZZZZZZZ...
TOO BAD IT'S STILL RAININ'. OTHERWISE THE CONSTRUCTION CATS'D BE IN VIEW ACROSS THE COURTYARD THERE, WORKIN' ON BOMB REPAIRS.
I INVITED ONE OF 'EM INTO A ROOM LAST WEEK, AN' GUESS WHAT?
HE PULLED A REEFER OUT OF HIS POCKET AN' WE SPENT TEN MINUTES HAVIN' THE SEXIEST TIME TWO MEN EVER HAD WITH THEIR PANTS ON.
LES... I'VE GOTTA SAY SOME-THING.
WHAT'S THAT?
I LOVE YOU.
NO, YOU DON'T.
BUT DON'T FEEL STUPID FOR THINKIN' YOU DO, TEMPORARILY. BELIEVE ME, I'VE BEEN THERE!

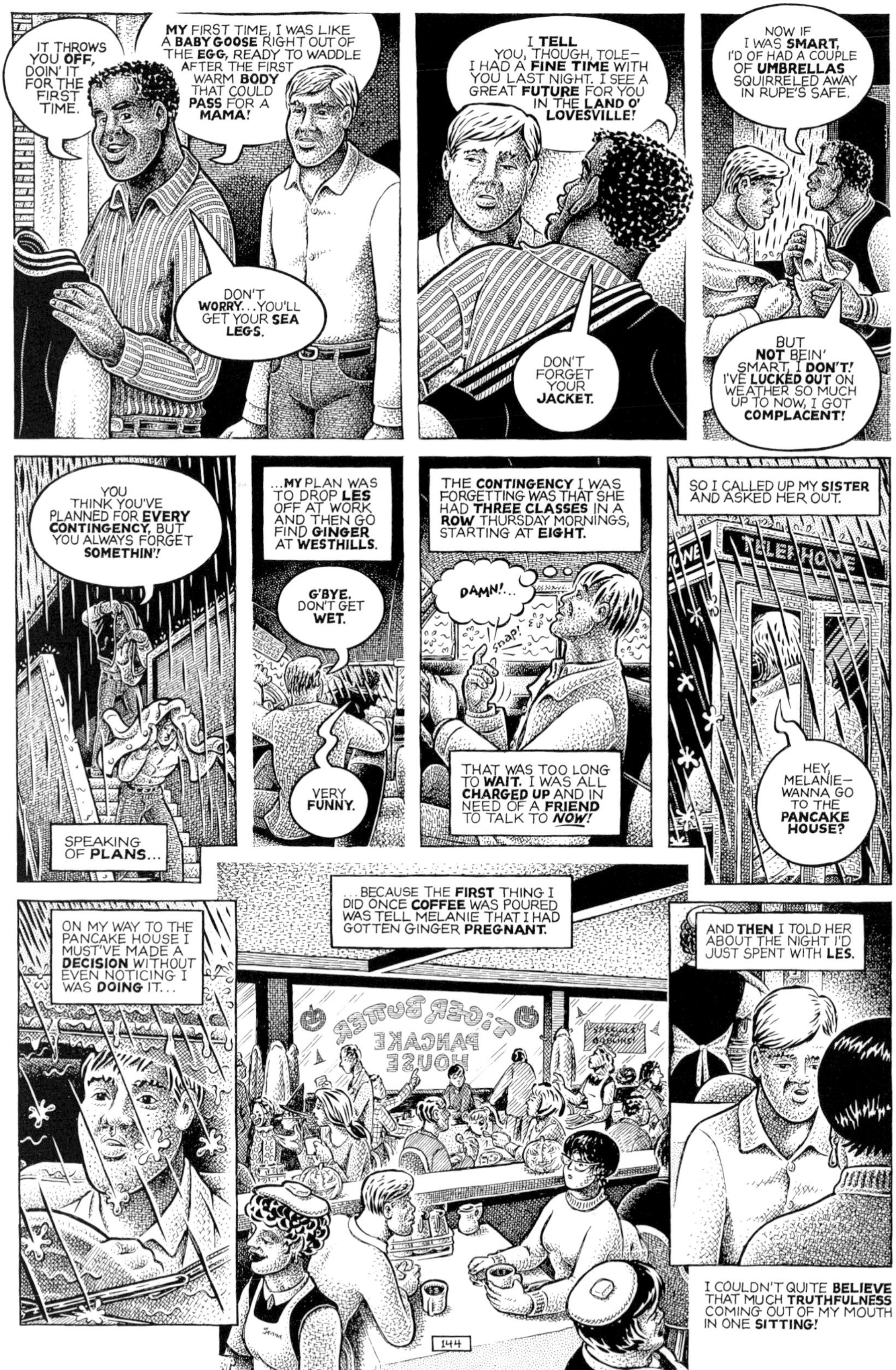
IT THROWS YOU OFF, DOIN' IT FOR THE FIRST TIME.
MY FIRST TIME, I WAS LIKE A BABY GOOSE RIGHT OUT OF THE EGG, READY TO WADDLE AFTER THE FIRST WARM BODY THAT COULD PASS FOR A MAMA!
DON'T WORRY... YOU'LL GET YOUR SEA LEGS.
I TELL YOU, THOUGH, TOLE— I HAD A FINE TIME WITH YOU LAST NIGHT. I SEE A GREAT FUTURE FOR YOU IN THE LAND O' LOVESVILLE!
DON'T FORGET YOUR JACKET.
NOW IF I WAS SMART, I'D OF HAD A COUPLE OF UMBRELLAS SQUIRRELED AWAY IN RUPE'S SAFE.
BUT NOT BEIN' SMART, I DON'T! I'VE LUCKED OUT ON WEATHER SO MUCH UP TO NOW, I GOT COMPLACENT!
YOU THINK YOU'VE PLANNED FOR EVERY CONTINGENCY, BUT YOU ALWAYS FORGET SOMETHIN'!
SPEAKING OF PLANS...
...MY PLAN WAS TO DROP LES OFF AT WORK AND THEN GO FIND GINGER AT WESTHILLS.
G'BYE. DON'T GET WET.
VERY FUNNY.
THE CONTINGENCY I WAS FORGETTING WAS THAT SHE HAD THREE CLASSES IN A ROW THURSDAY MORNINGS, STARTING AT EIGHT.
DAMN!...
snap!
THAT WAS TOO LONG TO WAIT. I WAS ALL CHARGED UP AND IN NEED OF A FRIEND TO TALK TO NOW!
SO I CALLED UP MY SISTER AND ASKED HER OUT.
HEY, MELANIE— WANNA GO TO THE PANCAKE HOUSE?
ON MY WAY TO THE PANCAKE HOUSE I MUST'VE MADE A DECISION WITHOUT EVEN NOTICING I WAS DOING IT...
...BECAUSE THE FIRST THING I DID ONCE COFFEE WAS POURED WAS TELL MELANIE THAT I HAD GOTTEN GINGER PREGNANT.
TIGER BUTTER PANCAKE HOUSE
SPECIALS GOBLINS!
AND THEN I TOLD HER ABOUT THE NIGHT I'D JUST SPENT WITH LES.
I COULDN'T QUITE BELIEVE THAT MUCH TRUTHFULNESS COMING OUT OF MY MOUTH IN ONE SITTING!

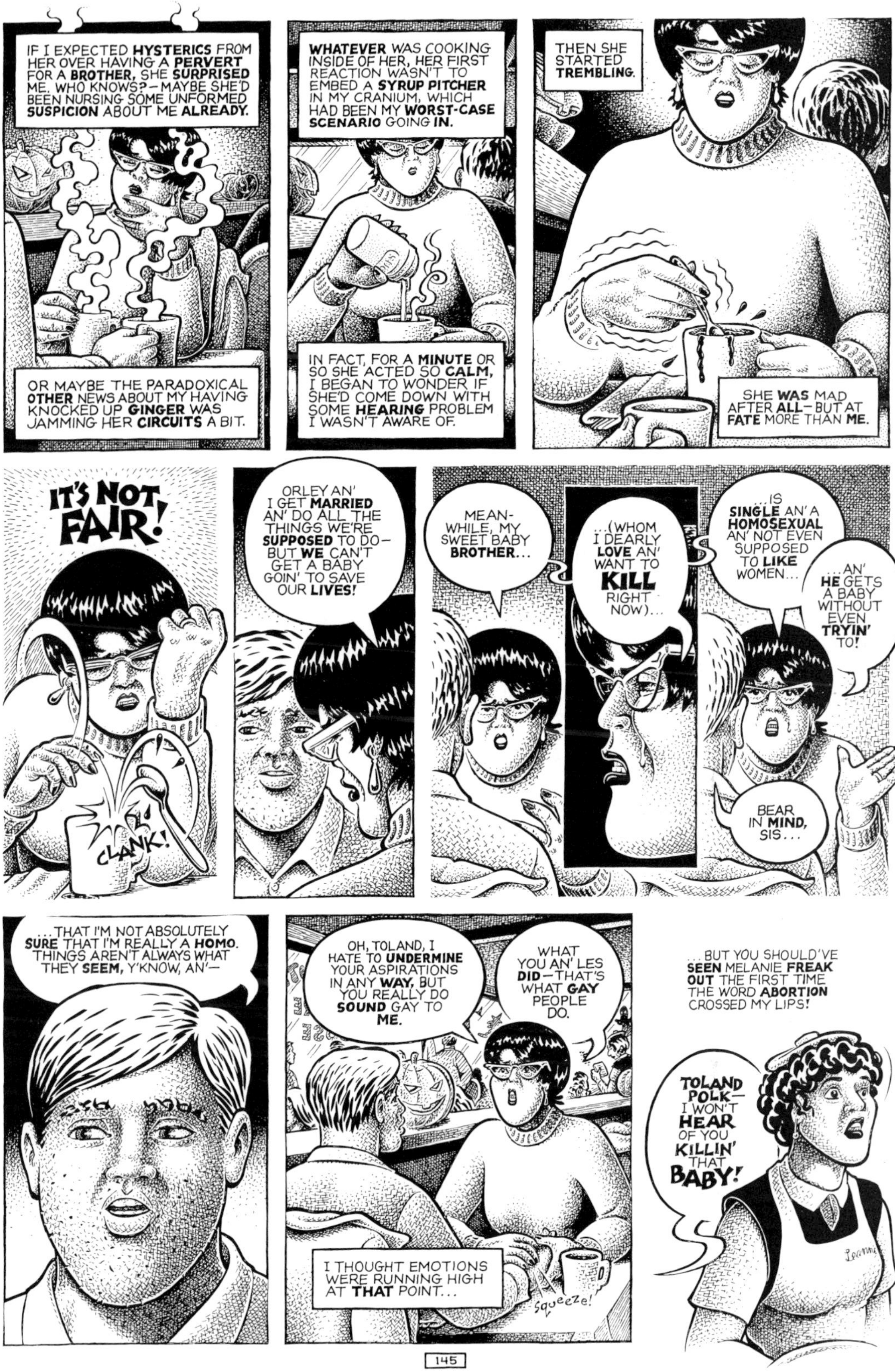
IF I EXPECTED **HYSTERICS** FROM HER OVER HAVING A **PERVERT** FOR A **BROTHER**, SHE **SURPRISED** ME. WHO KNOWS?—MAYBE SHE'D BEEN NURSING SOME UNFORMED **SUSPICION** ABOUT ME **ALREADY**.
OR MAYBE THE PARADOXICAL **OTHER** NEWS ABOUT MY HAVING KNOCKED UP **GINGER** WAS JAMMING HER **CIRCUITS** A BIT.
WHATEVER WAS COOKING INSIDE OF HER, HER FIRST REACTION WASN'T TO EMBED A **SYRUP PITCHER** IN MY CRANIUM, WHICH HAD BEEN MY **WORST-CASE SCENARIO** GOING **IN**.
IN FACT, FOR A **MINUTE** OR SO SHE ACTED SO **CALM**, I BEGAN TO WONDER IF SHE'D COME DOWN WITH SOME **HEARING** PROBLEM I WASN'T AWARE OF.
THEN SHE STARTED **TREMBLING**.
SHE **WAS** MAD AFTER **ALL**—BUT AT **FATE** MORE THAN **ME**.
IT'S NOT FAIR!
CLANK!
ORLEY AN' I GET **MARRIED** AN' DO ALL THE THINGS WE'RE **SUPPOSED** TO DO—BUT **WE** CAN'T GET A BABY GOIN' TO SAVE OUR **LIVES**!
MEAN-WHILE, MY SWEET BABY **BROTHER**...
...(WHOM I DEARLY **LOVE** AN' WANT TO **KILL** RIGHT NOW)...
...IS **SINGLE** AN' A **HOMOSEXUAL** AN' NOT EVEN SUPPOSED TO **LIKE** WOMEN...
...AN' **HE** GETS A BABY WITHOUT EVEN **TRYIN'** TO!
BEAR IN **MIND**, SIS...
...THAT I'M NOT ABSOLUTELY **SURE** THAT I'M REALLY A **HOMO**. THINGS AREN'T ALWAYS WHAT THEY **SEEM**, Y'KNOW, AN'—
OH, TOLAND, I HATE TO **UNDERMINE** YOUR ASPIRATIONS IN ANY **WAY**, BUT YOU REALLY DO **SOUND** GAY TO **ME**.
WHAT YOU AN' LES **DID**—THAT'S WHAT **GAY** PEOPLE DO.
I THOUGHT EMOTIONS WERE RUNNING HIGH AT **THAT** POINT...
squeeze!
...BUT YOU SHOULD'VE **SEEN** MELANIE **FREAK OUT** THE FIRST TIME THE WORD **ABORTION** CROSSED MY LIPS!
TOLAND POLK—I WON'T **HEAR** OF YOU **KILLIN'** THAT **BABY**!

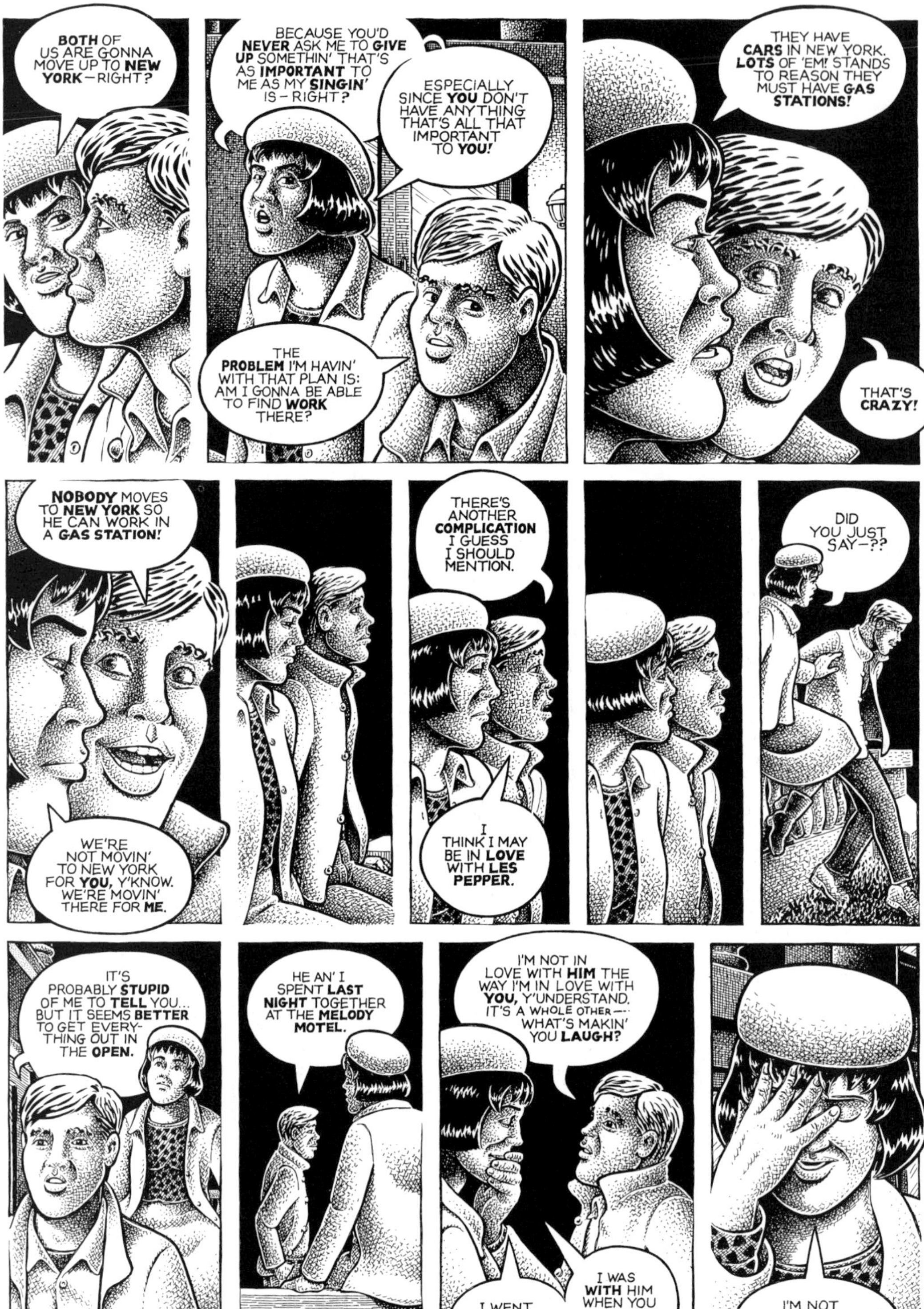
BOTH OF US ARE GONNA MOVE UP TO NEW YORK – RIGHT?
BECAUSE YOU'D NEVER ASK ME TO GIVE UP SOMETHIN' THAT'S AS IMPORTANT TO ME AS MY SINGIN' IS – RIGHT?
ESPECIALLY SINCE YOU DON'T HAVE ANYTHING THAT'S ALL THAT IMPORTANT TO YOU!
THE PROBLEM I'M HAVIN' WITH THAT PLAN IS: AM I GONNA BE ABLE TO FIND WORK THERE?
THEY HAVE CARS IN NEW YORK. LOTS OF 'EM! STANDS TO REASON THEY MUST HAVE GAS STATIONS!
THAT'S CRAZY!
NOBODY MOVES TO NEW YORK SO HE CAN WORK IN A GAS STATION!
WE'RE NOT MOVIN' TO NEW YORK FOR YOU, Y'KNOW. WE'RE MOVIN' THERE FOR ME.
THERE'S ANOTHER COMPLICATION I GUESS I SHOULD MENTION.
I THINK I MAY BE IN LOVE WITH LES PEPPER.
DID YOU JUST SAY–??
IT'S PROBABLY STUPID OF ME TO TELL YOU... BUT IT SEEMS BETTER TO GET EVERYTHING OUT IN THE OPEN.
HE AN' I SPENT LAST NIGHT TOGETHER AT THE MELODY MOTEL.
I'M NOT IN LOVE WITH HIM THE WAY I'M IN LOVE WITH YOU, Y'UNDERSTAND. IT'S A WHOLE OTHER— WHAT'S MAKIN' YOU LAUGH?
I WENT TO BED WITH RILEY LAST NIGHT.
I WAS WITH HIM WHEN YOU PHONED.
I'M NOT REALLY LAUGHIN'. THIS IS ALL JUST SO —

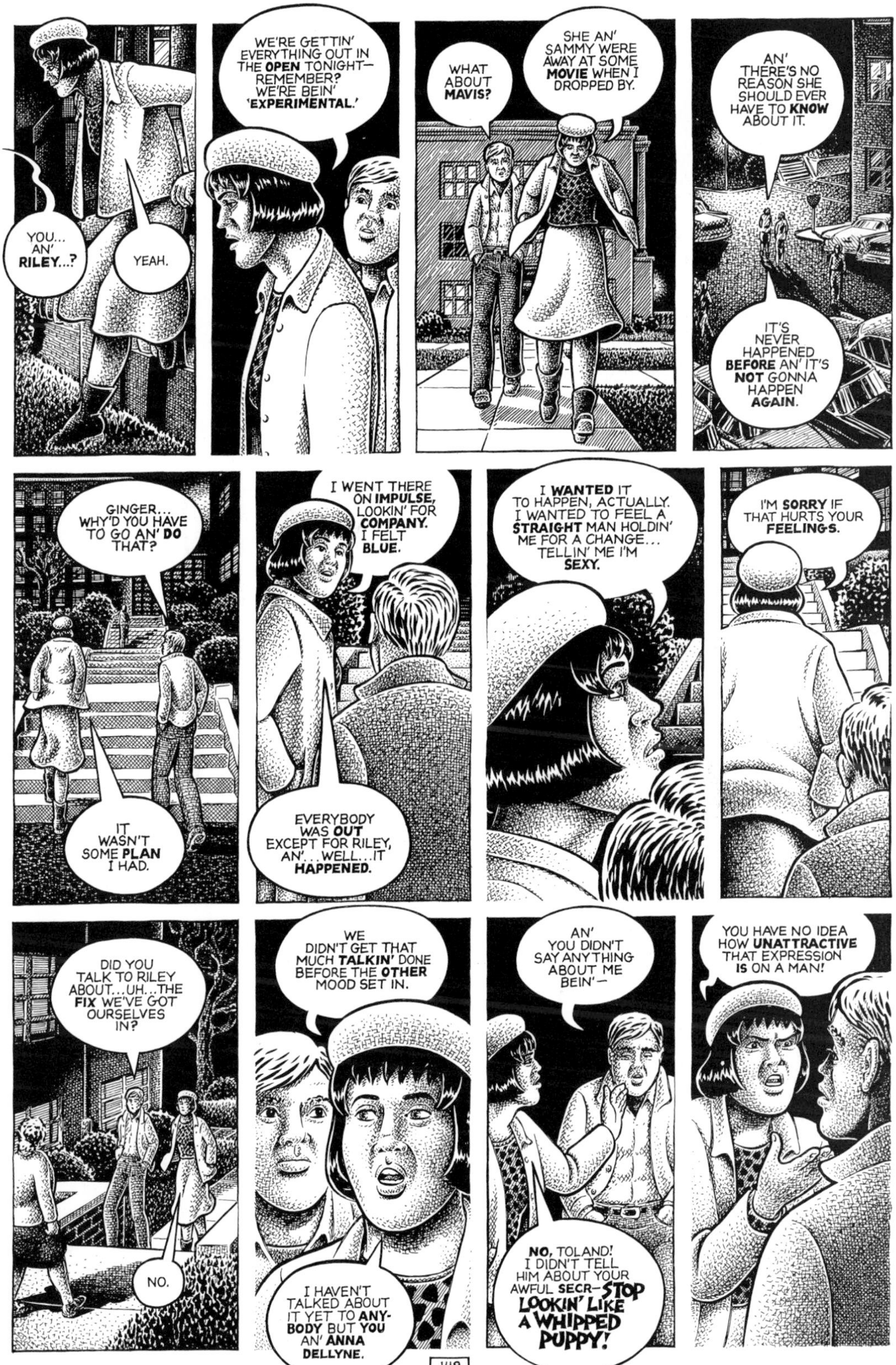
YOU... AN' RILEY...?
YEAH.
WE'RE GETTIN' EVERYTHING OUT IN THE OPEN TONIGHT— REMEMBER? WE'RE BEIN' 'EXPERIMENTAL.'
WHAT ABOUT MAVIS?
SHE AN' SAMMY WERE AWAY AT SOME MOVIE WHEN I DROPPED BY.
AN' THERE'S NO REASON SHE SHOULD EVER HAVE TO KNOW ABOUT IT.
IT'S NEVER HAPPENED BEFORE AN' IT'S NOT GONNA HAPPEN AGAIN.
GINGER... WHY'D YOU HAVE TO GO AN' DO THAT?
IT WASN'T SOME PLAN I HAD.
I WENT THERE ON IMPULSE, LOOKIN' FOR COMPANY. I FELT BLUE.
EVERYBODY WAS OUT EXCEPT FOR RILEY, AN'...WELL...IT HAPPENED.
I WANTED IT TO HAPPEN, ACTUALLY. I WANTED TO FEEL A STRAIGHT MAN HOLDIN' ME FOR A CHANGE... TELLIN' ME I'M SEXY.
I'M SORRY IF THAT HURTS YOUR FEELINGS.
DID YOU TALK TO RILEY ABOUT...UH...THE FIX WE'VE GOT OURSELVES IN?
NO.
WE DIDN'T GET THAT MUCH TALKIN' DONE BEFORE THE OTHER MOOD SET IN.
I HAVEN'T TALKED ABOUT IT YET TO ANYBODY BUT YOU AN' ANNA DELLYNE.
AN' YOU DIDN'T SAY ANYTHING ABOUT ME BEIN'—
NO, TOLAND! I DIDN'T TELL HIM ABOUT YOUR AWFUL SECR—STOP LOOKIN' LIKE A WHIPPED PUPPY!
YOU HAVE NO IDEA HOW UNATTRACTIVE THAT EXPRESSION IS ON A MAN!

YOU WERE OUT WARMIN' THE BEDSPRINGS WITH **LES** LAST NIGHT. WHAT'VE **YOU** GOT TO COMPLAIN ABOUT?

RILEY'S MY **BEST** FRIEND!

AN' **LES** IS ONE OF **MY** BEST FRIENDS!

SO IS **MAVIS!** AN' **SAMMY!**

WE'RE **ALL** OF US 'BEST FRIENDS' AROUND HERE!

I'M **GOIN'** IN.

GINGER—**WAIT.**

DO YOU **MIND** IF I...?

IT'S TOO **SOON** BY A **LONG** SHOT TO FEEL ANYTHING **KICKIN'.**

I KNOW. HE PROBABLY HASN'T EVEN FIGURED OUT FOR **HIMSELF** YET THAT HE **EXISTS!** OR **SHE** EXISTS.

STILL—

GO AHEAD AN' **FEEL.** WHOEVER'S **IN** THERE IS YOURS, **TOO.**

WHAT IT **REMINDS** ME OF IS TIMES I'VE LAID ON THE **GROUND** AT NIGHT, LOOKIN' UP AT THE **STARS** AN' WONDERIN' IF THERE ARE ANY **LITTLE GREEN PEOPLE** FROM **OTHER PLANETS** UP THERE.

COULD BE YOU'RE LOOKIN' ONE OF 'EM RIGHT IN THE **EYE**—BUT HE'S SO **FAR AWAY** AN' **TINY,** THERE'S NO WAY OF **KNOWIN'.**

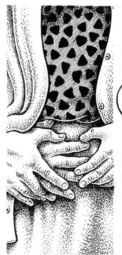

COMIN' FROM THE TWO OF **US,** THIS ONE MIGHT JUST AS **WELL** BE FROM ANOTHER PLANET!

WE'RE A **PAIR,** ALL RIGHT!

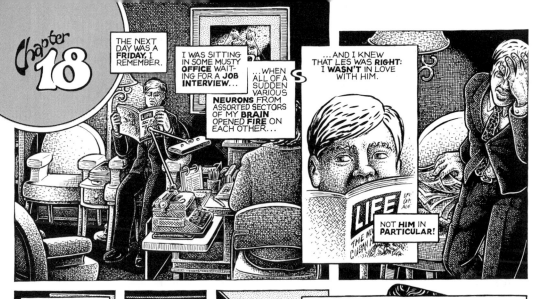

Chapter **18**

THE NEXT DAY WAS A **FRIDAY**, I REMEMBER.

I WAS SITTING IN SOME MUSTY **OFFICE** WAITING FOR A **JOB INTERVIEW**...

...WHEN ALL OF A SUDDEN VARIOUS **NEURONS** FROM ASSORTED SECTORS OF MY **BRAIN** OPENED **FIRE** ON EACH OTHER...

...AND I KNEW THAT LES WAS **RIGHT**: I **WASN'T** IN LOVE WITH HIM.

NOT **HIM** IN **PARTICULAR**!

SOME **EMOTIONS** I DIDN'T **UNDERSTAND** TOOK HOLD OF ME...

MR. POLK...?

...AND I **BOLTED** OUT THE **DOOR**.

THE **MAGAZINE** I'D BEEN LEAFING THROUGH HAD HAD A PHOTOGRAPH OF **SAL MINEO** IN IT.

WHICH REMINDED ME OF THE NIGHT I'D GONE TO SEE 'REBEL WITHOUT A CAUSE' A FEW YEARS BACK...

...AND COME HOME UNABLE TO THINK ABOUT **ANYTHING** EXCEPT WANTING TO HOLD JAMES DEAN'S DARK-EYED FRIEND IN MY **ARMS** AND **COMFORT** HIM.

IT COULDN'T BE '**LOVE**' I FELT, COULD IT? NOT FOR A **MOVIE ACTOR** I WAS NEVER GONNA BE WITHIN A **THOUSAND MILES** OF... AND NOT WITH **LES PEPPER**, EITHER!

'**LOVE**' HAD TO BE SOMETHING **ELSE**!

SOMETHING YOU COULD FIT INTO **SONG LYRICS** AND DANCE TO!

WHAT I WAS FEELING WAS A YEARNING **ACHE** THAT HAD TO DO WITH **MORE** THAN SOME **ONE GUY** I'D HAD MY ARMS AROUND IN A **MOTEL**.

I SAT ON MY **CAR FENDER** AND WATCHED THE RUSH HOUR **TRAFFIC** BUILD.

A PERSON COULD **HOP** RIGHT OUT INTO THE **MIDDLE** OF IT IF HE WANTED TO.

ONE WELL-TIMED **CARTWHEEL** AND IT'D BE **HELLO·O·O, OBLIVION**!

I WASN'T LOOKING **FORWARD** TO DRIVING BACK TO THE **WHEELERY**.

NOTHING THERE WAS THE WAY IT **USED** TO BE ANYMORE.

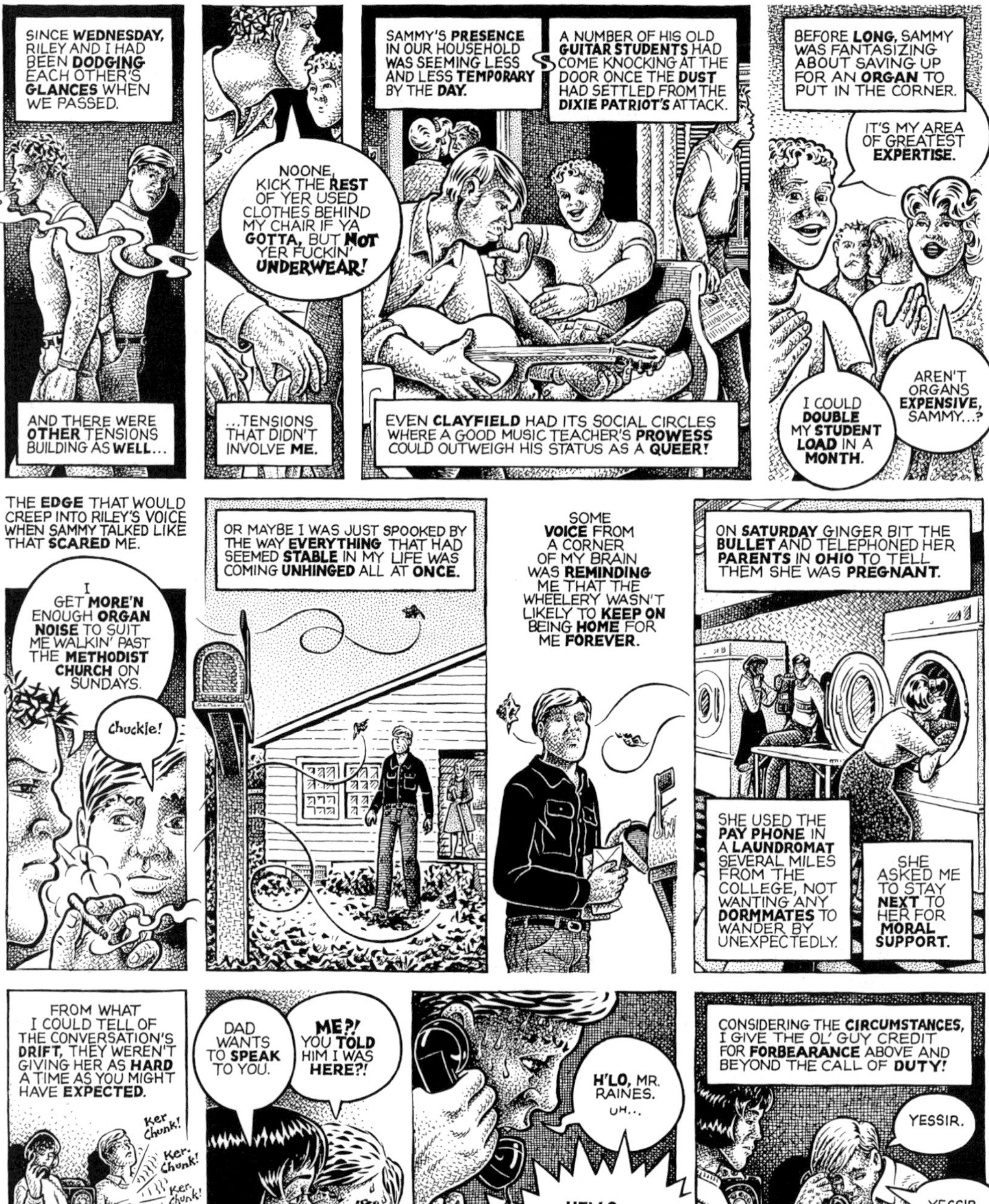
SINCE WEDNESDAY, RILEY AND I HAD BEEN DODGING EACH OTHER'S GLANCES WHEN WE PASSED.
AND THERE WERE OTHER TENSIONS BUILDING AS WELL...
NOONE, KICK THE REST OF YER USED CLOTHES BEHIND MY CHAIR IF YA GOTTA, BUT NOT YER FUCKIN' UNDERWEAR!
...TENSIONS THAT DIDN'T INVOLVE ME.
SAMMY'S PRESENCE IN OUR HOUSEHOLD WAS SEEMING LESS AND LESS TEMPORARY BY THE DAY.
A NUMBER OF HIS OLD GUITAR STUDENTS HAD COME KNOCKING AT THE DOOR ONCE THE DUST HAD SETTLED FROM THE DIXIE PATRIOT'S ATTACK.
EVEN CLAYFIELD HAD ITS SOCIAL CIRCLES WHERE A GOOD MUSIC TEACHER'S PROWESS COULD OUTWEIGH HIS STATUS AS A QUEER!
BEFORE LONG, SAMMY WAS FANTASIZING ABOUT SAVING UP FOR AN ORGAN TO PUT IN THE CORNER.
IT'S MY AREA OF GREATEST EXPERTISE.
AREN'T ORGANS EXPENSIVE, SAMMY...?
I COULD DOUBLE MY STUDENT LOAD IN A MONTH.
THE EDGE THAT WOULD CREEP INTO RILEY'S VOICE WHEN SAMMY TALKED LIKE THAT SCARED ME.
I GET MORE'N ENOUGH ORGAN NOISE TO SUIT ME WALKIN' PAST THE METHODIST CHURCH ON SUNDAYS.
Chuckle!
OR MAYBE I WAS JUST SPOOKED BY THE WAY EVERYTHING THAT HAD SEEMED STABLE IN MY LIFE WAS COMING UNHINGED ALL AT ONCE.
SOME VOICE FROM A CORNER OF MY BRAIN WAS REMINDING ME THAT THE WHEELERY WASN'T LIKELY TO KEEP ON BEING HOME FOR ME FOREVER.
ON SATURDAY GINGER BIT THE BULLET AND TELEPHONED HER PARENTS IN OHIO TO TELL THEM SHE WAS PREGNANT.
SHE USED THE PAY PHONE IN A LAUNDROMAT SEVERAL MILES FROM THE COLLEGE, NOT WANTING ANY DORMMATES TO WANDER BY UNEXPECTEDLY.
SHE ASKED ME TO STAY NEXT TO HER FOR MORAL SUPPORT.
FROM WHAT I COULD TELL OF THE CONVERSATION'S DRIFT, THEY WEREN'T GIVING HER AS HARD A TIME AS YOU MIGHT HAVE EXPECTED.
Ker Chunk!
Ker-Chunk!
Ker-Chunk!
DAD WANTS TO SPEAK TO YOU.
ME?! YOU TOLD HIM I WAS HERE?!
HE GUESSED.
H'LO, MR. RAINES. UH...
HELLO, TOLAND. IT'S GOOD TO TALK TO YOU AT LAST. GINGER'S TOLD US A LOT ABOUT YOU, SON, AND YOU'VE ALWAYS SOUNDED LIKE A RESPONSIBLE KIND OF FELLOW WHO'D WANT TO DO THE RIGHT THING....
Ker-Chunk!
Ker-Chunk!!
CONSIDERING THE CIRCUMSTANCES, I GIVE THE OL' GUY CREDIT FOR FORBEARANCE ABOVE AND BEYOND THE CALL OF DUTY!
YESSIR.
YESSIR.
THAT SOUNDS GOOD TO ME, SIR.
HE SAID THAT HE AND GINGER'S MOTHER WOULD MAKE A TRIP SOUTH VERY SHORTLY SO THAT WE COULD ALL STRATEGIZE TOGETHER ABOUT WHAT TO DO NEXT.

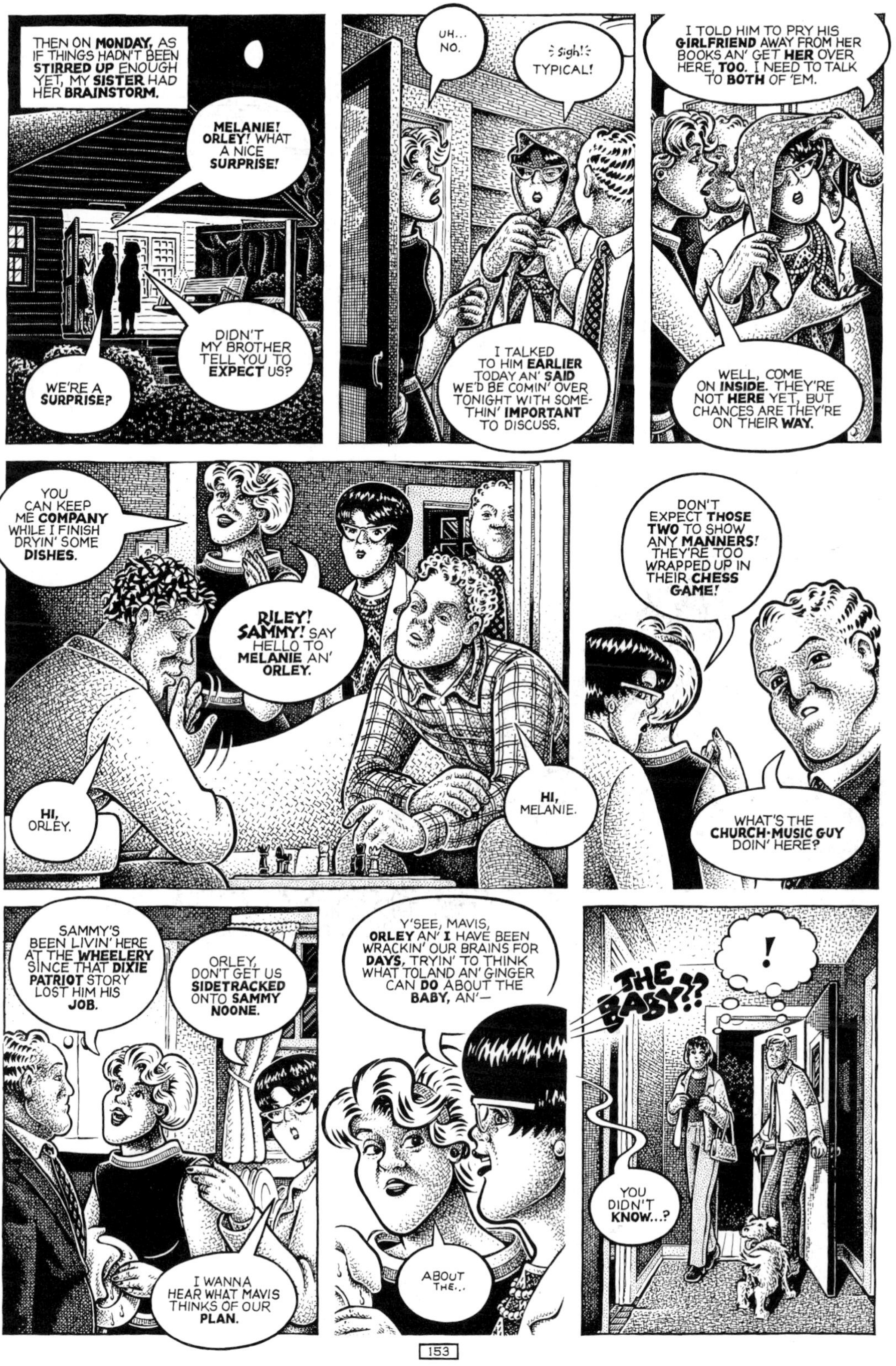
THEN ON MONDAY, AS IF THINGS HADN'T BEEN STIRRED UP ENOUGH YET, MY SISTER HAD HER BRAINSTORM.
MELANIE! ORLEY! WHAT A NICE SURPRISE!
WE'RE A SURPRISE?
DIDN'T MY BROTHER TELL YOU TO EXPECT US?
UH... NO.
Sigh! TYPICAL!
I TALKED TO HIM EARLIER TODAY AN' SAID WE'D BE COMIN' OVER TONIGHT WITH SOME-THIN' IMPORTANT TO DISCUSS.
I TOLD HIM TO PRY HIS GIRLFRIEND AWAY FROM HER BOOKS AN' GET HER OVER HERE, TOO. I NEED TO TALK TO BOTH OF 'EM.
WELL, COME ON INSIDE. THEY'RE NOT HERE YET, BUT CHANCES ARE THEY'RE ON THEIR WAY.
YOU CAN KEEP ME COMPANY WHILE I FINISH DRYIN' SOME DISHES.
RILEY! SAMMY! SAY HELLO TO MELANIE AN' ORLEY.
HI, ORLEY.
HI, MELANIE.
DON'T EXPECT THOSE TWO TO SHOW ANY MANNERS! THEY'RE TOO WRAPPED UP IN THEIR CHESS GAME!
WHAT'S THE CHURCH-MUSIC GUY DOIN' HERE?
SAMMY'S BEEN LIVIN' HERE AT THE WHEELERY SINCE THAT DIXIE PATRIOT STORY LOST HIM HIS JOB.
ORLEY, DON'T GET US SIDETRACKED ONTO SAMMY NOONE.
I WANNA HEAR WHAT MAVIS THINKS OF OUR PLAN.
Y'SEE, MAVIS, ORLEY AN' I HAVE BEEN WRACKIN' OUR BRAINS FOR DAYS, TRYIN' TO THINK WHAT TOLAND AN' GINGER CAN DO ABOUT THE BABY, AN'—
ABOUT THE...
THE BABY??
!
YOU DIDN'T KNOW...?

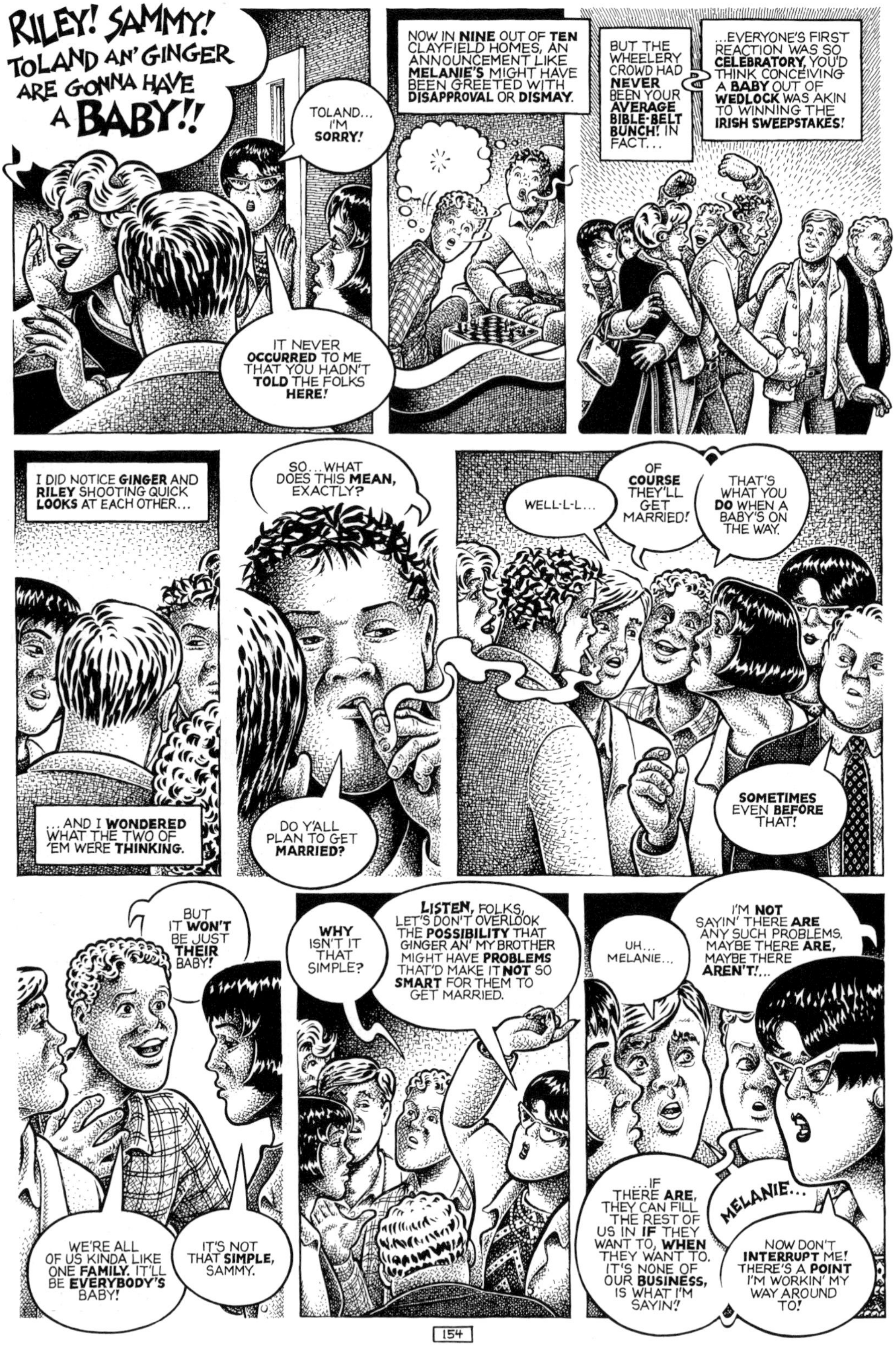
RILEY! SAMMY! TOLAND AN' GINGER ARE GONNA HAVE A BABY!!
TOLAND... I'M SORRY!
IT NEVER OCCURRED TO ME THAT YOU HADN'T TOLD THE FOLKS HERE!
NOW IN NINE OUT OF TEN CLAYFIELD HOMES, AN ANNOUNCEMENT LIKE MELANIE'S MIGHT HAVE BEEN GREETED WITH DISAPPROVAL OR DISMAY.
BUT THE WHEELERY CROWD HAD NEVER BEEN YOUR AVERAGE BIBLE-BELT BUNCH! IN FACT...
...EVERYONE'S FIRST REACTION WAS SO CELEBRATORY, YOU'D THINK CONCEIVING A BABY OUT OF WEDLOCK WAS AKIN TO WINNING THE IRISH SWEEPSTAKES!
I DID NOTICE GINGER AND RILEY SHOOTING QUICK LOOKS AT EACH OTHER...
...AND I WONDERED WHAT THE TWO OF 'EM WERE THINKING.
SO...WHAT DOES THIS MEAN, EXACTLY?
DO Y'ALL PLAN TO GET MARRIED?
WELL-L-L...
OF COURSE THEY'LL GET MARRIED!
THAT'S WHAT YOU DO WHEN A BABY'S ON THE WAY.
SOMETIMES EVEN BEFORE THAT!
BUT IT WON'T BE JUST THEIR BABY!
WE'RE ALL OF US KINDA LIKE ONE FAMILY. IT'LL BE EVERYBODY'S BABY!
IT'S NOT THAT SIMPLE, SAMMY.
WHY ISN'T IT THAT SIMPLE?
LISTEN, FOLKS, LET'S DON'T OVERLOOK THE POSSIBILITY THAT GINGER AN' MY BROTHER MIGHT HAVE PROBLEMS THAT'D MAKE IT NOT SO SMART FOR THEM TO GET MARRIED.
UH... MELANIE...
I'M NOT SAYIN' THERE ARE ANY SUCH PROBLEMS. MAYBE THERE ARE, MAYBE THERE AREN'T!...
...IF THERE ARE, THEY CAN FILL THE REST OF US IN IF THEY WANT TO, WHEN THEY WANT TO. IT'S NONE OF OUR BUSINESS, IS WHAT I'M SAYIN'!
MELANIE...
NOW DON'T INTERRUPT ME! THERE'S A POINT I'M WORKIN' MY WAY AROUND TO!

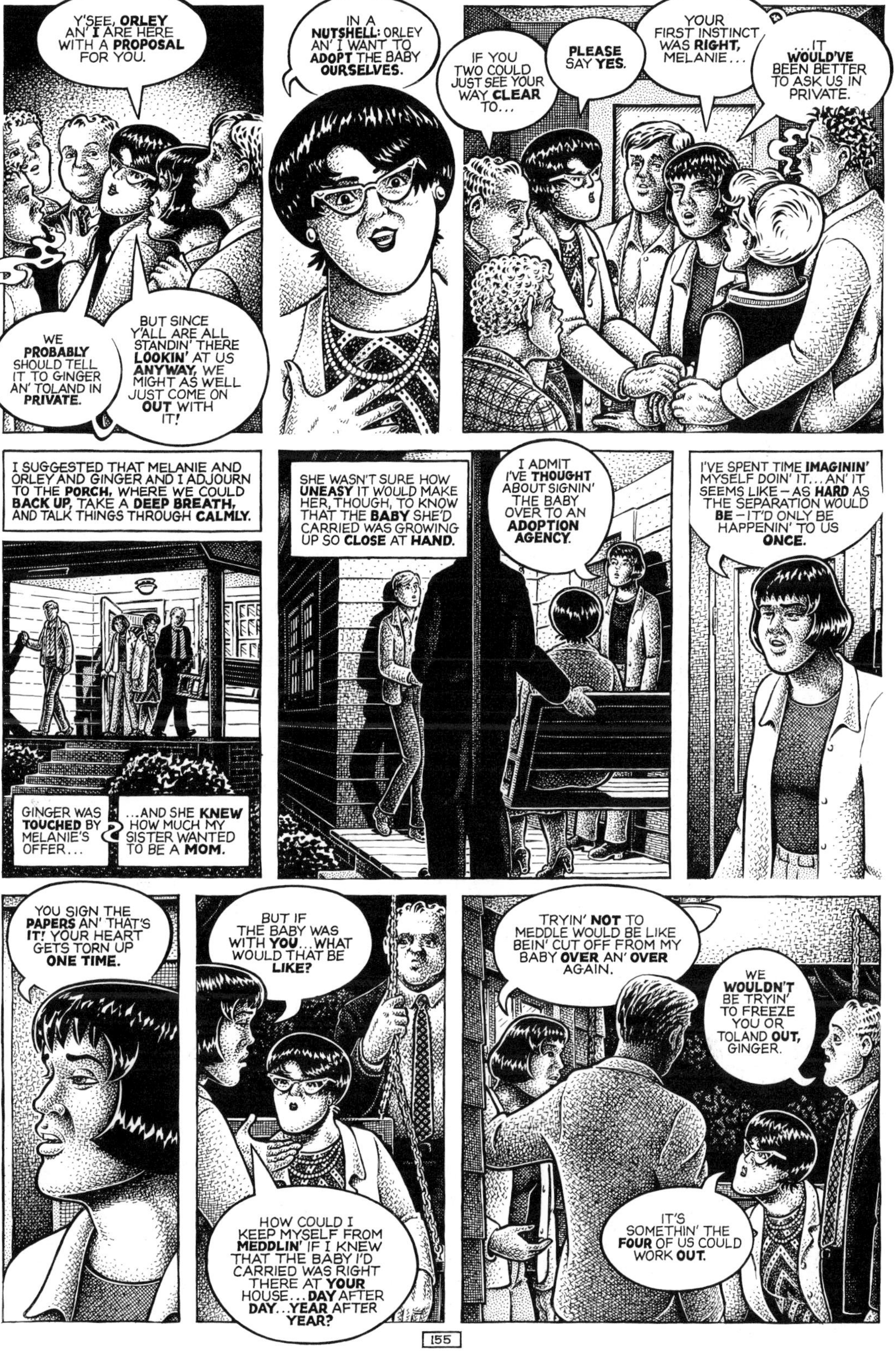
Y'SEE, ORLEY AN' I ARE HERE WITH A PROPOSAL FOR YOU.
WE PROBABLY SHOULD TELL IT TO GINGER AN' TOLAND IN PRIVATE.
BUT SINCE Y'ALL ARE ALL STANDIN' THERE LOOKIN' AT US ANYWAY, WE MIGHT AS WELL JUST COME ON OUT WITH IT!
IN A NUTSHELL: ORLEY AN' I WANT TO ADOPT THE BABY OURSELVES.
IF YOU TWO COULD JUST SEE YOUR WAY CLEAR TO...
PLEASE SAY YES.
YOUR FIRST INSTINCT WAS RIGHT, MELANIE...
...IT WOULD'VE BEEN BETTER TO ASK US IN PRIVATE.
I SUGGESTED THAT MELANIE AND ORLEY AND GINGER AND I ADJOURN TO THE PORCH, WHERE WE COULD BACK UP, TAKE A DEEP BREATH, AND TALK THINGS THROUGH CALMLY.
GINGER WAS TOUCHED BY MELANIE'S OFFER...
...AND SHE KNEW HOW MUCH MY SISTER WANTED TO BE A MOM.
SHE WASN'T SURE HOW UNEASY IT WOULD MAKE HER, THOUGH, TO KNOW THAT THE BABY SHE'D CARRIED WAS GROWING UP SO CLOSE AT HAND.
I ADMIT I'VE THOUGHT ABOUT SIGNIN' THE BABY OVER TO AN ADOPTION AGENCY.
I'VE SPENT TIME IMAGININ' MYSELF DOIN' IT... AN' IT SEEMS LIKE — AS HARD AS THE SEPARATION WOULD BE — IT'D ONLY BE HAPPENIN' TO US ONCE.
YOU SIGN THE PAPERS AN' THAT'S IT! YOUR HEART GETS TORN UP ONE TIME.
BUT IF THE BABY WAS WITH YOU... WHAT WOULD THAT BE LIKE?
HOW COULD I KEEP MYSELF FROM MEDDLIN' IF I KNEW THAT THE BABY I'D CARRIED WAS RIGHT THERE AT YOUR HOUSE... DAY AFTER DAY... YEAR AFTER YEAR?
TRYIN' NOT TO MEDDLE WOULD BE LIKE BEIN' CUT OFF FROM MY BABY OVER AN' OVER AGAIN.
WE WOULDN'T BE TRYIN' TO FREEZE YOU OR TOLAND OUT, GINGER.
IT'S SOMETHIN' THE FOUR OF US COULD WORK OUT.

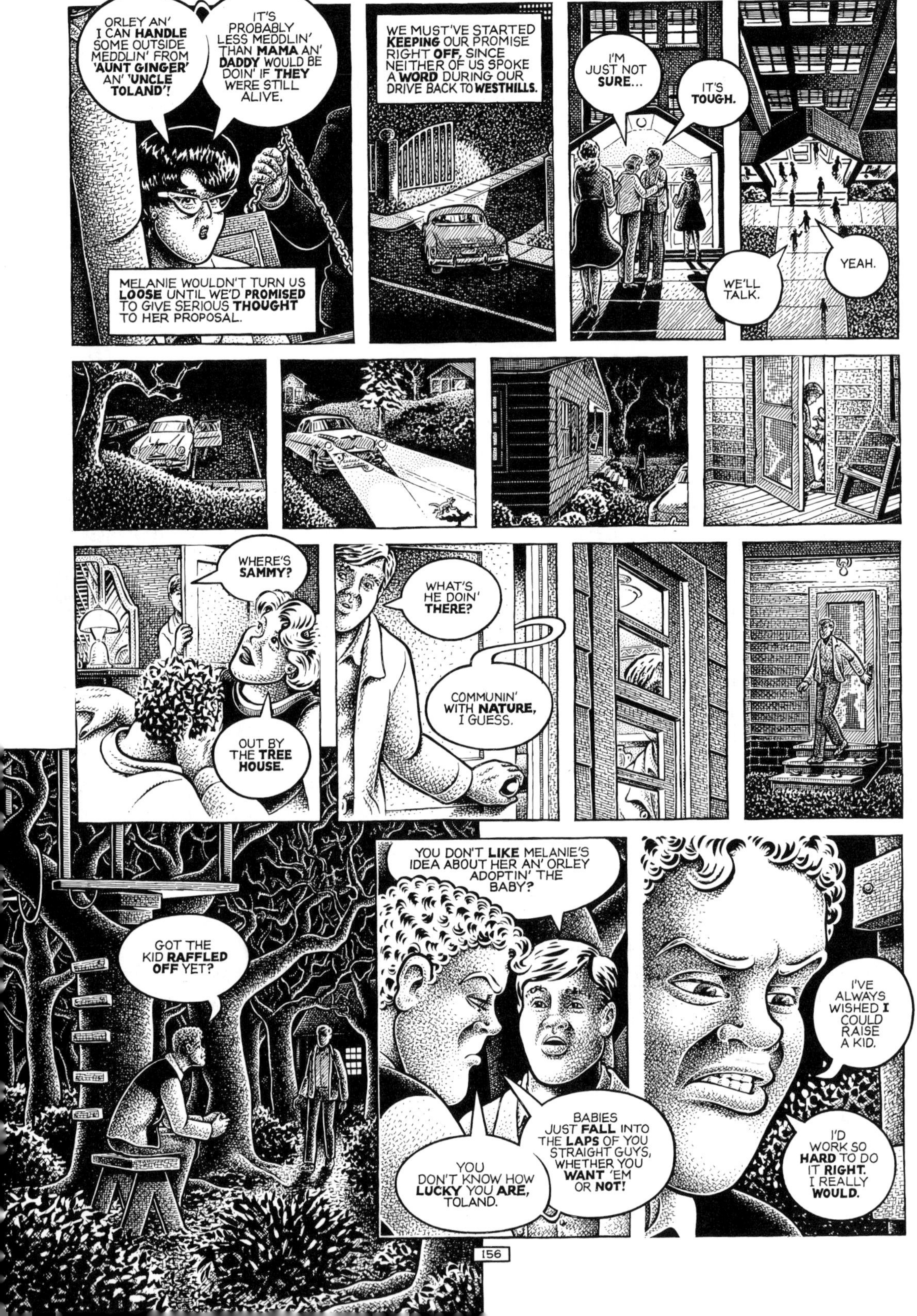
ORLEY AN' I CAN **HANDLE** SOME OUTSIDE MEDDLIN' FROM **'AUNT GINGER'** AN' **'UNCLE TOLAND'**!
IT'S PROBABLY LESS MEDDLIN' THAN **MAMA** AN' **DADDY** WOULD BE DOIN' IF **THEY** WERE STILL ALIVE.
MELANIE WOULDN'T TURN US **LOOSE** UNTIL WE'D **PROMISED** TO GIVE SERIOUS **THOUGHT** TO HER PROPOSAL.
WE MUST'VE STARTED **KEEPING** OUR PROMISE RIGHT **OFF**, SINCE NEITHER OF US SPOKE A **WORD** DURING OUR DRIVE BACK TO **WESTHILLS**.
I'M JUST NOT **SURE**...
IT'S **TOUGH.**
WE'LL TALK.
YEAH.
WHERE'S **SAMMY?**
OUT BY THE **TREE HOUSE.**
WHAT'S HE DOIN' **THERE?**
COMMUNIN' WITH **NATURE**, I GUESS.
GOT THE KID **RAFFLED OFF** YET?
YOU DON'T **LIKE** MELANIE'S IDEA ABOUT HER AN' ORLEY ADOPTIN' THE BABY?
YOU DON'T KNOW HOW **LUCKY** YOU **ARE**, TOLAND.
BABIES JUST **FALL** INTO THE **LAPS** OF YOU STRAIGHT GUYS, WHETHER YOU **WANT** 'EM OR **NOT**!
I'VE ALWAYS WISHED **I** COULD RAISE A KID.
I'D WORK SO **HARD** TO DO IT **RIGHT**. I REALLY **WOULD.**

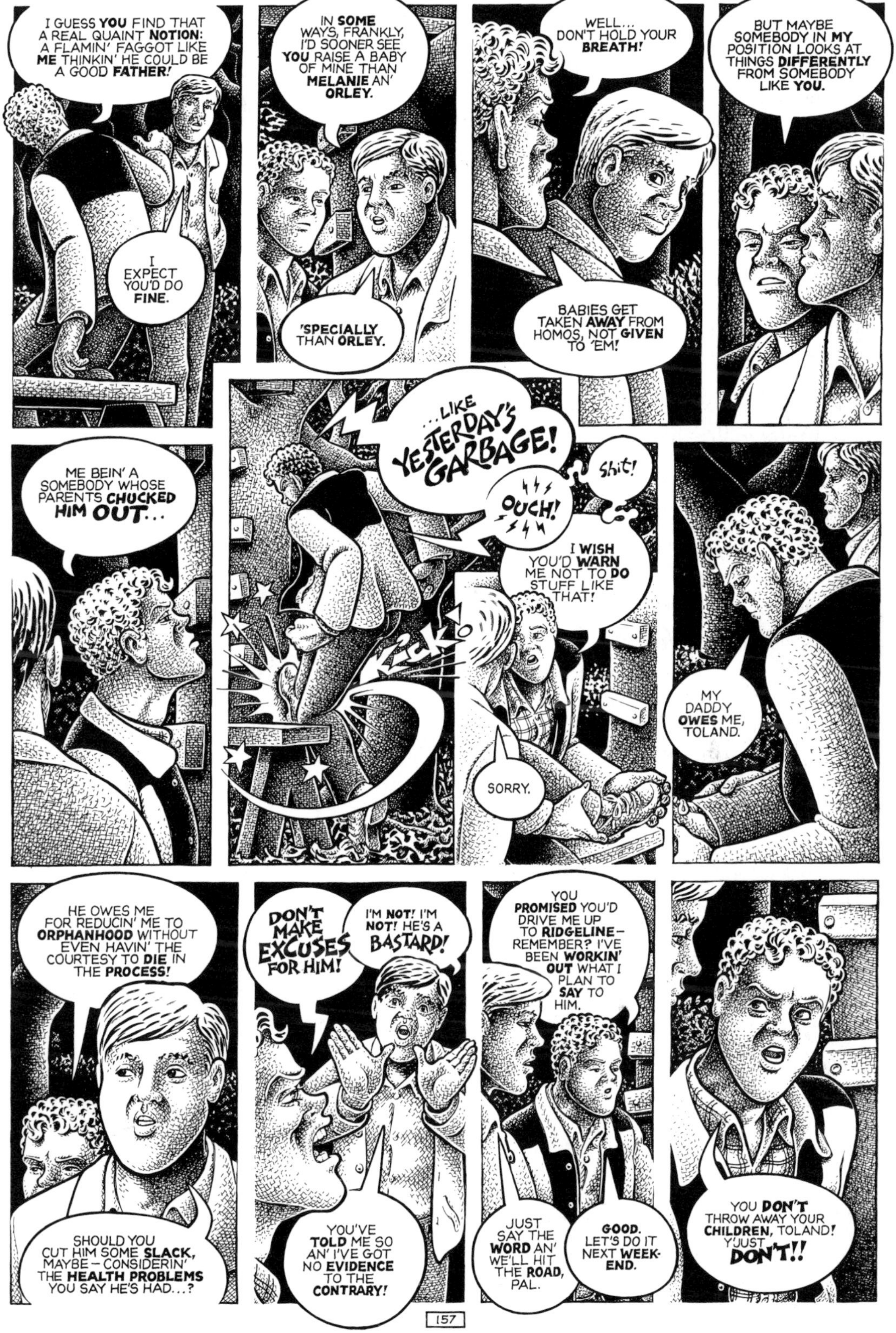
I GUESS YOU FIND THAT A REAL QUAINT NOTION: A FLAMIN' FAGGOT LIKE ME THINKIN' HE COULD BE A GOOD FATHER!
I EXPECT YOU'D DO FINE.
IN SOME WAYS, FRANKLY, I'D SOONER SEE YOU RAISE A BABY OF MINE THAN MELANIE AN' ORLEY.
'SPECIALLY THAN ORLEY.
WELL... DON'T HOLD YOUR BREATH!
BABIES GET TAKEN AWAY FROM HOMOS, NOT GIVEN TO 'EM!
BUT MAYBE SOMEBODY IN MY POSITION LOOKS AT THINGS DIFFERENTLY FROM SOMEBODY LIKE YOU.
ME BEIN' A SOMEBODY WHOSE PARENTS CHUCKED HIM OUT...
...LIKE YESTERDAY'S GARBAGE!
KICK!
OUCH!
SHIT!
I WISH YOU'D WARN ME NOT TO DO STUFF LIKE THAT!
SORRY.
MY DADDY OWES ME, TOLAND.
HE OWES ME FOR REDUCIN' ME TO ORPHANHOOD WITHOUT EVEN HAVIN' THE COURTESY TO DIE IN THE PROCESS!
SHOULD YOU CUT HIM SOME SLACK, MAYBE — CONSIDERIN' THE HEALTH PROBLEMS YOU SAY HE'S HAD...?
DON'T MAKE EXCUSES FOR HIM!
I'M NOT! I'M NOT! HE'S A BASTARD!
YOU'VE TOLD ME SO AN' I'VE GOT NO EVIDENCE TO THE CONTRARY!
YOU PROMISED YOU'D DRIVE ME UP TO RIDGELINE— REMEMBER? I'VE BEEN WORKIN' OUT WHAT I PLAN TO SAY TO HIM.
JUST SAY THE WORD AN' WE'LL HIT THE ROAD, PAL.
GOOD. LET'S DO IT NEXT WEEK-END.
YOU DON'T THROW AWAY YOUR CHILDREN, TOLAND! Y'JUST DON'T!!

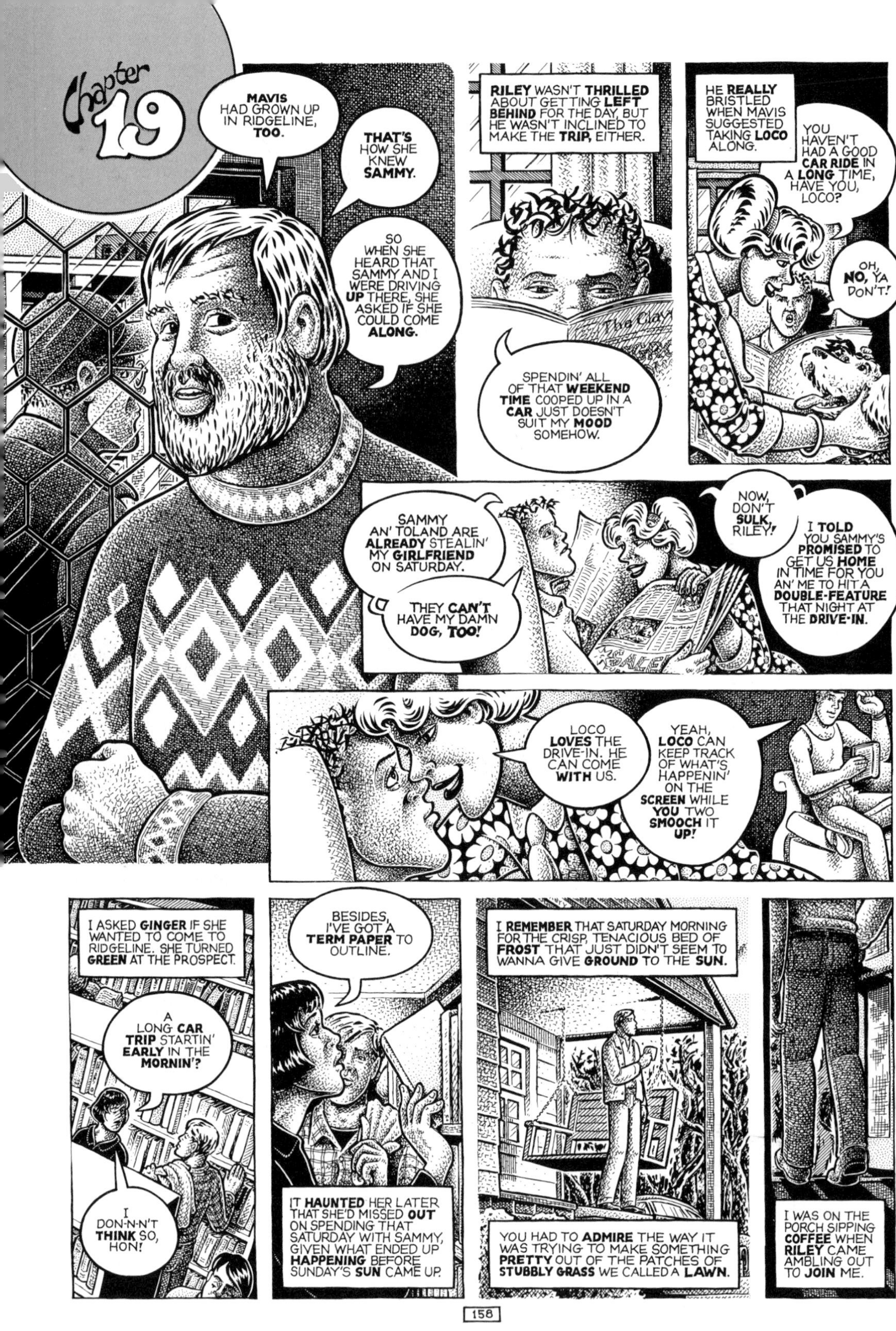
Chapter 19
MAVIS HAD GROWN UP IN RIDGELINE, TOO.
THAT'S HOW SHE KNEW SAMMY.
SO WHEN SHE HEARD THAT SAMMY AND I WERE DRIVING UP THERE, SHE ASKED IF SHE COULD COME ALONG.
RILEY WASN'T THRILLED ABOUT GETTING LEFT BEHIND FOR THE DAY, BUT HE WASN'T INCLINED TO MAKE THE TRIP, EITHER.
SPENDIN' ALL OF THAT WEEKEND TIME COOPED UP IN A CAR JUST DOESN'T SUIT MY MOOD SOMEHOW.
HE REALLY BRISTLED WHEN MAVIS SUGGESTED TAKING LOCO ALONG.
YOU HAVEN'T HAD A GOOD CAR RIDE IN A LONG TIME, HAVE YOU, LOCO?
OH, NO, YA DON'T!
SAMMY AN' TOLAND ARE ALREADY STEALIN' MY GIRLFRIEND ON SATURDAY.
THEY CAN'T HAVE MY DAMN DOG, TOO!
NOW, DON'T SULK, RILEY!
I TOLD YOU SAMMY'S PROMISED TO GET US HOME IN TIME FOR YOU AN' ME TO HIT A DOUBLE-FEATURE THAT NIGHT AT THE DRIVE-IN.
LOCO LOVES THE DRIVE-IN. HE CAN COME WITH US.
YEAH, LOCO CAN KEEP TRACK OF WHAT'S HAPPENIN' ON THE SCREEN WHILE YOU TWO SMOOCH IT UP!
I ASKED GINGER IF SHE WANTED TO COME TO RIDGELINE. SHE TURNED GREEN AT THE PROSPECT.
A LONG CAR TRIP STARTIN' EARLY IN THE MORNIN'?
I DON-N-N'T THINK SO, HON!
BESIDES, I'VE GOT A TERM PAPER TO OUTLINE.
IT HAUNTED HER LATER THAT SHE'D MISSED OUT ON SPENDING THAT SATURDAY WITH SAMMY, GIVEN WHAT ENDED UP HAPPENING BEFORE SUNDAY'S SUN CAME UP.
I REMEMBER THAT SATURDAY MORNING FOR THE CRISP, TENACIOUS BED OF FROST THAT JUST DIDN'T SEEM TO WANNA GIVE GROUND TO THE SUN.
YOU HAD TO ADMIRE THE WAY IT WAS TRYING TO MAKE SOMETHING PRETTY OUT OF THE PATCHES OF STUBBLY GRASS WE CALLED A LAWN.
I WAS ON THE PORCH SIPPING COFFEE WHEN RILEY CAME AMBLING OUT TO JOIN ME.

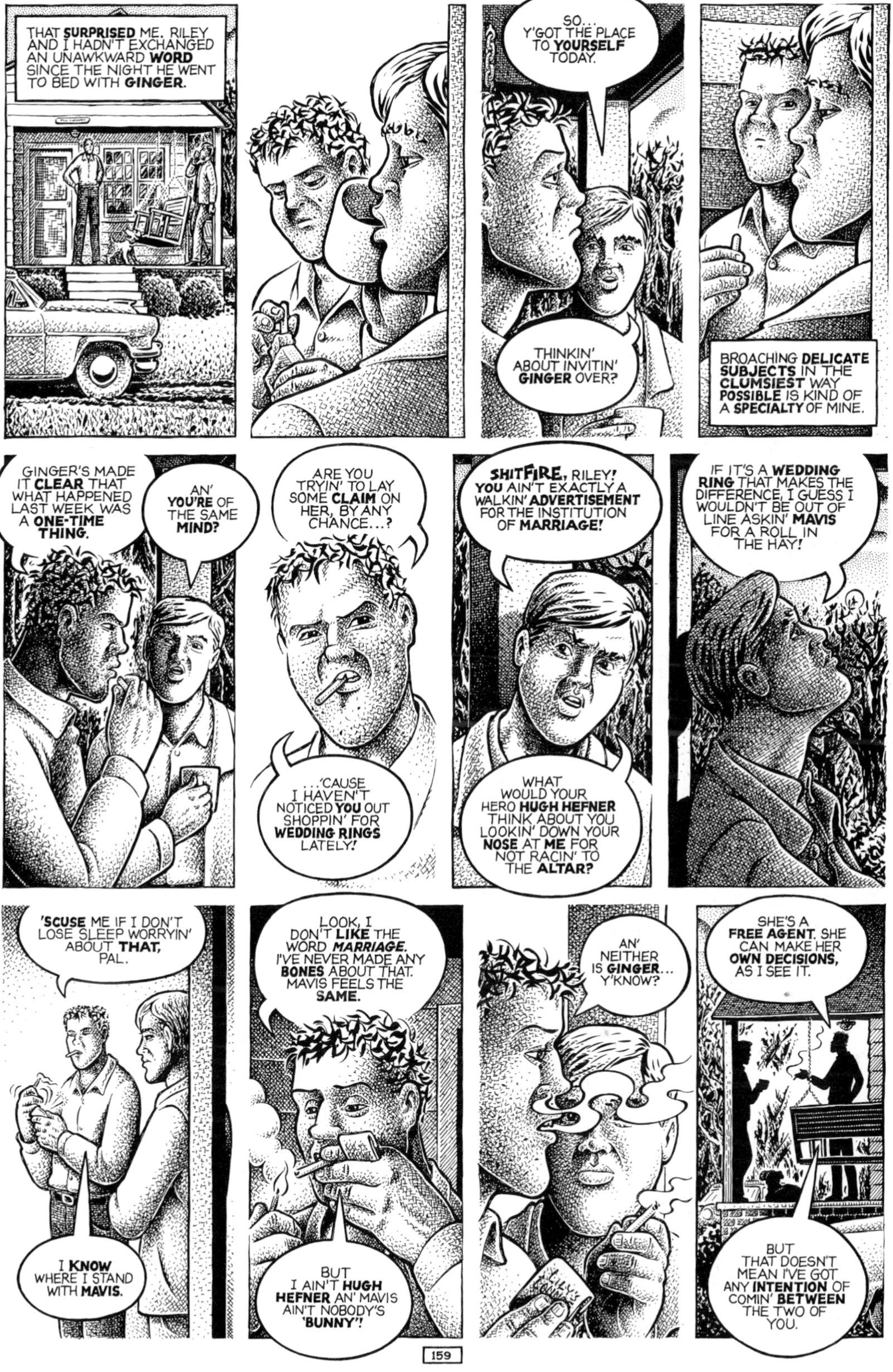
THAT SURPRISED ME. RILEY AND I HADN'T EXCHANGED AN UNAWKWARD WORD SINCE THE NIGHT HE WENT TO BED WITH GINGER.
SO... Y'GOT THE PLACE TO YOURSELF TODAY.
THINKIN' ABOUT INVITIN' GINGER OVER?
BROACHING DELICATE SUBJECTS IN THE CLUMSIEST WAY POSSIBLE IS KIND OF A SPECIALTY OF MINE.
GINGER'S MADE IT CLEAR THAT WHAT HAPPENED LAST WEEK WAS A ONE-TIME THING.
AN' YOU'RE OF THE SAME MIND?
ARE YOU TRYIN' TO LAY SOME CLAIM ON HER, BY ANY CHANCE...?
...'CAUSE I HAVEN'T NOTICED YOU OUT SHOPPIN' FOR WEDDING RINGS LATELY!
SHITFIRE, RILEY! YOU AIN'T EXACTLY A WALKIN' ADVERTISEMENT FOR THE INSTITUTION OF MARRIAGE!
WHAT WOULD YOUR HERO HUGH HEFNER THINK ABOUT YOU LOOKIN' DOWN YOUR NOSE AT ME FOR NOT RACIN' TO THE ALTAR?
IF IT'S A WEDDING RING THAT MAKES THE DIFFERENCE, I GUESS I WOULDN'T BE OUT OF LINE ASKIN' MAVIS FOR A ROLL IN THE HAY!
'SCUSE ME IF I DON'T LOSE SLEEP WORRYIN' ABOUT THAT, PAL.
I KNOW WHERE I STAND WITH MAVIS.
LOOK, I DON'T LIKE THE WORD MARRIAGE. I'VE NEVER MADE ANY BONES ABOUT THAT. MAVIS FEELS THE SAME.
BUT I AIN'T HUGH HEFNER AN' MAVIS AIN'T NOBODY'S 'BUNNY'!
AN' NEITHER IS GINGER... Y'KNOW?
SHE'S A FREE AGENT. SHE CAN MAKE HER OWN DECISIONS, AS I SEE IT.
BUT THAT DOESN'T MEAN I'VE GOT ANY INTENTION OF COMIN' BETWEEN THE TWO OF YOU.

'SPECIALLY WITH GINGER **PREGNANT**. **THAT** GOT SPRUNG ON ME OUTA **LEFT FIELD**!

OF COURSE, YOU AN' I **BOTH** KNOW THAT YOU CAN GET **BACK** AT ME IF YOU'RE SO INCLINED BY TELLIN' MAVIS ABOUT—

♪ O.K., TOLAND! ♪

SAMMY AN' I ARE **READY** TO **GO**!

Yurf!

NO, **NO**, LOCO. WE GO! **YOU DON'T GO** NOW! **YOU** GO LATER!

Woof! Woof!

OOPS! I ALMOST FORGOT MY **ENVELOPE**.

WHAT'S **IN** THAT PRECIOUS ENVELOPE OF YOURS **ANYWAY**?

YOU'LL SEE.

IT'S MY **SHOW-AN'-TELL**!

I WON'T SPILL ANY BEANS TO **MAVIS**. IT'S NOT MY **PLACE** TO.

'BYE, RILEY.

WE'LL SEE YOU **LATE** THIS **AFTERNOON**.

TURN ON THE **RADIO**, I WANT **MUSIC**!

♪ Walk Right In! Sit right down! Daddy, let your mind roll on!... ♪

RICK'S FOOD

Burma Shave

SAMMY HADN'T GIVEN HIS FOLKS A **WORD** OF **WARNING** THAT HE WAS ABOUT TO PAY THEM A **VISIT**.

HE DIDN'T WANT TO GIVE 'EM TIME TO DIG THE **BARBED WIRE** AND **LAND MINES** OUT OF STORAGE, HE SAID.

DINAH!

MISTER **SAMMY**! I DON'T BELIEVE WHAT I'M **SEEIN'**!

YOU COME HERE RIGHT THIS **MINUTE** AN' GIVE ME A **HUG**!

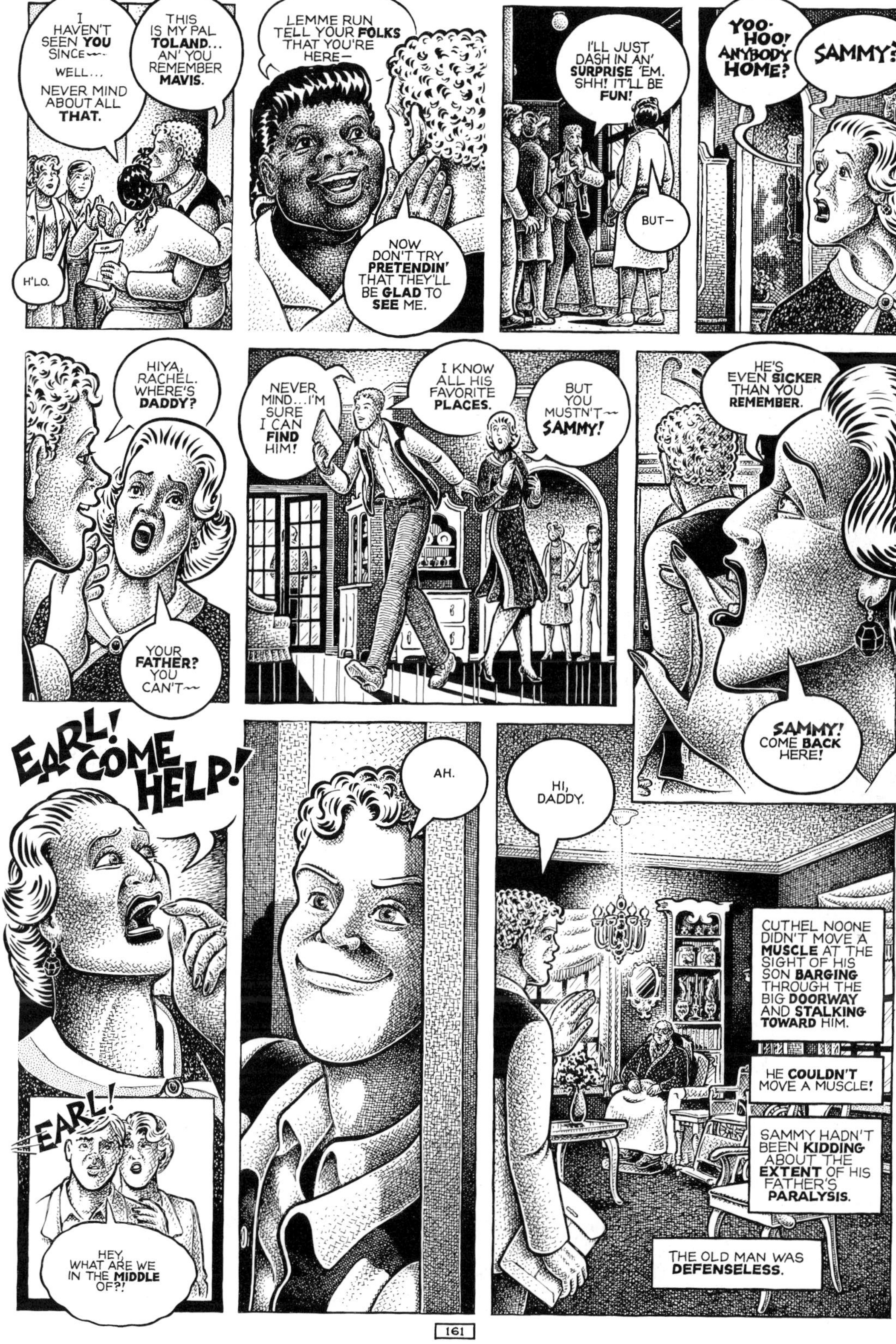
I HAVEN'T SEEN YOU SINCE~~ WELL... NEVER MIND ABOUT ALL THAT.
THIS IS MY PAL TOLAND... AN' YOU REMEMBER MAVIS.
H'LO.
LEMME RUN TELL YOUR FOLKS THAT YOU'RE HERE—
NOW DON'T TRY PRETENDIN' THAT THEY'LL BE GLAD TO SEE ME.
I'LL JUST DASH IN AN' SURPRISE 'EM. SHH! IT'LL BE FUN!
BUT—
YOO-HOO! ANYBODY HOME?
SAMMY?
HIYA, RACHEL. WHERE'S DADDY?
YOUR FATHER? YOU CAN'T~~
NEVER MIND... I'M SURE I CAN FIND HIM!
I KNOW ALL HIS FAVORITE PLACES.
BUT YOU MUSTN'T~~ SAMMY!
HE'S EVEN SICKER THAN YOU REMEMBER.
SAMMY! COME BACK HERE!
EARL! COME HELP!
EARL!
HEY, WHAT ARE WE IN THE MIDDLE OF?!
AH.
HI, DADDY.
CUTHEL NOONE DIDN'T MOVE A MUSCLE AT THE SIGHT OF HIS SON BARGING THROUGH THE BIG DOORWAY AND STALKING TOWARD HIM.
HE COULDN'T MOVE A MUSCLE!
SAMMY HADN'T BEEN KIDDING ABOUT THE EXTENT OF HIS FATHER'S PARALYSIS.
THE OLD MAN WAS DEFENSELESS.

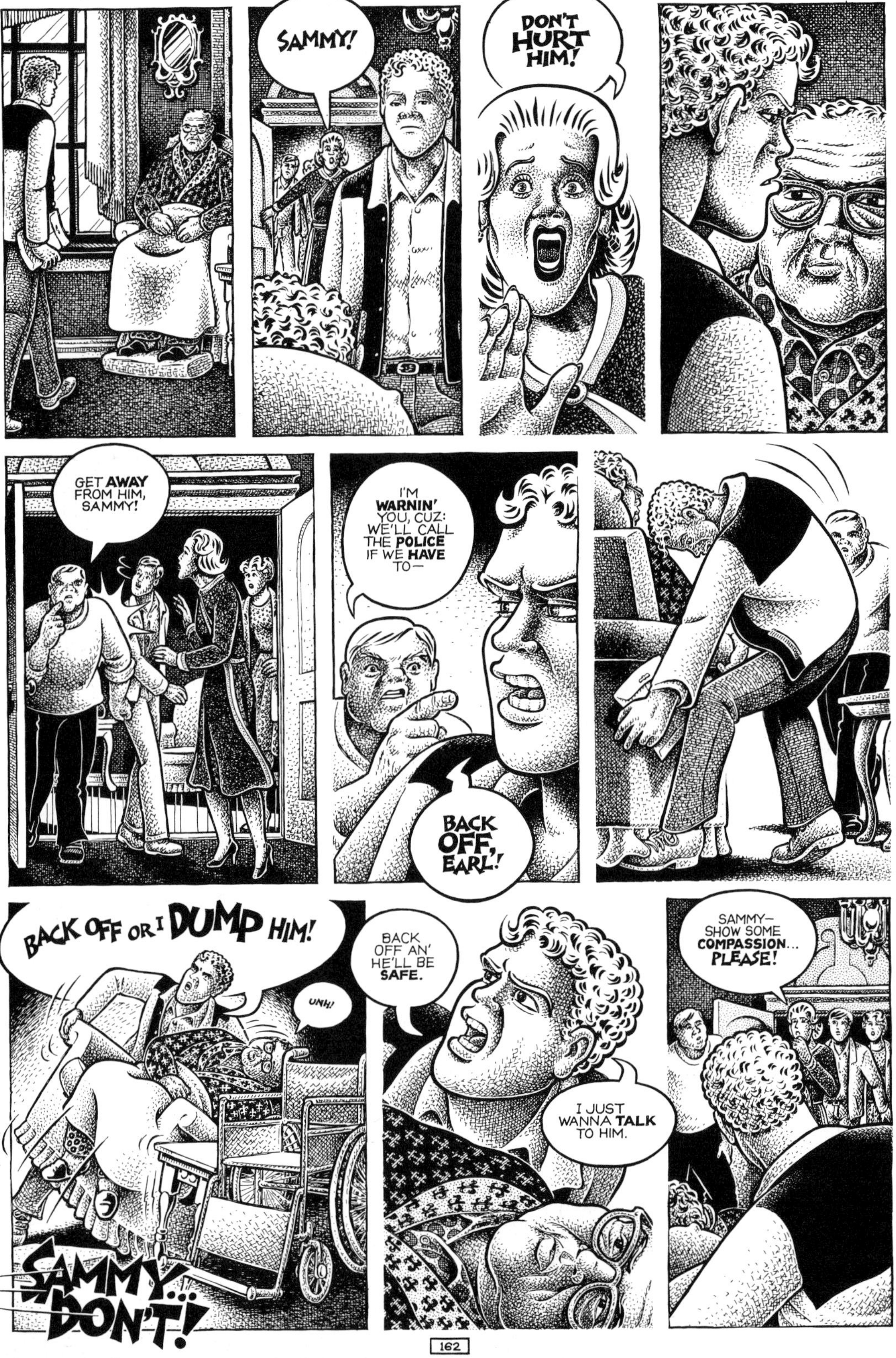
SAMMY!
DON'T HURT HIM!
GET AWAY FROM HIM, SAMMY!
I'M WARNIN' YOU, CUZ: WE'LL CALL THE POLICE IF WE HAVE TO—
BACK OFF, EARL!
BACK OFF OR I DUMP HIM!
UNH!
SAMMY... DON'T!
BACK OFF AN' HE'LL BE SAFE.
I JUST WANNA TALK TO HIM.
SAMMY— SHOW SOME COMPASSION... PLEASE!

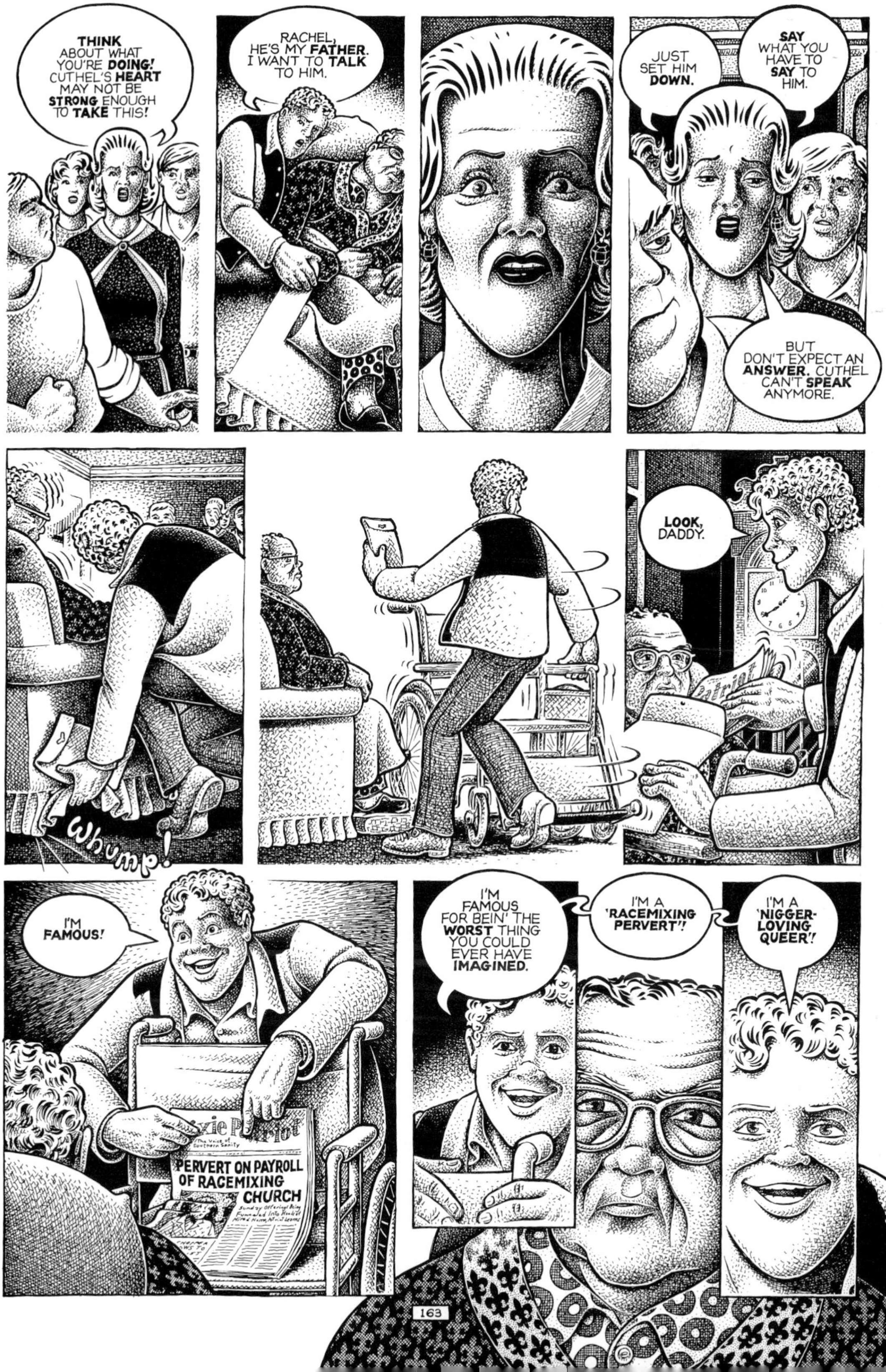
THINK ABOUT WHAT YOU'RE DOING! CUTHEL'S HEART MAY NOT BE STRONG ENOUGH TO TAKE THIS!
RACHEL, HE'S MY FATHER. I WANT TO TALK TO HIM.
JUST SET HIM DOWN.
SAY WHAT YOU HAVE TO SAY TO HIM.
BUT DON'T EXPECT AN ANSWER. CUTHEL CAN'T SPEAK ANYMORE.
Whump!
LOOK, DADDY.
Patriot
I'M FAMOUS!
The Voice of Southern Sanity
PERVERT ON PAYROLL OF RACEMIXING CHURCH
I'M FAMOUS FOR BEIN' THE WORST THING YOU COULD EVER HAVE IMAGINED.
I'M A 'RACEMIXING PERVERT'!
I'M A 'NIGGER-LOVING QUEER'!

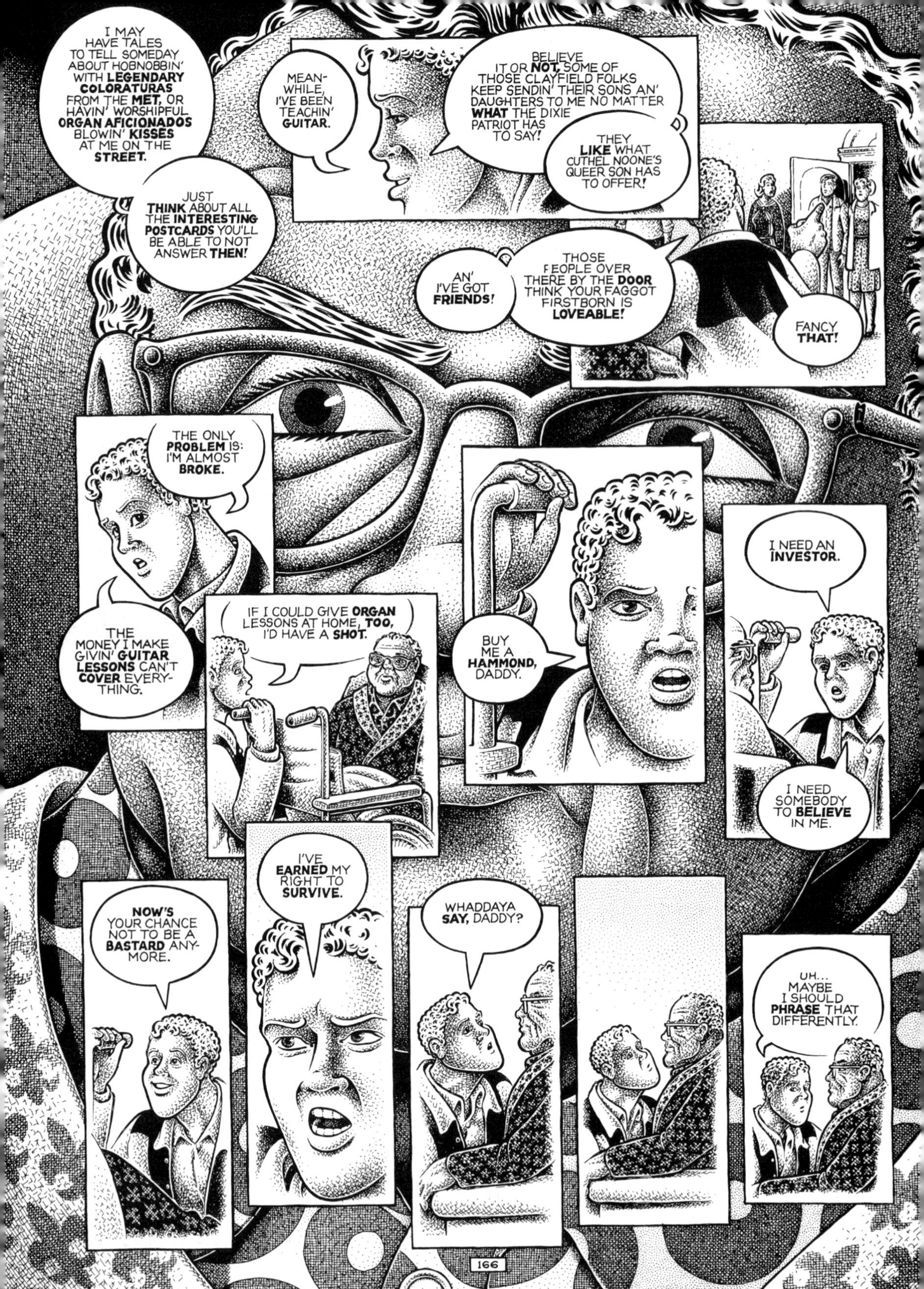
I MAY HAVE TALES TO TELL SOMEDAY ABOUT HOBNOBBIN' WITH **LEGENDARY COLORATURAS** FROM THE **MET**, OR HAVIN' WORSHIPFUL **ORGAN AFICIONADOS** BLOWIN' **KISSES** AT ME ON THE **STREET**.
JUST **THINK** ABOUT ALL THE **INTERESTING POSTCARDS** YOU'LL BE ABLE TO NOT ANSWER **THEN**!
MEAN-WHILE, I'VE BEEN TEACHIN' **GUITAR**.
BELIEVE IT OR **NOT**, SOME OF THOSE CLAYFIELD FOLKS KEEP SENDIN' THEIR SONS AN' DAUGHTERS TO ME NO MATTER **WHAT** THE DIXIE PATRIOT HAS TO SAY!
THEY **LIKE** WHAT CUTHEL NOONE'S QUEER SON HAS TO OFFER!
AN' I'VE GOT **FRIENDS**!
THOSE PEOPLE OVER THERE BY THE **DOOR** THINK YOUR FAGGOT FIRSTBORN IS **LOVEABLE**!
FANCY **THAT**!
THE ONLY **PROBLEM** IS: I'M ALMOST **BROKE**.
THE MONEY I MAKE GIVIN' **GUITAR LESSONS** CAN'T **COVER** EVERY-THING.
IF I COULD GIVE **ORGAN** LESSONS AT HOME, **TOO**, I'D HAVE A **SHOT**.
BUY ME A **HAMMOND**, DADDY.
I NEED AN **INVESTOR**.
I NEED SOMEBODY TO **BELIEVE** IN ME.
NOW'S YOUR CHANCE NOT TO BE A **BASTARD** ANY-MORE.
I'VE **EARNED** MY RIGHT TO **SURVIVE**.
WHADDAYA **SAY**, DADDY?
UH... MAYBE I SHOULD **PHRASE** THAT DIFFERENTLY.

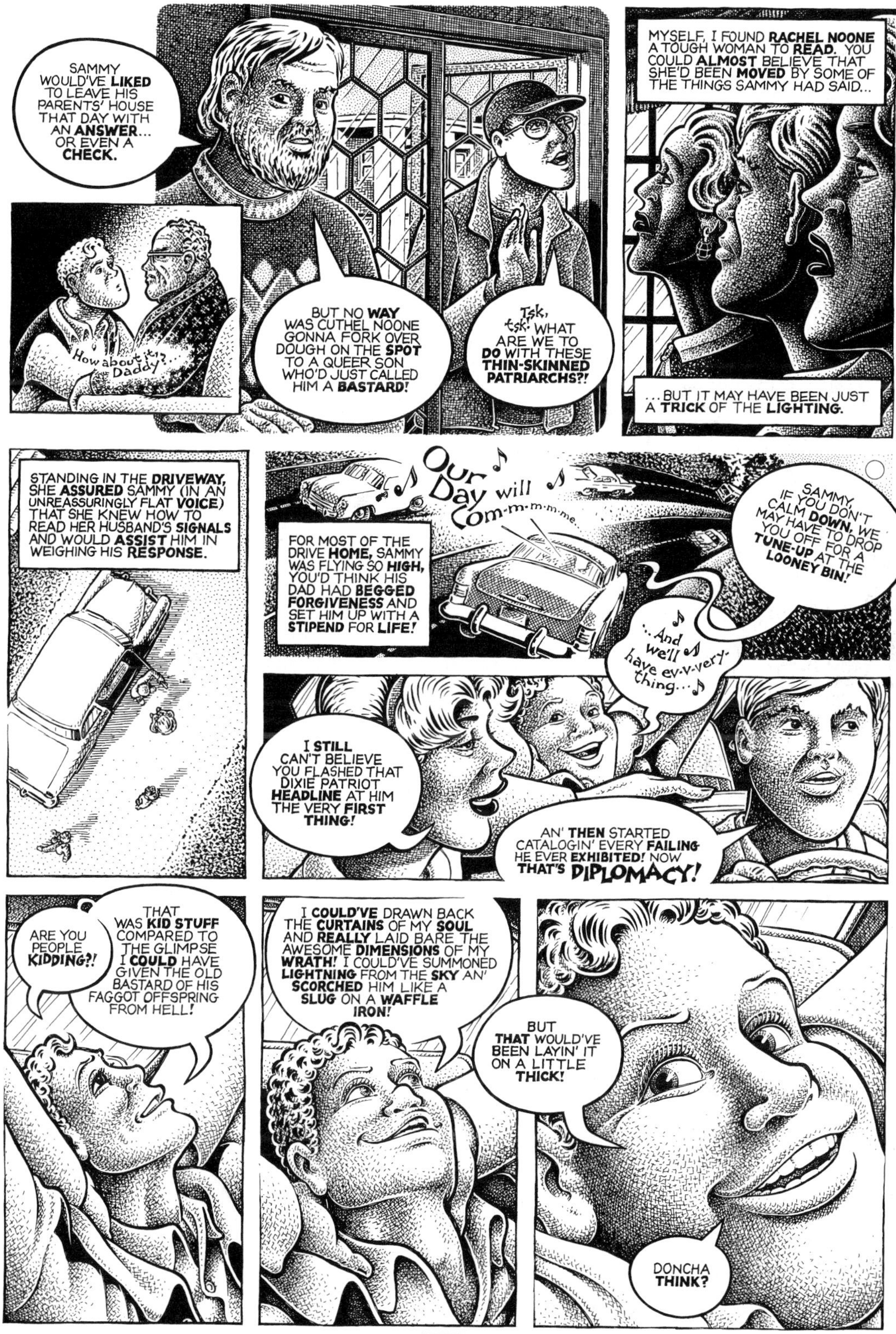
SAMMY WOULD'VE **LIKED** TO LEAVE HIS PARENTS' HOUSE THAT DAY WITH AN **ANSWER**... OR EVEN A **CHECK.**
How about it, Daddy?..
BUT NO **WAY** WAS CUTHEL NOONE GONNA FORK OVER DOUGH ON THE **SPOT** TO A QUEER SON WHO'D JUST CALLED HIM A **BASTARD!**
Tsk, tsk. WHAT ARE WE TO **DO** WITH THESE **THIN-SKINNED PATRIARCHS?!**
MYSELF, I FOUND **RACHEL NOONE** A TOUGH WOMAN TO **READ.** YOU COULD **ALMOST** BELIEVE THAT SHE'D BEEN **MOVED** BY SOME OF THE THINGS SAMMY HAD SAID...
...BUT IT MAY HAVE BEEN JUST A **TRICK** OF THE **LIGHTING.**
STANDING IN THE **DRIVEWAY,** SHE **ASSURED** SAMMY (IN AN UNREASSURINGLY FLAT **VOICE**) THAT SHE KNEW HOW TO READ HER HUSBAND'S **SIGNALS** AND WOULD **ASSIST** HIM IN WEIGHING HIS **RESPONSE.**
Our Day will Com-m-m-m-me...
FOR MOST OF THE DRIVE **HOME,** SAMMY WAS FLYING SO **HIGH,** YOU'D THINK HIS DAD HAD **BEGGED FORGIVENESS** AND SET HIM UP WITH A **STIPEND** FOR **LIFE!**
SAMMY, IF YOU DON'T CALM **DOWN,** WE MAY HAVE TO DROP YOU OFF FOR A **TUNE-UP** AT THE **LOONEY BIN!**
..And we'll have ev-v-very-thing...
I **STILL** CAN'T BELIEVE YOU FLASHED THAT DIXIE PATRIOT **HEADLINE** AT HIM THE VERY **FIRST THING!**
AN' **THEN** STARTED CATALOGIN' EVERY **FAILING** HE EVER **EXHIBITED!** NOW **THAT'S DIPLOMACY!**
ARE YOU PEOPLE **KIDDING?!**
THAT WAS **KID STUFF** COMPARED TO THE GLIMPSE I **COULD** HAVE GIVEN THE OLD BASTARD OF HIS FAGGOT OFFSPRING FROM HELL!
I **COULD'VE** DRAWN BACK THE **CURTAINS** OF MY **SOUL** AND **REALLY** LAID BARE THE AWESOME **DIMENSIONS** OF MY **WRATH!** I COULD'VE SUMMONED **LIGHTNING** FROM THE **SKY** AN' **SCORCHED** HIM LIKE A **SLUG** ON A **WAFFLE IRON!**
BUT **THAT** WOULD'VE BEEN LAYIN' IT ON A LITTLE **THICK!**
DONCHA **THINK?**

Chapter 20

WHEN WE GOT BACK TO THE **WHEELERY**, I TELEPHONED **GINGER** AND TOLD HER ALL ABOUT OUR WEIRD TRIP TO **RIDGELINE.**

THEN WE MOVED ON TO **OTHER** SUBJECTS AND I LOST TRACK OF **TIME** ...'TIL **MAVIS** BROKE IN.

TOLAND, I'M **SORRY**... I'VE JUST **GOTTA** INTERRUPT YOU.

HOLD ON A SEC, GINGER, **MAVIS** WANTS SOMETHIN'.

BE A HONEY AN' GO **LOOK IN** ON **SAMMY.** I'D DO IT, BUT I'VE GOT **SUPPER** COMIN' OFF THE STOVE.

WHY? WHAT'S WITH **SAMMY?**

HE'S BEEN HITTIN' THE **BOTTLE** SO HARD SINCE WE GOT HOME, IT'S **WORRYIN'** ME.

REALLY? I THOUGHT HE WAS IN A **GREAT** MOOD.

MAYBE HE'S JUST **CELEBRATIN'.**

COULD **BE**...BUT IT DOESN'T HAVE THAT **FEEL** TO ME.

I'VE GOTTA **GO,** GINGER.

YOU'RE LOOKIN' DOWNRIGHT **STONKERED,** FELLA.

SHOULD YOU MAYBE SLOW **DOWN**...?

JUST **WINDIN'** DOWN FROM A **THRILL-PACKED** DAY!

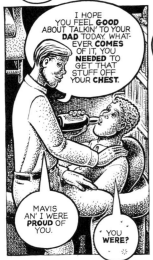

I HOPE YOU FEEL **GOOD** ABOUT TALKIN' TO YOUR **DAD** TODAY. WHATEVER **COMES** OF IT, YOU **NEEDED** TO GET THAT STUFF OFF YOUR **CHEST.**

MAVIS AN' I WERE **PROUD** OF YOU.

YOU **WERE?**

WHAT A **COINCIDENCE!** *I* WAS PROUD OF MYSELF, **TOO!**

THE **ONLY** THING THAT WOULD'VE MADE ME **PROUDER** WOULD BE IF I'D **DRIBBLED** THE OL' BASTARD AROUND THE ROOM LIKE A **BASKETBALL** AN' **DROP-KICKED** HIM OUT THE **WINDOW!**

BUT IF I'D DONE **THAT,** HE MIGHT NOT'VE GIVEN ME MY **HAMMOND!**

I **THINK** I'M GONNA PUT IT **RIGHT**... OVER... **THERE**...

LOOK, IT'S **SUPPERTIME.** THINK YOU CAN WOBBLE YOUR WAY TO THE **KITCHEN?**

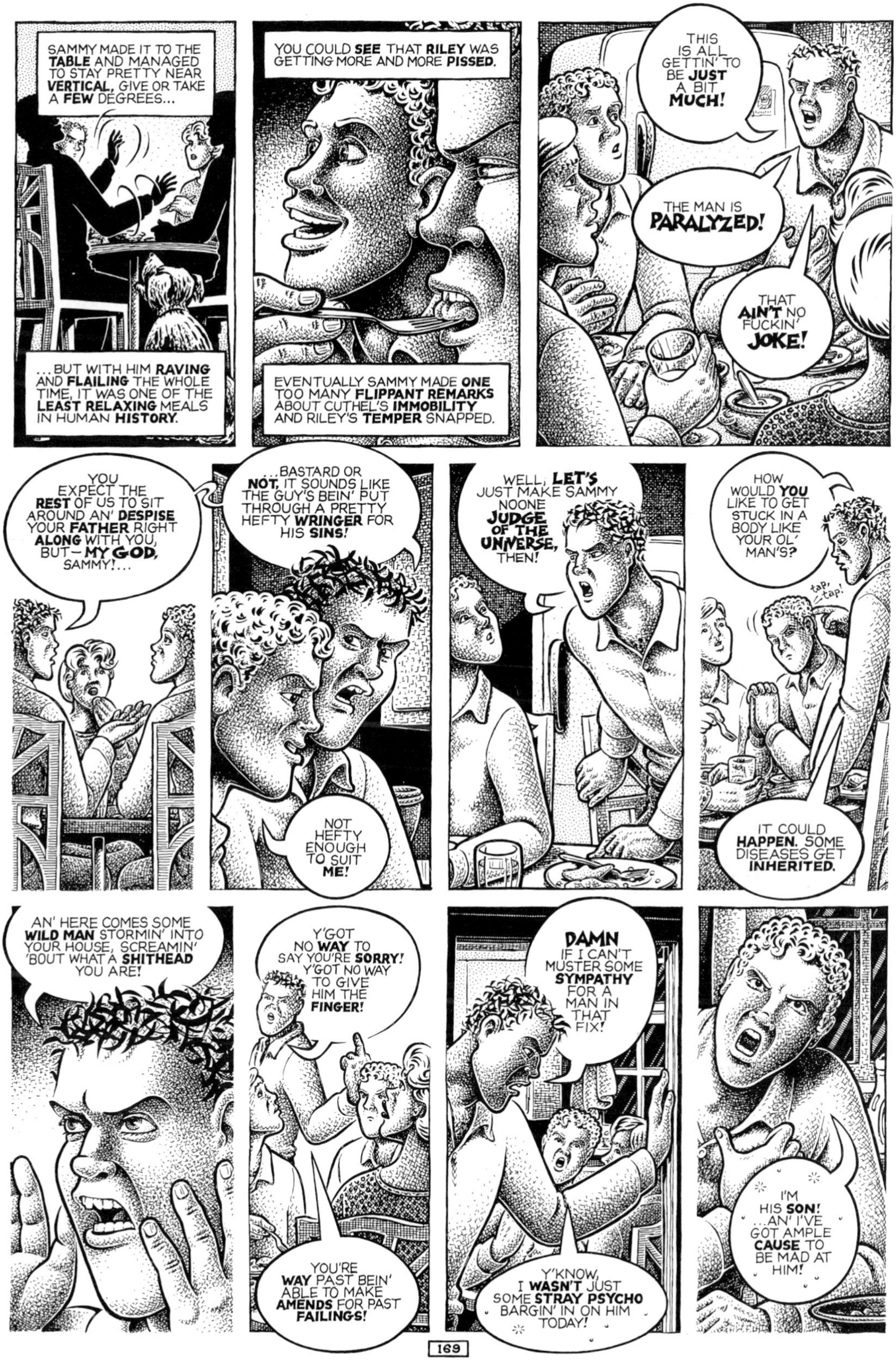

SAMMY MADE IT TO THE TABLE AND MANAGED TO STAY PRETTY NEAR VERTICAL, GIVE OR TAKE A FEW DEGREES...
...BUT WITH HIM RAVING AND FLAILING THE WHOLE TIME, IT WAS ONE OF THE LEAST RELAXING MEALS IN HUMAN HISTORY.
YOU COULD SEE THAT RILEY WAS GETTING MORE AND MORE PISSED.
EVENTUALLY SAMMY MADE ONE TOO MANY FLIPPANT REMARKS ABOUT CUTHEL'S IMMOBILITY AND RILEY'S TEMPER SNAPPED.
THIS IS ALL GETTIN' TO BE JUST A BIT MUCH!
THE MAN IS PARALYZED!
THAT AIN'T NO FUCKIN' JOKE!
YOU EXPECT THE REST OF US TO SIT AROUND AN' DESPISE YOUR FATHER RIGHT ALONG WITH YOU, BUT— MY GOD, SAMMY!...
...BASTARD OR NOT, IT SOUNDS LIKE THE GUY'S BEIN' PUT THROUGH A PRETTY HEFTY WRINGER FOR HIS SINS!
NOT HEFTY ENOUGH TO SUIT ME!
WELL, LET'S JUST MAKE SAMMY NOONE JUDGE OF THE UNIVERSE, THEN!
HOW WOULD YOU LIKE TO GET STUCK IN A BODY LIKE YOUR OL' MAN'S?
tap, tap!
IT COULD HAPPEN. SOME DISEASES GET INHERITED.
AN' HERE COMES SOME WILD MAN STORMIN' INTO YOUR HOUSE, SCREAMIN' 'BOUT WHAT A SHITHEAD YOU ARE!
Y'GOT NO WAY TO SAY YOU'RE SORRY! Y'GOT NO WAY TO GIVE HIM THE FINGER!
YOU'RE WAY PAST BEIN' ABLE TO MAKE AMENDS FOR PAST FAILINGS!
DAMN IF I CAN'T MUSTER SOME SYMPATHY FOR A MAN IN THAT FIX!
Y'KNOW, I WASN'T JUST SOME STRAY PSYCHO BARGIN' IN ON HIM TODAY!
I'M HIS SON! ...AN' I'VE GOT AMPLE CAUSE TO BE MAD AT HIM!

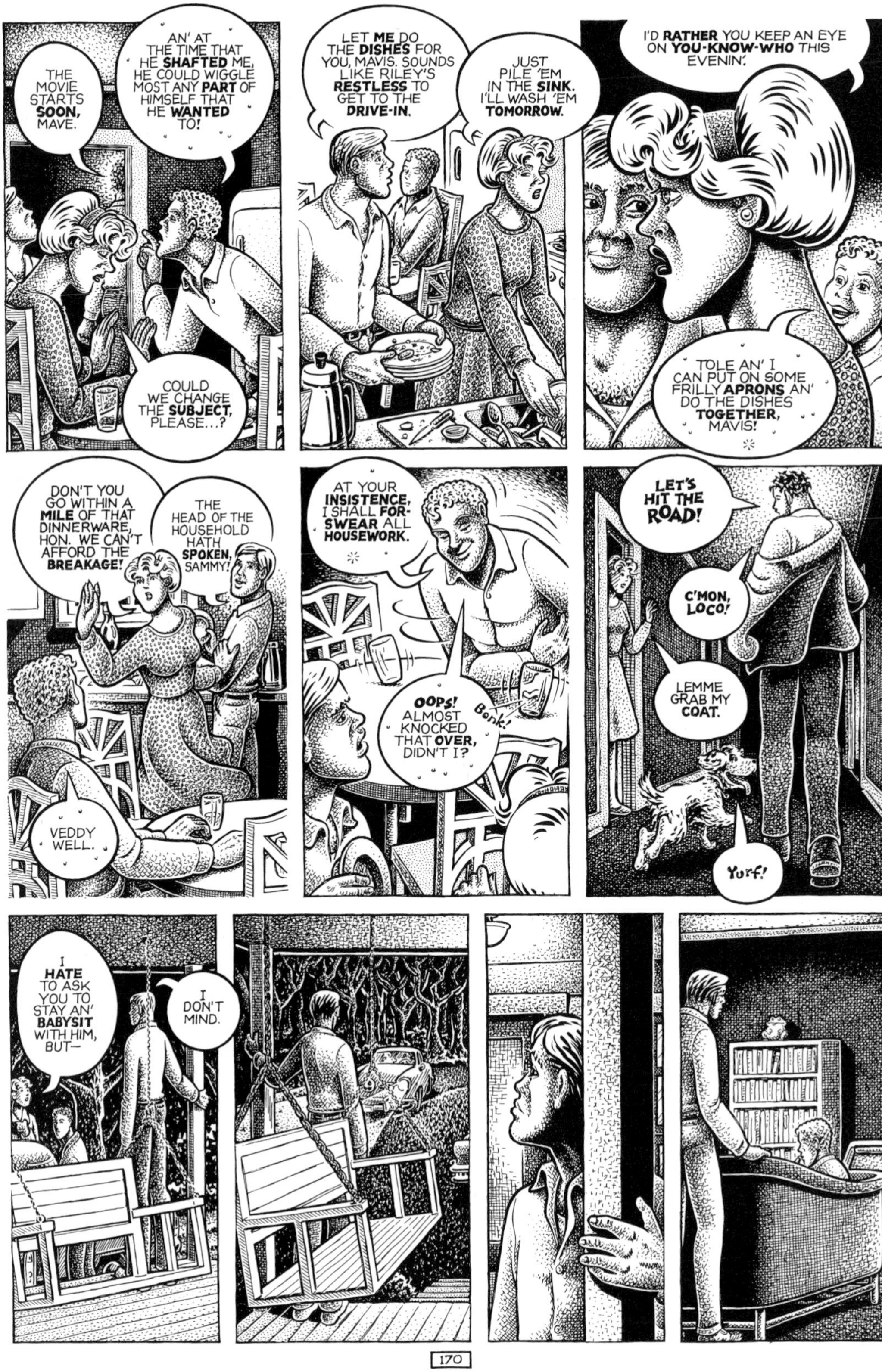
THE MOVIE STARTS SOON, MAVE.
AN' AT THE TIME THAT HE SHAFTED ME, HE COULD WIGGLE MOST ANY PART OF HIMSELF THAT HE WANTED TO!
COULD WE CHANGE THE SUBJECT, PLEASE...?
LET ME DO THE DISHES FOR YOU, MAVIS. SOUNDS LIKE RILEY'S RESTLESS TO GET TO THE DRIVE-IN.
JUST PILE 'EM IN THE SINK. I'LL WASH 'EM TOMORROW.
I'D RATHER YOU KEEP AN EYE ON YOU-KNOW-WHO THIS EVENIN'.
TOLE AN' I CAN PUT ON SOME FRILLY APRONS AN' DO THE DISHES TOGETHER, MAVIS!
DON'T YOU GO WITHIN A MILE OF THAT DINNERWARE, HON. WE CAN'T AFFORD THE BREAKAGE!
THE HEAD OF THE HOUSEHOLD HATH SPOKEN, SAMMY!
VEDDY WELL.
AT YOUR INSISTENCE, I SHALL FORSWEAR ALL HOUSEWORK.
OOPS! ALMOST KNOCKED THAT OVER, DIDN'T I?
Bonk!
LET'S HIT THE ROAD!
C'MON, LOCO!
LEMME GRAB MY COAT.
Yurf!
I HATE TO ASK YOU TO STAY AN' BABYSIT WITH HIM, BUT—
I DON'T MIND.

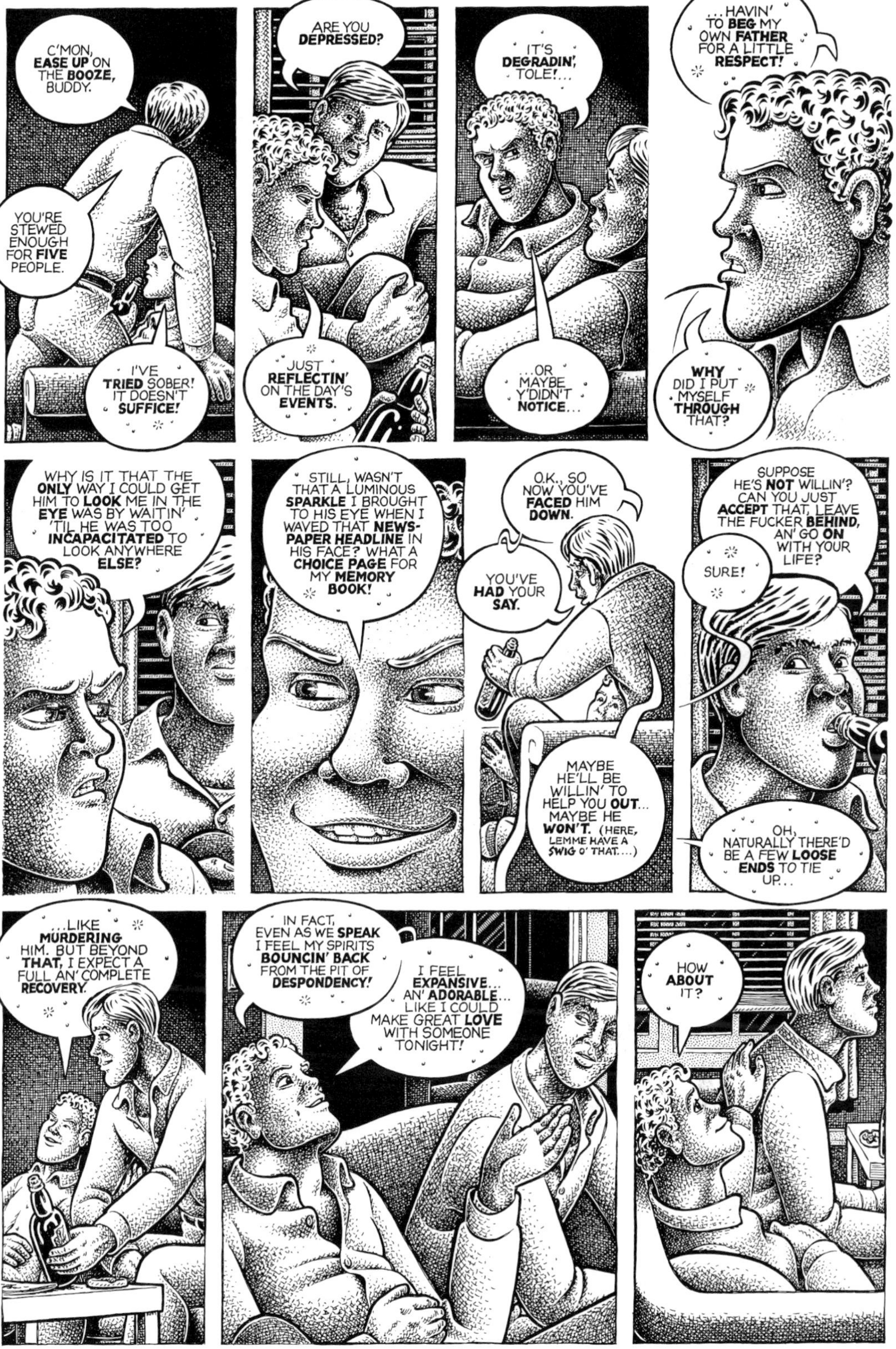
C'MON, EASE UP ON THE BOOZE, BUDDY.
YOU'RE STEWED ENOUGH FOR FIVE PEOPLE.
I'VE TRIED SOBER! IT DOESN'T SUFFICE!
ARE YOU DEPRESSED?
JUST REFLECTIN' ON THE DAY'S EVENTS.
IT'S DEGRADIN', TOLE!...
...OR MAYBE Y'DIDN'T NOTICE...
...HAVIN' TO BEG MY OWN FATHER FOR A LITTLE RESPECT!
WHY DID I PUT MYSELF THROUGH THAT?
WHY IS IT THAT THE ONLY WAY I COULD GET HIM TO LOOK ME IN THE EYE WAS BY WAITIN' 'TIL HE WAS TOO INCAPACITATED TO LOOK ANYWHERE ELSE?
STILL, WASN'T THAT A LUMINOUS SPARKLE I BROUGHT TO HIS EYE WHEN I WAVED THAT NEWS-PAPER HEADLINE IN HIS FACE? WHAT A CHOICE PAGE FOR MY MEMORY BOOK!
O.K., SO NOW YOU'VE FACED HIM DOWN.
YOU'VE HAD YOUR SAY.
MAYBE HE'LL BE WILLIN' TO HELP YOU OUT... MAYBE HE WON'T. (HERE, LEMME HAVE A SWIG O' THAT....)
SUPPOSE HE'S NOT WILLIN'? CAN YOU JUST ACCEPT THAT, LEAVE THE FUCKER BEHIND, AN' GO ON WITH YOUR LIFE?
SURE!
OH, NATURALLY THERE'D BE A FEW LOOSE ENDS TO TIE UP...
...LIKE MURDERING HIM. BUT BEYOND THAT, I EXPECT A FULL AN' COMPLETE RECOVERY.
IN FACT, EVEN AS WE SPEAK I FEEL MY SPIRITS BOUNCIN' BACK FROM THE PIT OF DESPONDENCY!
I FEEL EXPANSIVE... AN' ADORABLE... LIKE I COULD MAKE GREAT LOVE WITH SOMEONE TONIGHT!
HOW ABOUT IT?

WHAT? WITH ME??

COME ON, TOLAND. IT'LL FEEL GREAT!

BE EXPERIMENTAL. TRY A KISS. I PROMISE YOU IT'LL BE SUPER!

NOT A GOOD IDEA, PAL!

C'MON.

IT'S A GOOD TIME TO PLAY.

NOBODY'S HERE.

JUST A KISS, FOR STARTERS.

HEY! SAMMY!

THAT'S ENOUGH!

I'M SERIOUS!

STOP IT!

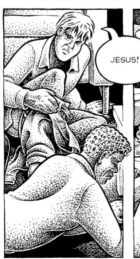

JESUS!

SIGH!... IT'D BE REALLY NICE TO MAKE LOVE WITH SOMEONE TONIGHT. SOMEONE WHO'S A FRIEND.

IT'D BE JUST LOVELY.

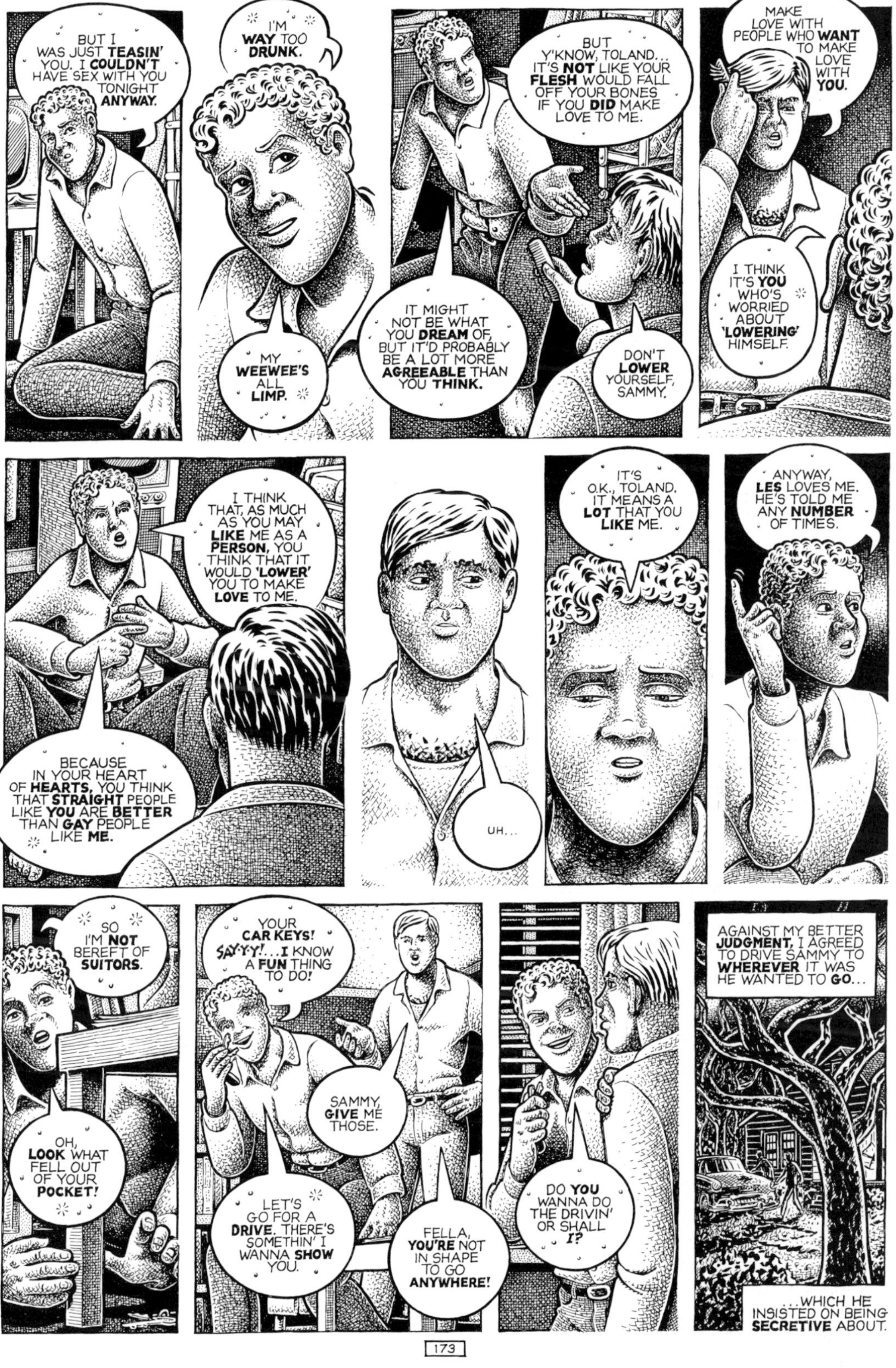
BUT I WAS JUST **TEASIN'** YOU. I **COULDN'T** HAVE SEX WITH YOU TONIGHT **ANYWAY.**
I'M **WAY** TOO **DRUNK.**
MY **WEEWEE'S** ALL **LIMP.**
BUT Y'KNOW, TOLAND... IT'S **NOT** LIKE YOUR **FLESH** WOULD FALL OFF YOUR BONES IF YOU **DID** MAKE LOVE TO ME.
IT MIGHT NOT BE WHAT YOU **DREAM** OF, BUT IT'D PROBABLY BE A LOT MORE **AGREEABLE** THAN YOU **THINK.**
DON'T **LOWER** YOURSELF, SAMMY.
MAKE LOVE WITH PEOPLE WHO **WANT** TO MAKE LOVE WITH **YOU.**
I THINK IT'S **YOU** WHO'S WORRIED ABOUT **'LOWERING'** HIMSELF.
I THINK THAT, AS MUCH AS YOU MAY **LIKE** ME AS A **PERSON,** YOU THINK THAT IT WOULD **'LOWER'** YOU TO MAKE **LOVE** TO ME.
BECAUSE IN YOUR HEART OF **HEARTS,** YOU THINK THAT **STRAIGHT** PEOPLE LIKE **YOU** ARE **BETTER** THAN **GAY** PEOPLE LIKE **ME.**
UH...
IT'S O.K., TOLAND. IT MEANS A **LOT** THAT YOU **LIKE** ME.
ANYWAY, **LES** LOVES ME. HE'S TOLD ME ANY **NUMBER** OF TIMES.
SO I'M **NOT** BEREFT OF **SUITORS.**
OH, **LOOK** WHAT FELL OUT OF YOUR **POCKET!**
YOUR **CAR KEYS!** SAY-Y-Y!... I KNOW A **FUN** THING TO DO!
SAMMY, **GIVE** ME THOSE.
LET'S GO FOR A **DRIVE.** THERE'S SOMETHIN' I WANNA **SHOW** YOU.
FELLA, **YOU'RE** NOT IN SHAPE TO GO **ANYWHERE!**
DO **YOU** WANNA DO THE DRIVIN' OR SHALL ***I?***
AGAINST MY BETTER **JUDGMENT,** I AGREED TO DRIVE SAMMY TO **WHEREVER** IT WAS HE WANTED TO **GO...**
...WHICH HE INSISTED ON BEING **SECRETIVE** ABOUT.

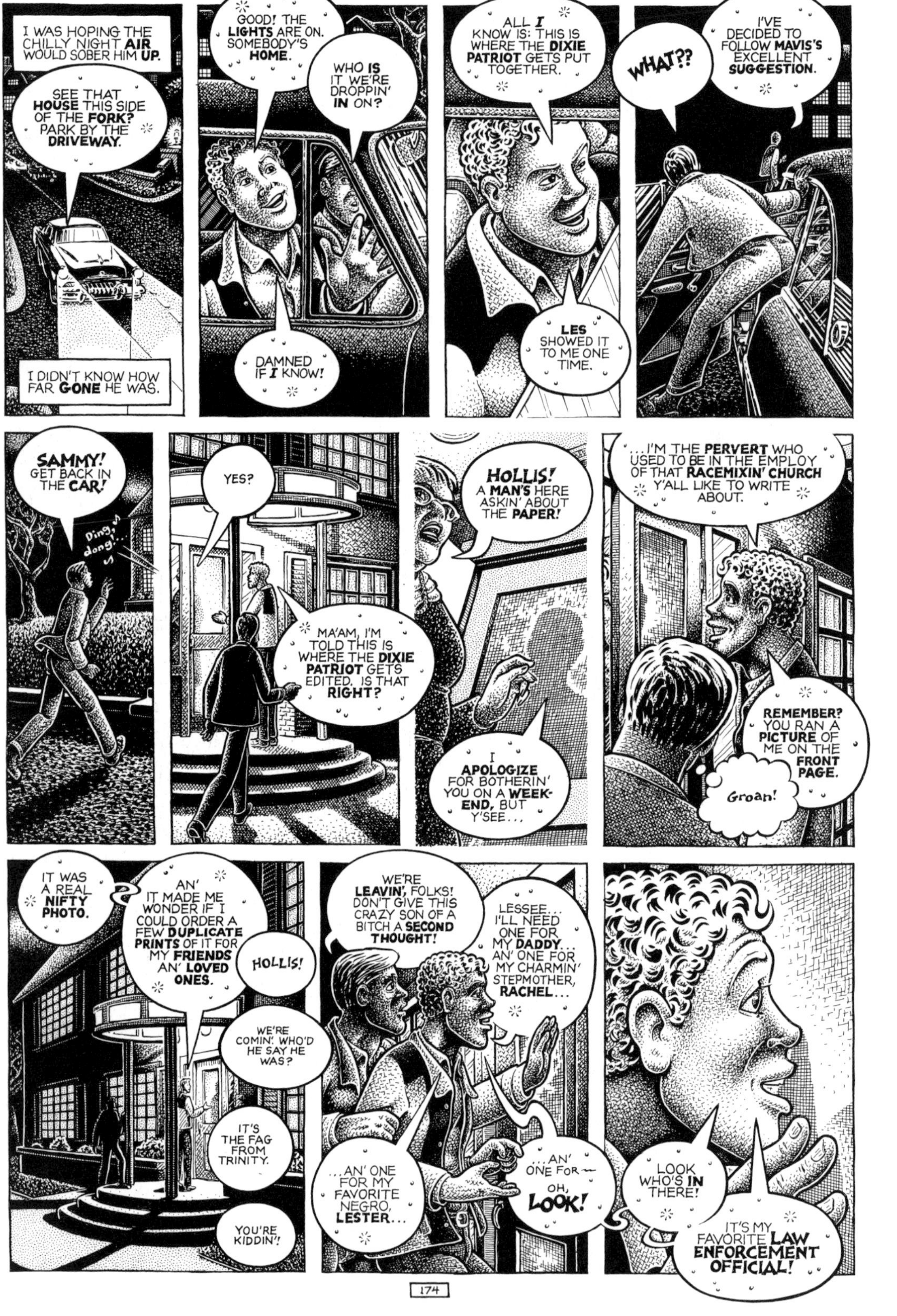
I WAS HOPING THE CHILLY NIGHT AIR WOULD SOBER HIM UP.
SEE THAT HOUSE THIS SIDE OF THE FORK? PARK BY THE DRIVEWAY.
I DIDN'T KNOW HOW FAR GONE HE WAS.
GOOD! THE LIGHTS ARE ON. SOMEBODY'S HOME.
WHO IS IT WE'RE DROPPIN' IN ON?
DAMNED IF I KNOW!
ALL I KNOW IS: THIS IS WHERE THE DIXIE PATRIOT GETS PUT TOGETHER.
LES SHOWED IT TO ME ONE TIME.
WHAT??
I'VE DECIDED TO FOLLOW MAVIS'S EXCELLENT SUGGESTION.
SAMMY! GET BACK IN THE CAR!
Ding, dong!...
YES?
MA'AM, I'M TOLD THIS IS WHERE THE DIXIE PATRIOT GETS EDITED. IS THAT RIGHT?
HOLLIS! A MAN'S HERE ASKIN' ABOUT THE PAPER!
I APOLOGIZE FOR BOTHERIN' YOU ON A WEEK-END, BUT Y'SEE...
...I'M THE PERVERT WHO USED TO BE IN THE EMPLOY OF THAT RACEMIXIN' CHURCH Y'ALL LIKE TO WRITE ABOUT.
REMEMBER? YOU RAN A PICTURE OF ME ON THE FRONT PAGE.
Groan!
IT WAS A REAL NIFTY PHOTO.
AN' IT MADE ME WONDER IF I COULD ORDER A FEW DUPLICATE PRINTS OF IT FOR MY FRIENDS AN' LOVED ONES.
HOLLIS!
WE'RE COMIN'. WHO'D HE SAY HE WAS?
IT'S THE FAG FROM TRINITY.
YOU'RE KIDDIN'!
WE'RE LEAVIN', FOLKS! DON'T GIVE THIS CRAZY SON OF A BITCH A SECOND THOUGHT!
LESSEE... I'LL NEED ONE FOR MY DADDY... AN' ONE FOR MY CHARMIN' STEPMOTHER, RACHEL...
...AN' ONE FOR MY FAVORITE NEGRO, LESTER...
...AN' ONE FOR— OH, LOOK!
LOOK WHO'S IN THERE!
IT'S MY FAVORITE LAW ENFORCEMENT OFFICIAL!

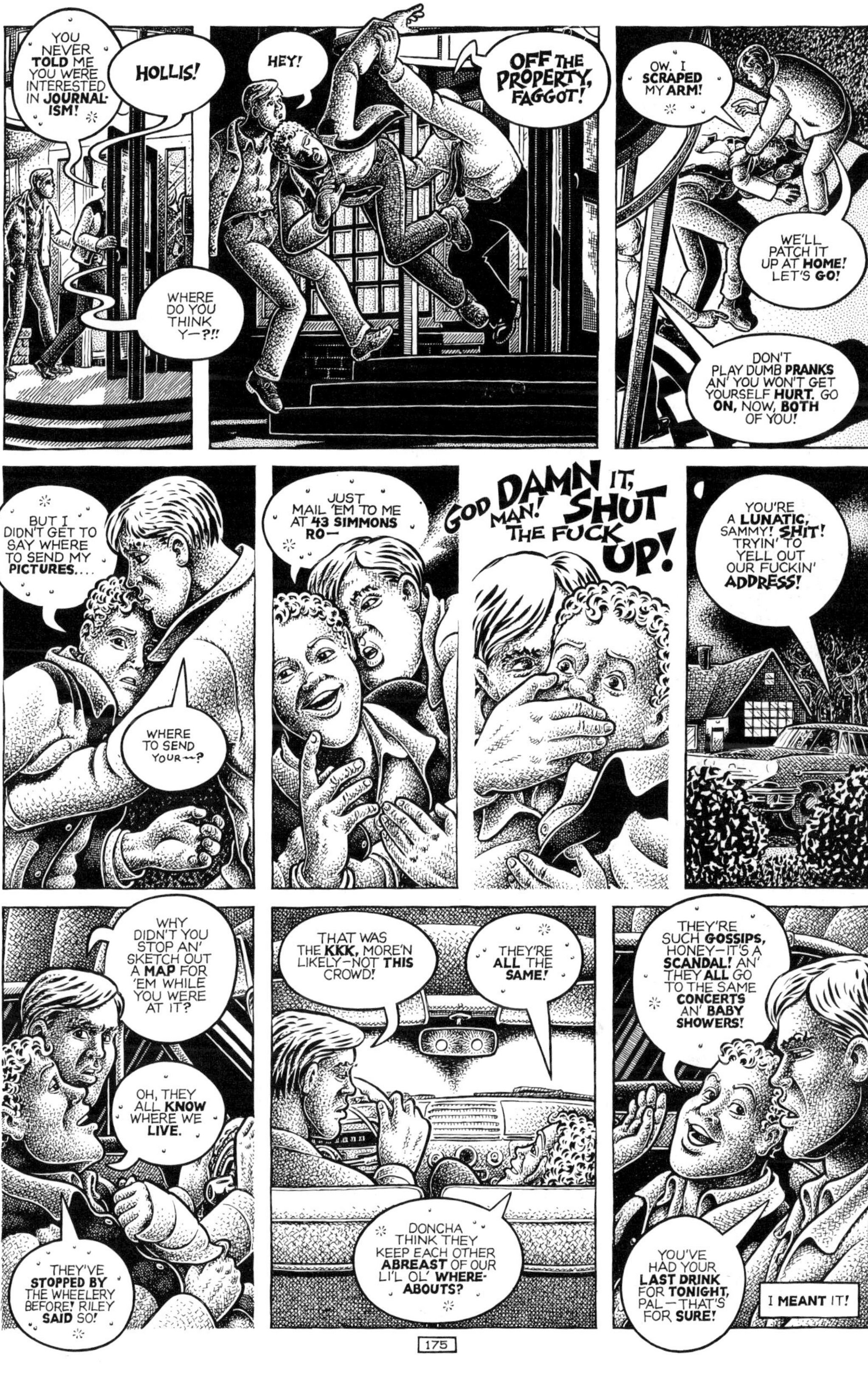

YOU NEVER TOLD ME YOU WERE INTERESTED IN JOURNALISM!
HOLLIS!
WHERE DO YOU THINK Y—?!!
HEY!
OFF THE PROPERTY, FAGGOT!
OW. I SCRAPED MY ARM!
WE'LL PATCH IT UP AT HOME! LET'S GO!
DON'T PLAY DUMB PRANKS AN' YOU WON'T GET YOURSELF HURT. GO ON, NOW, BOTH OF YOU!
BUT I DIDN'T GET TO SAY WHERE TO SEND MY PICTURES....
WHERE TO SEND YOUR—?
JUST MAIL 'EM TO ME AT 43 SIMMONS RO—
GOD DAMN IT, MAN! SHUT THE FUCK UP!
YOU'RE A LUNATIC, SAMMY! SHIT! TRYIN' TO YELL OUT OUR FUCKIN' ADDRESS!
WHY DIDN'T YOU STOP AN' SKETCH OUT A MAP FOR 'EM WHILE YOU WERE AT IT?
OH, THEY ALL KNOW WHERE WE LIVE.
THEY'VE STOPPED BY THE WHEELERY BEFORE! RILEY SAID SO!
THAT WAS THE KKK, MORE'N LIKELY—NOT THIS CROWD!
THEY'RE ALL THE SAME!
DONCHA THINK THEY KEEP EACH OTHER ABREAST OF OUR LI'L OL' WHERE-ABOUTS?
THEY'RE SUCH GOSSIPS, HONEY—IT'S A SCANDAL! AN' THEY ALL GO TO THE SAME CONCERTS AN' BABY SHOWERS!
YOU'VE HAD YOUR LAST DRINK FOR TONIGHT, PAL—THAT'S FOR SURE!
I MEANT IT!

WHEN WE GOT **HOME**, I SET ABOUT CONFISCATING EVERY DROP OF **ALCOHOL** ON THE **PREMISES**...

*DON'T PUT YOURSELF **OUT** SO, TOLAND.*

...EXCEPT FOR THE **'RUBBING'** KIND WE DOUSED ON SAMMY'S **SCRAPES**.

I SHOVED THE JUMBLE OF **CANS** AND **BOTTLES** UNDER MY **BED**, SO SAMMY COULDN'T GET **AT** 'EM EVEN AFTER I'D GONE TO **SLEEP**.

*YOU'RE SUCH A **BUSY BEE!***

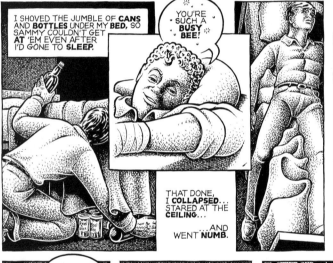

THAT DONE, I **COLLAPSED**... STARED AT THE **CEILING**...

...AND WENT **NUMB**.

MY MIND **DRIFTED** AND **SPUN**...

...'TIL I HEARD A **NOISE**...

...WHICH I TOOK TO BE SAMMY **BARFING** OUT IN THE **YARD**.

SAMMY...?

I WALKED OUT THE **BACK DOOR** TO MAKE SURE HE FELT **STEADY** ENOUGH TO GET BACK **INSIDE**.

AND THAT'S ALL I **REMEMBER**.

KRAK

176

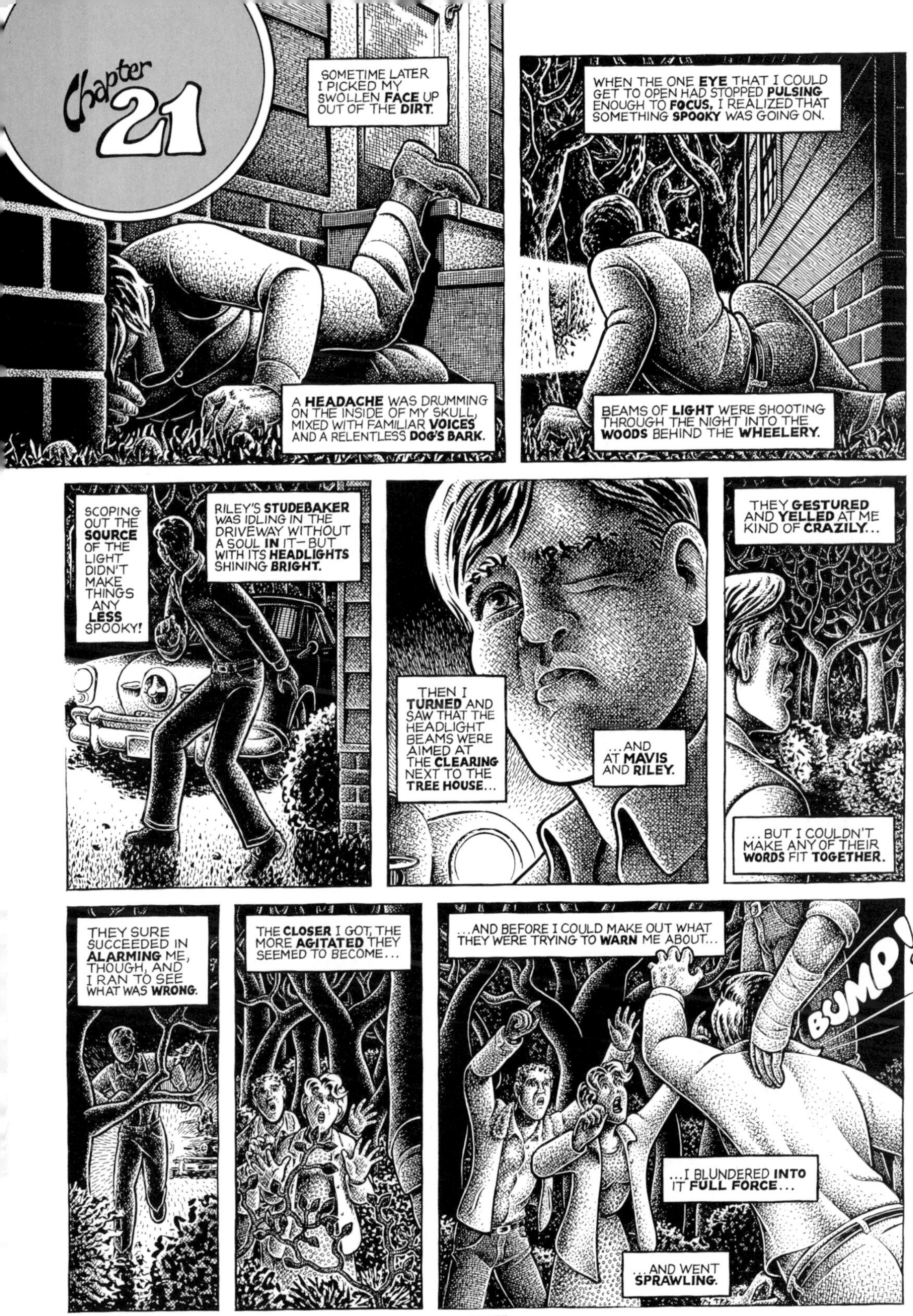
Chapter 21
SOMETIME LATER I PICKED MY SWOLLEN FACE UP OUT OF THE DIRT.
A HEADACHE WAS DRUMMING ON THE INSIDE OF MY SKULL, MIXED WITH FAMILIAR VOICES AND A RELENTLESS DOG'S BARK.
WHEN THE ONE EYE THAT I COULD GET TO OPEN HAD STOPPED PULSING ENOUGH TO FOCUS, I REALIZED THAT SOMETHING SPOOKY WAS GOING ON.
BEAMS OF LIGHT WERE SHOOTING THROUGH THE NIGHT INTO THE WOODS BEHIND THE WHEELERY.
SCOPING OUT THE SOURCE OF THE LIGHT DIDN'T MAKE THINGS ANY LESS SPOOKY!
RILEY'S STUDEBAKER WAS IDLING IN THE DRIVEWAY WITHOUT A SOUL IN IT— BUT WITH ITS HEADLIGHTS SHINING BRIGHT.
THEN I TURNED AND SAW THAT THE HEADLIGHT BEAMS WERE AIMED AT THE CLEARING NEXT TO THE TREE HOUSE...
...AND AT MAVIS AND RILEY.
THEY GESTURED AND YELLED AT ME KIND OF CRAZILY...
...BUT I COULDN'T MAKE ANY OF THEIR WORDS FIT TOGETHER.
THEY SURE SUCCEEDED IN ALARMING ME, THOUGH, AND I RAN TO SEE WHAT WAS WRONG.
THE CLOSER I GOT, THE MORE AGITATED THEY SEEMED TO BECOME...
...AND BEFORE I COULD MAKE OUT WHAT THEY WERE TRYING TO WARN ME ABOUT...
BUMP!
...I BLUNDERED INTO IT FULL FORCE...
...AND WENT SPRAWLING.

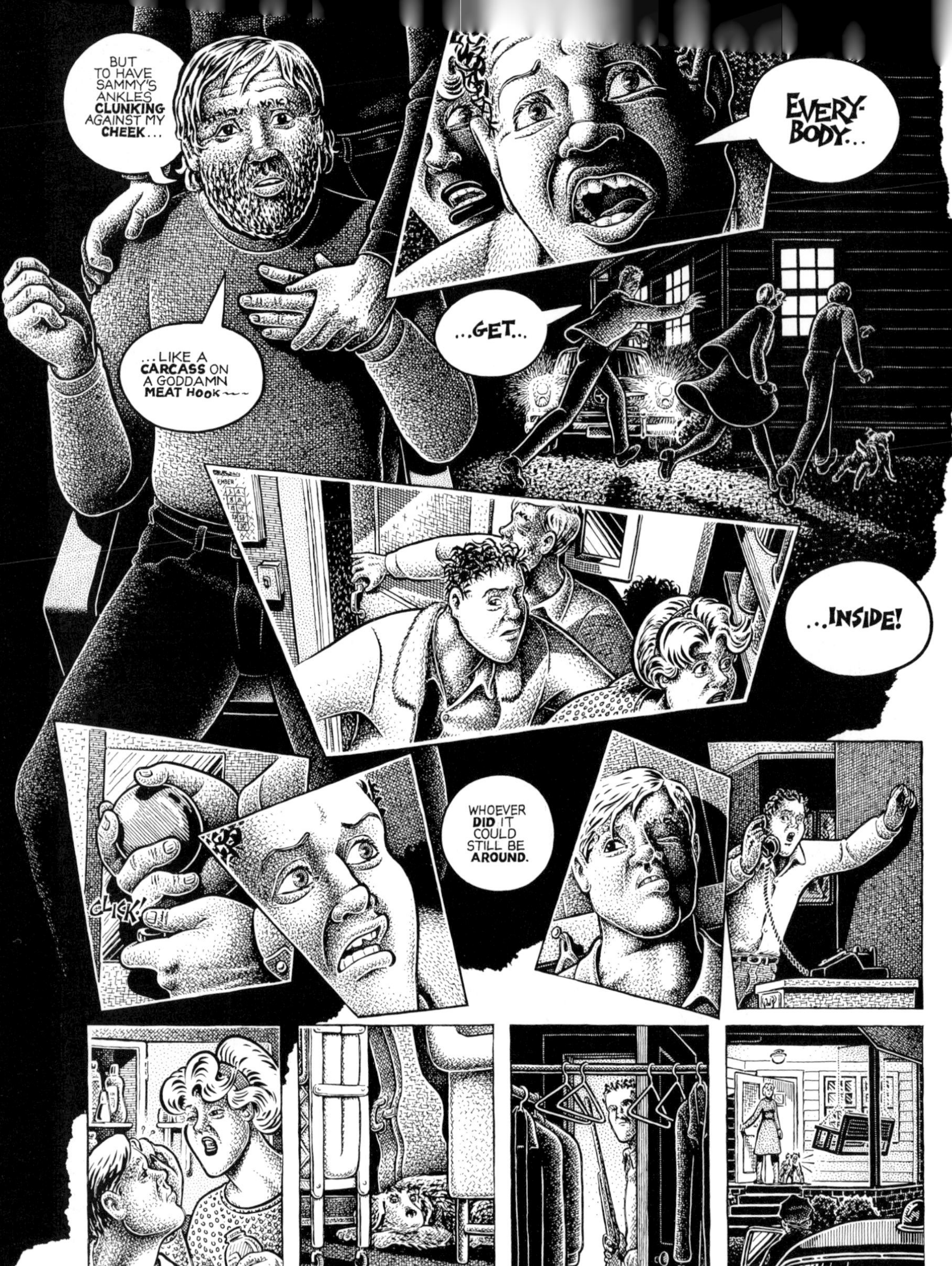

BUT TO HAVE SAMMY'S ANKLES CLUNKING AGAINST MY CHEEK...
EVERY-BODY...
...GET...
...LIKE A CARCASS ON A GODDAMN MEAT HOOK
...INSIDE!
CLICK!
WHOEVER DID IT COULD STILL BE AROUND.

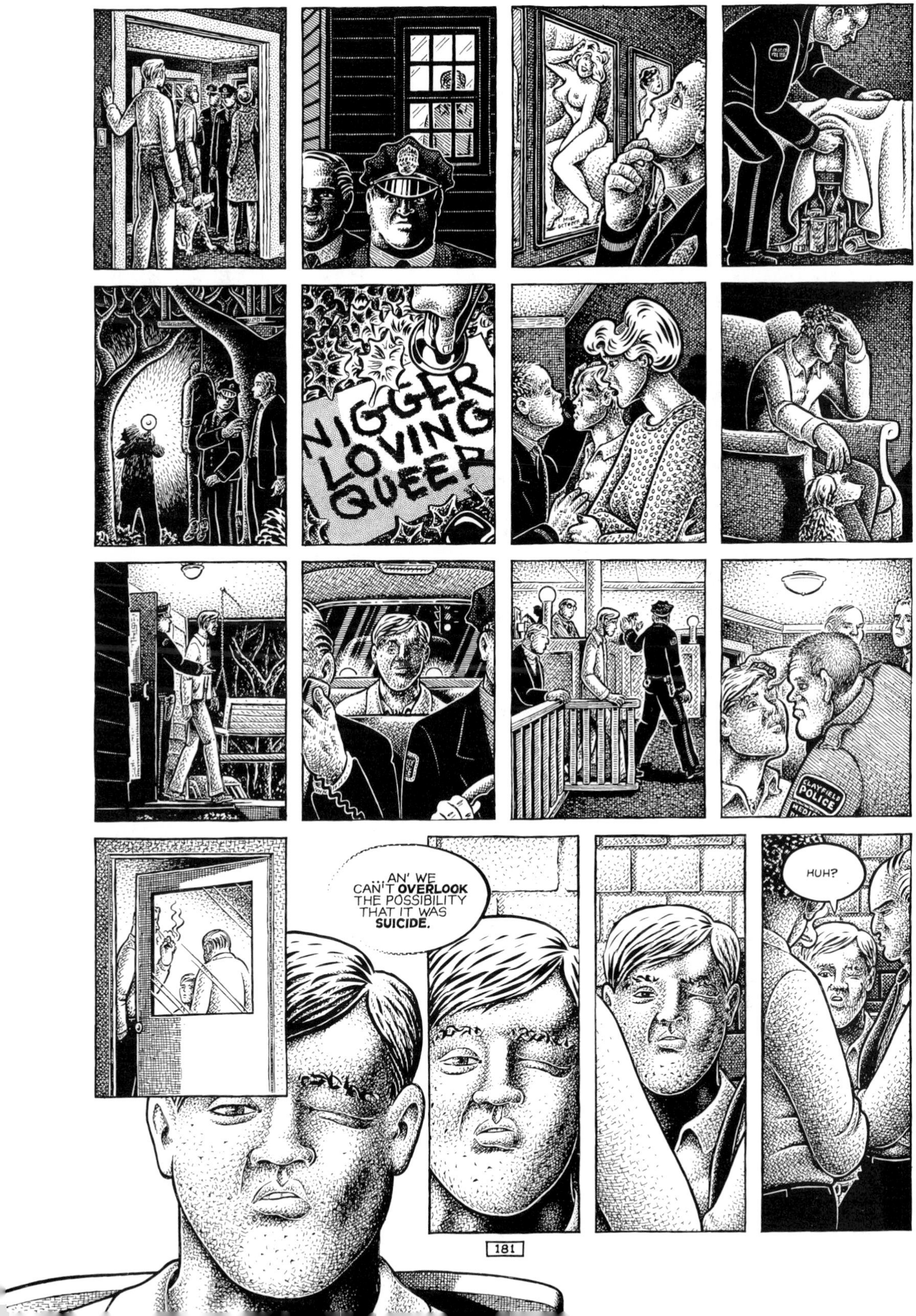
NIGGER LOVING QUEER
CLAYFIELD POLICE
...AN' WE CAN'T **OVERLOOK** THE POSSIBILITY THAT IT WAS **SUICIDE.**
HUH?

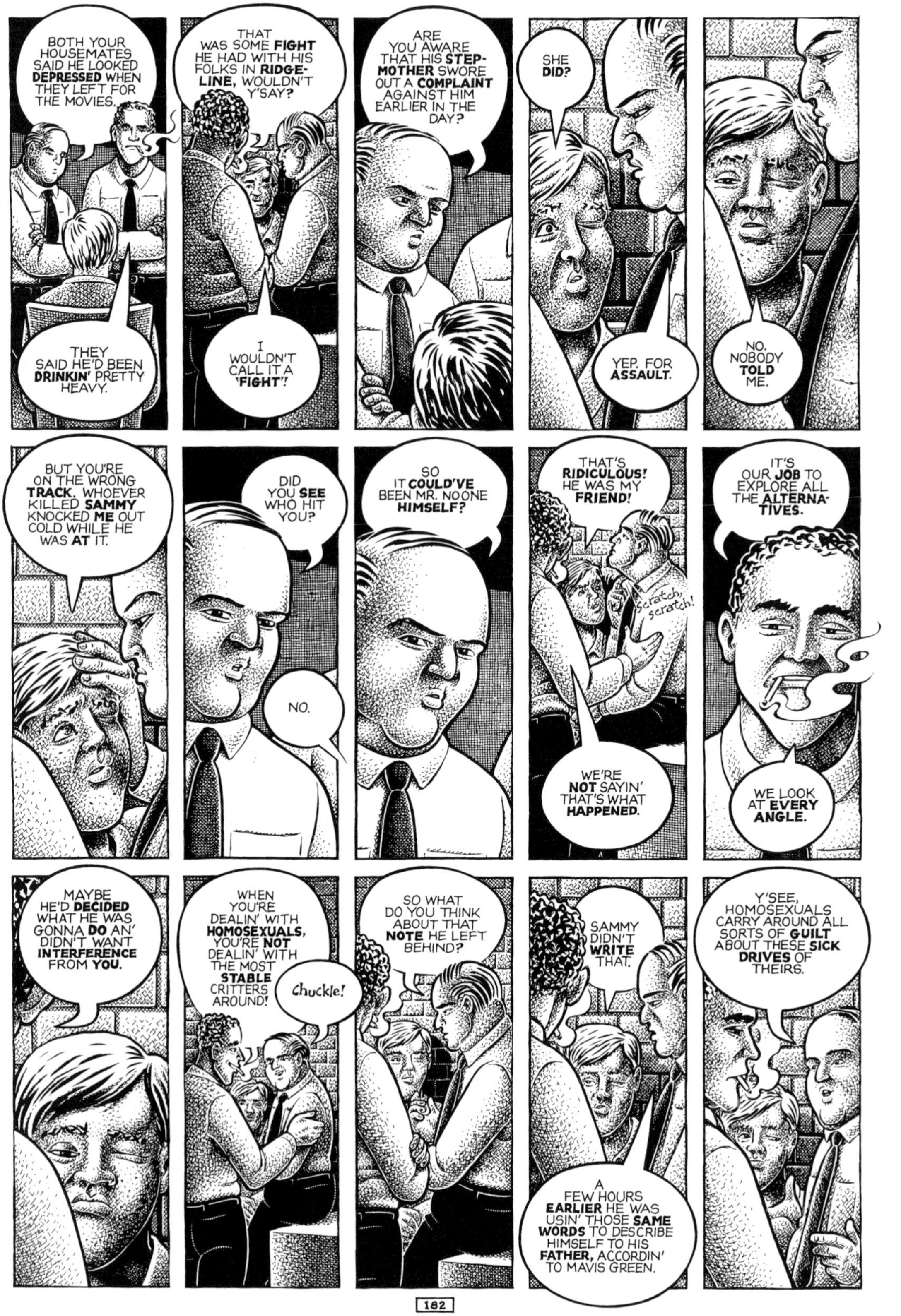
BOTH YOUR HOUSEMATES SAID HE LOOKED DEPRESSED WHEN THEY LEFT FOR THE MOVIES.
THEY SAID HE'D BEEN DRINKIN' PRETTY HEAVY.
THAT WAS SOME FIGHT HE HAD WITH HIS FOLKS IN RIDGE-LINE, WOULDN'T Y'SAY?
I WOULDN'T CALL IT A 'FIGHT'!
ARE YOU AWARE THAT HIS STEP-MOTHER SWORE OUT A COMPLAINT AGAINST HIM EARLIER IN THE DAY?
SHE DID?
YEP. FOR ASSAULT.
NO. NOBODY TOLD ME.
BUT YOU'RE ON THE WRONG TRACK. WHOEVER KILLED SAMMY KNOCKED ME OUT COLD WHILE HE WAS AT IT.
DID YOU SEE WHO HIT YOU?
NO.
SO IT COULD'VE BEEN MR. NOONE HIMSELF?
THAT'S RIDICULOUS! HE WAS MY FRIEND!
Scratch, scratch!
WE'RE NOT SAYIN' THAT'S WHAT HAPPENED.
IT'S OUR JOB TO EXPLORE ALL THE ALTERNA-TIVES.
WE LOOK AT EVERY ANGLE.
MAYBE HE'D DECIDED WHAT HE WAS GONNA DO AN' DIDN'T WANT INTERFERENCE FROM YOU.
WHEN YOU'RE DEALIN' WITH HOMOSEXUALS, YOU'RE NOT DEALIN' WITH THE MOST STABLE CRITTERS AROUND!
Chuckle!
SO WHAT DO YOU THINK ABOUT THAT NOTE HE LEFT BEHIND?
SAMMY DIDN'T WRITE THAT.
A FEW HOURS EARLIER HE WAS USIN' THOSE SAME WORDS TO DESCRIBE HIMSELF TO HIS FATHER, ACCORDIN' TO MAVIS GREEN.
Y'SEE, HOMOSEXUALS CARRY AROUND ALL SORTS OF GUILT ABOUT THESE SICK DRIVES OF THEIRS.

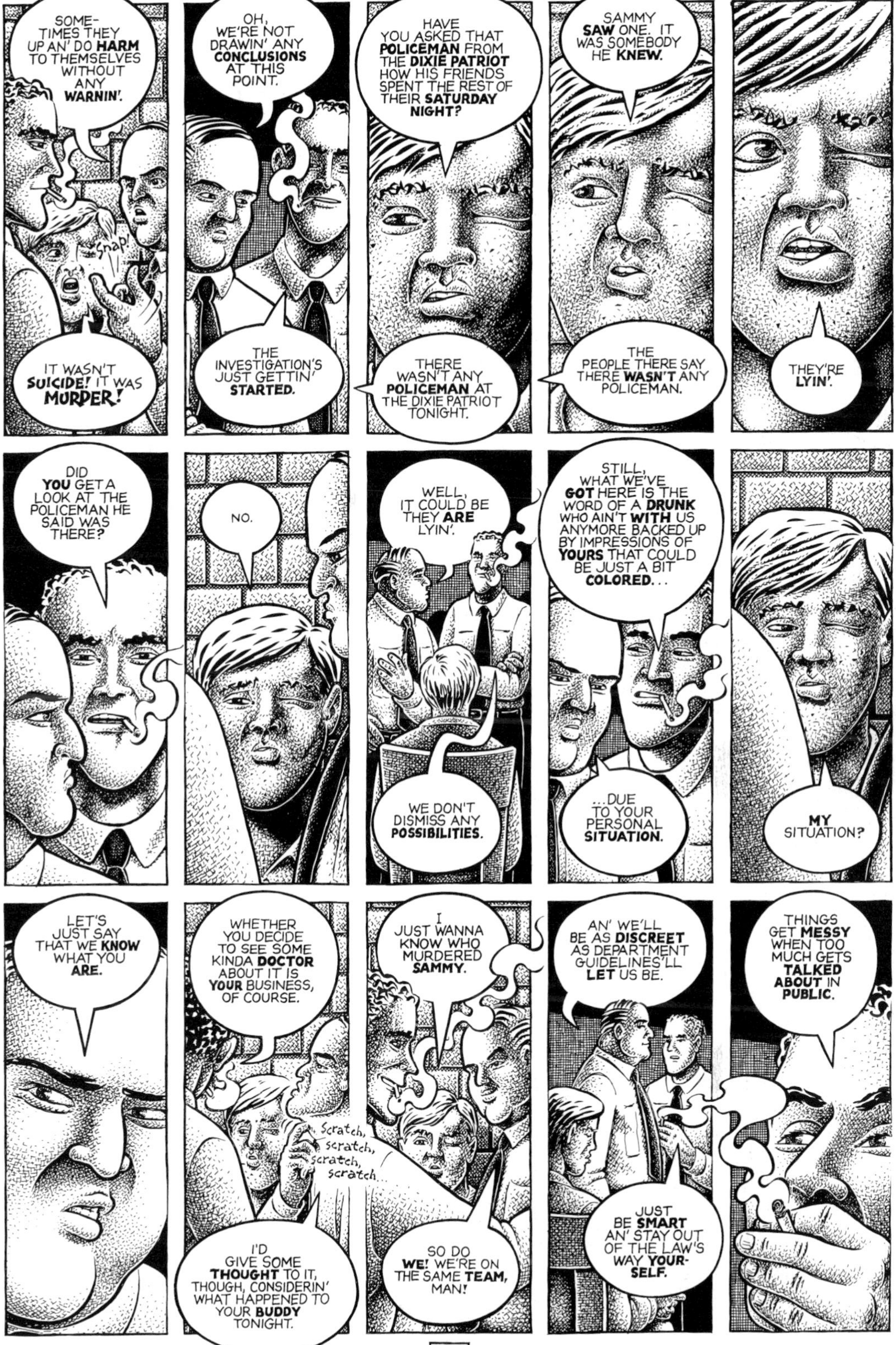
SOMETIMES THEY UP AN' DO HARM TO THEMSELVES WITHOUT ANY WARNIN'.
Snap!
IT WASN'T SUICIDE! IT WAS MURDER!
OH, WE'RE NOT DRAWIN' ANY CONCLUSIONS AT THIS POINT.
THE INVESTIGATION'S JUST GETTIN' STARTED.
HAVE YOU ASKED THAT POLICEMAN FROM THE DIXIE PATRIOT HOW HIS FRIENDS SPENT THE REST OF THEIR SATURDAY NIGHT?
THERE WASN'T ANY POLICEMAN AT THE DIXIE PATRIOT TONIGHT.
SAMMY SAW ONE. IT WAS SOMEBODY HE KNEW.
THE PEOPLE THERE SAY THERE WASN'T ANY POLICEMAN.
THEY'RE LYIN'.
DID YOU GET A LOOK AT THE POLICEMAN HE SAID WAS THERE?
NO.
WELL, IT COULD BE THEY ARE LYIN'.
WE DON'T DISMISS ANY POSSIBILITIES.
STILL, WHAT WE'VE GOT HERE IS THE WORD OF A DRUNK WHO AIN'T WITH US ANYMORE BACKED UP BY IMPRESSIONS OF YOURS THAT COULD BE JUST A BIT COLORED...
...DUE TO YOUR PERSONAL SITUATION.
MY SITUATION?
LET'S JUST SAY THAT WE KNOW WHAT YOU ARE.
WHETHER YOU DECIDE TO SEE SOME KINDA DOCTOR ABOUT IT IS YOUR BUSINESS, OF COURSE.
Scratch, scratch, scratch, scratch...
I'D GIVE SOME THOUGHT TO IT, THOUGH, CONSIDERIN' WHAT HAPPENED TO YOUR BUDDY TONIGHT.
I JUST WANNA KNOW WHO MURDERED SAMMY.
SO DO WE! WE'RE ON THE SAME TEAM, MAN!
AN' WE'LL BE AS DISCREET AS DEPARTMENT GUIDELINES'LL LET US BE.
JUST BE SMART AN' STAY OUT OF THE LAW'S WAY YOURSELF.
THINGS GET MESSY WHEN TOO MUCH GETS TALKED ABOUT IN PUBLIC.

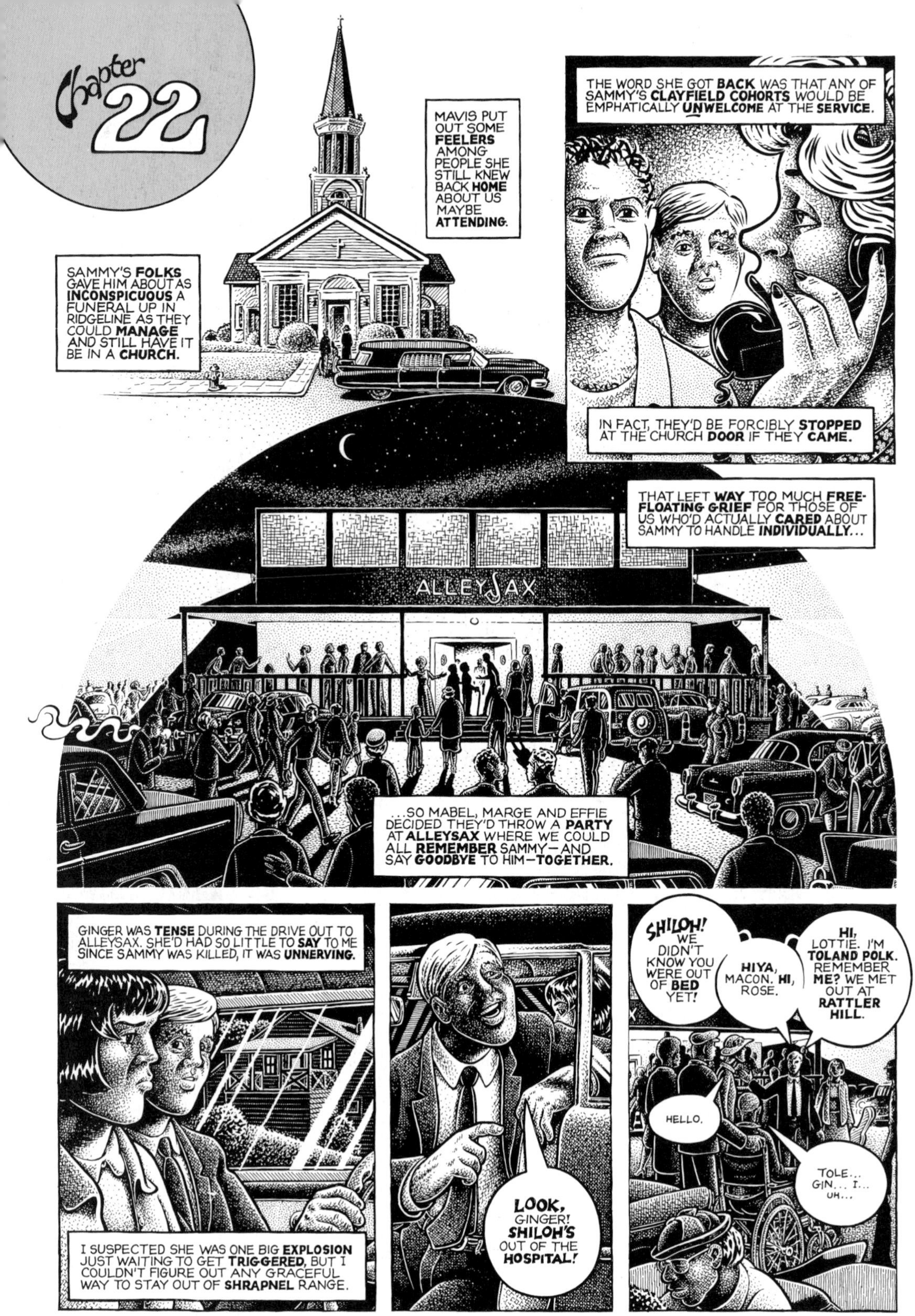
Chapter 22
SAMMY'S FOLKS GAVE HIM ABOUT AS INCONSPICUOUS A FUNERAL UP IN RIDGELINE AS THEY COULD MANAGE AND STILL HAVE IT BE IN A CHURCH.
MAVIS PUT OUT SOME FEELERS AMONG PEOPLE SHE STILL KNEW BACK HOME ABOUT US MAYBE ATTENDING.
THE WORD SHE GOT BACK WAS THAT ANY OF SAMMY'S CLAYFIELD COHORTS WOULD BE EMPHATICALLY UNWELCOME AT THE SERVICE.
IN FACT, THEY'D BE FORCIBLY STOPPED AT THE CHURCH DOOR IF THEY CAME.
THAT LEFT WAY TOO MUCH FREE-FLOATING GRIEF FOR THOSE OF US WHO'D ACTUALLY CARED ABOUT SAMMY TO HANDLE INDIVIDUALLY...
ALLEYSAX
...SO MABEL, MARGE AND EFFIE DECIDED THEY'D THROW A PARTY AT ALLEYSAX WHERE WE COULD ALL REMEMBER SAMMY—AND SAY GOODBYE TO HIM—TOGETHER.
GINGER WAS TENSE DURING THE DRIVE OUT TO ALLEYSAX. SHE'D HAD SO LITTLE TO SAY TO ME SINCE SAMMY WAS KILLED, IT WAS UNNERVING.
I SUSPECTED SHE WAS ONE BIG EXPLOSION JUST WAITING TO GET TRIGGERED, BUT I COULDN'T FIGURE OUT ANY GRACEFUL WAY TO STAY OUT OF SHRAPNEL RANGE.
LOOK, GINGER! SHILOH'S OUT OF THE HOSPITAL!
SHILOH! WE DIDN'T KNOW YOU WERE OUT OF BED YET!
HIYA, MACON. HI, ROSE.
HI, LOTTIE. I'M TOLAND POLK. REMEMBER ME? WE MET OUT AT RATTLER HILL.
HELLO.
TOLE... GIN... I... UH...

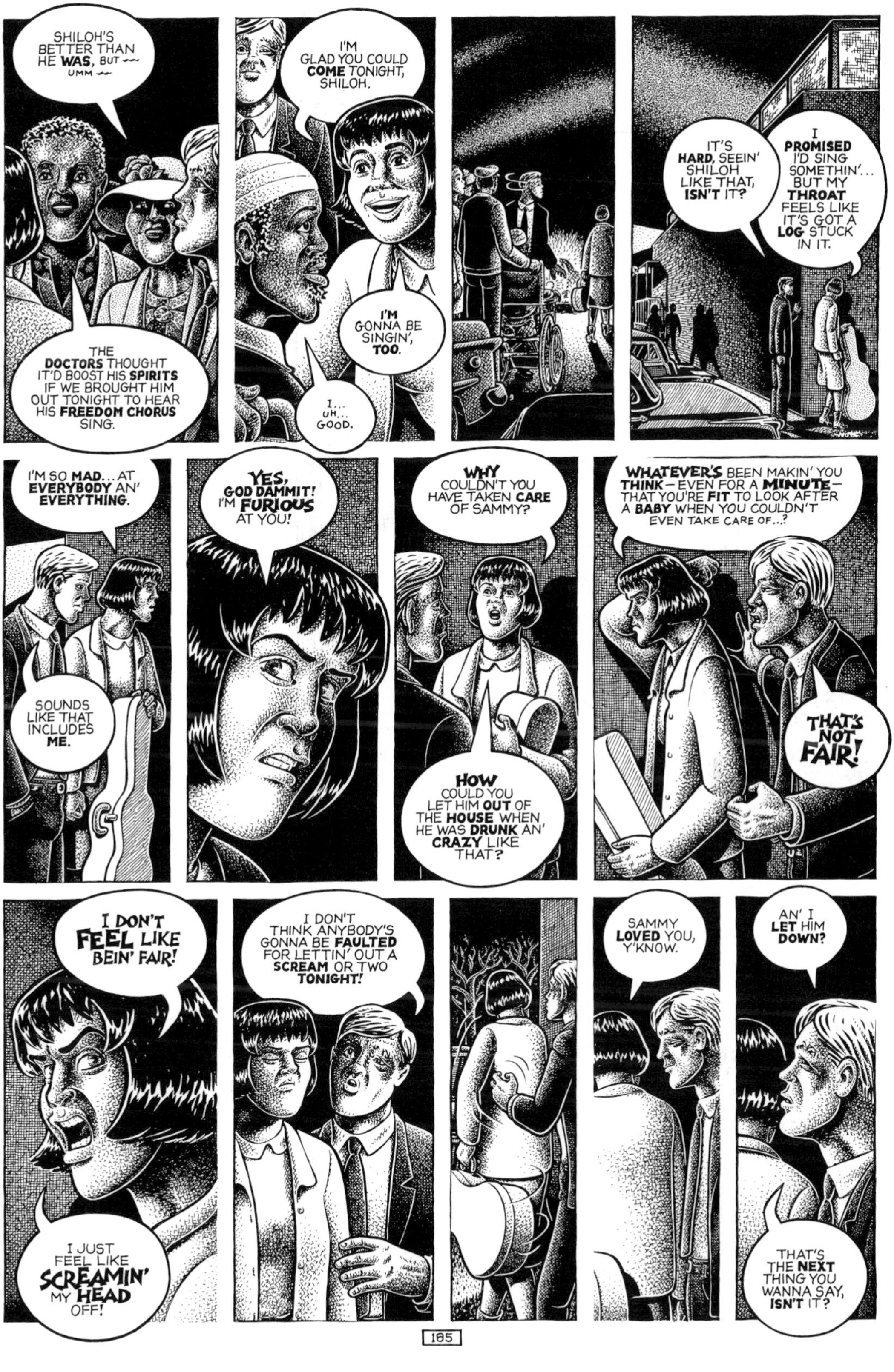
SHILOH'S BETTER THAN HE WAS, BUT ~~ UMM ~~
THE DOCTORS THOUGHT IT'D BOOST HIS SPIRITS IF WE BROUGHT HIM OUT TONIGHT TO HEAR HIS FREEDOM CHORUS SING.
I'M GLAD YOU COULD COME TONIGHT, SHILOH.
I'M GONNA BE SINGIN', TOO.
I... UH... GOOD.
IT'S HARD, SEEIN' SHILOH LIKE THAT, ISN'T IT?
I PROMISED I'D SING SOMETHIN'... BUT MY THROAT FEELS LIKE IT'S GOT A LOG STUCK IN IT.
I'M SO MAD... AT EVERYBODY AN' EVERYTHING.
SOUNDS LIKE THAT INCLUDES ME.
YES, GOD DAMMIT! I'M FURIOUS AT YOU!
WHY COULDN'T YOU HAVE TAKEN CARE OF SAMMY?
HOW COULD YOU LET HIM OUT OF THE HOUSE WHEN HE WAS DRUNK AN' CRAZY LIKE THAT?
WHATEVER'S BEEN MAKIN' YOU THINK—EVEN FOR A MINUTE—THAT YOU'RE FIT TO LOOK AFTER A BABY WHEN YOU COULDN'T EVEN TAKE CARE OF...?
THAT'S NOT FAIR!
I DON'T FEEL LIKE BEIN' FAIR!
I JUST FEEL LIKE SCREAMIN' MY HEAD OFF!
I DON'T THINK ANYBODY'S GONNA BE FAULTED FOR LETTIN' OUT A SCREAM OR TWO TONIGHT!
SAMMY LOVED YOU, Y'KNOW.
AN' I LET HIM DOWN?
THAT'S THE NEXT THING YOU WANNA SAY, ISN'T IT?

HER **BACK** WAS TO ME. SHE WAS **GIGGLING** AT SOME **JOKE** THAT HAD JUST BEEN CRACKED BY ONE OF THE **STAGEHANDS.**

CONSIDERING THE **MEMORIES** WE SHARED, I WAS SURE I COULD COAX A REFLEXIVE **SMILE** AND **EMBRACE** OUT OF HER BY SIMPLY **STEPPING** INTO THE **LIGHT.**

I DIDN'T **DO** IT, THOUGH.

I SAVORED THE SOUND OF HER **BANTER** FOR A FEW SECONDS, THEN TURNED AND WALKED BACK OUT ONTO THE **SIDEWALK.**

SOMEHOW I **KNEW** THAT— **SMILE** OR **NO** SMILE—IF I STEPPED INTO THAT ROOM WITH GINGER, THERE WOULD BE A **CHASM** BETWEEN US BEYOND **IGNORING.**

AND THE **PARADOX** OF IT IS **THIS:**

IN A **SPOTLIGHT,** WITH A FEW **DOZEN** (OR A **HUNDRED** OR A **THOUSAND)** OTHER AUDIENCE MEMBERS **ALONG** FOR THE **RIDE...**

..How our noble brother fell...

...SHE'LL **ALWAYS** BE ABLE TO STRETCH OUT THOSE SOFT **ARMS** OF HERS AND **DRAW** ME RIGHT **IN...**

...AS IF **NOTHING** ABOUT OUR LOVE WAS **COMPLICATED** AND **EVERYTHING** ABOUT OUR TIME TOGETHER WAS **ETERNAL.**

ESMERELDUS IS COMIN' UP HERE NOW. SHE'S GOT **ANOTHER** SONG FOR YOU THAT WAS A FAVORITE OF SAMMY'S.

GINGER, YOUR **PIPES** GIVE ME **PALPITA-TIONS!**

Squeeze!

click!

LISTEN, I CAN'T GO **ON** UNTIL I **SAY** SOMETHIN' TO Y'ALL...AN' TO **SAMMY,** TOO.

IT'S ABOUT A **SACRIFICE** I'M PREPARED TO MAKE.

AN' SAMMY, DON'T THINK I CAN'T **FEEL** YOU UP THERE **FIDGETIN'** AN' **TWIDDLIN'** YOUR FLUFFY NEW **WINGS** AN' WONDERIN' WHEN THE **HELL** THIS QUEEN IS GONNA GET **ON** WITH HER **ACT!**

BUT I'M THINKIN' THAT I MAY HAFTA **DISAPPOINT** YOU.

Y'SEE, EVEN THOUGH I'VE **ALREADY** GONE TO THE TROUBLE OF PUTTIN' ON MY **WIG** AN' ALL OF THIS GORGEOUS **MAKEUP...**

...AN' EVEN THOUGH GOD **KNOWS** THAT NOBODY'S MORE INCLINED TO **HOG** A SPOT-**LIGHT** THAN **I** AM...

...WE ALL KNOW THAT THE LADY WHO'LL **OWN** THIS SONG **FOREVER** IS RIGHT HERE **WITH** US IN THIS **ROOM.**

EVERYBODY **KNOWS** WHO I'M **TALKIN'** ABOUT.

IF **SHE'D** BE **WILLIN'** TO COME UP HERE AN' PERFORM THIS SONG **INSTEAD** OF ME...

...**SHE** WOULDN'T EVEN HAVE TO **LIP-SYNC!**

COME ON AN' **DO** IT, ANNA DELLYNE. EVERY-BODY WOULD **LOVE** FOR YOU TO.

PLEASE --

-- **YOU** GO AHEAD AN' HAVE **FUN** WITH IT, ESMERELDUS. I'LL STAND **BACK.**

O.K., HONEY.

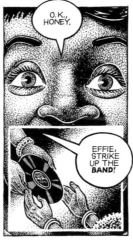

EFFIE, STRIKE UP THE **BAND!**

♪ Got a feeling there's a Secret in the Air... ♪

♪ Nods and whispers among my sisters here and there... ♪

♪ Awkward pauses... Eyes averted... Little warnings, oddly worded... ♪

♪ Can the truth be all that hard to bear...? ♪

AND THEN CAME THE TIME WHEN SEVERAL OF SAMMY'S **FRIENDS** WERE SLATED TO SHARE **PERSONAL REMINISCENCES** ABOUT HIM.

OTHERS WENT **AHEAD** OF ME.

IT WAS **HOPELESS** TRYING TO LISTEN TO WHAT **THEY** WERE SAYING WITH MY **OWN** TURN COMING UP.

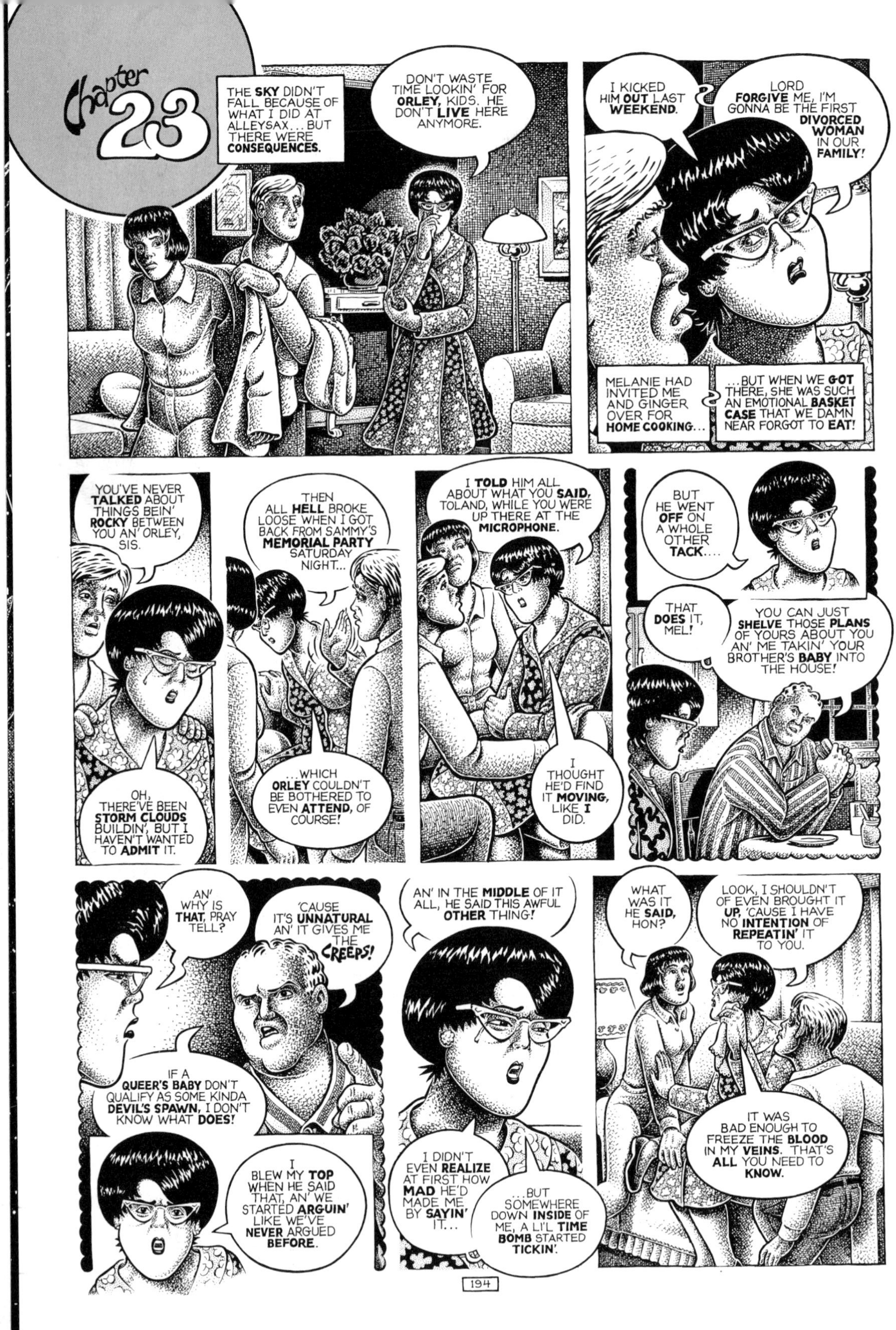

Chapter 23
THE SKY DIDN'T FALL BECAUSE OF WHAT I DID AT ALLEYSAX... BUT THERE WERE CONSEQUENCES.
DON'T WASTE TIME LOOKIN' FOR ORLEY, KIDS. HE DON'T LIVE HERE ANYMORE.
I KICKED HIM OUT LAST WEEKEND.
LORD FORGIVE ME, I'M GONNA BE THE FIRST DIVORCED WOMAN IN OUR FAMILY!
MELANIE HAD INVITED ME AND GINGER OVER FOR HOME COOKING...
...BUT WHEN WE GOT THERE, SHE WAS SUCH AN EMOTIONAL BASKET CASE THAT WE DAMN NEAR FORGOT TO EAT!
YOU'VE NEVER TALKED ABOUT THINGS BEIN' ROCKY BETWEEN YOU AN' ORLEY, SIS.
OH, THERE'VE BEEN STORM CLOUDS BUILDIN', BUT I HAVEN'T WANTED TO ADMIT IT.
THEN ALL HELL BROKE LOOSE WHEN I GOT BACK FROM SAMMY'S MEMORIAL PARTY SATURDAY NIGHT...
...WHICH ORLEY COULDN'T BE BOTHERED TO EVEN ATTEND, OF COURSE!
I TOLD HIM ALL ABOUT WHAT YOU SAID, TOLAND, WHILE YOU WERE UP THERE AT THE MICROPHONE.
I THOUGHT HE'D FIND IT MOVING, LIKE I DID.
BUT HE WENT OFF ON A WHOLE OTHER TACK....
THAT DOES IT, MEL!
YOU CAN JUST SHELVE THOSE PLANS OF YOURS ABOUT YOU AN' ME TAKIN' YOUR BROTHER'S BABY INTO THE HOUSE!
AN' WHY IS THAT, PRAY TELL?
'CAUSE IT'S UNNATURAL AN' IT GIVES ME THE CREEPS!
IF A QUEER'S BABY DON'T QUALIFY AS SOME KINDA DEVIL'S SPAWN, I DON'T KNOW WHAT DOES!
I BLEW MY TOP WHEN HE SAID THAT, AN' WE STARTED ARGUIN' LIKE WE'VE NEVER ARGUED BEFORE.
AN' IN THE MIDDLE OF IT ALL, HE SAID THIS AWFUL OTHER THING!
I DIDN'T EVEN REALIZE AT FIRST HOW MAD HE'D MADE ME BY SAYIN' IT...
...BUT SOMEWHERE DOWN INSIDE OF ME, A LI'L TIME BOMB STARTED TICKIN'.
WHAT WAS IT HE SAID, HON?
LOOK, I SHOULDN'T OF EVEN BROUGHT IT UP, 'CAUSE I HAVE NO INTENTION OF REPEATIN' IT TO YOU.
IT WAS BAD ENOUGH TO FREEZE THE BLOOD IN MY VEINS. THAT'S ALL YOU NEED TO KNOW.

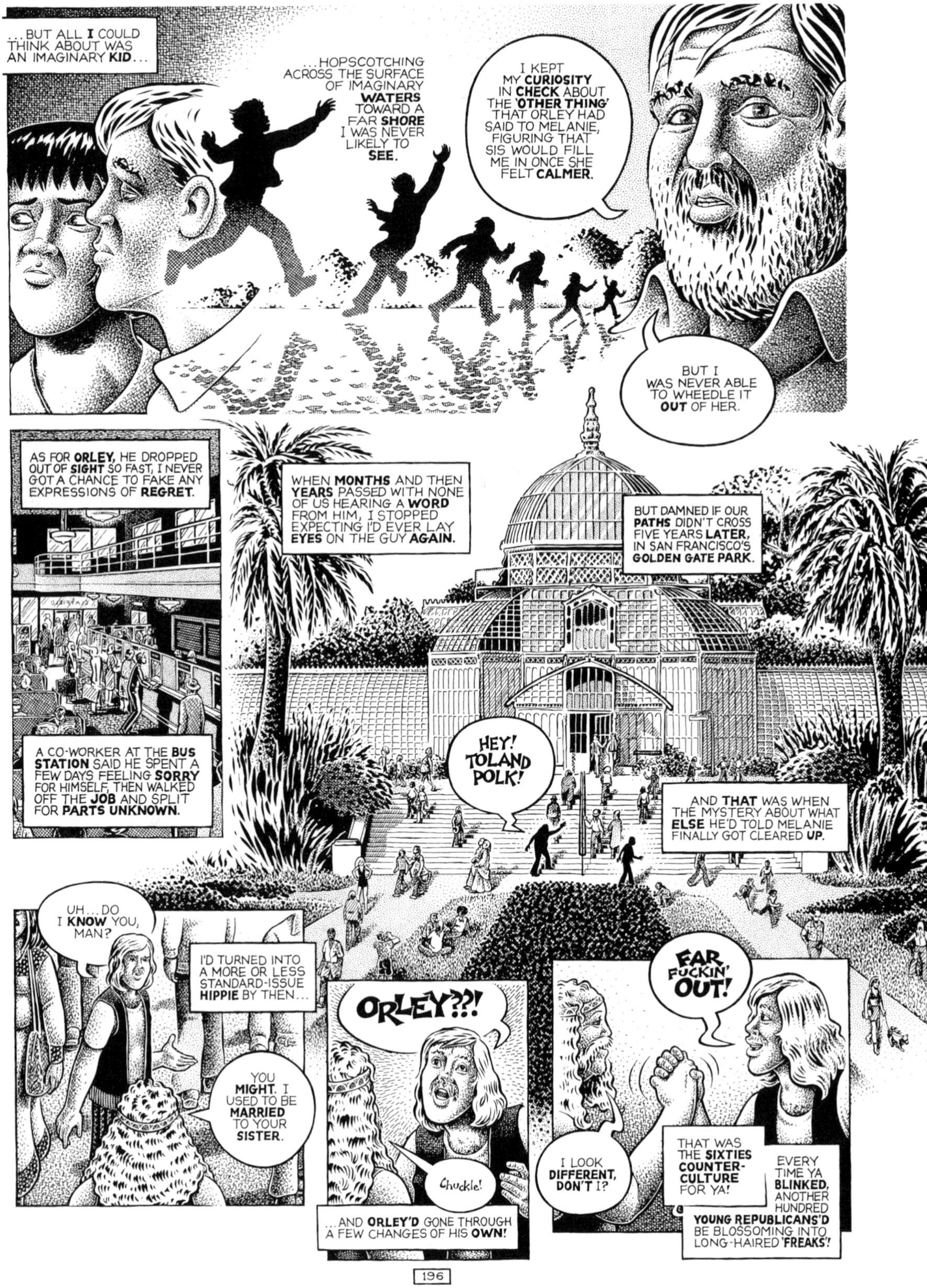
...BUT ALL I COULD THINK ABOUT WAS AN IMAGINARY KID...
...HOPSCOTCHING ACROSS THE SURFACE OF IMAGINARY WATERS TOWARD A FAR SHORE I WAS NEVER LIKELY TO SEE.
I KEPT MY CURIOSITY IN CHECK ABOUT THE 'OTHER THING' THAT ORLEY HAD SAID TO MELANIE, FIGURING THAT SIS WOULD FILL ME IN ONCE SHE FELT CALMER.
BUT I WAS NEVER ABLE TO WHEEDLE IT OUT OF HER.
AS FOR ORLEY, HE DROPPED OUT OF SIGHT SO FAST, I NEVER GOT A CHANCE TO FAKE ANY EXPRESSIONS OF REGRET.
A CO-WORKER AT THE BUS STATION SAID HE SPENT A FEW DAYS FEELING SORRY FOR HIMSELF, THEN WALKED OFF THE JOB AND SPLIT FOR PARTS UNKNOWN.
WHEN MONTHS AND THEN YEARS PASSED WITH NONE OF US HEARING A WORD FROM HIM, I STOPPED EXPECTING I'D EVER LAY EYES ON THE GUY AGAIN.
BUT DAMNED IF OUR PATHS DIDN'T CROSS FIVE YEARS LATER, IN SAN FRANCISCO'S GOLDEN GATE PARK.
HEY! TOLAND POLK!
AND THAT WAS WHEN THE MYSTERY ABOUT WHAT ELSE HE'D TOLD MELANIE FINALLY GOT CLEARED UP.
UH...DO I KNOW YOU, MAN?
I'D TURNED INTO A MORE OR LESS STANDARD-ISSUE HIPPIE BY THEN...
YOU MIGHT. I USED TO BE MARRIED TO YOUR SISTER.
ORLEY??!
Chuckle!
...AND ORLEY'D GONE THROUGH A FEW CHANGES OF HIS OWN!
FAR FUCKIN' OUT!
I LOOK DIFFERENT, DON'T I?
THAT WAS THE SIXTIES COUNTER-CULTURE FOR YA!
EVERY TIME YA BLINKED, ANOTHER HUNDRED YOUNG REPUBLICANS'D BE BLOSSOMING INTO LONG-HAIRED 'FREAKS'!

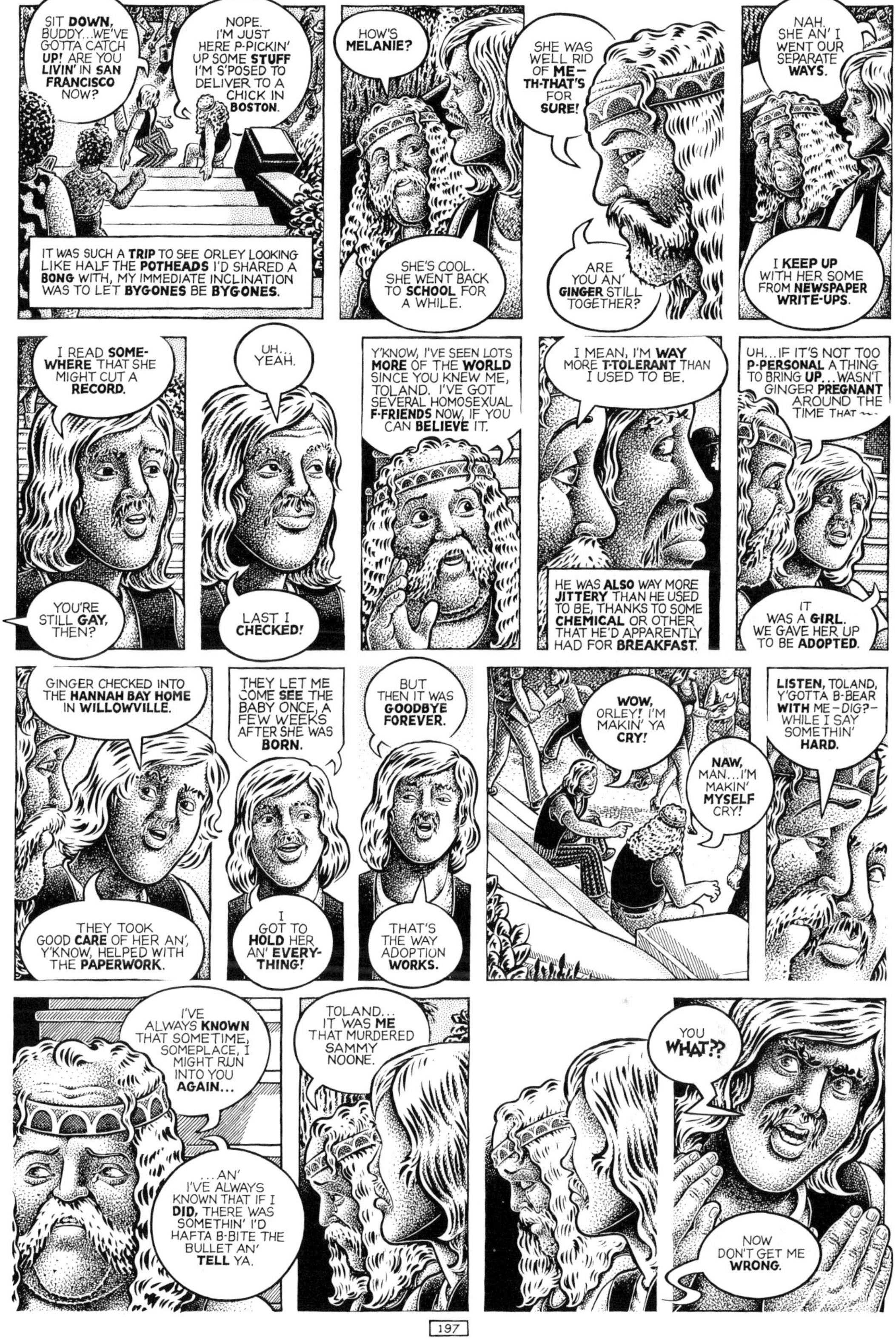
SIT DOWN, BUDDY... WE'VE GOTTA CATCH UP! ARE YOU LIVIN' IN SAN FRANCISCO NOW?
NOPE. I'M JUST HERE P-PICKIN' UP SOME STUFF I'M S'POSED TO DELIVER TO A CHICK IN BOSTON.
IT WAS SUCH A TRIP TO SEE ORLEY LOOKING LIKE HALF THE POTHEADS I'D SHARED A BONG WITH, MY IMMEDIATE INCLINATION WAS TO LET BYGONES BE BYGONES.
HOW'S MELANIE?
SHE'S COOL. SHE WENT BACK TO SCHOOL FOR A WHILE.
SHE WAS WELL RID OF ME— TH-THAT'S FOR SURE!
ARE YOU AN' GINGER STILL TOGETHER?
NAH. SHE AN' I WENT OUR SEPARATE WAYS.
I KEEP UP WITH HER SOME FROM NEWSPAPER WRITE-UPS.
I READ SOMEWHERE THAT SHE MIGHT CUT A RECORD.
YOU'RE STILL GAY, THEN?
UH... YEAH.
LAST I CHECKED!
Y'KNOW, I'VE SEEN LOTS MORE OF THE WORLD SINCE YOU KNEW ME, TOLAND. I'VE GOT SEVERAL HOMOSEXUAL F-FRIENDS NOW, IF YOU CAN BELIEVE IT.
I MEAN, I'M WAY MORE T-TOLERANT THAN I USED TO BE.
HE WAS ALSO WAY MORE JITTERY THAN HE USED TO BE, THANKS TO SOME CHEMICAL OR OTHER THAT HE'D APPARENTLY HAD FOR BREAKFAST.
UH... IF IT'S NOT TOO P-PERSONAL A THING TO BRING UP... WASN'T GINGER PREGNANT AROUND THE TIME THAT ~~
IT WAS A GIRL. WE GAVE HER UP TO BE ADOPTED.
GINGER CHECKED INTO THE HANNAH BAY HOME IN WILLOWVILLE.
THEY TOOK GOOD CARE OF HER AN', Y'KNOW, HELPED WITH THE PAPERWORK.
THEY LET ME COME SEE THE BABY ONCE, A FEW WEEKS AFTER SHE WAS BORN.
I GOT TO HOLD HER AN' EVERYTHING!
BUT THEN IT WAS GOODBYE FOREVER.
THAT'S THE WAY ADOPTION WORKS.
WOW, ORLEY! I'M MAKIN' YA CRY!
NAW, MAN... I'M MAKIN' MYSELF CRY!
LISTEN, TOLAND, Y'GOTTA B-BEAR WITH ME—DIG?— WHILE I SAY SOMETHIN' HARD.
I'VE ALWAYS KNOWN THAT SOMETIME, SOMEPLACE, I MIGHT RUN INTO YOU AGAIN...
...AN' I'VE ALWAYS KNOWN THAT IF I DID, THERE WAS SOMETHIN' I'D HAFTA B-BITE THE BULLET AN' TELL YA.
TOLAND... IT WAS ME THAT MURDERED SAMMY NOONE.
YOU WHAT??
NOW DON'T GET ME WRONG.

I WASN'T PART OF THE GANG THAT **HUNG** HIM! NO **WAY!**

BUT THERE **WAS** SOMETHIN' I **DID**....

JESUS! AM I GONNA HAVE THE B-BALLS TO ACTUALLY **TELL** YOU THIS...?

REMEMBER THE N-NIGHT WHEN THEY RAN **FILM** OF SAMMY ON THE **TV NEWS** AN' HE WAS BAD-MOUTHIN' **SUTTON CHOPPER?**

WELL, WATCHIN' THAT MADE ME SO **MAD,** I COULDN'T **SEE** STRAIGHT!

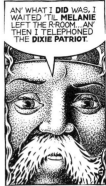
AN' WHAT I **DID** WAS, I WAITED 'TIL **MELANIE** LEFT THE R-ROOM...AN' THEN I TELEPHONED THE **DIXIE PATRIOT.**

I TOLD WHOEVER CAME ON THE **L-LINE** THAT THE **RACE-MIXER** WHO'D JUST B-BEEN ON TV WAS AS **QUEER** AS A **THREE-DOLLAR BILL**...

...AN' THAT THEY COULD FIND HIM PLAYIN' THE **ORGAN** EVERY **S-SUNDAY** AT **TRINITY EPISCOPAL.**

I CAN'T PLAY **INNO-CENT.**

I **KNEW** IT'D DRIVE 'EM **C-CRAZY** TO HEAR THAT.

IT WAS A PURE ACT OF **MEANNESS** TOWARD SAMMY...'CAUSE OF THE **PREJUDICES** I HAD.

AN' MY **CONSCIENCE** TELLS ME THAT IF I **HADN'T** MADE THAT CALL, SAMMY MIGHT'VE SLIPPED BY AS JUST ONE MORE STRAY **'T-TRAITOR** TO THE **WHITE RACE'** FOR THE REDNECKS TO **C-CURSE** AT AN' THEN **FORGET.**

BUT WITH ME PUTTIN' OUT THE **W-WORD** THAT HE WAS A **QUEER** AN' A LOCAL **CH-CHURCH ORGANIST** TO **BOOT**...

...WELL, IT DON'T TAKE A **G-GENIUS** TO KNOW HOW **THAT'D** STICK IN THEIR CRAWS!

SO IT WAS **ME** THAT MADE SAMMY A **TARGET,** Y'SEE?

THERE'S NO **SEPARATIN'** WHAT **I** DID FROM WHAT HAPPENED **LATER.**

THE **GUILT** I FEEL, TOLAND... IT'S J-JUST **TERRIBLE!**

WELL, I'VE **TOLD** YA NOW.

GIMME CREDIT FOR EITHER **G-GUTS** OR **STUPIDITY!**

I KNOW IT'S **ASKIN'** TOO MUCH FOR YOU NOT TO **H-HATE** ME, BUT—

YOU'RE **RIGHT,** ORLEY. I'M NOT **SAINT** ENOUGH NOT TO HATE YOU.

I **LOVED** SAMMY. HE WAS A GOOD **FRIEND** AN' HE MADE ME **BRAVER** THAN I WOULD'VE BEEN OTHER-**WISE.**

I DUNNO IF I'LL END UP HATIN' YOU OVER THE **LONG** HAUL. IT'LL TAKE ME A **WHILE** TO WORK THAT OUT.

...BUT **'TIL FURTHER NOTICE**...

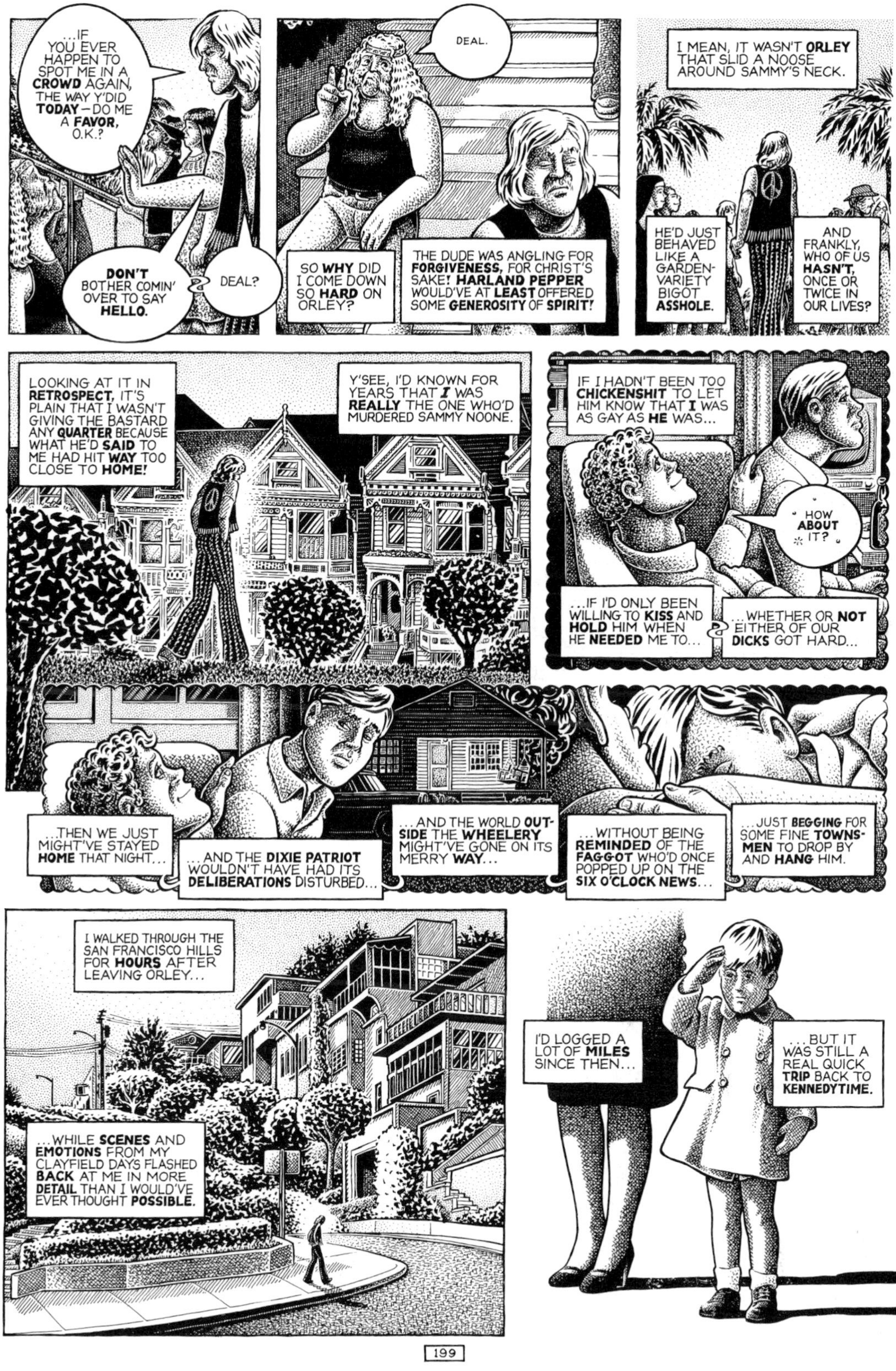
...IF YOU EVER HAPPEN TO SPOT ME IN A CROWD AGAIN, THE WAY Y'DID TODAY—DO ME A FAVOR, O.K.?
DON'T BOTHER COMIN' OVER TO SAY HELLO.
DEAL?
DEAL.
SO WHY DID I COME DOWN SO HARD ON ORLEY?
THE DUDE WAS ANGLING FOR FORGIVENESS, FOR CHRIST'S SAKE! HARLAND PEPPER WOULD'VE AT LEAST OFFERED SOME GENEROSITY OF SPIRIT!
I MEAN, IT WASN'T ORLEY THAT SLID A NOOSE AROUND SAMMY'S NECK.
HE'D JUST BEHAVED LIKE A GARDEN-VARIETY BIGOT ASSHOLE.
AND FRANKLY, WHO OF US HASN'T, ONCE OR TWICE IN OUR LIVES?
LOOKING AT IT IN RETROSPECT, IT'S PLAIN THAT I WASN'T GIVING THE BASTARD ANY QUARTER BECAUSE WHAT HE'D SAID TO ME HAD HIT WAY TOO CLOSE TO HOME!
Y'SEE, I'D KNOWN FOR YEARS THAT I WAS REALLY THE ONE WHO'D MURDERED SAMMY NOONE.
IF I HADN'T BEEN TOO CHICKENSHIT TO LET HIM KNOW THAT I WAS AS GAY AS HE WAS...
HOW ABOUT IT?
...IF I'D ONLY BEEN WILLING TO KISS AND HOLD HIM WHEN HE NEEDED ME TO...
...WHETHER OR NOT EITHER OF OUR DICKS GOT HARD...
...THEN WE JUST MIGHT'VE STAYED HOME THAT NIGHT...
...AND THE DIXIE PATRIOT WOULDN'T HAVE HAD ITS DELIBERATIONS DISTURBED...
...AND THE WORLD OUTSIDE THE WHEELERY MIGHT'VE GONE ON ITS MERRY WAY...
...WITHOUT BEING REMINDED OF THE FAGGOT WHO'D ONCE POPPED UP ON THE SIX O'CLOCK NEWS...
...JUST BEGGING FOR SOME FINE TOWNSMEN TO DROP BY AND HANG HIM.
I WALKED THROUGH THE SAN FRANCISCO HILLS FOR HOURS AFTER LEAVING ORLEY...
...WHILE SCENES AND EMOTIONS FROM MY CLAYFIELD DAYS FLASHED BACK AT ME IN MORE DETAIL THAN I WOULD'VE EVER THOUGHT POSSIBLE.
I'D LOGGED A LOT OF MILES SINCE THEN...
...BUT IT WAS STILL A REAL QUICK TRIP BACK TO KENNEDYTIME.

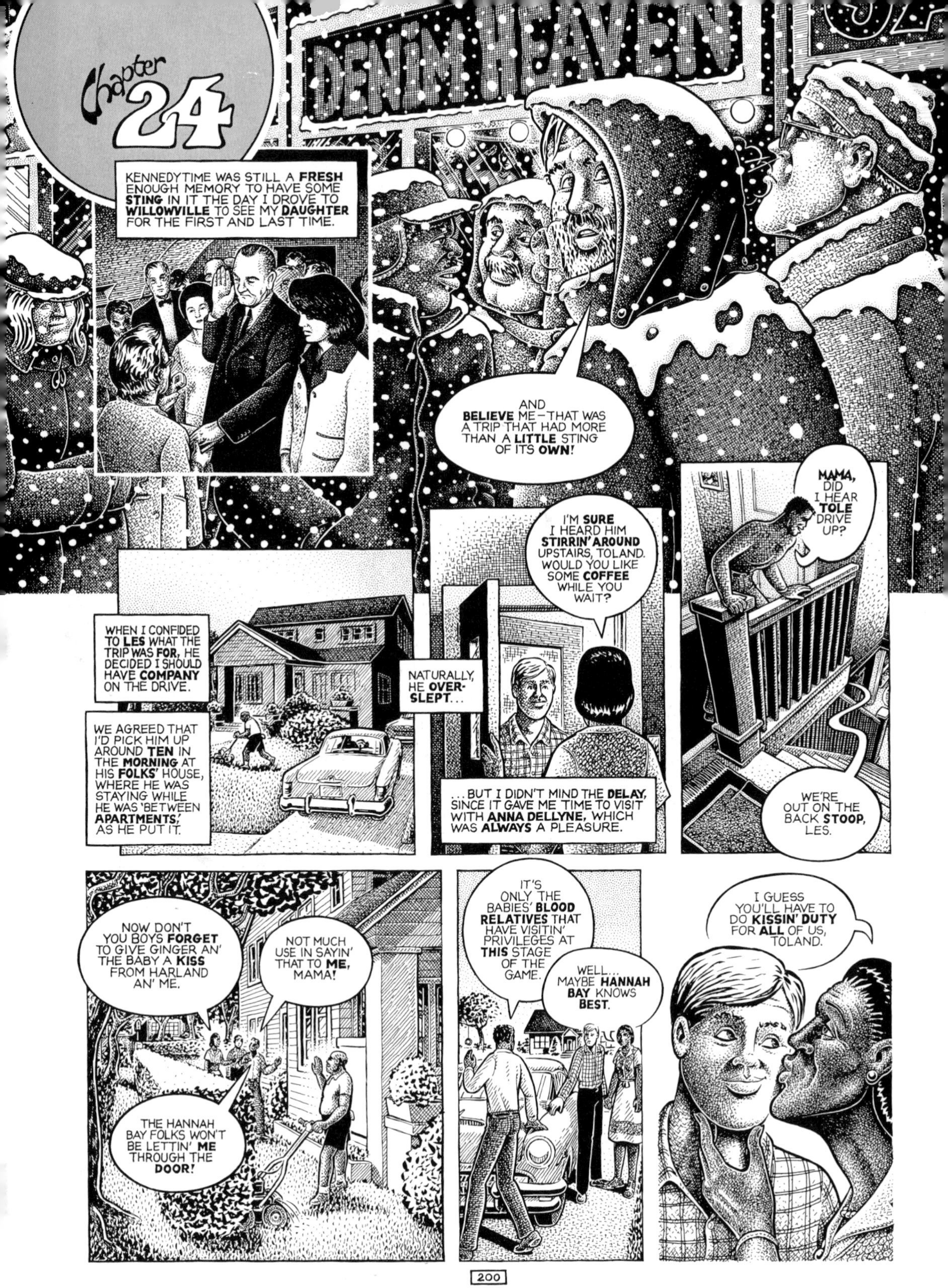

Chapter 24
DENIM HEAVEN
KENNEDYTIME WAS STILL A FRESH ENOUGH MEMORY TO HAVE SOME STING IN IT THE DAY I DROVE TO WILLOWVILLE TO SEE MY DAUGHTER FOR THE FIRST AND LAST TIME.
AND BELIEVE ME—THAT WAS A TRIP THAT HAD MORE THAN A LITTLE STING OF ITS OWN!
WHEN I CONFIDED TO LES WHAT THE TRIP WAS FOR, HE DECIDED I SHOULD HAVE COMPANY ON THE DRIVE.
WE AGREED THAT I'D PICK HIM UP AROUND TEN IN THE MORNING AT HIS FOLKS' HOUSE, WHERE HE WAS STAYING WHILE HE WAS 'BETWEEN APARTMENTS,' AS HE PUT IT.
NATURALLY, HE OVER-SLEPT...
I'M SURE I HEARD HIM STIRRIN' AROUND UPSTAIRS, TOLAND. WOULD YOU LIKE SOME COFFEE WHILE YOU WAIT?
...BUT I DIDN'T MIND THE DELAY, SINCE IT GAVE ME TIME TO VISIT WITH ANNA DELLYNE, WHICH WAS ALWAYS A PLEASURE.
MAMA, DID I HEAR TOLE DRIVE UP?
WE'RE OUT ON THE BACK STOOP, LES.
NOW DON'T YOU BOYS FORGET TO GIVE GINGER AN' THE BABY A KISS FROM HARLAND AN' ME.
NOT MUCH USE IN SAYIN' THAT TO ME, MAMA!
THE HANNAH BAY FOLKS WON'T BE LETTIN' ME THROUGH THE DOOR!
IT'S ONLY THE BABIES' BLOOD RELATIVES THAT HAVE VISITIN' PRIVILEGES AT THIS STAGE OF THE GAME.
WELL... MAYBE HANNAH BAY KNOWS BEST.
I GUESS YOU'LL HAVE TO DO KISSIN' DUTY FOR ALL OF US, TOLAND.

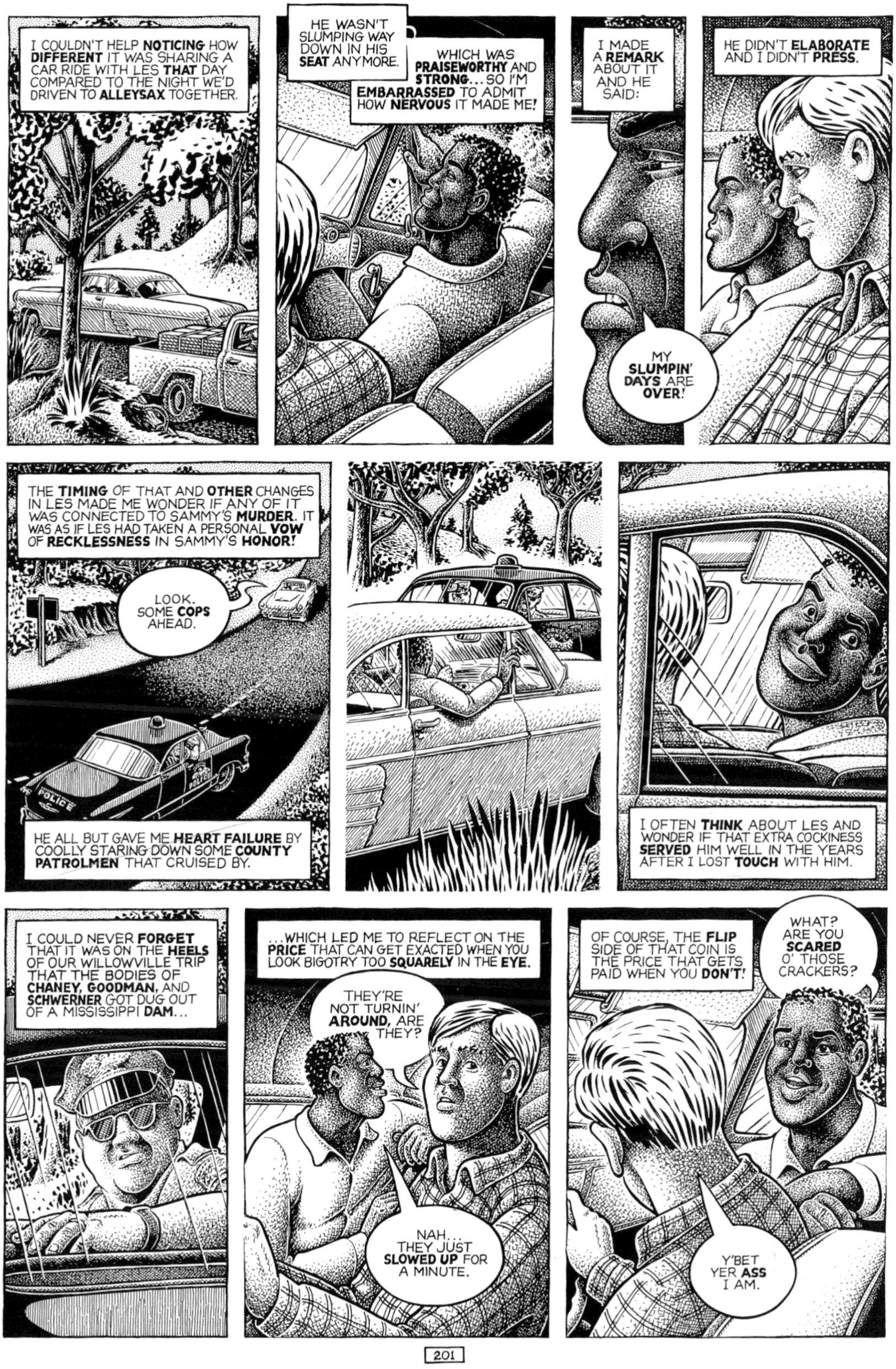
I COULDN'T HELP NOTICING HOW DIFFERENT IT WAS SHARING A CAR RIDE WITH LES THAT DAY COMPARED TO THE NIGHT WE'D DRIVEN TO ALLEYSAX TOGETHER.
HE WASN'T SLUMPING WAY DOWN IN HIS SEAT ANYMORE.
WHICH WAS PRAISEWORTHY AND STRONG... SO I'M EMBARRASSED TO ADMIT HOW NERVOUS IT MADE ME!
I MADE A REMARK ABOUT IT AND HE SAID:
MY SLUMPIN' DAYS ARE OVER!
HE DIDN'T ELABORATE AND I DIDN'T PRESS.
THE TIMING OF THAT AND OTHER CHANGES IN LES MADE ME WONDER IF ANY OF IT WAS CONNECTED TO SAMMY'S MURDER. IT WAS AS IF LES HAD TAKEN A PERSONAL VOW OF RECKLESSNESS IN SAMMY'S HONOR!
LOOK. SOME COPS AHEAD.
POLICE
HE ALL BUT GAVE ME HEART FAILURE BY COOLLY STARING DOWN SOME COUNTY PATROLMEN THAT CRUISED BY.
I OFTEN THINK ABOUT LES AND WONDER IF THAT EXTRA COCKINESS SERVED HIM WELL IN THE YEARS AFTER I LOST TOUCH WITH HIM.
I COULD NEVER FORGET THAT IT WAS ON THE HEELS OF OUR WILLOWVILLE TRIP THAT THE BODIES OF CHANEY, GOODMAN, AND SCHWERNER GOT DUG OUT OF A MISSISSIPPI DAM...
...WHICH LED ME TO REFLECT ON THE PRICE THAT CAN GET EXACTED WHEN YOU LOOK BIGOTRY TOO SQUARELY IN THE EYE.
THEY'RE NOT TURNIN' AROUND, ARE THEY?
NAH... THEY JUST SLOWED UP FOR A MINUTE.
OF COURSE, THE FLIP SIDE OF THAT COIN IS THE PRICE THAT GETS PAID WHEN YOU DON'T!
WHAT? ARE YOU SCARED O' THOSE CRACKERS?
Y'BET YER ASS I AM.

THERE WAS A ROADSIDE **DINER** THAT RAEBURN'S **SISTER** COOKED FOR, SITUATED A MILE OR SO UP THE **HIGHWAY** FROM THE **UNWED MOTHERS' HOME** I WAS GOING TO.

Bobbie Q's

LES HAD TELEPHONED **AHEAD** TO SEE IF HE COULD HANG OUT IN THE **KITCHEN** WITH HER WHILE **I** WAS VISITING WITH **GINGER.**

WELL... BEAR **UP,** MAN.

AN' TELL GINGER THAT ALL THE **PEPPERS** SAY HI.

THE HANNAH BAY HOME

in memory of an Angel

TOLAND! WE'RE GLAD YOU COULD **COME.**

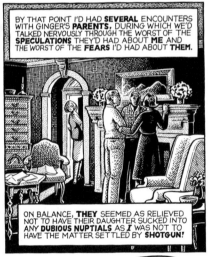

BY THAT POINT I'D HAD **SEVERAL** ENCOUNTERS WITH GINGER'S **PARENTS,** DURING WHICH WE'D TALKED NERVOUSLY THROUGH THE WORST OF THE **SPECULATIONS** THEY'D HAD ABOUT **ME** AND THE WORST OF THE **FEARS** I'D HAD ABOUT **THEM.**

ON BALANCE, **THEY** SEEMED AS RELIEVED NOT TO HAVE THEIR DAUGHTER SUCKED INTO ANY **DUBIOUS NUPTIALS** AS **I** WAS NOT TO HAVE THE MATTER SETTLED BY **SHOTGUN!**

MR. POLK, I'M **IVY** McGINNIS.

SHALL I TAKE YOU TO **GINGER** AND THE **BABY?**

H'LO.

LOOK AT HER, TOLAND. CAN YOU **BELIEVE** IT?

AM I ALLOWED TO **HOLD** HER?

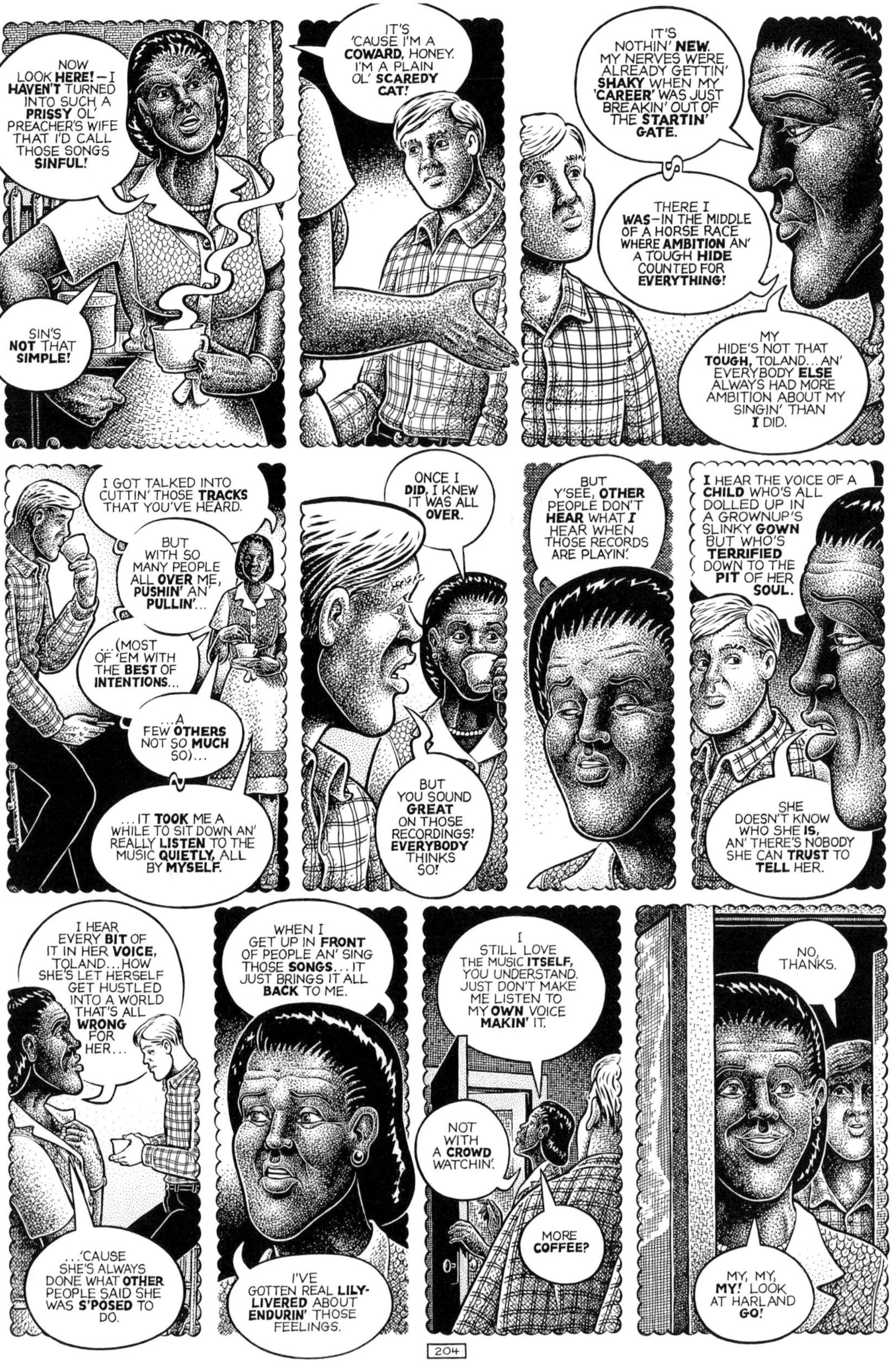
NOW LOOK HERE! — I HAVEN'T TURNED INTO SUCH A PRISSY OL' PREACHER'S WIFE THAT I'D CALL THOSE SONGS SINFUL!
SIN'S NOT THAT SIMPLE!
IT'S 'CAUSE I'M A COWARD, HONEY. I'M A PLAIN OL' SCAREDY CAT!
IT'S NOTHIN' NEW. MY NERVES WERE ALREADY GETTIN' SHAKY WHEN MY 'CAREER' WAS JUST BREAKIN' OUT OF THE STARTIN' GATE.
THERE I WAS—IN THE MIDDLE OF A HORSE RACE WHERE AMBITION AN' A TOUGH HIDE COUNTED FOR EVERYTHING!
MY HIDE'S NOT THAT TOUGH, TOLAND... AN' EVERYBODY ELSE ALWAYS HAD MORE AMBITION ABOUT MY SINGIN' THAN I DID.
I GOT TALKED INTO CUTTIN' THOSE TRACKS THAT YOU'VE HEARD.
BUT WITH SO MANY PEOPLE ALL OVER ME, PUSHIN' AN' PULLIN'...
...(MOST OF 'EM WITH THE BEST OF INTENTIONS...
...A FEW OTHERS NOT SO MUCH SO)...
...IT TOOK ME A WHILE TO SIT DOWN AN' REALLY LISTEN TO THE MUSIC QUIETLY, ALL BY MYSELF.
ONCE I DID, I KNEW IT WAS ALL OVER.
BUT YOU SOUND GREAT ON THOSE RECORDINGS! EVERYBODY THINKS SO!
BUT Y'SEE, OTHER PEOPLE DON'T HEAR WHAT I HEAR WHEN THOSE RECORDS ARE PLAYIN'.
I HEAR THE VOICE OF A CHILD WHO'S ALL DOLLED UP IN A GROWNUP'S SLINKY GOWN BUT WHO'S TERRIFIED DOWN TO THE PIT OF HER SOUL.
SHE DOESN'T KNOW WHO SHE IS, AN' THERE'S NOBODY SHE CAN TRUST TO TELL HER.
I HEAR EVERY BIT OF IT IN HER VOICE, TOLAND... HOW SHE'S LET HERSELF GET HUSTLED INTO A WORLD THAT'S ALL WRONG FOR HER...
...'CAUSE SHE'S ALWAYS DONE WHAT OTHER PEOPLE SAID SHE WAS S'POSED TO DO.
WHEN I GET UP IN FRONT OF PEOPLE AN' SING THOSE SONGS... IT JUST BRINGS IT ALL BACK TO ME.
I'VE GOTTEN REAL LILY-LIVERED ABOUT ENDURIN' THOSE FEELINGS.
I STILL LOVE THE MUSIC ITSELF, YOU UNDERSTAND. JUST DON'T MAKE ME LISTEN TO MY OWN VOICE MAKIN' IT.
NOT WITH A CROWD WATCHIN'.
MORE COFFEE?
NO, THANKS.
MY, MY, MY! LOOK AT HARLAND GO!

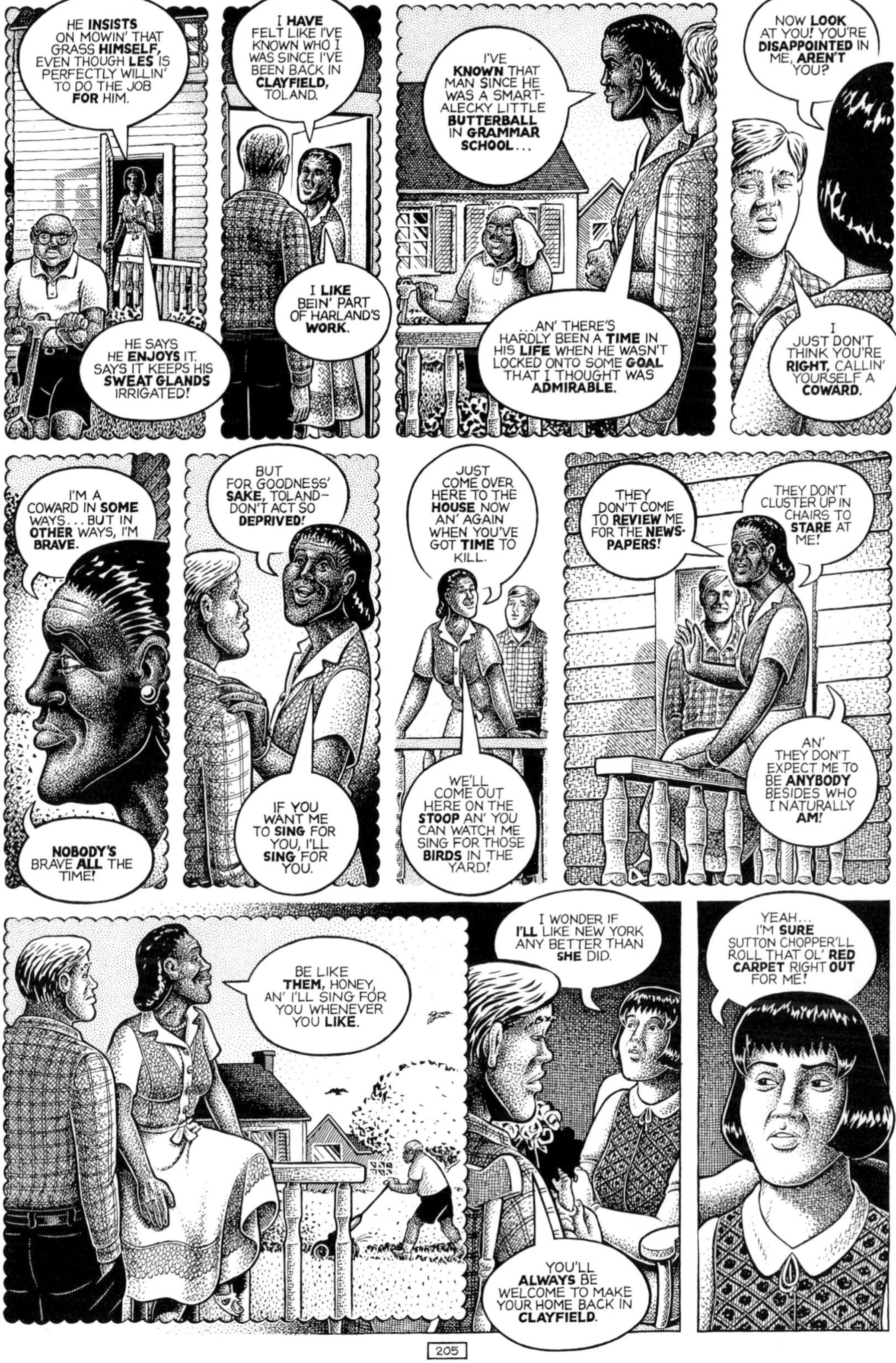
HE **INSISTS** ON MOWIN' THAT GRASS **HIMSELF,** EVEN THOUGH **LES** IS PERFECTLY WILLIN' TO DO THE JOB **FOR** HIM.
HE SAYS HE **ENJOYS** IT. SAYS IT KEEPS HIS **SWEAT GLANDS** IRRIGATED!
I **HAVE** FELT LIKE I'VE KNOWN WHO I WAS SINCE I'VE BEEN BACK IN **CLAYFIELD,** TOLAND.
I **LIKE** BEIN' PART OF HARLAND'S **WORK**.
I'VE **KNOWN** THAT MAN SINCE HE WAS A SMART-ALECKY LITTLE **BUTTERBALL** IN **GRAMMAR SCHOOL**...
...AN' THERE'S HARDLY BEEN A **TIME** IN HIS **LIFE** WHEN HE WASN'T LOCKED ONTO SOME **GOAL** THAT I THOUGHT WAS **ADMIRABLE**.
NOW **LOOK** AT YOU! YOU'RE **DISAPPOINTED** IN ME, **AREN'T** YOU?
I JUST DON'T THINK YOU'RE **RIGHT,** CALLIN' YOURSELF A **COWARD**.
I'M A COWARD IN **SOME** WAYS... BUT IN **OTHER** WAYS, I'M **BRAVE**.
NOBODY'S BRAVE **ALL** THE TIME!
BUT FOR GOODNESS' **SAKE,** TOLAND— DON'T ACT SO **DEPRIVED!**
IF YOU WANT ME TO **SING** FOR YOU, I'LL **SING** FOR YOU.
JUST COME OVER HERE TO THE **HOUSE** NOW AN' AGAIN WHEN YOU'VE GOT **TIME** TO KILL.
WE'LL COME OUT HERE ON THE **STOOP** AN' YOU CAN WATCH ME SING FOR THOSE **BIRDS** IN THE YARD!
THEY DON'T COME TO **REVIEW** ME FOR THE **NEWS-PAPERS!**
THEY DON'T CLUSTER UP IN CHAIRS TO **STARE** AT ME!
AN' THEY DON'T EXPECT ME TO BE **ANYBODY** BESIDES WHO I NATURALLY **AM!**
BE LIKE **THEM,** HONEY, AN' I'LL SING FOR YOU WHENEVER YOU **LIKE**.
I WONDER IF **I'LL** LIKE NEW YORK ANY BETTER THAN **SHE** DID.
YOU'LL **ALWAYS** BE WELCOME TO MAKE YOUR HOME BACK IN **CLAYFIELD**.
YEAH... I'M **SURE** SUTTON CHOPPER'LL ROLL THAT OL' **RED CARPET** RIGHT **OUT** FOR ME!

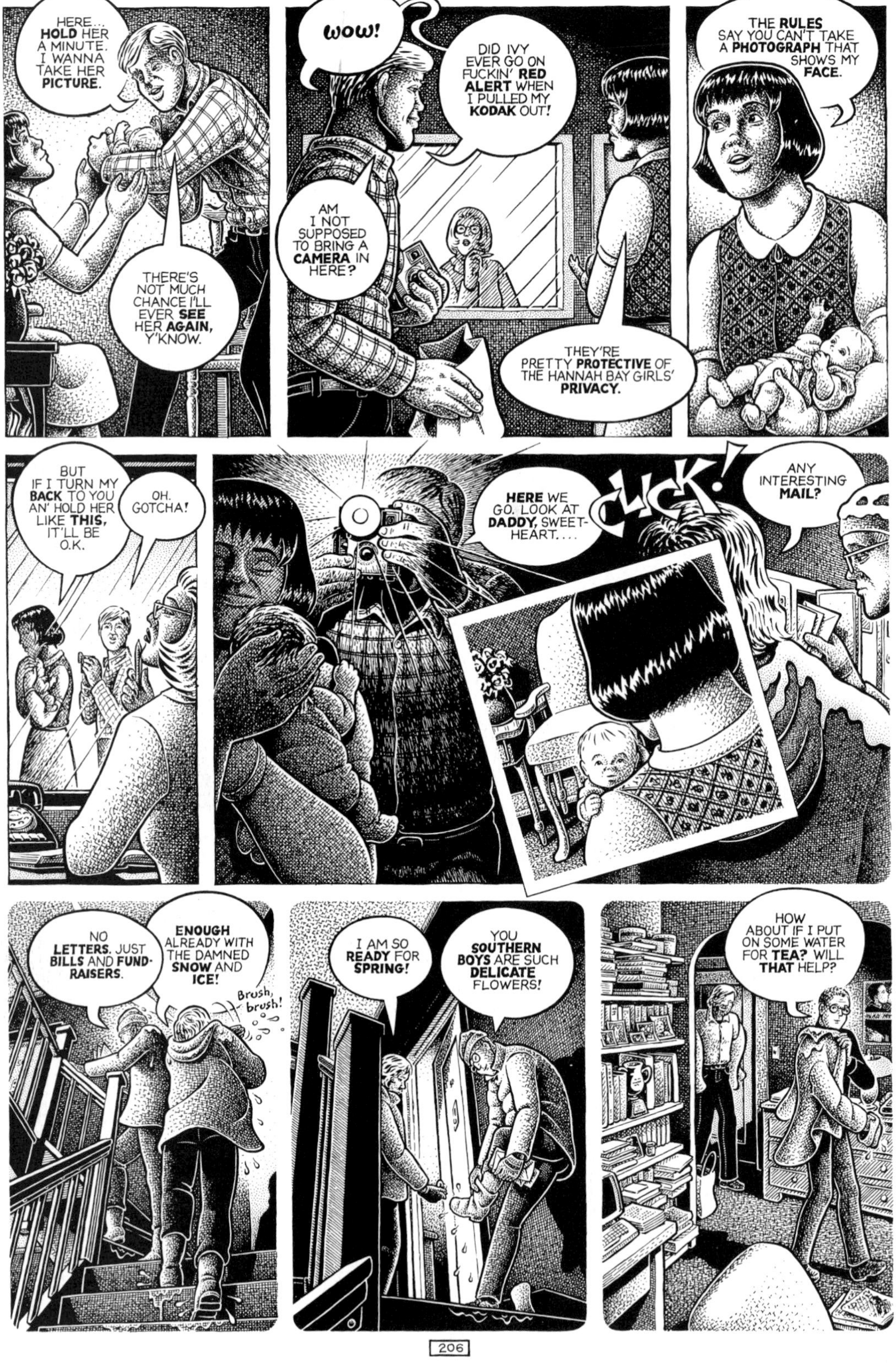

HERE... HOLD HER A MINUTE. I WANNA TAKE HER PICTURE.
THERE'S NOT MUCH CHANCE I'LL EVER SEE HER AGAIN, Y'KNOW.
WOW!
DID IVY EVER GO ON FUCKIN' RED ALERT WHEN I PULLED MY KODAK OUT!
AM I NOT SUPPOSED TO BRING A CAMERA IN HERE?
THEY'RE PRETTY PROTECTIVE OF THE HANNAH BAY GIRLS' PRIVACY.
THE RULES SAY YOU CAN'T TAKE A PHOTOGRAPH THAT SHOWS MY FACE.
BUT IF I TURN MY BACK TO YOU AN' HOLD HER LIKE THIS, IT'LL BE O.K.
OH. GOTCHA!
HERE WE GO. LOOK AT DADDY, SWEETHEART....
CLICK!
ANY INTERESTING MAIL?
NO LETTERS. JUST BILLS AND FUND-RAISERS.
ENOUGH ALREADY WITH THE DAMNED SNOW AND ICE!
Brush, brush!
I AM SO READY FOR SPRING!
YOU SOUTHERN BOYS ARE SUCH DELICATE FLOWERS!
HOW ABOUT IF I PUT ON SOME WATER FOR TEA? WILL THAT HELP?

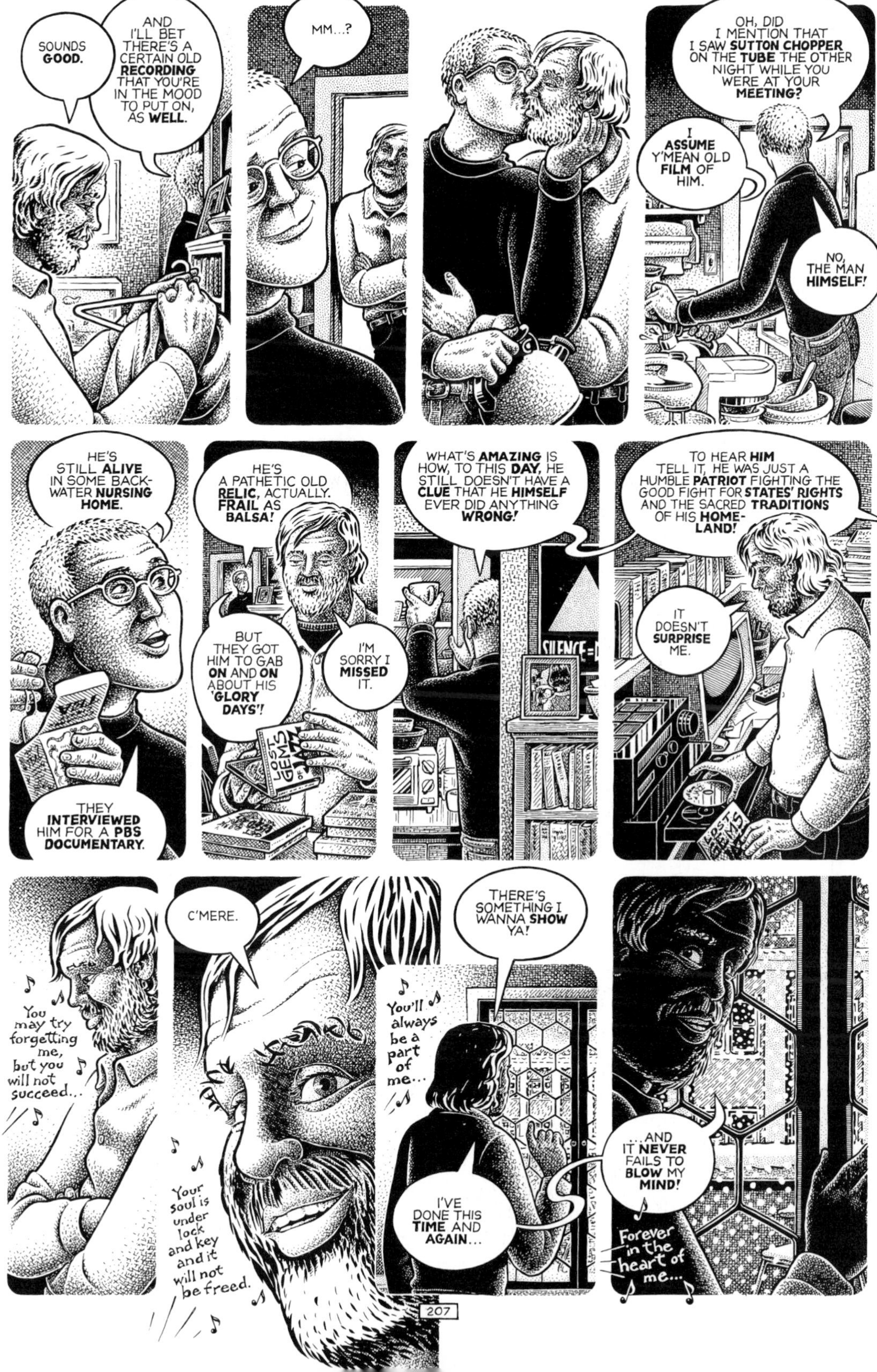
SOUNDS GOOD.
AND I'LL BET THERE'S A CERTAIN OLD RECORDING THAT YOU'RE IN THE MOOD TO PUT ON, AS WELL.
MM...?
OH, DID I MENTION THAT I SAW SUTTON CHOPPER ON THE TUBE THE OTHER NIGHT WHILE YOU WERE AT YOUR MEETING?
I ASSUME Y'MEAN OLD FILM OF HIM.
NO, THE MAN HIMSELF!
HE'S STILL ALIVE IN SOME BACK-WATER NURSING HOME.
THEY INTERVIEWED HIM FOR A PBS DOCUMENTARY.
HE'S A PATHETIC OLD RELIC, ACTUALLY. FRAIL AS BALSA!
BUT THEY GOT HIM TO GAB ON AND ON ABOUT HIS 'GLORY DAYS'!
I'M SORRY I MISSED IT.
LOST GEMS OF JAZZ
WHAT'S AMAZING IS HOW, TO THIS DAY, HE STILL DOESN'T HAVE A CLUE THAT HE HIMSELF EVER DID ANYTHING WRONG!
SILENCE=D
TO HEAR HIM TELL IT, HE WAS JUST A HUMBLE PATRIOT FIGHTING THE GOOD FIGHT FOR STATES' RIGHTS AND THE SACRED TRADITIONS OF HIS HOME-LAND!
IT DOESN'T SURPRISE ME.
LOST GEMS
You may try forgetting me, but you will not succeed...
C'MERE.
Your soul is under lock and key and it will not be freed.
THERE'S SOMETHING I WANNA SHOW YA!
You'll always be a part of me...
I'VE DONE THIS TIME AND AGAIN...
...AND IT NEVER FAILS TO BLOW MY MIND!
Forever in the heart of me...

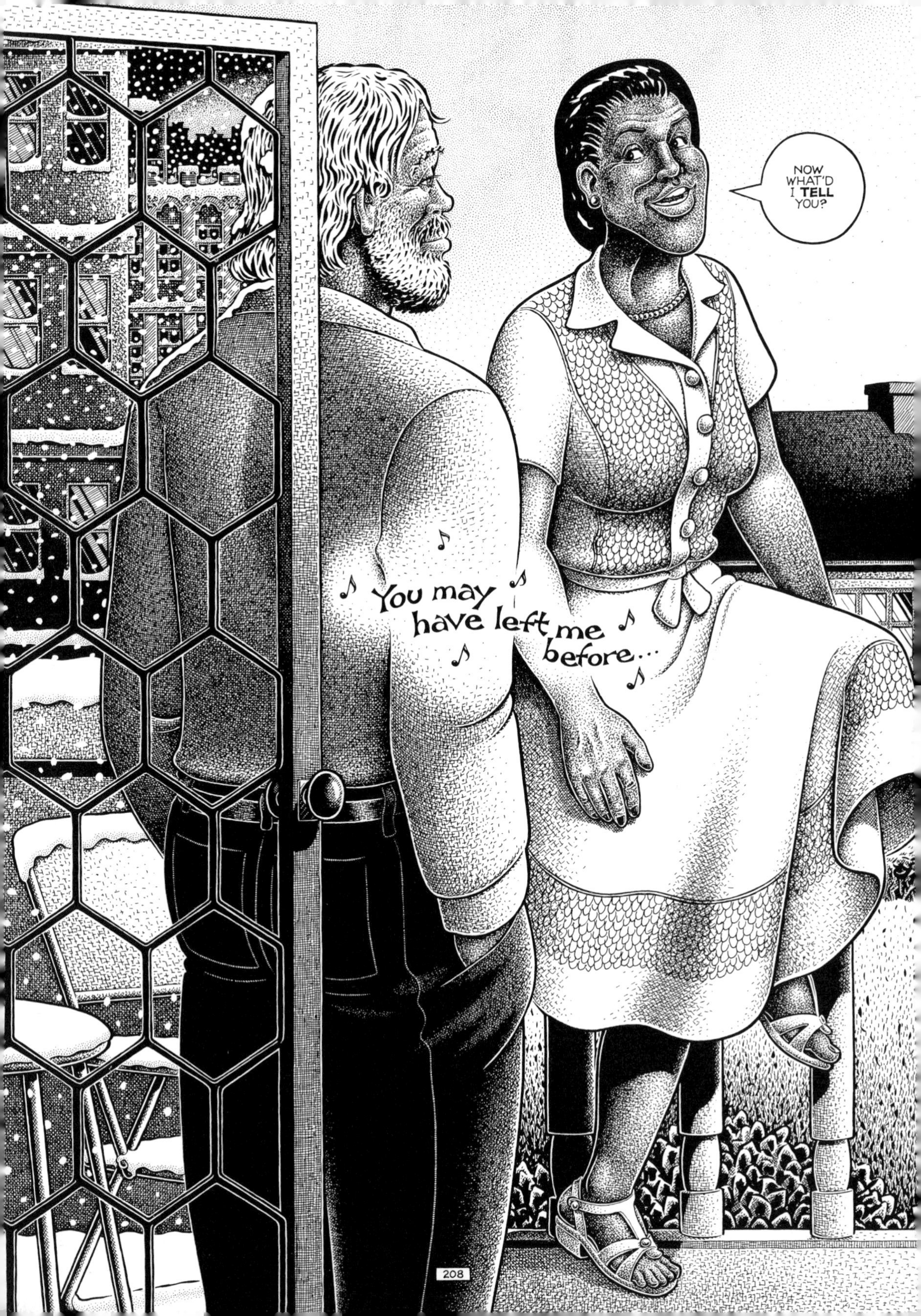

NOW WHAT'D I **TELL** YOU?
You may have left me before...

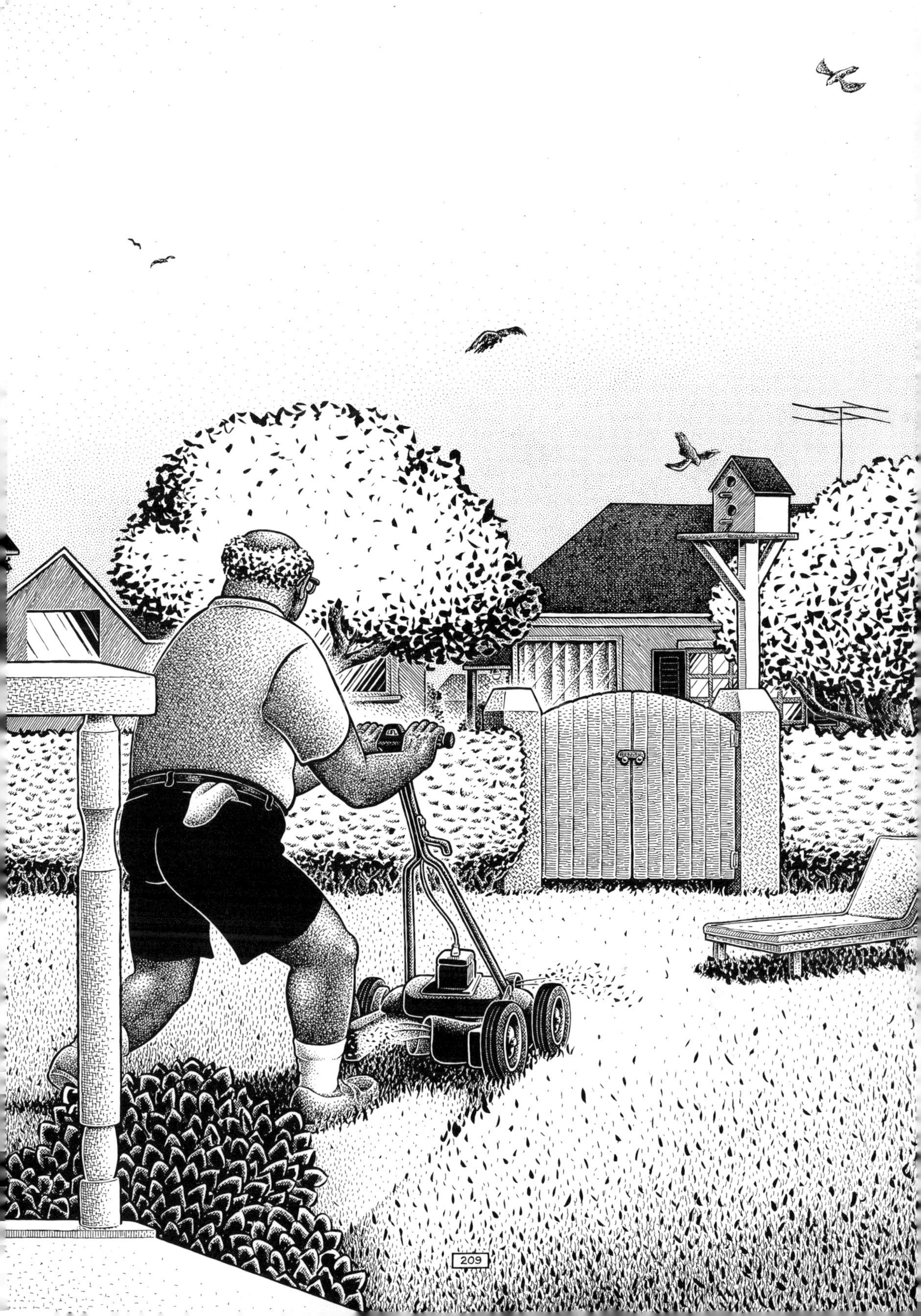

♪ ♪

...But you can't leave me behind. ♪

♪

♪

A C K N O W L E D G M E N T S

Stuck Rubber Baby is a work of fiction, not autobiography. Its characters are inventions of mine, and Clayfield is a make-believe city.

That said, it's doubtful I'd have been moved to write and draw this graphic novel if I hadn't come of age in Birmingham, Alabama, during the early '60s. My own experiences as well as those of old friends and new acquaintances who were kind enough to share their memories with me have served as springboards for various incidents in my narrative, as have the news accounts that I and a nation watched together. I'm grateful to the following individuals for setting aside time to tell me tales: Bob Bailey; Irene Beavers; Clyde and Linda Buzzard; Nina Cain; Dr. Dodson Curry; William A. Dry; John Fuller; Harry Garwood; Mary Larsen; Bill Miller; Bertram N. Perry; Cora Pitt; Perry Schwartz; Jim and Eileen Walbert; Jack Williamson; and Thomas E. Wrenn.

Let me emphasize that none of the individuals cited above had any hand in the actual development of my storyline nor any opportunity to evaluate the liberties I've taken in bringing my own point of view to the fictional incidents loosely inspired by their accounts. Any errors of history or perceived wrong-headedness of interpretation should be laid at my door, not theirs.

Others have aided me, too, in varying ways. Much help was provided at the outset by Marvin Whiting, the Birmingham Public Library's distinguished archivist. I have turned for enlightenment on technical points of law to David Fleischer and to David Hansell. Ed Still provided background on the history of Jim Crow laws. John Gillick helped me with guns; Diana Arecco provided architectural reference; and Murdoch Matthew and Gary Gilbert instructed me on Episcopalian matters. Mary McClain, Stephen Solomita, Dennis O'Neil and John Townsend also provided important nuggets of information.

I'm grateful to Harvey Pekar for answering my questions about jazz lore and to Wade Black of Bozart Mountain/Jade Films for letting me photograph his old movie cameras for reference. And it's by the good graces of Morton J. Savada of Records Revisited in Manhattan that Anna Dellyne's record labels and sleeves have a touch of authenticity.

I'm especially indebted to Leonard Shiller of the Antique Auto Association of Brooklyn, Inc., for cheerfully escorting me from garage to garage in his borough as I photographed not only classic cars but also his fascinating cache of gas pumps, washing machines, vacuum cleaners, scooters, bicycles, beverage trucks, fire engines and other collectibles from a bygone era.

I owe thanks to those who admitted me into their private domains so I could snap reference photos of old furniture, appliances, and representative bits of architecture: Arthur Davis and Ellen Elliott; David Nimmons and David Fleischer; Howie Katz; Elyse Taylor and Leonard Shiller; and Tony Ward and Richard Goldstein. And I'm grateful as well for the special contributions of Grady Clarkson, Tim J. Luddy, and David Hutchison.

I want to thank Andrew Helfer and Bronwyn Taggart, respectively the group editor and editor of Paradox Press, for supporting *Stuck Rubber Baby* unwaveringly during its extended incubation and for allowing me great artistic autonomy in its execution. I'm indebted to Mark Nevelow, the founding editor-in-chief of Piranha Press (Paradox's predecessor), who said yes in 1990 to my proposal for a graphic novel embodying themes that might have tempted a less adventurous editor to stand back, and whose subsequent feedback contributed to a sturdier narrative; and to Margaret Clark, Ms. Taggart's predecessor as editor, for her helpfulness while in that position. My agent, Mike Friedrich of Star∗Reach Productions, Inc., has been an effective problem solver and a valued advisor with regard to both pictures and text. And I'm especially grateful to my longtime friend Martha Thomases, publicity manager of DC Comics, for the help she has provided on too many fronts to mention here, as well as for her seminal insistence, in the face of my initial skepticism, that space might exist at the House of Superman for an underground cartoonist's pursuit of a labor of love.

When I started *Stuck Rubber Baby*, I thought I could do it in two years. It took four. Thus was precipitated a personal budgetary crisis of unnerving proportions, one that forced an unwelcome diversion of energy into the search for enough supplemental funds to cover two unanticipated years of full-time drawing.

Accustomed as I am to creating art in relative solitude, it's been disorienting to find myself so dependent on assistance from others. But dependent I've been, and it's with deep gratitude that I catalog here the varied ways that friends and creative colleagues have gone to bat for me during difficult times.

Most of the forms I filled out in applying for foundation grants asked for letters of endorsement from individuals of creative accomplishment. The following people wrote such letters in my behalf: Stephen R. Bissette; Martin Duberman; Will Eisner; Harvey Fierstein; Richard Goldstein; Maurice Horn; Scott McCloud; Ida Panicelli; and Harvey Pekar.

When things seemed most precarious, a fundraising tactic was devised

by which individuals could become "sponsors" of this book through the purchase
of original artwork from it — at higher than market value and in advance of its
even being drawn. In support of this tactic, a letter of endorsement for *Stuck
Rubber Baby* was drafted and signed by fifteen writers, artists, film and
TV producers, and other cultural leaders. Those who signed that letter were:
Michael Feingold; Matt Foreman; David Frankel; Richard Goldstein; Arnie
Kantrowitz; Tony Kushner; Harvey Marks; Lawrence D. Mass; Jed Mattes;
Armistead Maupin; Michael Musto; Robert Newman; John Scagliotti; Randy
Shilts; and John Wessel. Crucial technical tasks related to fundraising were
performed by Tony Ward, Jennifer Camper, Robert Hanna, and Suk Choi of Box
Graphics, Inc. I appreciate the willingness of Paul Levitz, the executive vice-
president and publisher of DC Comics, to sanction the bending of some normal
company practices in the assembly of our fundraising prospectus.

I am deeply grateful to the individual sponsors themselves, whose
advance purchases of original art from this graphic novel made the completion of
Stuck Rubber Baby possible. They are:

Fred Adams
Allan Cruse
Kevin Eastman
Richard Goldstein
Tony Kushner
Stanley Reed
Martha Thomases and John R. Tebbel
Bob Wingate

Additional support for this project was provided by:

Joan Cullman
Glenn Izutsu
Chopeta Lyons
The Anderson Prize Foundation

Let me finish by thanking Ed Sedarbaum, my companion of sixteen
years, for his unshakable belief in me and in the merits of this graphic novel;
for the concrete help he offered when practical problems loomed; and for the
encouragement and thoughtful feedback he has provided as successive chapters
have been offered for his assessment.

Howard Cruse
July 1995

MARY JACOBS LIBRARY
64 WASHINGTON ST.
ROCKY HILL, NJ 08553

ABOUT THE AUTHOR

Howard Cruse, creator of *Barefootz* and *Wendel* and the founding editor of *Gay Comix*, is an Alabama preacher's kid who counted *The Baptist Student* among his cartoon markets while still in high school. Since then his comic strips and cartoon illustrations have appeared in dozens of national magazines, underground comic books, and anthologies as well as in six book collections of his own. He and his partner of thirty years, political activist Ed Sedarbaum, are now married and living in northwestern Massachusetts.